CONTENTS

INTRODUCTION

The Mediterranean diet has been around since the 1960s, based on the diet of the countries lining the Mediterranean Sea. When experts in dieting rank dietary regimens, the Mediterranean diet often takes the first place. At least, it usually shares top honors with the diets that focus on natural foods such as fruits, vegetables, and whole grains. The Mediterranean diet doesn't explicitly exclude any food group; it simply promotes better food choices such as replacing bad fats with good fats, red meat with seafood and so on. It promotes foods that are as close to their natural state as possible. The Mediterranean diet is one of the easiest diets to follow, as well as one of the best diets for a wide range of chronic diseases. It has been shown to lower risk of diabetes, cardiovascular disease, and cancer. The Mediterranean diet may help you lose unwanted pounds and slow the aging process by five to ten years. But what makes the eating habits of the Italians and Greeks such a genius diet plan is that it's not just about food; it's a whole lifestyle!

The Mediterranean Diet: Why it's Not Just a Diet, More a Way of Life

I've spent a good portion of my life trying to lose weight and then, struggling to maintain my healthy weight. I tried almost all popular weight loss diets until my mid-thirties. The truth is that the number on the scales went down occasionally and I managed to fit into my skinny jeans for some period. I've tried to stick to the golden rules of dieting – eat fewer calories than you burn off, drink plenty of water, exercise, same old same old every day. In fact, I've spent over 15 years of my life being miserable, fighting with a yo-yo dieting. Sometimes I have eaten nothing for the whole day, drinking only water and a little bit of juices. I felt like a hamster on a wheel! I wanted to scream. "I am sick and tired of dieting!" Finally, I gave up dieting and decided to find a sustainable healthy eating plan. I set off on a quest to understand my body and weight loss mechanism. Shortly afterwards, I discovered the Mediterranean diet, a healthy diet plan that is known for its long-term sustainability. And voila! The secret to a healthy diet and weight loss is simpler than I ever though!

What to eat and avoid on the Mediterranean diet? The Mediterranean diet focuses on consuming natural or "real" foods such as fruits, vegetables, nuts, whole grains, beans, and healthy fats such as olive oil, avocado, and seeds. Further, you can consume beef, dairy, eggs, and red wine in moderation.

The list of unhealthy foods includes trans fats (such as margarine), refined oils (soybean oil, cottonseed oil, canola oil,), processed meat (such as a hot dog), sugar-sweetened beverages, refined grains (such as white bread) and highly processed foods. In other words, opt for clean eating and consuming foods that are minimally processed and rich in naturally occurring nutrients.

Since I love to eat mostly vegetarian foods, this is one of the few diets I could actually follow without going on a "real diet". Restrictive diets can be challenging and intimidating for me. Do not eat carbs, do not eat fat, do not eat sugar, do not dine out, do not have fun! Too many don'ts! The Mediterranean diet is all about clean eating without strict rules. This diet does not exclude any food group and it does not count macros or calories. But, do not get me wrong, this is not a permission to sit on your couch and eat a whole bag of chips. This dietary regimen helped me to understand how food makes my body stronger or weaker. Adopting the Mediterranean meal plan can be an effective way to lose weight naturally and spontaneously as well as improve your overall health. It means relying less on processed items and cooking food at home, making you less likely to feel restricted and more likely to follow an eating plan in the long run. Why this is not just a way of eating? The Mediterranean lifestyle includes family meals, daily exercise, and enjoying your diet plan!

Major Benefits of the Mediterranean Diet

What makes the Mediterranean diet so loved by dieters and nutrition experts? Here are the top 3 benefits of the Mediterranean diet.

Health Benefits.

In the 1950s and '60s, scientists found that people in Mediterranean countries had the lowest risk of developing cardiovascular disease due to their specific diet. This dietary regimen is well balanced, encouraging the consumption of antioxidant-rich foods such as fresh fruits, vegetables, legumes, nuts, seeds, and herbs. It also encourages the regular intake of omega-3 fatty acids that can be found in fish and seafood. The Mediterranean diet also includes the consumption of lots and lots of water.

Many studies have shown that a Mediterranean-style diet can significantly lower the risk of major cardiovascular diseases such as a heart attack or stroke. Its positive impact on heart health can be linked to fewer cardiovascular disease risk factors such as obesity. Omega-3 fatty acids can significantly reduce the so-called bad LDL cholesterol and increase HDL cholesterol (good cholesterol). In addition, this diet plan has been shown to reduce cancer risk. In fact, omega-3 fatty acids can lower inflammation that can cause DNA damage and lead to serious diseases including cancer. This DNA damage can lead to other autoimmune diseases such as rheumatoid arthritis and lupus, too. Many studies have found that people on the Mediterranean diet had a better gut health than those eating a typical Western diet. Water and fiber from vegetables can help eliminate toxins from the gastrointestinal tract, which is a boon to digestive health.

When it comes to your mental health, the Mediterranean diet can improve your memory and brain health. This eating pattern may prevent cognitive decline and Alzheimer's disease. Higher consumption of antioxidants, found in Mediterranean fruits and vegetables, has been proven to boost your overall mental health.

Thanks to many studies, the Mediterranean diet was associated with an increased life span. The Mediterranean diet is all about the simple idea that the food can either destroy your body or cure it. At the end of the day, it all comes down to your health and happiness. The Mediterranean diet is one of the best natural remedies for many modern diseases!

Anti-Aging Benefits.

When your body is well hydrated and nourished, it has a good circulation and blood flow, which can help your skin glow. Vegetables and greens have been shown to balance gut bacteria, which is the secret to glowing skin and beautiful hair. Fruits, vegetables and nuts are loaded with vitamins and minerals that can improve your skin health in many ways. Drinking water and consuming good oils can help plump up skin cells, which minimizes the appearance of acne and wrinkles. As a staple of the Mediterranean diet, good-quality olive oil has significant antioxidant effects that may be beneficial for the skin and hair. Plus, olive oil contains vitamins A, D, and E. It is well known that people have used vitamin E to treat a variety of skin conditions and reduce wrinkles and fine lines. Olive oil and coconut oil can be used to treat bacterial infections of the skin due to their antibacterial effects.

As we said before, the Mediterranean emphasizes consuming large amount of water. Water supports detoxification and helps flush impurities out of your body, which is usually shown on our largest organ – our skin! I like sipping warm lemon water to help my body detoxify first thing in the morning. Lemon is rich in vitamin C that can neutralize free radicals and boost collagen production in the skin. Plus, warm lemon water is beneficial for weight loss. This leads us to my next point, the third crucial advantage of the Mediterranean diet – weight loss.

Weight Loss.

It is not something new – the Mediterranean diet has been associated with weight loss in many studies. It makes sense that high-fiber and water-rich foods keep you full longer, making you less likely to gain weight. This type of diet also improves glucose intolerance and reduces type 2 diabetes-related health complications.

There are a few tricks that help me maintain my weight on the Mediterranean diet for years.

1. I eat vegetables as a main course. I usually have a stew, soup, or casserole for lunch. Accompanied by a piece of good feta cheese, these meals are low in calories and high in fiber, which can help your body improve metabolism and burn belly fat faster;

2. I consume olive oil, nuts and avocado in moderation. A good fat such as olive oil does not make you fat; however, you should limit your oil consumption to 3 tablespoons per day;

3. I learned to simplify my diet by planning my meals and keeping pantry staples at my fingertips. These staples include canned tomatoes, whole grains, olive oil, and seafood;

4. Exercise is the key to good health and longer life. Besides being good for your health, moving around is beneficial for your healthy weight. Walking, doing chores, climbing stairs, doing gardening, all that matters. The good news is... even if you don't follow the Mediterranean diet strictly, simply eating more of the natural foods is an outstanding achievement!

3-WEEK MEAL PLAN

This is a sample menu for three weeks on the Mediterranean diet. Recipe Number is written before the recipe name, so you can easily find it within the book (note this is recipe number, not page number).

DAY 1
Breakfast – 10. Broccoli Frittata with Ricotta Salad
Snack – 274. Homemade Potato Chips
Lunch – 183. Chicken Wings with Kalamata Olives; 1 handful of iceberg lettuce
Dinner – 379. Giant Bean in Tomato Sauce

DAY 2
Breakfast – 11. Grilled Salmon Melt Sandwiches; 1 shake with 1/2 cup of coconut milk and protein powder
Lunch – 370. Oven-Roasted Cauliflower with Tahini Sauce; 319. Fennel Quinoa Salad
Dinner – 139. Couscous with Tuna and Basil; 1 serving of cabbage salad
Dessert – 497. Classic Orange Cheesecake

DAY 3
Breakfast – 3. Poached Eggs on Toast
Lunch – 53. Classic Tomato and Orzo Soup; 109. Roasted Eggplant with Herbs
Snack – 279. Easy Three Layer Dip
Dinner – 335. Moroccan Couscous Salad

DAY 4
Breakfast – 5. Greek-Style Pancakes with Blueberries
Lunch – 5. Greek-Style Pancakes with Blueberries; 1 serving of coleslaw
Dinner – 226. Herb Mozzarella Chicken with Olives
Dessert – 501. Turkish Baked Pudding (Sütlaç)

DAY 5
Breakfast – 30. Caprese Egg Cups; 1/2 cup Greek yogurt
Snack – 276. Grilled Street Corn
Lunch – 377. White Bean Soup with Kale and Cheese; 1 serving of brown rice
Dinner – 397. Double-Cheese Broccoli Casserole

DAY 6
Breakfast – 20. Authentic Yiaourti Me Meli; 1 hard-boiled egg
Lunch – 50. Spanish-Style Sausage Soup with Garbanzos; 344. Italian Corn Muffins
Dinner – 385. Spicy BBQ Tofu Steaks; 1 serving of lettuce leaves
Dessert – 478. The Best Chocolate Quinoa Cake Ever

DAY 7
Breakfast – 6. Egg Cups with Tuna and Tomato; 1 toast
Lunch – 241. Chunky Beef and Cannellini Bean Casserole; 1 large tomato
Dinner – 430. Roasted Veggie Rotini Salad
Dessert – 466. Creamed Fruit Salad

DAY 8
Breakfast – Scrambled eggs; 1 tomato; 1 pitta bread
Lunch – 217. Italian Chicken and Tortellini Soup
Dinner – 455. Traditional Cacio e Pepe
Dessert – 492. Chocolate Fudge Ice Pops

DAY 9
Breakfast – 12. Greek Pita Tostadas; 1/2 cup of unsweetened almond milk
Lunch – 86. Lebanese Split Pea Soup; 88. Shawarma Salad Bowl
Snack – 283. Layered Hummus and Turkey Dip
Dinner – 349. Polenta and Mushroom Tart

DAY 10
Breakfast – 8. Green Apple Smoothie
Snack – 275. Cheesy Zucchini Sticks
Lunch – 54. Greek Avgolemono Soup with Pastina; 325. Cornbread with Feta and Sun-Dried Tomatoes
Dinner – 164. Baked Seafood Manicotti

DAY 11
Breakfast – 7. Traditional Shakshuka with a Twist; 1 toast
Lunch – 68. Traditional Minestrone Soup; 97. Fried Zucchini and Parmesan Cakes
Snack – 281. Herb Potato Wedges
Dinner – 356. Brown Rice Salad

DAY 12
Breakfast – 13. Dad's Cloud Eggs
Snack – 290. Garlic Carrots with Yogurt Dip
Lunch – 263. London Broil with Herbs and Feta Cheese; 324. Traditional Pita Bread
Dinner – 375. Grilled Tofu with Swiss Chard
DAY 13
Breakfast – 9. Savory Crêpe with Goat Cheese
Lunch – 149. Parmesan Prawn Casserole; 101. Roasted Sweet Potato Salad
Dinner – 360. Italian-Style Polenta Pie
Dessert – 487. Koufeto with Walnuts
DAY 14
Breakfast – 21. Tahini & Feta Toast
Lunch – 233. Herb and Wine Beef Stew; 1 handful of baby spinach with 1 teaspoon of mustard and 1 teaspoon of olive oil
Dinner – 211. Saucy Chicken Creole; 353. Classic Freekeh Salad
Dessert – 469. Turkish-Style Chocolate Halva
DAY 15
Breakfast – 14. Cheese and Bacon Wraps; 1 tomato
Lunch – 52. Rich Quinoa, Bean and Vegetable Soup; 61. Tuna Salad with Homemade Salsa
Snack – 278. Roasted Parmesan Carrots
Dinner – 414. Vegetarian Skillet Pizza
DAY 16
Breakfast – 43. Hash Brown and Sardine Casserole
Lunch – 99. Grilled Vegetable Kabobs; 57. Dijon Potato Salad
Dinner – 359. Old-Fashioned Barley Pilaf with Vegetables
Dessert – 479. Creamy Apricot and Almond Dessert
DAY 17
Breakfast – 15. Traditional Socca with Spinach; 1/2 cup Greek yogurt
Lunch – 96. Grilled Hash Brown Burgers; 58. Decadent Green Bean Salad
Dinner – 163. Creamed Shrimp with Linguine
Dessert – 481. Traditional Greek Prune Compote
DAY 18
Breakfast – 1. Labneh with Herbs and Toasted Nuts; 533. Red Fruit Salad
Lunch – 515. Tuna and Feta Cheese Lettuce Wraps; 376. Green Beans with Halloumi Cheese
Snack – 289. Greek-Style Potato Bites
Dinner – 142. Authentic Greek Calamari; 1 serving of lettuce salad
DAY 19
Breakfast – 502. Favorite Homemade Granola
Lunch – 70. Mac and Cheese Soup with Spinach; 73. Asparagus and Sardine Salad
Dinner – 120. Moroccan-Style Millet with Roasted Carrots
Dessert – 467. Mini Orange Tarts
DAY 20
Breakfast – 17. Sardine Salad Sandwiches
Lunch – 243. Beef and Mushroom Mélange; 1 tomato
Snack – 285. Zucchini Chips with Pine Nuts
Dinner – 452. Avocado, Poppy Seed and Farfalle Salad
DAY 21
Breakfast – 42. French Toast with Cranberries
Lunch – 49. Greek-Style Summer Salad; 346. Bulgur and Bean Soup
Snack – 301. Avocado and Ricotta Bruschetta
Dinner – 416. Traditional Spaghetti Bolognese

BREAKFAST

Labneh with Herbs and Toasted Nuts

(Ready in about 15 minutes + chilling time | Servings 4)
Per serving: Calories: 243; Fat: 16.8g; Carbs: 9.3g; Protein: 16.7g

Ingredients
16 ounces Greek-style yogurt
1/2 teaspoon sea salt
1/2 cup almonds, chopped
1/2 cup walnuts, chopped
8 fresh mint leaves, chopped
8 large basil leaves, chopped
1 teaspoon fresh dill, stems removed, chopped

Directions
Add the yogurt and salt to a large mixing bowl.
Line another bowl with several layers of cheesecloth; then, carefully pour the yogurt into the cheesecloth. Tie the cheesecloth and set it aside in your refrigerator to drain for about 24 hours.
Meanwhile, toast your nuts in a nonstick skillet over a moderate flame until fragrant and golden brown, stirring continuously.
Garnish your labneh with the fresh herbs and toasted nuts; serve with toasted pita bread, if desired. Enjoy!

Breakfast Salad with Eggs and Brown Rice

(Ready in about 40 minutes | Servings 3)
Per serving: Calories: 532; Fat: 27.3g; Carbs: 60g; Protein: 14.9g

Ingredients
1 cup brown rice
2 large-sized eggs
1 cup Iceberg lettuce
2 cups baby spinach
2 cups arugula
1 medium-sized tomato, cut into sliced
1 English cucumber, sliced
1 avocado
2 tablespoons basil leaves, chopped
1 tablespoon fresh parsley, chopped
1/2 cup Kalamata olives, pitted and sliced
1 fresh lemon, freshly squeezed
1 tablespoon extra-virgin olive oil
Sea salt and freshly ground black pepper, to taste
4 ounces feta cheese, crumbled

Directions
Bring the rice, 2 cups of water, and 1/4 teaspoon of sea salt to a boil. Cover, and reduce the temperature to a simmer; let it simmer for 30 minutes and remove from the heat. Fluff your rice and transfer it to a nice salad bowl.
Then, place the eggs in a saucepan and cover them with water by 1 inch. Bring the water to a rolling boil over high heat.

Boil the eggs, covered, for about 7 minutes over medium-high heat. Peel the eggs and slice them into wedges.
Add the fresh Iceberg lettuce, baby spinach, arugula, tomatoes, cucumber, avocado, basil, parsley, and olives to the salad bowl with the cooked rice.
Drizzle fresh lemon juice and extra-virgin olive oil over the ingredients. Season with salt and pepper to taste and toss to combine well. Top with the reserved eggs and feta cheese and serve immediately.

Poached Eggs on Toast

(Ready in about 15 minutes | Servings 1)
Per serving: Calories: 397; Fat: 24.4g; Carbs: 29.1g; Protein: 16.6g

Ingredients
2 eggs
Sea salt and ground black pepper, to taste
2 bread slices
1/2 avocado, pitted and mashed
1/2 teaspoon squeezed lemon juice
1 teaspoon everything bagel seasoning

Directions
Crack your egg into a bowl.
Bring a pan of water to a simmer. Carefully fold the eggs into the pan.
Cook the eggs for 2 minutes; heat off; leave the pan for about 9 minutes. Remove the eggs from the water with a slotted spoon; pat the eggs dry with a paper towel.
Toast the bread to your desired doneness; now, top each slice of bread with the mashed avocado.
Sprinkle with lemon juice and everything bagel seasoning.
Top with poached eggs and season with salt and pepper to taste. Bon appétit!

Smoked Salmon on Toast

(Ready in about 15 minutes | Servings 2)
Per serving: Calories: 524; Fat: 24.1g; Carbs: 45.7g; Protein: 31.8g

Ingredients
2 tablespoons butter
2 tablespoons plain flour
1/4 cup cream of celery soup
1/4 cup coconut milk
5 ounces sweet corn kernels, thawed
8 ounces smoked salmon
1/4 teaspoon cayenne pepper
1/4 teaspoon dried rosemary
1/4 teaspoon dried marjoram
Sea salt and ground black pepper, to taste
4 slices rye bread, toasted

Directions

Melt the butter in a nonstick skillet over a moderate flame. Whisk in the flour, stirring frequently, to avoid lumps.

Gradually pour in the soup and milk, and continue to cook for about 10 minutes until the sauce has thickened and reduced.

Stir in the corn, salmon and spices, and continue simmering for 5 minutes more or until thoroughly heated.

Divide the smoked salmon mixture between toasted bread slices and serve warm. Enjoy!

Greek-Style Pancakes with Blueberries

(Ready in about 30 minutes | Servings 3)
Per serving: Calories: 272; Fat: 6.5g; Carbs: 42.2g; Protein: 11.1g

Ingredients
1 cup all-purpose flour
1 teaspoon baking powder
1/4 teaspoon coarse sea salt
1 tablespoon granulated sugar
2 eggs, whisked
1/2 cup milk
1/2 cup Greek-style yogurt
A few drizzles of fresh lemon juice
1 tablespoon coconut oil, melted
1/2 cup blueberries

Directions
In a mixing bowl, thoroughly combine all dry ingredients. Gradually and carefully add in the eggs, milk and 1/4 cup of Greek-style yogurt.

Then, whip the batter with a hand mixer until you have a really smooth texture.

Add in a few drizzles of fresh lemon juice. Allow the batter to rest for 15 minutes.

Brush a pancake griddle with a little bit of coconut oil. Pour about 1/4 cup of the batter onto the hot griddle and cook until the bubbles on top burst and then, they create holes.

Garnish your pancakes with the remaining Greek-style yogurt and blueberries. Enjoy!

Egg Cups with Tuna and Tomato

(Ready in about 25 minutes | Servings 4)
Per serving: Calories: 178; Fat: 9.6g; Carbs: 2.8g; Protein: 19.5g

Ingredients
5 large eggs
1/4 teaspoon red pepper flakes, crushed
Sea salt and ground black pepper, to taste
1 medium-sized tomato, chopped
6 ounces canned tuna, drained and flakes
1/4 cup pecorino cheese, shredded
2 tablespoons fresh basil leaves

Directions
Begin by preheating your oven to 370 degrees F. Brush a muffin tin with a nonstick spray.

Beat the eggs with red pepper, salt, and black pepper, and pour the mixture into the cups.

Add in the tomato, canned tuna, and cheese. Bake the egg cups for about 16 minutes until the eggs are set and tops are a light golden brown.

Allow the egg cups to cool for 5 to 6 minutes before unmolding and serving. Garnish with fresh basil leaves and serve. Bon appétit!

Traditional Shakshuka with a Twist

(Ready in about 15 minutes | Servings 2)
Per serving: Calories: 444; Fat: 32g; Carbs: 17.4g; Protein: 22.3g

Ingredients
2 tablespoons olive oil, divided
1 red onion, chopped
1 Italian pepper, diced
1 chili pepper, seeded and chopped
1 teaspoon fresh garlic, minced
2 tomatoes, diced
Salt and freshly ground black pepper, to taste
1/2 teaspoon ras el hanout
4 eggs
1/2 cup halloumi cheese, crumbled
1 tablespoon fresh dill, coarsely chopped

Directions
Heat the olive oil in a saucepan over a moderate heat. Now, sauté the onion, peppers, and garlic for 2 to 3 minutes.

Fold in the diced tomatoes, salt, black pepper, and ras el hanout; continue to cook for a further 8 minutes. Break the eggs into the saucepan, cover, and cook until your desired doneness is reached.

Garnish with cheese and fresh dill and serve warm. Enjoy!

Green Apple Smoothie

(Ready in about 5 minutes | Servings 1)
Per serving: Calories: 266; Fat: 4.7g; Carbs: 54g; Protein: 6.8g

Ingredients
1 banana
1 cup lettuce
1 green apple
1/2 teaspoon fresh ginger, peeled and minced
1 orange, peeled
1/2 cup almond milk
2 dates, pitted
A few fresh mint leaves

Directions
Process all of the above ingredients in your blender until creamy, uniform and smooth.

Pour the smoothie into a tall glass, garnish with fresh mint leaves, and serve immediately. Enjoy!

Savory Crêpe with Goat Cheese

(Ready in about 15 minutes | Servings 4)
Per serving: Calories: 393; Fat: 20.2g; Carbs: 44.4g; Protein: 10.8g

Ingredients
1 ½ cups all-purpose flour
1/4 teaspoon sea salt

1/4 teaspoon granulated sugar
4 tablespoons extra-virgin olive oil, plus extra to drizzle
4 tablespoons olive paste
3 handfuls arugula
2 ounces sun-dried tomatoes in oil, chopped
1/2 cup goat cheese, room temperature
Directions
Sift the flour into a mixing bowl; add in the sea salt and granulated sugar; gradually pour in the water and 2 tablespoons of olive oil until smooth and well combined.

Brush a frying pan with a little bit of olive oil. Fry each pancake for about 3 minutes on each side or until cooked through.

Repeat with the remaining batter, brushing the pan with a small amount of the olive oil.

Spread the olive paste over each pancake. Garnish each pancake with arugula, sun-dried tomatoes, and goat cheese. Bon appétit!

Broccoli Frittata with Ricotta Salad
(Ready in about 15 minutes | Servings 3)
Per serving: Calories: 274; Fat: 19.5g; Carbs: 6.1g; Protein: 18.3g
Ingredients
1 tablespoon olive oil
1 small-sized red onion, chopped
1 cup broccoli florets
6 large-sized eggs
1/2 cup ricotta salata cheese, crumbled
1/2 teaspoon dread basil
1/2 teaspoon dried oregano
1/2 teaspoon rosemary
1/4 teaspoon red pepper flakes, crushed
Sea salt and ground black pepper, to taste
Directions
In an ovenproof skillet, heat the olive oil until sizzling. Once hot, sauté the onion and broccoli florets until they've softened.

Next, beat the eggs, ricotta salata cheese, and spices in a mixing dish.

Pour the egg mixture over the sautéed vegetables in the skillet. Bake your frittata in the preheated oven at 395 degrees F for about 10 minutes,

For a crispy top, broil your frittata under the preheated broiler for 2 minutes. Bon appétit!

Grilled Salmon Melt Sandwiches
(Ready in about 10 minutes | Servings 2)
Per serving: Calories: 364; Fat: 17.5g; Carbs: 30.9g; Protein: 19.7g
Ingredients
3 ounces canned salmon
2 ounces halloumi cheese, sliced
1/2 small cucumber, sliced
1/2 tomato, sliced
Salt and freshly ground black pepper, to taste
1 tablespoon fresh chives, chopped
1 tablespoon extra-virgin olive oil

4 slices Mediterranean olive bread
Directions
Top the slices of bread with the salmon, cheese, cucumber and tomato. Sprinkle salt and pepper over the veggies.

Garnish with fresh chives and top with the remaining bread slices.

Preheat the olive oil in a grilling pan over a moderate flame; once hot, toast the bread slices for 2 minutes on each side until it's golden brown and crisp on top. Bon appétit!

Greek Pita Tostadas
(Ready in about 10 minutes | Servings 3)
Per serving: Calories: 334; Fat: 17.7g; Carbs: 27.1g; Protein: 16.5g
Ingredients
1 tablespoon olive oil
1 bell pepper, seeded and diced
1/2 red onion, finely chopped
1 small-sized zucchini, diced
6 eggs
4 tablespoons sour cream
1/2 teaspoon oregano
1/2 teaspoon rosemary
Sea salt, to season
1 small tomato, diced
3 whole wheat flat Greek pitas
1/3 cup hummus
Directions
Preheat the olive oil in a frying pan over medium-high heat; then, sauté the pepper, onion, and zucchini until they've softened.

In a mixing bowl, whisk the eggs with sour cream until well combined; pour the egg mixture into the pan and sprinkle oregano, rosemary, and salt over everything.

In the meantime, place your pitas on a baking sheet and bake for about 5 minutes or until lightly browned.

Top each tostada with hummus and egg mixture; garnish with tomato and eat warm. Enjoy!

Dad's Cloud Eggs
(Ready in about 15 minutes | Servings 2)
Per serving: Calories: 495; Fat: 25.7g; Carbs: 32.8g; Protein: 31.5g
Ingredients
4 eggs
1/4 teaspoon sea salt
1 teaspoon Dijon mustard
4 ounces Parmesan cheese, grated
4 slices rye bread
1 small tomato, sliced
Directions
Crack the eggs and separate the yolks from the whites; reserve the yolks in a cup.

Add the salt and Dijon mustard to the whites. Beat the egg whites until stiff peaks.

Coat a baking pan with parchment paper. Spoon the egg white mixture onto the pan, forming the "nests". Cook the nests until slightly golden on the top about 3 minutes. Create a furrow in the center of each nest and place them on the bread slices.

Now, carefully add yolks to each egg cloud and transfer the pan to the preheated oven.

Bake the cloud eggs at 360 degrees F for about 5 minutes. Top with parmesan cheese and serve with fresh tomatoes. Bon appétit!

Cheese and Bacon Wraps

(Ready in about 10 minutes | Servings 2)
Per serving: Calories: 577; Fat: 43.5g; Carbs: 28.5g; Protein: 20.1g

Ingredients
2 slices bacon
2 eggs
3 tablespoons Greek-style yogurt
2 tablespoons butter
Sea salt and ground black pepper, to taste
2 flatbreads
1/4 cup Pecorino cheese, shredded
1/2 avocado, pitted and sliced

Directions
Preheat a frying pan over medium-high heat and cook the bacon until crisp about 6 minutes; crumble with a fork and reserve.

Beat the eggs and yogurt with a balloon whisk until well combined.

In the same frying pan, melt the butter and cook the eggs until set; season the eggs with salt and pepper.

Assemble the warps: In the center of each flatbread, layer bacon, eggs, cheese, and sliced avocado. Roll them up and serve warm. Enjoy!

Traditional Socca with Spinach

(Ready in about 40 minutes | Servings 3)
Per serving: Calories: 207; Fat: 8.9g; Carbs: 19.4g; Protein: 10.7g

Ingredients
1 cup besan (chickpea flour)
1 cup sparkling water
1 tablespoon fresh lemon juice
1 teaspoon olive oil
A pinch of granulated sugar
A pinch of salt
1 teaspoon za'atar
1 cup spinach, chopped
1/2 cup feta cheese, crumbled

Directions
Whisk the flour, sparkling water, lemon juice, olive oil, sugar, and salt until well combined. Allow the batter to rest for about 30 minutes.

Add in the za'atar and spinach and stir again to combine well.

Pour the batter into a lightly greased baking pan and transfer it to the preheated oven.

Bake your socca for about 10 minutes until the top begins to blister. Cut into wedges just before serving. Serve with crumbled feta cheese and enjoy!

Tuna and Corn Fritters

(Ready in about 15 minutes | Servings 3)
Per serving: Calories: 381; Fat: 16.4g; Carbs: 32.4g; Protein: 27g

Ingredients
1 egg
1 teaspoon balsamic vinegar
2 tablespoons pecorino cheese, grated
6 tablespoons Italian bread crumbs
10 ounces canned tuna, drained
2 ounces sweet corn kernels, thawed
2 tablespoons sweet onions, chopped
1 teaspoon fresh garlic, chopped
Sea salt and ground black pepper, to taste
2 tablespoons olive oil

Directions
Whisk the eggs and vinegar until pale and frothy; stir in the pecorino cheese, bread crumbs, tuna, corn, sweet onions, garlic, salt, and black pepper. Stir to combine well.

Form the tuna mixture into equal balls and flatten them to make the patties.

Then, heat the olive oil in a frying pan over a moderately high heat.

Once hot, fry the fritters until golden brown and thoroughly cooked, about 10 minutes; make sure to turn your fritters over to promote even cooking. Bon appétit!

Sardine Salad Sandwiches

(Ready in about 10 minutes | Servings 3)
Per serving: Calories: 536; Fat: 37.1g; Carbs: 28.6g; Protein: 21.1g

Ingredients
8 ounces canned sardines in tomato sauce, drained, bones removed, and flaked
1/2 cup mayonnaise
1 bell pepper, sliced
1/2 teaspoon garlic, pressed
1 small-sized red onion, sliced
1 tablespoon red wine vinegar
1 tablespoon caper, drained
6 slices rye bread

Directions
Thoroughly combine the canned sardines, mayonnaise, pepper, garlic, onion, red wine, and caper.

Assemble sandwiches with the chilled salad and serve immediately. Bon appétit!

Spanish-Style Toasted Bread

(Ready in about 5 minutes | Servings 1)
Per serving: Calories: 414; Fat: 16.8g; Carbs: 44.1g; Protein: 22.6g

Ingredients
2 slices whole-grain bread

2 ounces soft cheese
2 ounces fresh mixed berries
1 teaspoon pepitas, chopped
Directions
Preheat a lightly greased nonstick skillet over a moderately high heat.
Once hot, toast the bread slices on each side until they are golden brown and crisp on top.
Top each toasted slice of bread with soft cheese, mixed berries, and chopped pepitas.
Bon appétit!

Traditional Kagianas with Cherry Tomatoes

(Ready in about 10 minutes | Servings 2)
Per serving: Calories: 364; Fat: 22.6g; Carbs: 23.1g; Protein: 18.3g
Ingredients
1 tablespoon olive oil
2 stalks green onion, chopped
8 ounces cherry tomatoes, sliced in half
4 large eggs
1/2 teaspoon dried oregano
1 teaspoon fresh mint
Sea salt and ground black pepper, to taste
2 ounces feta, crumbled
Directions
Heat the olive oil in a pan over medium flame, and then, sauté the onion until tender and fragrant, about 2 minutes.
Add in the tomatoes and continue to sauté for another 2 minutes.
Beat the eggs in a small dish and pour into the pan; increase the heat and stir your eggs quickly with a spoon carefully, making sure not to smash the tomatoes.
Cook until the eggs are slightly thickened. Sprinkle with oregano, mint, salt, and black pepper.
Garnish with crumbled feta and serve warm. Enjoy!

Authentic Yiaourti Me Meli

(Ready in about 10 minutes | Servings 4)
Per serving: Calories: 266; Fat: 13.6g; Carbs: 28.7g; Protein: 11.7g
Ingredients
1 cup walnuts
2 cups Greek-style yogurt, strained
1/3 cup honey
Directions
Heat a frying pan over medium-high heat. Add the walnuts to the hot pan. Toast your walnuts, stirring continuously until the walnuts start to brown and smell toasted for 4 to 5 minutes.
Chop the walnuts and set them aside.
Divide the strained Greek yogurt between four serving bowls; top the yogurt with toasted walnuts and honey and serve immediately.

Tahini & Feta Toast

(Ready in about 10 minutes | Servings 2)

Per serving: Calories: 246; Fat: 12.6g; Carbs: 23.3g; Protein: 9.7g
Ingredients
4 slices crusty bread
4 teaspoons tahini paste (sesame butter)
1 medium tomato, sliced
2 ounces feta cheese, crumbled
1 tablespoon fresh basil leaves, roughly chopped
Directions
Toast your bread on a hot and dry frying pan until golden brown, about 3 minutes per side.
Now, spread each slice of bread with the tahini or sesame butter.
Top the toasted bread with tomato and crumbled feta cheese. Garnish with fresh basil and serve immediately.
Bon appétit!

Aromatic Granola with Walnuts and Coconut

(Ready in about 1 hour 25 minutes | Servings 10)
Per serving: Calories: 480; Fat: 28.6g; Carbs: 46g; Protein: 13.7g
Ingredients
4 cups rolled oats
2 cups walnuts, roughly chopped
1/2 cup pumpkin seeds
1/2 cup sunflower seeds
1 cup coconut flakes
1/2 cup coconut sugar
1/2 cup extra-virgin olive oil
1/2 teaspoon cinnamon
1/2 teaspoon cardamom
1/4 teaspoon grated nutmeg
1/4 teaspoon ground cloves
A pinch of salt
Directions
Start by preheating your oven to 250 degrees F.
In a mixing bowl, thoroughly combine the oats, walnuts, seeds, coconut flakes, and coconut sugar.
Then, gradually stir in the remaining ingredients and stir to combine well.
Spread the mixture onto a parchment-lined baking sheet.
Bake your granola in the preheated oven for 1 hour and 20 minutes, stirring every 30 minutes to promote even cooking. Enjoy!

Eliopsomo (Olive and Herb Bread)

(Ready in about 2 hours | Servings 8)
Per serving: Calories: 336; Fat: 14.4g; Carbs: 45.5g; Protein: 8.1g
Ingredients
2 cups plain flour
1 ¾ cups whole-wheat flour
1/4 ounce instant dry yeast
1 cup lukewarm water
1/4 cup extra-virgin olive oil
1 ½ teaspoons sea salt
1 teaspoon honey

1 tablespoon dried rosemary
1 tablespoon dried oregano
1 tablespoon dried basil
A pinch of freshly grated nutmeg
A pinch of ground cloves
1 cup olives, pitted and chopped
4 ounces halloumi cheese

Directions

Thoroughly combine the flour and instant yeast; gradually, pour in the water and olive oil.

Now, add in the salt, and honey and mix to combine well.

Transfer your dough to a floured working surface. Now, knead and stretch the dough for several times until it is elastic and smooth.

Roll the dough in a ball and cover with plastic wrap; let it rest in a warm place for about an hour.

Divide the ball into two separate balls. Stretch the ball using a rolling pin and top each of them with herbs and olives. Form the pieces of dough into balls again.

Let the balls rest for about 30 minutes. Then, bake your bread in the preheated oven at 420 degrees F for 30 to 35 minutes.

Serve with halloumi cheese and enjoy!

Mom's Breakfast Tomatoes

(Ready in about 35 minutes | Servings 4)

Per serving: Calories: 245; Fat: 16.8g; Carbs: 9.2g; Protein: 14.7g

Ingredients

4 tomatoes, tops, seeds, and pulp removed
4 teaspoons olive oil
4 eggs
1/4 teaspoon sea salt
1/4 teaspoon ground black pepper
1/4 teaspoon cayenne pepper
4 ounces parmesan cheese, grated

Directions

Start by preheating your over to 370 degrees F. Line a baking pan with the parchment paper.

Place your tomatoes on the baking pan and brush them with olive oil. Crack one egg into each tomato. Sprinkle the salt, black pepper, and cayenne pepper on them.

Roast the stuffed tomatoes for about 30 minutes, rotating the pan halfway through the cooking time.

Top the warm tomatoes with the grated parmesan cheese; serve warm or at room temperature. Bon appétit!

Tuna, Kale and Yogurt Pie

(Ready in about 40 minutes | Servings 6)

Per serving: Calories: 514; Fat: 32.6g; Carbs: 39.5g; Protein: 17.6g

Ingredients

1 tablespoon olive oil
1 red onion, chopped
1/2 teaspoon fresh garlic, chopped
1 rosemary sprig, leaves picked

1 thyme sprig, leaves picked
10 ounces canned tuna, drained
1 pound button mushrooms, chopped
Sea salt and ground black pepper, to taste
1 cup Greek-style yogurt
1 teaspoon yellow mustard
2 cups loosely packed kale
1 pound puff pastry, rolled into a circle
1 teaspoon olive oil

Directions

Heat olive oil in an oven-proof dish. Now, sauté the onion for 2 to 3 minutes until tender and translucent.

Now, stir in the garlic, rosemary, thyme, and continue to sauté an additional 30 seconds until aromatic.

Add in the canned tuna, mushrooms, salt, and black pepper. Remove the dish from the heat and stir in the yogurt, mustard, and kale. Cover with the puff pastry, pressing into the sides of the dish.

Mix 1 teaspoon of olive oil with 2 tablespoons of water.

Drizzle the top of your pie with the olive oil mixture. Bake in the preheated oven at 390 degrees F for 30 to 35 minutes until it is puffed up and golden. Bon appétit!

Authentic Greek Spanakopita

(Ready in about 45 minutes | Servings 4)

Per serving: Calories: 438; Fat: 28.2g; Carbs: 32.5g; Protein: 16.9g

Ingredients

2 tablespoons olive oil
1 red onion, chopped
1 teaspoon garlic, minced
1 ½ pounds spinach, chopped
1 teaspoon basil
1/2 teaspoon oregano
Sea salt and ground black pepper, to taste
1 cup Greek-style yogurt
2 eggs
8 phyllo sheets
4 tablespoons extra-virgin olive oil

Directions

Start by preheating your oven to 350 degrees F. Then, grease the sides and bottom of a baking pan with a nonstick cooking oil.

Heat 2 tablespoons of olive oil in a frying pan over moderately high heat. Sauté the onion and garlic until tender and aromatic.

Now, stir in the spinach, basil, oregano, salt, and black pepper, and continue to sauté for a further 2 to 3 minutes. Heat off.

Then, beat the yogurt with eggs until frothy and well combined. Stir in the spinach mixture.

Place a sheet of phyllo in the prepared baking pan and brush with a little bit of extra-virgin olive oil. Repeat with 3 more phyllo sheets.

Spoon the spinach mixture onto the phyllo sheets. Cover with the remaining phyllo sheets brushing each one with olive oil.

Tuck the overhanging phyllo sheets into the pan.

Bake your spanakopita in the preheated oven for about 35 minutes, until golden on the top. Remove your spanakopita from the oven and let it cool slightly before slicing and serving. Enjoy!

Breakfast Zucchini Patties

(Ready in about 15 minutes | Servings 3)

Per serving: Calories: 268; Fat: 18g; Carbs: 15.1g; Protein: 10.6g

Ingredients
1 large zucchini, grated
1 egg, beaten
1 small shallot, chopped
1 garlic clove, minced
1/4 cup chickpea flour
1/4 cup all-purpose flour
1/2 cup pecorino cheese, grated
1/3 cup soft Mediterranean cheese
Sea salt and ground black pepper, to taste
2 tablespoons olive oil

Directions
Thoroughly combine the zucchini, beaten eggs, shallot, garlic, flour, cheese, salt, and pepper in a bowl.
Heat olive oil in a frying pan over medium-high heat.
Drop the zucchini mixture by heaping tablespoonfuls onto the hot oil; fry the zucchini patties for about 3 minutes per side or until golden.
Serve with chilled yogurt or tahini sauce if desired. Bon appétit!

Traditional Greek Spanakokeftethes

(Ready in about 15 minutes | Servings 2)

Per serving: Calories: 394; Fat: 26.4g; Carbs: 22.9g; Protein: 19.5g

Ingredients
9 cups packed spinach
1 medium-sized leek, chopped
2 garlic cloves, minced
1/2 teaspoon cumin seeds
1/4 teaspoon fennel seeds
2 tablespoons dill, chopped
2 tablespoons fresh basil, chopped
2 large eggs, beaten
1/2 cup Parmesan cheese, grated
Sea salt and ground black pepper, to taste
1/2 cup breadcrumbs
2 tablespoons olive oil

Directions
In a large pot, heat the spinach in water until it wilts; strain well.
Thoroughly combine the spinach with leeks, garlic, cumin seeds, fennel seeds, dill, and basil.
Gradually, stir in the eggs and cheese, and mix until everything is well combined. Season with salt and black pepper.
Next, shape the mixture into equal patties. Cover them with the breadcrumbs, pressing to coat well.

Heat the olive oil in a nonstick skillet over a moderately high heat; cook the patties for about 3 minutes per side. Serve warm and enjoy!

Menemen (Turkish Omelet)

(Ready in about 15 minutes | Servings 2)

Per serving: Calories: 344; Fat: 24.4g; Carbs: 15.7g; Protein: 16.5g

Ingredients
2 tablespoons olive oil
1/2 red onion, chopped
2 cloves garlic, chopped
1 bell pepper, chopped
1 Anaheim pepper, chopped
2 tomatoes, chopped
Sea salt and ground black pepper, to taste
1/4 teaspoon cayenne pepper
5 eggs
1 tablespoon fresh parsley, chopped
1 tablespoon fresh mint, chopped

Directions
Heat olive oil in a frying pan over a moderately heat. Now, sauté the vegetables until they've softened.
Using a spoon, create the holes in the mixture; crack an egg into each hole. Sprinkle the salt, black pepper, and cayenne pepper on them.
Turn the temperature to a simmer and continue to cook for about 9 minutes or until eggs are cooked to your desired doneness.
Garnish with parsley and mint leaves and serve immediately.

Caprese Egg Cups

(Ready in about 20 minutes | Servings 6)

Per serving: Calories: 380; Fat: 25.7g; Carbs: 7.6g; Protein: 28.5g

Ingredients
12 fresh mozzarella mini balls
12 eggs
12 teaspoons pesto sauce
12 grape tomatoes, cut in half
Sea salt and freshly ground black pepper, to taste
1 teaspoon garlic powder
1 cup parmesan cheese, grated
1 tablespoon balsamic vinegar
2 tablespoons fresh Italian parsley, roughly chopped

Directions
Start by preheating your oven to 350 degrees F.
Spritz a muffin tin with a nonstick cooking spray.
Divide the mozzarella balls, eggs, pesto sauce, and tomatoes between 12 muffin cups. Sprinkle the salt, black pepper, and garlic powder over them.
Top with parmesan cheese and transfer the muffin tin to the preheated oven. Bake your cups for about 15 minutes.
Garnish with a few drizzles of balsamic vinegar and fresh Italian parsley. Bon appétit!

Cheesy Carrot Croquettes

(Ready in about 15 minutes | Servings 4)

Per serving: Calories: 388; Fat: 22.4g; Carbs: 32.2g; Protein: 15.5g

Ingredients

2 carrots, grated
1 red onion, chopped
4 ounces pecorino cheese, grated
1 tablespoon lemon zest
2 tablespoons all-purpose flour
2 eggs, whisked
1/4 teaspoon dried dill weed
1/2 teaspoon ground cumin
Sea salt and ground black pepper, to taste
2 tablespoons olive oil
4 hamburger buns
2 ounces Kalamata olives, pitted and sliced
1 tomato, sliced

Directions

Thoroughly combine the carrots, onion, cheese, lemon zest, flour, eggs, dill, ground cumin, salt, and black pepper in a bowl.

Now, using oiled hands, shape the mixture into equal balls and flatten them lightly.

Heat the olive oil in a frying pan over medium-high heat. Cook the croquettes for 4 to 5 minutes until they're nicely browned on all sides, turning them over to ensure even cooking.

Place your croquettes on hamburger buns, garnish with olives and tomatoes and serve warm. Bon appétit!

Italian Zucchini and Prosciutto Pie

(Ready in about 40 minutes | Servings 6)

Per serving: Calories: 228; Fat: 12.4g; Carbs: 17g; Protein: 10.4g

Ingredients

8 phyllo sheets
1 cup parmesan cheese, grated
1 tomato, chopped
1 zucchini, thinly sliced
4 ounces prosciutto, diced
1 teaspoon Italian seasoning
2 tablespoons olive oil combined with 4 tablespoons warm water
1 egg yolk, whisked

Directions

Start by preheating the oven to 390 degrees F. Brush the sides and bottom of baking dish with a nonstick cooking spray.

In a bowl, combine the parmesan cheese, tomato, zucchini, prosciutto, and Italian seasoning.

Place a sheet of phyllo in the prepared baking pan and brush with the olive oil mixture. Repeat with 3 more phyllo sheets.

Spoon the zucchini mixture onto the phyllo sheets. Cover with the remaining phyllo sheets, brushing each one with the olive oil mixture.

Tuck the overhanging phyllo sheets into the pan. Brush the top of your pie with the whisked egg yolk. Bake your pie in the preheated oven for about 35 minutes until golden on the top. Remove your pie

from the oven and let it cool slightly before slicing and serving. Enjoy!

Herb and Sun-Dried Tomato Bread

(Ready in about 2 hours | Servings 8)

Per serving: Calories: 178; Fat: 7.2g; Carbs: 24.7g; Protein: 3.6g

Ingredients

2 cups plain flour
1/4 ounce instant dry yeast
1 ½ teaspoons sea salt
1 teaspoon brown sugar
1/4 cup extra-virgin olive oil
1 cup lukewarm water
2 ounces sun-dried tomatoes, chopped
1 tablespoon dried rosemary
1 tablespoon dried basil
1 tablespoon dried oregano

Directions

Thoroughly combine the flour and instant yeast; add in the salt and sugar and mix to combine well.

Gradually, pour in the olive oil and water.

Transfer your dough to a floured working surface. Knead and stretch the dough for several times until it is elastic and smooth.

Roll the dough into a ball and cover with plastic wrap; let it rest in a warm place for about an hour.

Stretch the ball using a rolling pin and place sun-dried tomatoes and herbs on the top.

Let the ball rest for about 30 minutes. Then, bake your bread in the preheated oven at 420 degrees F for 30 to 35 minutes or until a tester comes out dry and clean.

Serve with feta cheese and olives, if desired. Bon appétit!

Breakfast Polenta with Scrambled Eggs

(Ready in about 20 minutes | Servings 3)

Per serving: Calories: 564; Fat: 27.2g; Carbs: 57g; Protein: 21.9g

Ingredients

1 cup water
3 cups vegetable broth
2 cups milk
1 ½ cups polenta
1/2 cup soft Mediterranean cheese
1/2 cup pecorino cheese
2 tablespoons olive oil
3 spring onion stalks, sliced
1 teaspoon garlic, pressed
1 bell pepper, cut into strips
3 eggs, lightly beaten
Sea salt and ground black pepper, to taste
1 large tomato, sliced

Directions

Add the milk, broth, and water to a saucepan and bring to a boil. Slowly and gradually, stir in the polenta and bring to a rolling boil.

Immediately reduce the heat to a simmer and cook, stirring constantly with a wire whisk, for about 10 minutes until the polenta has thickened.

Add in the cheese and remove from the heat.

Heat olive oil in a frying pan; now, sauté the onion, garlic, and peppers until they are tender. Pour in the eggs and continue to cook, stirring frequently, until the eggs are set or about 5 minutes.

Divide your polenta between three serving plates; top each of them with the egg/vegetable mixture and season with salt and black pepper.

Garnish with fresh tomato and serve immediately.

Fluffy Mini Frittatas

(Ready in about 15 minutes | Servings 4)
Per serving: Calories: 247; Fat: 17.3g; Carbs: 6.3g; Protein: 16.7g
Ingredients
8 eggs
1/3 cup creme fraiche
Sea salt and ground black pepper, to taste
1/2 teaspoon cayenne pepper, to taste
1 bell pepper, chopped
1/3 cup sun-dried tomatoes, chopped
1/2 cup pecorino cheese, grated
1/4 cup green olives, pitted and sliced
2 tablespoons scallions, chopped
2 tablespoons Italian parsley, roughly chopped
Directions
Beat the eggs, creme fraiche, and spices in a mixing dish.

Pour the egg mixture into the lightly greased muffin cups. Evenly distribute the remaining ingredients between the muffin cups.

Bake the mini frittatas in the preheated oven at 380 degrees F for about 10 minutes,

For a crispy top, broil your frittatas under the preheated broiler for 2 minutes. Bon appétit!

Scrambled Eggs with Asparagus and Goat Cheese

(Ready in about 15 minutes | Servings 4)
Per serving: Calories: 466; Fat: 36.3g; Carbs: 5.4g; Protein: 29.1g
Ingredients
8 eggs, beaten
1/4 cup Greek-style yogurt
1/2 teaspoon red pepper flakes, crushed
Sea salt and ground black pepper, to taste
2 tablespoons olive oil, divided
1 cup asparagus spears, finely chopped
1 cup goat cheese, crumbled
Directions
Using a wire whisk, thoroughly combine the eggs, yogurt, red pepper, salt, and black pepper.

Heat the olive oil in a frying pan over medium flame. Once hot, add the asparagus to the pan and continue to cook for 7 to 8 minutes or until the eggs begin to set.

Garnish with goat cheese and serve immediately. Bon appétit!

Easy Caprese Toast

(Ready in about 5 minutes | Servings 2)
Per serving: Calories: 206; Fat: 11.3g; Carbs: 20.1g; Protein: 6.1g
Ingredients
2 slices rye bread
1/2 avocado, peeled and mashed
2 tablespoons feta cheese
1 tomato, sliced
Flaked sea salt and black pepper, to taste
1 heaping tablespoon basil leaves
Directions
Toast the bread slices on each side until they are golden brown and crisp on top.

Top each toasted slice of bread with the mashed avocado, feta cheese and tomatoes; sprinkle salt and pepper on them.

Garnish with fresh basil leaves and serve immediately. Bon appétit!

Oatmeal with Figs and Pistachios

(Ready in about 10 minutes | Servings 3)
Per serving: Calories: 532; Fat: 9.3g; Carbs: 95.1g; Protein: 21.1g
Ingredients
3 cups of water
1 ½ cups rolled oats
1/2 teaspoon ground cinnamon
1/4 teaspoon freshly grated nutmeg
1/4 teaspoon ground cloves
7 medium-sized fresh figs, chopped
6 ounces Greek yogurt
3 tablespoons pistachios, shelled and roughly chopped
3 tablespoons honey
Directions
Bring the water to a rolling boil; immediately, turn the heat to medium; stir in the rolled oats and cook for about 5 minutes, stirring periodically.

Stir the cinnamon, nutmeg, and cloves into the hot oatmeal.

Divide your oatmeal between individual bowls. Top each serving with the other ingredients and serve immediately. Enjoy!

Crunch Cereal with Cranberries

(Ready in about 30 minutes | Servings 15)
Per serving: Calories: 316; Fat: 15.1g; Carbs: 37.2g; Protein: 10.2g
Ingredients
4 cups rolled oats
1 cup wheat germ
1/2 cup sunflower seeds
1/2 cup finely chopped almonds
1/2 cup finely chopped walnuts
1 teaspoon salt
1/2 cup brown sugar

1/2 cup olive oil
1/2 teaspoon cardamom
1/2 teaspoon grated nutmeg
1 teaspoon crystallized ginger
1 teaspoon ground cinnamon
1 teaspoon vanilla extract
1 cup cranberries
Directions
Start by preheating the oven to 320 degrees F. Then, coat a large baking sheet with parchment paper.
Mix all ingredients, except for the cranberries, until everything is well combined. Spread it out evenly on the prepared baking sheets.
Bake the crunch cereal in the preheated oven for about 25 minutes until toasted and crispy, stirring every 10 minutes.
Allow the crunch cereal to cool; then, add in the cranberries and stir to combine. Bon appétit!

Spanish Chorizo Egg Cups

(Ready in about 15 minutes | Servings 4)
Per serving: Calories: 246; Fat: 17.2g; Carbs: 5.8g; Protein: 15.7g
Ingredients
7 large eggs, beaten
4 ounces chorizo sausage, chopped
1 Spanish pepper, chopped
1 jalapeno peppers, chopped
1 Spanish onion, chopped
1 tablespoon fresh cilantro, chopped
1/2 teaspoon garlic, minced
Sea salt and ground black pepper, to taste
Directions
Beat the eggs in a mixing bowl.
Pour the eggs into lightly greased muffin cups. Evenly distribute the remaining ingredients between the muffin cups.
Bake the egg cups in the preheated oven at 390 degrees F for about 10 minutes,
For a crispy top, broil the egg cups under the preheated broiler for 2 minutes. Bon appétit!

Authentic Mediterranean Strata

(Ready in about 45 minutes | Servings 4)
Per serving: Calories: 456; Fat: 19.8g; Carbs: 43g; Protein: 26.3g
Ingredients
1 teaspoon olive oil
1/2 pound olive bread, cubed
1/2 pound cooked turkey sausage, crumbled
1 Spanish pepper, chopped
1 jalapeno pepper, chopped
1/4 cup kalamata olives, pitted and quartered
1 garlic clove, chopped
4 medium-sized eggs
1 cup half and half
1/2 cup asiago cheese, shredded
1 teaspoon dried marjoram leaves
Sea salt and ground black pepper, to taste
Directions

Start by preheating your oven to 340 degrees F. Then, brush the insides of four ramekins with olive oil. Then, divide the bread, sausage, peppers, olives, and garlic between the prepared ramekins.
In a mixing bowl, beat the eggs with half and half until well combined; add in the cheese, marjoram, salt, and black pepper. Pour this mixture into the ramekins.
Bake your strata in the preheated oven for about 40 minutes. Transfer to a wire rack and allow your strata to rest for a few minutes before serving. Bon appétit!

French Toast with Cranberries

(Ready in about 45 minutes | Servings 2)
Per serving: Calories: 445; Fat: 14.1g; Carbs: 58.3g; Protein: 20.3g
Ingredients
2 eggs
A pinch of flaked sea salt
A pinch of freshly grated nutmeg
1/2 teaspoon ground cinnamon
1/4 cup milk
4 tablespoons brown sugar
4 slices multi grain bread
4 teaspoons dried cranberries
Directions
In a mixing bowl, beat the eggs, salt, nutmeg, cinnamon, milk, and brown sugar.
Dip each bread slice in the spiced egg mixture, coating well on both sides.
Preheat a griddle pan over a moderately high heat and cook the French toast until it is golden brown or about 6 minutes.
Garnish with dried cranberries and serve. Enjoy!

Hash Brown and Sardine Casserole

(Ready in about 55 minutes | Servings 4)
Per serving: Calories: 555; Fat: 31.6g; Carbs: 34.1g; Protein: 34.3g
Ingredients
12 ounces frozen hash browns
8 ounces canned sardines, drained, deboned and flaked
1 red onion, chopped
1 teaspoon Dijon mustard
6 eggs
1/2 cup Greek yogurt
1/2 teaspoon dried basil
1/2 teaspoon dried oregano
1/2 teaspoon dried marjoram
1/2 teaspoon cayenne pepper
Sea salt and ground black pepper, to taste
4 ounces Asiago cheese, shredded
Directions
Mix the hash browns, sardines, onions, and mustard in a bowl and transfer the mixture to a lightly oiled casserole dish.
In a mixing bowl, beat the eggs, Greek yogurt, spices, and cheese.

Distribute the egg mixture evenly over the hash brown layer.

Bake your casserole in the preheated oven at 360 degrees F for about 50 minutes or until heated through. Bon appétit!

Morning Bread Pudding with Kale

(Ready in about 1 hour | Servings 4)

Per serving: Calories: 582; Fat: 24.1g; Carbs: 68.5g; Protein: 24.3g

Ingredients

2 tablespoons olive oil
1 loaf rye bread
2 cloves garlic, pressed
8 ounces kale, torn into pieces
1 Italian pepper, chopped
1 large tomato, chopped
1/2 cup black olives, pitted and roughly chopped
Sea salt and ground black pepper, to taste
4 eggs
1 cup milk
1/2 cuppecorino cheese, grated

Directions

Start by preheating your oven to 340 degrees F. Then, brush the inside of a baking dish with 1 tablespoon of the olive oil.

Then, place the bread, garlic, kale, pepper, tomatoes, and olives in the prepared baking dish. Drizzle the remaining tablespoon of olive oil on them and season with salt and pepper to taste.

In a mixing bowl, beat the eggs with milk; now, pour this mixture into the baking dish.

Bake the bread pudding in the preheated oven for about 40 minutes. Top the bread pudding with the grated cheese and continue to bake an additional 5 to 7 minutes or until the cheese is bubbly.

Transfer to a wire rack and allow the bread pudding to rest for 5 to 10 minutes before cutting and serving. Bon appétit!

Breakfast Tortilla Española

(Ready in about 25 minutes | Servings 2)

Per serving: Calories: 552; Fat: 35.1g; Carbs: 43.3g; Protein: 16.3g

Ingredients

1/4 cup olive oil
1 pound potatoes, peeled and sliced
1/2 red onion, chopped
1 garlic clove, minced
4 eggs
Salt and freshly ground black pepper, to taste

Directions

Heat the olive oil in a frying pan over a moderate flame. Once hot, cook the potato slice, stirring and turning periodically, until they've softened or about 10 minutes.

Add in the onion and garlic; continue to cook for 2 minutes more or until fragrant.

Meanwhile, beat the eggs until pale and frothy and pour the mixture into the frying pan. Cook your tortilla for about 4 minutes, and then, reduce the heat to medium-low. Cook for a further 4 to 5 minutes. Season your tortilla with salt and black pepper and serve warm.

SOUPS & SALADS

Red Lentil and Vegetable Soup

(Ready in about 25 minutes | Servings 4)

Per serving: Calories: 295; Fat: 6.5g; Carbs: 45.4g; Protein: 16.8g

Ingredients

1 tablespoon olive oil
1 red onion, chopped
1 medium zucchini, diced
1 celery stalk with leaves, chopped
1 carrot, peeled, chopped
6 ounces button mushrooms, chopped
1 teaspoon garlic, minced
1 tablespoon fresh basil
1 tablespoon fresh parsley
1 teaspoon fresh rosemary
Sea salt and ground black pepper, to taste
1/2 teaspoon turmeric powder
1/2 teaspoon cayenne pepper
2 tomatoes, chopped
8 ounces red lentils, rinsed and drained
4 cups vegetable broth

Directions

Heat the olive oil in a soup pot over medium-high heat. Once hot, sauté the onion until just tender and translucent.

Now, add in the zucchini, celery, and carrots and continue to sauté an additional 3 minutes until they are just tender. Add a splash of vegetable broth, if needed.

Stir in the mushrooms, garlic and herbs, and continue to cook for a minute or so until fragrant.

Add in the salt, black pepper, turmeric powder, cayenne pepper, tomatoes, red lentils, and vegetable broth.

Turn the heat to a simmer and let it cook for 15 to 20 minutes or until the lentils have softened and your soup is cooked through. Enjoy!

Sicilian Sausage and Cannellini Bean Soup

(Ready in about 30 minutes | Servings 3)

Per serving: Calories: 426; Fat: 35g; Carbs: 12.7g; Protein: 18g

Ingredients

1 tablespoon olive oil
1/2 pound Italian sausage
1/2 teaspoon garlic powder
1/2 teaspoon dried basil
1/2 teaspoon dried marjoram
1/2 teaspoon dried savory
1/2 teaspoon red pepper flakes
3 cups chicken stock, preferably homemade
6 ounces canned Italian-style stewed tomatoes
6 ounces canned Cannellini beans, drained
2 cups kale, torn into smaller pieces
Sea salt and ground black pepper, to taste
2 ounces Parmigiano-Reggiano cheese, freshly grated

Directions

Heat the olive oil in a Dutch oven until sizzling; once hot, brown the sausage for 3 minutes, crumbling with a fork.

Add in the garlic powder, basil, marjoram, dried savory, red pepper, chicken stock and stewed tomatoes. Continue to simmer, covered, for 12 to 13 minutes.

Stir in the canned beans and kale and continue to simmer for 10 minutes more; heat off. Season with salt and pepper to taste.

Ladle the soup into individual serving bowls and top each serving with the grated Parmigiano-Reggiano cheese.

Bon appétit!

Fattoush (Traditional Lebanese Salad)

(Ready in about 10 minutes | Servings 2)

Per serving: Calories: 336; Fat: 15g; Carbs: 43.9g; Protein: 7.7g

Ingredients

1 Lebanese cucumber, peeled and diced
1 medium-sized tomato, finely diced
1 small-sized red onion, chopped
1/2 chili pepper, chopped
2 tablespoons fresh parsley, finely chopped
2 tablespoons fresh mint, finely chopped
2 tablespoons fresh basil, finely chopped
2 tablespoons fresh lemon juice
2 tablespoons extra-virgin olive oil
1/2 teaspoon sumac
Sea salt and freshly ground pepper, to taste
1 teaspoon stone-ground mustard
2 (6-inch) Lebanese pita breads, cut into wedges

Directions

In a salad bowl, toss the cucumber, tomato, red onion, chili pepper, parsley, mint, and basil; toss to combine well.

Make the dressing by whisking the lemon juice, olive oil, sumac, salt, black pepper, and mustard.

Meanwhile, toast the bread in a nonstick skillet over a moderately high flame.

Dress the salad and top each serving with the toasted wedges of Lebanese pita bread. Enjoy!

Greek-Style Summer Salad

(Ready in about 10 minutes | Servings 4)

Per serving: Calories: 328; Fat: 21.5g; Carbs: 24g; Protein: 11.2g

Ingredients

2 tomatoes, diced
1 Greek cucumber, sliced
1 bell pepper, sliced
2 handfuls baby spinach leaves
1 red onion, thinly sliced
1 cup radishes, sliced
8 ounces canned red kidney beans, drained
1 cup feta cheese, crumbled
4 tablespoons extra-virgin olive oil

1 lime, freshly squeezed
1 teaspoon dried Greek oregano
1 tablespoon mint
1 teaspoon dried basil
1/2 teaspoon dried dill weed
1/2 teaspoon ground thyme
1 garlic clove, pressed
1 tablespoon honey

Directions

Toss all ingredients, except for the feta cheese, in a large salad bowl. Toss to combine well.

Divide the salad between four individual bowls and top each of them with crumbled feta cheese. Eat immediately.

Spanish-Style Sausage Soup with Garbanzos

(Ready in about 30 minutes | Servings 4)

Per serving: Calories: 320; Fat: 21.8g; Carbs: 21.2g; Protein: 15.6g

Ingredients

1 teaspoon olive oil
1/2 pound andouille sausage, sliced
1/2 medium leek onion, diced
1 Spanish pepper, sliced
2 carrots, sliced
4 cups roasted vegetable broth
1 teaspoon hot sauce
1/2 teaspoon cayenne pepper
1/2 teaspoon saffron
2 cans garbanzo beans, drained and rinsed
Sea salt and ground black pepper, to taste

Directions

Heat the olive oil in a Dutch oven until sizzling; once hot, brown the sausage for 3 minutes, crumbling with a fork.

Stir in the leek, pepper, and carrots and continue to sauté for 3 minutes longer until tender and aromatic. Add in the vegetables broth, hot sauce, cayenne pepper, and saffron and continue to simmer, covered, for about 15 minutes.

Stir in the canned garbanzo beans and continue to simmer for 7 to 8 minutes more; heat off. Season with salt and pepper to taste.

Ladle the soup into individual serving bowls and top each serving with some extra hot sauce, if desired. Enjoy!

Authentic Greek Khoriatiki (Anchovy Salad)

(Ready in about 10 minutes | Servings 4)

Per serving: Calories: 370; Fat: 29.5g; Carbs: 5.9g; Protein: 20.9g

Ingredients

4 anchovy fillets
2 ripe tomatoes, diced
1 Greek cucumber, sliced
1 red onion, thinly sliced
1/2 teaspoon garlic, minced
4 tablespoons extra-virgin olive oil

2 tablespoons red wine vinegar
1 tablespoon lemon juice
1 tablespoon fresh Greek oregano, finely chopped
1 tablespoon fresh basil, finely chopped
1 tablespoon fresh parsley, finely chopped
1 teaspoon fresh dill
Sea salt and ground black pepper, to season
4 ounces halloumi cheese, cubed
1/2 cup Greek olives, pitted and sliced

Directions

Grill the anchovy fillets over a hot charcoal fire or in a grill pan for about 2 minutes per side, or until the flesh becomes white. Reserve.

In a salad bowl, place all of the vegetables and toss to combine. Then, add in the olive oil, vinegar, lemon juice, and seasonings.

Toss to combine well. Mound the salad on a platter. Top the salad with grilled anchovy fillets. Garnish the salad with halloumi cheese and Greek olives and serve immediately.

Rich Quinoa, Bean and Vegetable Soup

(Ready in about 30 minutes | Servings 4)

Per serving: Calories: 395; Fat: 12.9g; Carbs: 57g; Protein: 13.9g

Ingredients

2 tablespoons olive oil
1 medium-sized leek, chopped
2 carrots, trimmed and chopped
1 yellow squash, diced
3 garlic cloves, pressed
1/2 teaspoon dried marjoram
1/2 teaspoon dried oregano
1/2 teaspoon dried rosemary
1/2 teaspoon lemon thyme
1 teaspoon dried basil
2 ripe tomatoes, crushed
1 cup quinoa, rinsed
2 cups cream of onion soup
2 cups water
Cracked mixed peppercorns, to taste
1 bay laurel
10 ounces canned Great Northern beans, rinsed and drained

Directions

Heat the olive oil in a soup pot over medium-high heat. Once hot, sauté the leek until tender and fragrant.

Now, add in the carrots and yellow squash; continue to sauté an additional 3 to 4 minutes until they are just tender.

Stir in the garlic and herbs, and continue to cook for a minute or so, until aromatic. Add in the tomatoes, quinoa, soup, water, mixed peppercorns, and bay laurel.

Turn the heat to a simmer and let it cook for 15 to 20 minutes or until the quinoa has softened.

Afterwards, fold in the canned beans and let it simmer for 5 minutes longer until heated through. Enjoy!

Classic Tomato and Orzo Soup

(Ready in about 25 minutes | Servings 3)

Per serving: Calories: 197; Fat: 10.4g; Carbs: 21.2g; Protein: 6.2g

Ingredients

1 tablespoon olive oil
1/2 leek, chopped
1 zucchini, diced
1 cup orzo pasta
2 ripe tomatoes, chopped
3 cups vegetable broth
1/2 teaspoon dried rosemary
1 teaspoon dried basil
1 teaspoon dried oregano
Sea salt and ground black pepper, to taste
1/2 cup feta cheese, crumbled

Directions

In a soup pot, heat the olive oil over medium heat; now, sauté the leek and zucchini until they've softened, about 5 minutes. Add in the rinsed orzo pasta and continue to cook until it is lightly toasted.

Stir in the chopped tomatoes, vegetable broth, and seasonings; bring to a rolling boil, then, immediately turn the heat to a simmer.

Let it simmer, covered, until the orzo pasta is tender, for about 20 minutes. Ladle the soup into individual bowls and garnish with crumbled feta cheese. Bon appétit!

Greek Avgolemono Soup with Pastina

(Ready in about 20 minutes | Servings 4)

Per serving: Calories: 325; Fat: 16.4g; Carbs: 15.2g; Protein: 28.8g

Ingredients

4 cups chicken broth
1 cup pastina
Sea salt and ground black pepper, to taste
1 egg, at room temperature
1/4 cup fresh lemon juice
1 tablespoon extra-virgin olive oil
2 cups cooked rotisserie chicken, diced
2 tablespoons fresh dill, chopped

Directions

In a soup pot, bring the broth to a boil and add in the pasta. Now, cook your pasta until al dente, about 8 minutes. Season with salt and pepper and reduce the heat to a simmer.

In a mixing bowl, whisk together the egg and fresh lemon juice until well combined.

Spoon 1 cup of the hot broth into the egg/lemon mixture; now, whisk again to combine well. Add the egg/lemon mixture back to the simmering pot.

Add in the olive oil, chicken and dill and continue to simmer for about 5 minutes more or until the soup thickens as the eggs cook.

Taste, adjust seasonings, and ladle into individual bowls. Enjoy!

Mediterranean Spring Soup

(Ready in about 40 minutes | Servings 4)

Per serving: Calories: 189; Fat: 6.6g; Carbs: 23g; Protein: 9.8g

Ingredients

4 cups vegetable broth
1/2 cup brown rice
Sea salt and ground black pepper, to taste
1 tablespoon olive oil
2 spring onions, chopped
1 cup asparagus, trimmed and chopped
1 Italian pepper, sliced
2 spring garlic stalks, chopped
1 bay leaf
1 egg
2 tablespoons fresh parsley leaves, chopped

Directions

In a soup pot, bring the vegetable broth to a boil and add in the rice. Now, cook the rice for about 15 minutes.

Season with salt and pepper and reduce the heat to a simmer. Add in the olive oil, spring onions, asparagus, Italian pepper, garlic, and bay leaf.

Continue to simmer, covered, for 20 minutes more. Afterwards, whisk in the egg and continue to stir until well incorporated and cooked through, for 5 to 6 minutes more.

Taste, adjust seasonings, and ladle into individual bowls. Garnish with fresh parsley leaves and eat warm. Bon appétit!

Middle Eastern Chickpea Salad (Balela)

(Ready in about 10 minutes | Servings 4)

Per serving: Calories: 302; Fat: 17.6g; Carbs: 26g; Protein: 8.8g

Ingredients

2 cups chickpeas, boiled and rinsed
1 Italian pepper, chopped
1 Lebanese cucumber, diced
2 medium-sized ripe tomatoes, diced
1 red onion, sliced
1/4 cup sun-dried tomatoes in olive oil, drained and chopped
1/4 cup Kalamata olives, pitted and sliced
2 tablespoons Italian parsley leaves, chopped
2 tablespoons basil leaves, chopped
4 tablespoons extra virgin olive oil
1 tablespoon balsamic
1 tablespoon fresh lemon juice
1 teaspoon fresh garlic, pressed
1/2 teaspoon ground sumac
Sea salt and black pepper, to taste

Directions

Toss the chickpeas, vegetables, and herbs in a large salad bowl.

In a small mixing dish, whisk the remaining ingredients until well combined.

Dress your salad and serve immediately. Bon appétit!

Dijon Potato Salad

(Ready in about 20 minutes + chilling time | Servings 4)

Per serving: Calories: 309; Fat: 18.2g; Carbs: 33.6g; Protein: 4.1g

Ingredients

1 ½ pounds Yukon gold potatoes, unpeeled and sliced
Sea salt and ground black pepper, to taste
1 celery ribs, chopped
1 tablespoon capers, drained
1 red onion, sliced
1/3 cup extra-virgin olive oil
2 tablespoons balsamic vinegar
1 tablespoon lemon juice
1 tablespoon Dijon mustard
1/2 teaspoon ground sumac
1/4 cup fresh dill, chopped

Directions

Place the potatoes in a stockpot and add the water to cover by 1 inch. Bring to a rolling boil and then, turn to a simmer.

Let it simmer until your potatoes are tender for about 15 minutes. Peel the skins from your potatoes and transfer them to a salad bowl. Let it cool completely.

Season your potatoes with salt and black pepper. Add in the celery, capers, and red onion, gently toss to combine.

Then, in a mixing bowl, thoroughly combine the olive oil, balsamic vinegar, lemon juice, mustard, and sumac.

Dress your salad and serve garnished with freshly chopped dill. Bon appétit!

Decadent Green Bean Salad

(Ready in about 20 minutes + chilling time | Servings 4)

Per serving: Calories: 169; Fat: 18.2g; Carbs: 33.6g; Protein: 4.1g

Ingredients

1 cup water
1 ½ pounds green beans, trimmed and cut into bite-sized pieces
Sea salt and ground black pepper, to taste
1/2 cup almonds, sliced
1 teaspoon fresh garlic, pressed
2 scallions, chopped
1 red pepper, sliced
2 tablespoons extra-virgin olive oil
1 tablespoon red wine vinegar
1 teaspoon stone-ground mustard
2 ounces feta cheese, crumbled

Directions

In a saucepan, cook the water and green beans over medium heat. Let it cook for about 10 minutes until the beans are al dente.

Drain and transfer to a salad bowl. Season your beans with salt and black pepper. Add in the garlic, scallions, red pepper; toss to combine well.

Meanwhile, toast the almonds in the preheated, dry skillet over medium-low heat for 5 to 6 minutes.

In a mixing dish, thoroughly combine the olive oil, vinegar, and mustard. Dress your salad.

Once the almonds are cool enough, transfer them to the salad bowl. Garnish your salad with the feta cheese and serve well chilled. Enjoy!

Roasted Asparagus Salad with Hard-Boiled Eggs

(Ready in about 20 minutes | Servings 4)

Per serving: Calories: 352; Fat: 25.2g; Carbs: 18.2g; Protein: 17g

Ingredients

1 teaspoon olive oil
1 ½ pounds fresh asparagus, trimmed and diced into bite-sized pieces
2 tomatoes, diced
1 red bell pepper, sliced
1 green bell pepper, sliced
1/2 teaspoon garlic, minced
2 scallion stalks, chopped
2 tablespoons white vine
4 tablespoons white vinegar
4 tablespoons extra-virgin olive oil
1 teaspoon honey
Salt and freshly ground black pepper, to taste
4 hard-boiled eggs
3 ounces halloumi cheese, crumbled

Directions

Brush the asparagus with 1 teaspoon of olive oil. Arrange the asparagus on a parchment-lined baking sheet and transfer it to the preheated oven.

Bake the asparagus at 425 degrees F for about 15 minutes or to your desired degree of tenderness.

Now, toss the asparagus with the tomatoes, peppers, garlic, and scallions.

In a small mixing bowl, whisk the wine, vinegar, olive oil, honey, salt, and black pepper. Now, dress the salad.

Top your salad with the hard-boiled eggs and halloumi cheese. Serve at room temperature.

Roasted Red Pepper and Tomato Soup

(Ready in about 1 hour 30 minutes | Servings 4)

Per serving: Calories: 169; Fat: 7.7g; Carbs: 19.8g; Protein: 7.3g

Ingredients

4 bell peppers
1 small-sized leek, chopped
1 tablespoon olive oil
3 cloves garlic, minced
2 cups vegetable broth
2 tablespoons tomato sauce
1/2 teaspoon hot paprika
1/2 teaspoon Greek oregano
1/2 teaspoon dried basil
1/2 teaspoon dried rosemary
1/2 teaspoon dried thyme
Sea salt and ground black pepper, to taste
2 ounces feta cheese, crumbled

Directions

Place the peppers on a parchment-lined baking sheet and transfer it to the preheated oven.

Roast the peppers at 375 degrees F for about 40 minutes. Then transfer the peppers to an airtight container or plastic bag.

Allow it to sit for 30 minutes, then, peel the peppers and remove the seeds and membranes.

Meanwhile, heat the oil in a soup pot over medium-high heat. Once hot, cook the garlic for a minute or so until tender and aromatic.

Transfer the peppers to the soup pot. Add in the vegetable broth, tomato sauce, and spices. Turn the heat to a simmer. Let it cook, covered, for about 20 minutes.

Then, blend your soup in a food processor and serve in individual bowls, garnished with chilled and crumbled feta cheese. Bon appétit!

Tuna Salad with Homemade Salsa

(Ready in about 10 minutes | Servings 4)
Per serving: Calories: 239; Fat: 8.7g; Carbs: 20.3g; Protein: 18.3g
Ingredients
8 ounces canned tuna in oil, drained
4 radishes, chopped
1/2 Greek cucumber, sliced
2 tomatoes, diced
1 red onion, chopped
1 teaspoon garlic, minced
2 tablespoons fresh mint, chopped
2 tablespoons fresh basil, chopped
2 tablespoons fresh parsley, chopped
4 Kalamata olives, pitted and chopped
1 chili pepper, minced
1 tablespoon extra-virgin olive oil
Sea salt and ground black pepper, to taste
Directions
Place the canned tuna, radishes and cucumber in a salad bowl.

In another bowl, make the salsa by whisking the remaining ingredients until well combined.

Pour the salsa into the salad bowl and gently stir to combine. Serve immediately and enjoy!

Sardine and Egg Salad

(Ready in about 10 minutes | Servings 4)
Per serving: Calories: 359; Fat: 20g; Carbs: 28.5g; Protein: 18.8g
Ingredients
6 eggs
1 celery with the leaves, chopped
1 cup grape tomatoes, halved
2 scallion stalks, sliced
2 tablespoons Italian parsley, chopped
1 tablespoon fresh basil, chopped
Sea salt and ground black pepper, to taste
1/2 teaspoon cayenne pepper
3 ounces canned sardines, chopped
1 tablespoon champagne vinegar
2 tablespoons fresh lime juice
3 tablespoons extra-virgin olive oil
1 teaspoon Dijon mustard

4 small-sized pitas, cut into wedges
Directions
Place the eggs in a saucepan and cover them with water by 1 inch. Bring the water to a rolling boil over high heat.

Boil the eggs, covered, for about 7 minutes over medium-high heat. Peel the eggs and slice them into wedges.

In a salad bowl, place the celery, tomatoes, scallions, herbs, spices, and canned sardines. Make the dressing: whisk the vinegar, lime juice, olive oil, and Dijon mustard.

Dress your salad and top with the reserved eggs. Garnish with warm pita wedges and serve.

Moroccan-Style Lentil Soup

(Ready in about 25 minutes | Servings 4)
Per serving: Calories: 265; Fat: 8.5g; Carbs: 39.3g; Protein: 10.8g
Ingredients
2 tablespoons olive oil
1 teaspoon ground cumin
1 teaspoon ground turmeric
1 small-sized leek, sliced
1 carrot, peeled and chopped
2 garlic cloves, pressed or minced
1/2 teaspoon Aleppo pepper, minced
1/2 pound plum tomatoes, chopped
1/2 cup brown lentils, soaked and rinsed
3 cups vegetable broth
Sea salt and ground black pepper, to taste
4 lemon wedges, for garnish
Directions
Heat 1 tablespoon of the olive oil in a soup pot over medium-high heat. Now, sauté the ground cumin and turmeric for 30 seconds or until fragrant.

Heat the remaining tablespoon of the olive oil and sauté the leek and carrot until just tender or about 3 minutes.

Stir in the garlic and Aleppo pepper; continue to sauté for a further 30 seconds, stirring constantly. Next, add in the plum tomatoes, lentils, and vegetable broth.

Turn the heat to a simmer and let it cook, covered, for 20 minutes more or until the lentils are tender. Season with salt and pepper to taste.

Ladle into four soup bowls and garnish them with lemon wedges. Serve hot.

Arborio Rice and White Bean Soup

(Ready in about 25 minutes | Servings 3)
Per serving: Calories: 385; Fat: 5.3g; Carbs: 73g; Protein: 13.3g
Ingredients
1 tablespoon olive oil
1 small-sized red onion, chopped
2 cloves garlic, minced
1/2 teaspoon dried Greek oregano
1/2 teaspoon dried basil
3 cups vegetable broth

1 cup water
2 bay leaf
3/4 cup Arborio rice
10 ounces canned white beans, rinsed
2 cups spinach, torn into pieces
Sea salt and ground black pepper, to taste
2 tablespoons fresh chives, chopped

Directions

Heat the olive oil in a Dutch oven over medium heat. Add in the onion, and sauté until it is tender and translucent, about 2-3 minutes. Stir in the garlic, oregano, and basil; continue to sauté until fragrant for about 1 minute.

Whisk in the vegetable broth, water, bay leaf, and bring it to a rapid boil. Stir in the rice and continue to cook for about 16 minutes.

Stir in the beans and spinach and continue to simmer for a further 2 to 3 minutes. Season with salt and black pepper and serve garnished with fresh chives. Enjoy!

Baby Red Potato Salad with Tuna

(Ready in about 20 minutes + chilling time | Servings 4)

Per serving: Calories: 317; Fat: 15.7g; Carbs: 35.4g; Protein: 12.5g

Ingredients

1 ½ pounds baby red potatoes, quartered
Sea salt and ground black pepper, to season
1/2 teaspoon red pepper flakes, crushed
4 scallion stalks, chopped
1 teaspoon garlic, crushed
1/2 teaspoon dried dill weed
1/2 teaspoon dried basil
1/2 teaspoon dried Greek oregano
1/3 cup Kalamata olives, pitted and sliced
1/4 cup extra-virgin olive oil
2 tablespoons white wine vinegar
1 tablespoon fresh lime juice
4 ounces canned tuna in water, drained and flaked

Directions

Place the potatoes in a stockpot and add the water to cover by 1 inch. Bring to a rolling boil and then, turn to a simmer.

Let it simmer until your potatoes are tender for about 15 minutes. Peel the skins from your potatoes and transfer them to a salad bowl. Let them cool completely.

Season your potatoes with salt, black pepper, and red pepper. Add in the scallions, garlic, dill, basil, oregano, and olives, gently toss to combine.

Then, in a mixing bowl, thoroughly combine the olive oil, vinegar, and lime juice.

Dress your salad and serve topped with canned tuna. Bon appétit!

Syrian Egg Salad with Za'atar Vinaigrette

(Ready in about 10 minutes + chilling time | Servings 4)

Per serving: Calories: 257; Fat: 22.2g; Carbs: 4.9g; Protein: 7.6g

Ingredients

5 eggs
2 cups Romaine lettuce, torn into pieces
1 cucumber, diced
2 tablespoons fresh parsley, minced
2 tablespoons fresh mint, minced
1 clove garlic, crushed
5 tablespoons olive oil
1 tablespoon za'atar
2 tablespoon fresh lime juice
2 tablespoons balsamic vinegar
Sea salt and black pepper, to taste

Directions

Place the eggs in a saucepan and cover them with water by 1 inch. Bring the water to a rolling boil over high heat.

Boil the eggs, covered, for about 7 minutes over medium-high heat. Peel the eggs and slice them into wedges.

Add the lettuce, cucumber, parsley, mint, and garlic to a nice salad bowl and toss to combine well.

To make the dressing, whisk the olive oil, za'atar, lime juice, balsamic vinegar, salt, and black pepper. Dress the salad and toss until everything is well coated.

Top your salad with the hard-boiled eggs and serve well-chilled.

Green Bean and Egg Salad

(Ready in about 20 minutes + chilling time | Servings 4)

Per serving: Calories: 255; Fat: 18.2g; Carbs: 15.6g; Protein: 9.1g

Ingredients

1 ½ pounds green beans, trimmed
4 eggs
Sea salt and freshly ground black pepper, to taste
1 cup cherry tomatoes, halved
1 small-sized red onion, chopped
1/4 cup extra-virgin olive oil
2 tablespoons red wine vinegar
1 tablespoon fresh parsley leaves, chopped
2 tablespoons fresh chives, chopped
1 tablespoon fresh basil, snipped
1 teaspoon garlic, minced
1/2 teaspoon hot paprika

Directions

In a saucepan, place the green beans and eggs. Cover them with cool water by 1 inch, and cook over medium heat. Let it cook for about 9 minutes.

Drain and transfer the green bean to a salad bowl. Peel the eggs, slice them into quarters, and reserve. Season your beans and eggs with salt and black pepper.

Add in the tomatoes, red onions, olive oil, vinegar, herbs, and garlic; toss to combine well.

Garnish your salad with the hard-boiled eggs, sprinkle hot paprika over them, and serve well-chilled. Enjoy!

Traditional Minestrone Soup

(Ready in about 25 minutes | Servings 4)

Per serving: Calories: 275; Fat: 9.1g; Carbs: 35.6g; Protein: 14.4g

Ingredients
1 tablespoon olive oil
1/2 red onion, diced
1 zucchini, diced
1 stalk celery, diced
2 cloves garlic, minced
1/2 teaspoon dried oregano
1/2 teaspoon dried parsley flakes
1/2 teaspoon dried basil
Sea salt and freshly ground pepper, to taste
1 plum tomato, diced
1 cup fire-roasted tomatoes, drained and diced
4 cups chicken broth
1 cup ditalini pasta
8 ounces canned cannellini beans, drained and rinsed
2 ounces halloumi cheese, crumbled
2 tablespoons fresh chives, roughly chopped

Directions
In a stockpot, heat the olive oil until sizzling. Once hot, sauté the onion until just tender and translucent, about 3 minutes.

Add in the zucchini and celery and continue to cook until they've softened.

Add in the garlic and continue to sauté an additional 30 seconds. Stir in the seasoning, tomatoes, broth, and ditalini pasta. Turn the heat to a simmer and let it cook for 15 minutes longer.

Add in the canned cannellini beans and let it simmer for 5 minutes more or until heated through.

Ladle your soup into individual bowls and garnish with cheese and fresh chives. Bon appétit!

Classic Seafood Gumbo

(Ready in about 30 minutes | Servings 4)
Per serving: Calories: 275; Fat: 9.1g; Carbs: 35.6g; Protein: 14.4g

Ingredients
2 tablespoons olive oil
2 tablespoons tapioca flour
1/2 cup leeks, chopped
1/2 cup celery, chopped
1/2 cup carrots, chopped
1 Serrano pepper, chopped
1 ½ cups okra, cut into bite-sized chunks
2 plum tomatoes, chopped
1 teaspoon garlic, minced
2 thyme sprigs
2 rosemary sprigs
4 cups vegetable broth
1 bay laurel
1 tablespoon gumbo file
1/2 teaspoon paprika
Sea salt and ground black pepper, to taste
1 pound shrimp, peeled and deveined
2 tablespoons fresh parsley leaves, finely chopped

Directions

In a Dutch oven, heat the olive oil over a moderately high heat. Once hot, cook the flour to form a thick paste. Add a splash od vegetables broth, if needed. Then, sauté the leeks, celery, carrots, Serrano pepper, and okra; continue to cook for 5 to 6 minutes. Add in the remaining ingredients, except for the shrimp and fresh parsley leaves.

Bring it to a rolling boil; immediately reduce the temperature to medium; let it simmer for 15 to 17 minutes.

Afterwards, add in the shrimp and continue to simmer for about 7 minutes until thoroughly cooked. Ladle into individual bowls and garnish with fresh parsley. Eat warm.

Mac and Cheese Soup with Spinach

(Ready in about 30 minutes | Servings 6)
Per serving: Calories: 245; Fat: 7.4g; Carbs: 29.6g; Protein: 14.4g

Ingredients
6 ounces dry cavatappi macaroni
1 teaspoon olive oil
1 red onion, chopped
1 cup celery with leaves, chopped
1 medium-sized zucchini, diced
1 carrot, chopped
1 teaspoon garlic, pressed
6 cups beef bone broth
Sea salt and ground black pepper, to taste
1/2 teaspoon dried dill
1/2 teaspoon cayenne pepper
2 cups spinach, torn into small pieces
1 cup Parmesan cheese, grated

Directions
Cook the macaroni according to the manufacturer's directions; drain ad reserve.

In a soup pot, heat the olive oil over medium-high heat. Now, sauté the onion, celery, zucchini, and carrot until they've softened.

Now, stir in the garlic and continue to sauté an additional 30 seconds or until aromatic.

Add in the broth, salt, black pepper, dill, cayenne pepper, and turn the heat to a simmer. Continue to simmer, covered, for about 15 minutes or until everything is cooked through.

Afterwards, stir in the spinach and the reserved macaroni. Fold in the grated Parmesan cheese.

Cover and let it stand for about 10 minutes until your spinach wilts and the cheese melts. Bon appétit!

Greek-Style Chicken Lemon Soup

(Ready in about 30 minutes | Servings 4)
Per serving: Calories: 322; Fat: 11.4g; Carbs: 33.9g; Protein: 20.4g

Ingredients
1 tablespoon olive oil
1/2 leek, chopped
1 zucchini, diced
1 celery with leaves, diced
2 garlic cloves, minced

1 sprig thyme
1 sprig rosemary
1 teaspoon Greek seasoning
Sea salt and ground black pepper, to taste
4 cups chicken broth
1 cup water
1/2 pound chicken breasts, diced
3/4 cup brown rice
1/4 cup lemon juice

Directions

In a soup pot, heat the olive oil over medium-high heat. Now, sauté the leek, zucchini, and celery, until they've softened.

Now, stir in the garlic and continue to sauté an additional 30 seconds or until fragrant.

Add in the seasonings, broth, water, chicken, and brown rice, and turn the heat to a simmer. Continue to simmer, covered, for about 25 minutes or until everything is cooked through.

Ladle into individual bowls and add a few drizzles of lemon juice to each serving. Enjoy!

Roasted Red Pepper and Chickpea Salad

(Ready in about 50 minutes | Servings 4)

Per serving: Calories: 385; Fat: 17.3g; Carbs: 47.1g; Protein: 13.3g

Ingredients

4 red bell peppers
1/2 pound chickpeas, soaked overnight
1 red onion, thinly sliced
1 Greek cucumber, diced
1 cup cherry tomatoes, halved
1/4 cup olive oil
2 tablespoons fresh lime juice
2 tablespoons red wine vinegar
1 teaspoon mustard

Directions

Place the peppers on a parchment-lined baking sheet and transfer it to the preheated oven.

Roast the peppers at 375 degrees F for about 40 minutes. Then, transfer the peppers to an airtight container or plastic bag.

Allow it to sit for 30 minutes, then, peel the peppers and remove the seeds and membranes. Cut the peppers into strips and transfer them to the salad bowl.

In the meantime, drain the soaked chickpeas and tip them into a stockpot. Cover the chickpeas with water by 1 inch. Bring the water to a rolling boil over high heat.

Immediately turn the heat to a simmer and cook for about 50 minutes. Transfer the cooked chickpeas to the salad bowl with the roasted peppers.

Stir in the remaining ingredients, toss to combine well, and serve. Bon appétit!

Asparagus and Sardine Salad

(Ready in about 20 minutes | Servings 2)

Per serving: Calories: 245; Fat: 18.7g; Carbs: 6.2g; Protein: 13.8g

Ingredients

1/2 pound asparagus spears, cut into bite-sized pieces
1 cup arugula
1 cup baby spinach
3 ounces sardines in oil, drained and chopped
1 tablespoons capers, drained
2 tablespoons olive oil
1 teaspoon Dijon mustard
1 tablespoon fresh lemon juice
1 tablespoon red wine vinegar
Sea salt and freshly ground black pepper, to taste

Directions

Brush the asparagus with 1 teaspoon of olive oil. Arrange the asparagus on a parchment-lined baking sheet and transfer it to the preheated oven.

Bake the asparagus at 425 degrees F for about 15 minutes or to your desired degree of tenderness.

Now, toss the asparagus with the remaining ingredients. Bon appétit!

Greek Orzo Salad

(Ready in about 10 minutes | Servings 4)

Per serving: Calories: 500; Fat: 19g; Carbs: 72.2g; Protein: 15.5g

Ingredients

3/4 pound orzo pasta
1 Greek cucumber, diced
2 ripe tomatoes, sliced
1 bell pepper, sliced
1 small red onion, thinly sliced
1 teaspoon garlic, pressed
1/3 cup Kalamata olives, pitted and sliced
1/4 cup balsamic vinegar
1/4 cup extra-virgin olive oil
2 ounces feta cheese, crumbled
2 tablespoons fresh parsley, roughly chopped

Directions

Cook the pasta according to the manufacturer's instructions. Let it cool to room temperature.

Toss the pasta with the vegetables and drizzle the olive oil and vinegar over them. Toss to combine well.

Garnish with feta cheese and fresh parsley and serve. Enjoy!

The Best Panzanella Salad Ever

(Ready in about 10 minutes | Servings 4)

Per serving: Calories: 382; Fat: 28.2g; Carbs: 20.3g; Protein: 11.5g

Ingredients

2 tablespoons olive oil
4 cups Italian bread, torn into bite-sized pieces
1/2 teaspoon garlic powder
Sea salt and cayenne pepper, to taste
1 bell pepper, sliced
2 medium-sized tomatoes, sliced
1 small-sized red onion. thinly sliced
1 tablespoon fresh basil, roughly chopped
1 tablespoon fresh parsley, roughly chopped
1 cup Asiago cheese, grated

1/4 cup mayonnaise

Directions

Preheat the olive oil in a nonstick skillet over medium-high heat. Now, toast the bread pieces for about 10 minutes.

Toss the remaining ingredients in a salad bowl; toss to combine well.

Top with the toasted bread and serve. Bon appétit!

Aïoli Potato Salad

(Ready in about 15 minutes + chilling time | Servings 3)

Per serving: Calories: 454; Fat: 39.2g; Carbs: 22.9g; Protein: 4.6g

Ingredients

2 cloves garlic, peeled
2 egg yolks
1/2 cup olive oil
Sea salt and ground black pepper, to taste
3/4 pound potatoes, halved
1 red onion, thinly sliced
1/2 teaspoon Dijon mustard
1/2 teaspoon garlic, minced
2 tablespoons fresh parsley, roughly chopped

Directions

Mix the garlic, egg yolks, olive oil, salt, and black pepper with an immersion blender until smooth and creamy.

Place the potatoes in a stockpot and add the water to cover by 1 inch. Bring to a rolling boil and then, turn to a simmer.

Let it simmer until your potatoes are tender for about 15 minutes. Peel the skins from your potatoes and transfer them to a salad bowl. Let them cool completely and cut into slices.

Add the onion, mustard, and garlic to the salad bowl; stir in the prepared aïoli and gently toss to combine well. Garnish with fresh parsley leaves and serve well chilled. Enjoy!

Tuna Salad with Tapenade Vinaigrette

(Ready in about 10 minutes | Servings 3)

Per serving: Calories: 366; Fat: 31.5g; Carbs: 6.5g; Protein: 11.5g

Ingredients

5 ounces canned tuna in oil, drained and chopped
1 red bell pepper, sliced
1 large-sized tomato, diced
2 tablespoons capers
1 small-sized red onion
Tapenade vinaigrette:
6 tablespoons olive oil
2 tablespoons red wine vinegar
1 teaspoon lemon zest
3 tablespoons black olive tapenade
1/4 teaspoon ground black pepper

Directions

Place the canned tuna, red bell pepper, tomato, capers, and onion in a salad bowl.

Mix all ingredients for the tapenade vinaigrette until everything is well combined.

Add the tapenade vinaigrette to the salad bowl and toss to combine well. Bon appétit!

Cannellini Bean and Spaghetti Soup

(Ready in about 25 minutes | Servings 4)

Per serving: Calories: 306; Fat: 6.9g; Carbs: 44.5g; Protein: 17.4g

Ingredients

1 tablespoon olive oil
1 small-sized leek, chopped
1 teaspoon garlic, pressed
2 tomatoes, crushed
3 cups chicken bone broth
1 cup water
1 teaspoon Greek seasoning mix
1 cup spaghetti
1 can (15-1/2 ounces) cannellini beans, rinsed and drained
4 tablespoons parmesan cheese, grated

Directions

In a Dutch oven, heat the olive oil over medium-high heat. Then, cook the leek until tender or about 3 minutes.

Stir in the garlic and continue to sauté for 30 seconds more or until aromatic.

Add in the tomatoes, chicken bone broth, water, and Greek seasoning mix and bring to a boil. Immediately reduce the heat to a simmer.

Add in the uncooked spaghetti and continue to simmer, partially covered, for about 15 minutes.

Add in the beans and continue to cook for 5 minutes longer or until everything is heated through. Ladle into individual bowls and serve garnished with grated parmesan cheese. Enjoy!

Seafood Soup with Gremolata Toast

(Ready in about 20 minutes | Servings 4)

Per serving: Calories: 327; Fat: 11.4g; Carbs: 31.6g; Protein: 25.4g

Ingredients

2 tablespoons olive oil
1 sweet onion, chopped
2 garlic cloves, minced
4 ripe tomatoes, chopped
1 cup water
1 cup clam juice
1/2 cup Greek white wine
1/2 pound codfish fillets, cut into bite-sized chunks
1/2 pound shrimp, deveined
1/2 fresh lemon, sliced
Gremolata toast:
1/2 baguette, sliced and toasted
1 tablespoon butter
1 teaspoon lemon zest
1 teaspoon garlic, minced
1 tablespoon parsley, minced

Directions

Heat the olive oil in a stockpot over medium-high heat. Now, cook the onion and garlic, adding a splash of wine, until aromatic or about 2 minutes.

Add in the tomatoes, water, clam juice, and white wine, and bring to a boil. Immediately reduce the heat to a simmer.

Let it simmer for about 8 minutes. After that, add in the codfish and shrimp and let it simmer for 5 to 6 minutes more.

Meanwhile, in a small bowl, thoroughly combine the butter, lemon zest, garlic, and parsley. Spread the butter mixture on the toasts.

Ladle your soup into individual bowls and serve with the gremolata toast and the lemon slices. Bon appétit!

Mushroom, Swiss Chard and White Bean Soup

(Ready in about 25 minutes | Servings 4)

Per serving: Calories: 318; Fat: 9.6g; Carbs: 39.7g; Protein: 20.3g

Ingredients

1 tablespoon olive oil
1 small-sized leek, chopped
1 carrot, chopped
1 summer squash, chopped
1 cup button mushrooms, sliced
2 garlic cloves, minced
4 cups beef bone broth
2 ripe tomatoes, chopped
1/2 teaspoon dried rosemary
1/2 teaspoon dried oregano
3 cups Swiss chard, torn into smaller pieces
1 can (15-1/2 ounces) white beans, rinsed and drained
Sea salt and ground black pepper, to taste
1/2 cup feta cheese, crumbled

Directions

Heat the oil in a large soup pot over medium-high heat. Now, sauté the leek, carrot, and summer squash for 2 to 3 minutes until they've softened.

Then, add in the mushrooms and garlic and continue to cook for about 2 minutes more until the mushrooms release the liquid and the garlic is aromatic.

Add in the broth, tomatoes, rosemary, and oregano and bring to a boil. Turn the heat to a simmer and let it cook for 5 minutes more.

Add in the chard and white beans and continue to cook for 10 minutes more or until thoroughly cooked. Season with salt and black pepper to taste.

Ladle your soup into individual bowls and serve garnished with crumbled feta cheese. Enjoy!

Creamed Shrimp Salad

(Ready in about 10 minutes | Servings 4)

Per serving: Calories: 158; Fat: 5.4g; Carbs: 1.3g; Protein: 24.8g

Ingredients

1 pound shrimp, cleaned and deveined
1 red onion, thinly sliced
1 celery stalk, chopped
1 cup arugula
4 tablespoons mayonnaise

4 tablespoons Greek-style yogurt
1/2 teaspoon dried oregano
1/2 teaspoon cayenne pepper
Sea salt and ground black pepper, to taste

Directions

Steam the shrimp for 5 to 6 minutes and allow them to cool completely.

In a salad bowl, place the onion, celery and arugula. Chop the shrimp and add them to the salad bowl.

Stir in the mayonnaise, yogurt, oregano, cayenne pepper, salt, and black pepper. Toss to combine well and place in your refrigerator until ready to serve. Taste, adjust the seasonings and serve well-chilled. Bon appétit!

Winter Salmon Salad with Aioli

(Ready in about 10 minutes | Servings 4)

Per serving: Calories: 294; Fat: 18.8g; Carbs: 5.5g; Protein: 24.3g

Ingredients

1 pound salmon fillets
1 small-sized red onion, chopped
1 carrot, chopped
4 tablespoons aioli
1/2 teaspoon cayenne pepper
1 tablespoon balsamic vinegar
1 teaspoon stone-ground mustard
2 ounces pickles, chopped
Sea salt and ground black pepper, to taste

Directions

Add the salmon to a simmering water and poach it until the salmon is opaque throughout, about 5 minutes; remove the salmon from the water and pat it dry with a kitchen towel.

Slice the poached salmon into bite-sized strips and add in the remaining ingredients.

Gently toss to coat and serve well-chilled. Enjoy!

Great Northern Bean Salad

(Ready in about 1 hour + chilling time | Servings 4)

Per serving: Calories: 484; Fat: 14.1g; Carbs: 68.6g; Protein: 24.7g

Ingredients

3/4 pound Great Northern beans, soaked overnight
1 cup grape tomatoes, halved
1 cucumber, thinly sliced
1 small-sized red onion, thinly sliced
1 teaspoon garlic, minced
1/2 cup black olives, pitted and sliced
2 Italian peppers, sliced
1/2 cup marinated artichokes, chopped
1/2 cup halloumi cheese, crumbled
Dressing:
4 tablespoons extra-virgin olive oil
2 tablespoons white vinegar
1/2 teaspoon ground cumin
1 teaspoon oregano
1 teaspoon rosemary

Flakes sea salt and freshly cracked black pepper, to taste

Directions

Drain your beans, add the fresh water and cook for about 60 minutes. Allow your beans to cool slightly before adding them to the salad bowl.

Add in the tomatoes, cucumber, onion, garlic, black olives, Italian peppers, and artichokes.

Then, whisk the dressing ingredients until everything is well combined.

Dress your salad and serve garnished with halloumi cheese. Enjoy!

Famous Clam Chowder

(Ready in about 20 minutes | Servings 4)

Per serving: Calories: 299; Fat: 5.8g; Carbs: 36.8g; Protein: 24.3g

Ingredients

1 tablespoon olive oil
1 small-sized red onion, chopped
1 Italian pepper, deveined and sliced
1 celery stalk, chopped
2 cups clam juice
1 cup fish broth
1 cup marinara sauce
1 cup Acini di pepe pasta
1 pound prawns, deveined, peeled and chopped
6 ounces canned clams, minced
1 teaspoon Italian seasoning mix

Directions

In a Dutch oven, heat the olive oil over a moderate flame. Once hot, sauté the onion, pepper, and celery until they are crisp-tender, about 4 minutes.

Pour in the clam juice, broth, marinara sauce, and Acini di pepe. Turn the heat to a simmer and let it cook, partially covered, for about 10 minutes.

Now, fold in the prawns and clams, and continue to cook for a further 3 minutes until they turn pink. Add in the Italian seasoning mix and stir to combine well. Bon appétit!

Favorite French Vichyssoise

(Ready in about 35 minutes | Servings 5)

Per serving: Calories: 191; Fat: 4.8g; Carbs: 35.2g; Protein: 3.7g

Ingredients

1 tablespoon olive oil
1 pound leeks, thinly sliced
1 pound new potatoes, scrubbed and sliced
1 teaspoon cayenne pepper
1/2 teaspoon dried oregano
1/2 teaspoon dried marjoram
1/2 teaspoon mustard seeds
Sea salt and ground black pepper, to taste

1/4 teaspoon dried thyme
1 bay laurel
5 cups vegetable broth
1/4 cup crème fraîche

Directions

In a Dutch oven, heat the olive oil over a moderate flame. Once hot, sauté the leeks until they are crisp-tender, about 3 minutes.

Add in the potatoes and continue to cook for 10 minutes more, adding a splash of vegetable broth.

Add in the seasoning and broth and bring to a boil. Immediately turn the heat to a simmer, place the lid slightly ajar, and continue to cook for a further 20 minutes. Discard the bay laurel.

Puree the soup in your blender until creamy and uniform. Str in the crème fraiche just before serving and enjoy!

Lebanese Split Pea Soup

(Ready in about 45 minutes | Servings 5)

Per serving: Calories: 353; Fat: 6.5g; Carbs: 56.7g; Protein: 19.8g

Ingredients

2 tablespoons olive oil
1 cup spring onions, diced
2 garlic cloves, minced
2 cups split peas, soaked overnight
1 cup fennel, chopped
6 cups water
1/2 teaspoon red pepper flakes
Sea salt and ground white pepper, to taste
2 bay laurels
1/2 teaspoon dried oregano
1/2 teaspoon dried basil
1/2 teaspoon dried thyme
A pinch of grated nutmeg
1/4 teaspoon ground cumin
2 carrots, diced
2 celery ribs, diced

Directions

In a soup pot, heat the olive oil over a moderately high heat. Now, sauté the onions and garlic until just tender and fragrant or about 2 minutes.

Add in the remaining ingredients and bring to a boil. Immediately turn the heat to a simmer, place the lid slightly ajar, and continue to cook for a further 40 minutes.

Discard the bay laurels and serve hot. Bon appétit!

Corn, Vegetable and Herb Chowder

(Ready in about 20 minutes | Servings 3)

Per serving: Calories: 215; Fat: 11.7g; Carbs: 21.7g; Protein: 8.8g

Ingredients

2 tablespoons olive oil
1 medium-sized leek, chopped
2 cloves garlic
1 stalk celery, chopped
3 ears corn, husked
4 ounces Swiss chard, turn into bite-sized pieces
1 large-sized zucchini, diced
1 tablespoon basil, chopped
2 tablespoons parsley, chopped
1 tablespoon tarragon, snipped
3 cups roasted vegetable broth

Directions

In a Dutch oven, heat the olive oil over a moderately high heat. Now, sauté the leek, garlic, and celery until crisp-tender or about 4 minutes.

Add in the husked corn kernels, Swiss chard, zucchini, basil, parsley, tarragon, and vegetable broth. Bring the mixture to a rolling boil.

Then, turn the heat to a simmer and continue to cook for about 10 minutes, or until the vegetables are tender.

Cut the corn kernels off the cob. Taste and adjust seasonings. Ladle your soup into individual bowls and serve warm.

Bon appétit!

Shawarma Salad Bowl

(Ready in about 20 minutes | Servings 4)
Per serving: Calories: 295; Fat: 17.7g; Carbs: 9.9g; Protein: 24.8g

Ingredients

1 pound chicken breast
1/2 teaspoon ground cumin
1/2 teaspoon turmeric powder
1 garlic clove, minced
Sea salt and ground black pepper, to taste
1 red onion, thinly sliced
2 tablespoons fresh lemon juice
2 tablespoons extra-virgin olive oil
1 cup baby spinach
1 cup arugula
1 cup buttermilk lettuce
2 plum tomatoes, diced
1/2 red onion, thinly sliced
1 garlic clove, minced
Sea salt and ground black pepper, to taste
1 teaspoon sumac

Directions

Place the chicken breast and aromatics in a saucepan. Pour in enough cool water to cover the chicken by 1 inch.

Bring the water to a boil; then, immediately turn the heat to a simmer and let it cook for 15 minutes or until no longer pink.

Slice the chicken into strips and reserve.
Place the other ingredients in a salad bowl and toss to combine. Top with the reserved chicken and serve.

Creamed New Potato Soup

(Ready in about 35 minutes | Servings 4)
Per serving: Calories: 204; Fat: 8.4g; Carbs: 22.7g; Protein: 9.6g

Ingredients

2 tablespoons olive oil
1/2 cup spring onions, sliced
1 pound new potatoes, scrubbed and sliced
1 teaspoon garlic, minced
1 thyme sprig
1 rosemary sprig
4 cups vegetable broth
1/2 cup Greek-style yogurt, well-chilled

Directions

In a Dutch oven, heat the olive oil over a moderate flame. Once hot, sauté the onions until they are just tender, about 2 to 3 minutes.

Add in the potatoes and continue to cook for 10 minutes more, adding a splash of vegetable broth. Add in the garlic, thyme, rosemary, and vegetable broth and bring to a boil. Immediately turn the heat to a simmer, place the lid slightly ajar, and continue to cook for a further 20 minutes.

Puree the soup in your blender until creamy and uniform. Ladle your soup into individual bowls and serve garnished with well-chilled yogurt.

Bon appétit!

Reach Two-Bean Salad

(Ready in about 10 minutes + chilling time | Servings 4)
Per serving: Calories: 305; Fat: 14.7g; Carbs: 33.1g; Protein: 13.3g

Ingredients

Salad:
8 ounces canned garbanzo beans, drained and rinsed
8 ounces canned red kidney beans, drained and rinsed
1/2 cup peppadew peppers, roughly chopped
1 Greek cucumber, diced
1/2 cup scallion, chopped
1 tablespoon caper, drained
5 fresh mint leaves, roughly chopped
5 fresh basil leaves, roughly chopped
Vinaigrette:
4 tablespoons extra-virgin olive oil
2 garlic cloves, pressed
1 teaspoon stone-ground mustard
1 tablespoon red wine vinegar
1 tablespoon fresh lemon juice
1 teaspoon honey

Sea salt and black pepper, to taste
Directions
Add all the ingredients for the salad and toss to combine.
Whisk the ingredients for your vinaigrette until everything is well incorporated. Dress your salad and serve well-chilled. Enjoy!

Za'atar Chickpea Salad

(Ready in about 50 minutes + chilling time | Servings 4)
Per serving: Calories: 606; Fat: 22.4g; Carbs: 81g; Protein: 24.9g
Ingredients
1 pound chickpeas, soaked overnight
2 Roma tomatoes, diced
1 Greek cucumber, chopped
1 Spanish pepper, deveined and sliced
1/2 cup scallions, sliced
1/2 cup black olives, pitted and sliced
Sea salt and ground black pepper, to taste
4 tablespoons extra-virgin olive oil
2 tablespoons fresh lime juice
2 tablespoons balsamic vinegar
1 tablespoon basil, chopped
1 tablespoon chives, chopped
1 tablespoon parsley, chopped
1/2 teaspoon za'atar
Sea salt and freshly ground black pepper, to taste
Directions
Drain the soaked chickpeas and tip them into a pot. Cover the chickpeas with water by 1 inch. Bring the water to a rolling boil over high heat.
Immediately turn the heat to a simmer and cook for about 50 minutes. Let the chickpeas cool completely.
Transfer the cooked chickpeas to the salad bowl.
Stir in the remaining ingredients, toss to combine well, and serve. Bon appétit!

VEGETABLES & SIDE DISHES

Authentic Salad-e Shirazi

(Ready in about 5 minutes + chilling time | Servings 4)
Per serving: Calories: 176; Fat: 14.2g; Carbs: 11.1g;
Protein: 2.2g
Ingredients
1 Greek cucumber, diced
2 ripe tomatoes, diced
1 small-sized red onions, chopped
1 Italian sweet pepper, deveined and sliced
1 tablespoon fresh parsley, chopped
1 tablespoon fresh basil, chopped
1 tablespoon fresh dill, chopped
Sea salt and ground black pepper, to taste
1/2 teaspoon Harissa spice
1/4 teaspoon ground cumin
1/2 teaspoon Dijon mustard
1 lemon, freshly squeezed
4 tablespoons extra-virgin olive oil
Directions
Place all the ingredients in a salad bowl; toss to
combine well.
Place the salad in your refrigerator until ready to
serve, taste and adjust the seasonings once the salad
is well-chilled.
Bon appétit!

Italian-Style Cheesy Roasted Peppers

(Ready in about 55 minutes | Servings 2)
Per serving: Calories: 310; Fat: 20.4g; Carbs: 28.1g;
Protein: 8.5g
Ingredients
4 sweet Italian peppers
1 chile pepper
2 tablespoons extra-virgin olive oil
2 garlic cloves, minced
1 tablespoon Italian spice mix
Sea salt and ground black pepper, to taste
1 tablespoon fresh basil, chopped
1 tablespoon fresh mint, chopped
1 tablespoon fresh parsley, chopped
2 ounces feta cheese, crumbled
Directions
Place the peppers on a parchment-lined baking pan.
Sprinkle the olive oil, garlic, Italian spice mix, salt,
and black pepper over them.
Bake the peppers at 420 degrees F for about 25
minutes. Allow the peppers to sit for 30 minutes,
then, peel them and remove the seeds and
membranes.
Garnish with fresh herbs and crumbled feta cheese.
Enjoy!

Moroccan-Style Carrot Soup

(Ready in about 25 minutes | Servings 3)
Per serving: Calories: 255; Fat: 15.7g; Carbs: 22.7g;
Protein: 8.1g
Ingredients
2 tablespoons olive oil
1 red onion, chopped
1 garlic clove, minced
3/4 pound carrots, trimmed and diced
3 cups vegetable broth
1 tablespoon honey
1/2 teaspoon coriander, ground
1/2 teaspoon Harissa spice
1/2 teaspoon paprika
3 tablespoons sesame seeds
Directions
Heat the olive oil in a Dutch oven over medium-high
heat. Now, sauté the onion, garlic, and carrots until
they are crisp-tender and fragrant or about 2
minutes.
Add in the broth and bring to a rapid boil.
Immediately turn the heat to a simmer and continue
to cook for 15 minutes more or until the liquid has
slightly reduced.
Puree the soup in your food processor or blender
until creamy and smooth.
Add in the honey, coriander, Harissa spice, and
paprika, and continue to simmer, partially covered,
for a further 3 minutes or until heated through.
Meanwhile, heat up a nonstick skillet over medium-
high heat and toast the sesame seeds for 3 minutes
until golden brown and fragrant, stirring
continuously.
Ladle warm soup into individual bowls and serve
garnished with toasted sesame seeds. Enjoy!

Batata Harra (Lebanese Skillet Potatoes)

(Ready in about 20 minutes | Servings 3)
Per serving: Calories: 475; Fat: 9.7g; Carbs: 89.3g;
Protein: 11g
Ingredients
4 medium-sized gold potatoes, peeled and quartered
2 tablespoons olive oil
3 tablespoons scallions, thinly sliced
2 garlic cloves, minced
Sea salt and ground black pepper, to season
1/2 teaspoon red pepper flakes
1/4 cup fresh parsley, chopped
1/4 cup fresh basil, chopped
1/2 teaspoon allspice
Directions
Place the potatoes in a saucepan with enough water
to cover them. Bring to a rolling boil, and continue to
cook the potatoes for 10 to 12 minutes.
Drain the potatoes and allow them to cool. Slice the
potatoes into bite-sized chunks.
Heat the olive oil in a nonstick skillet over a
moderately high heat. Now, sauté the scallions and
garlic for a minute or so until fragrant.
Add in the cooked potatoes and continue to sauté for
5 minutes more. Sprinkle the seasonings over your
potatoes and serve warm. Bon appétit!

Grilled Hash Brown Burgers

(Ready in about 15 minutes | Servings 3)
Per serving: Calories: 242; Fat: 0.3g; Carbs: 54.3g; Protein: 6.6g
Ingredients
2 medium potatoes, peeled and grated
1 small-size dried onion, chopped
2 cloves garlic, minced
1 cup Swiss chard, chopped
4 tablespoon plain flour
1/2 teaspoon dried basil
1/2 teaspoon dried marjoram
1/4 teaspoon cumin powder
1/2 teaspoon cayenne pepper
Se salt and ground black pepper, taste
Directions
Mix the ingredients until everything is well combined.
Shape the mixture into equal patties.
Set the grill to medium heat.
Grill your burgers for 4 to 5 minutes on each side.
Serve your burgers in hamburger buns and enjoy!

Fried Zucchini and Parmesan Cakes

(Ready in about 25 minutes | Servings 3)
Per serving: Calories: 319; Fat: 21.3g; Carbs: 17.1g; Protein: 14.6g
Ingredients
1 large zucchini, grated
1 teaspoon salt
2 eggs, whisked
1 red onion, minced
2 cloves garlic, minced
1 teaspoon dried dill
1/2 teaspoon cumin, ground
1/2 teaspoon dried rosemary
1 cup parmesan cheese, grated
Sea salt and freshly cracked black peppercorns, to taste
1/4 cup cornflour
1/2 teaspoon baking powder
2 tablespoons olive oil
Directions
Place the grated zucchini and 1 teaspoon of salt in a fine-mesh strainer; set it over a bowl. Let it stand for about 20 minutes.
Now, squeeze the excess liquid out of the zucchini using your hands.
Then, mix the grated zucchini with the eggs, red onion, garlic, dill, cumin, rosemary, cheese, salt, black peppercorns, cornflour, and baking powder.
Heat the olive oil in a frying pan over medium flame.
Drop 2 tablespoon sized portions into the pan, and flatten them slightly, using the back of a spoon.
Cook the cakes for about 3 minutes per side until golden brown. Bon appétit!

Quick and Simple Roasted Carrots

(Ready in about 30 minutes | Servings 3)
Per serving: Calories: 215; Fat: 14g; Carbs: 22.1g; Protein: 2.4g

Ingredients
1 ½ pounds carrots, cut into bite-sized pieces
3 tablespoons olive oil
2 garlic cloves, pressed
1/2 teaspoon ground turmeric
1/2 teaspoon harissa spice blend
Sea salt and fresh ground black pepper, to taste
Directions
Start by preheating your oven to 400 degrees F.
Toss the carrots with the remaining ingredients and place them on a lightly greased roasting pan.
Roast the carrots for about 25 minutes or until tender and slightly caramelized. Enjoy!

Grilled Vegetable Kabobs

(Ready in about 20 minutes | Servings 4)
Per serving: Calories: 143; Fat: 7.7g; Carbs: 15.3g; Protein: 8.1g
Ingredients
1 pound zucchini, sliced
1 pound small-sized button mushrooms, rinsed
1/2 pound bell peppers, sliced
1 cup red onion, cut into wedges
2 tablespoons olive oil
1 teaspoon ginger-garlic paste
1/2 teaspoon ground cumin
1/2 teaspoon cayenne pepper
1/2 teaspoon hot
Sea salt and freshly ground black pepper, to taste
Directions
Toss the vegetable with the remaining ingredients until well coated on all sides.
Tread your veggies onto bamboo skewers and place them on the preheated grill.
Grill the vegetable kabobs over medium heat for about 14 minutes, turning them every few minutes to promote even cooking. Bon appétit!

Aromatic Pecorino-Crusted Potatoes

(Ready in about 45 minutes | Servings 2)
Per serving: Calories: 543; Fat: 20.6g; Carbs: 75.3g; Protein: 16.5g
Ingredients
4 medium gold potatoes, peeled and sliced into bite-sized pieces
1/2 cup Pecorino Romano cheese, grated
1 teaspoon red pepper flakes, crushed
Sea salt and ground black pepper, to taste
1/2 teaspoon dried dill
1/2 teaspoon dried oregano
1/2 teaspoon dried thyme
1/2 teaspoon dried onion powder
1/2 teaspoon garlic powder
2 tablespoons olive oil
Directions
Toss the potatoes with the remaining ingredients until well coated on all sides.
Place your potatoes in a lightly oiled rimmed baking pan.

Bake your potatoes in the preheated oven at 420 degrees F for about 45 minutes, rotating the pan once or twice.
Bon appétit!

Roasted Sweet Potato Salad

(Ready in about 35 minutes | Servings 4)
Per serving: Calories: 333; Fat: 13.8g; Carbs: 46.3g; Protein: 6.9g
Ingredients
1 ½ pounds sweet potatoes, peeled and cut into bite-sized chunks
1/2 cup scallions, sliced
1 teaspoon garlic, minced
Coarse sea salt and ground black pepper, to taste
4 tablespoons extra-virgin olive oil
2 tablespoons white vinegar
6 ounces canned red kidney beans
2 tablespoons fresh parsley leaves, chopped
Directions
Toss the sweet potatoes with 1 tablespoon of the olive oil and place them on a parchment-lined roasting pan.
Roast your potatoes at 430 degrees F for about 35 minutes or until they've softened.
Toss the roasted potatoes with the remaining ingredients and serve at room temperature. Bon appétit!

Easy Cauliflower Parmigiana

(Ready in about 30 minutes | Servings 3)
Per serving: Calories: 233; Fat: 15.9g; Carbs: 16.4g; Protein: 8.4g
Ingredients
1 pound cauliflower florets
2 tablespoons olive oil
Sea salt and ground black pepper, to taste
1 teaspoon garlic powder
1/2 teaspoon shallot powder
1/2 teaspoon dried oregano
1/2 teaspoon dried basil
1/2 cup parmesan cheese, grated
1/4 cup tortilla chips, crushed
Directions
Start by preheating your oven to 395 degrees F.
Toss the cauliflower florets with the remaining ingredients; arrange the cauliflower florets onto a parchment-lined baking pan.
Roast the cauliflower florets in the preheated oven for about 25 minutes or until they're crisp-tender. Bon appétit!

Perfect Oven-Roasted Vegetables

(Ready in about 45 minutes | Servings 5)
Per serving: Calories: 333; Fat: 16.8g; Carbs: 38.8g; Protein: 10g
Ingredients
1 pound summer squash, cubed
1 yellow bell pepper, seeded and sliced
1 red bell pepper, seeded and sliced
1 green bell pepper, seeded and sliced
1 pound gold potatoes, peeled and cubed
8 ounces Campari tomatoes, whole
2 red onions, quartered
1 tablespoon Italian herb mix
1/2 teaspoon cayenne pepper
Sea salt and freshly ground black pepper, to taste
4 tablespoons olive oil
2 tablespoons balsamic vinegar
1 cup parmesan cheese, grated
Directions
Toss the vegetables, herbs, spices, olive oil, and balsamic vinegar in a baking pan.
Roast your veggies in the preheated oven at 425 degrees F for about 40 minutes, tossing every 10 minutes to ensure even cooking.
Serve the warm vegetables with a sprinkle of freshly grated Parmesan cheese. Bon appétit!

Italian-Style Roasted Baby Bella Mushrooms

(Ready in about 30 minutes | Servings 4)
Per serving: Calories: 158; Fat: 14.1g; Carbs: 7.5g; Protein: 3g
Ingredients
1 pound baby Bella mushrooms
4 tablespoons olive oil
1 teaspoon dried rosemary
1 teaspoon dried oregano
1 teaspoon dried basil
1 teaspoon dried thyme
1 teaspoon onion powder
4 cloves garlic, minced
1 teaspoon sweet smoked paprika
Sea salt and ground black pepper, to taste
Directions
Toss the mushrooms with the olive oil, herbs and spices.
Spread the mushrooms evenly on a large roasting pan.
Roast the mushrooms for about 30 minutes or until they have softened. Bon appétit!

Moroccan-Style Summer Squash

(Ready in about 30 minutes | Servings 4)
Per serving: Calories: 185; Fat: 12.9g; Carbs: 14g; Protein: 5.1g
Ingredients
1 pound summer squash, peeled, seeded, and cut into bite-sized cubes
2 tablespoons olive oil
1/2 teaspoon Moroccan spice mix
Sea salt and white pepper, to taste
4 ounces crumbled feta
Directions
Toss the summer squash with the olive oil, Moroccan spice mix, salt, and white pepper.
Roast the squash at 360 degrees F for about 25 minutes.
Garnish with crumbled feta and serve. Bon appétit!

Asparagus Roll Ups

(Ready in about 20 minutes | Servings 4)

Per serving: Calories: 545; Fat: 42.4g; Carbs: 31.7g; Protein: 11.2g

Ingredients

8 asparagus spears, trimmed
1 tablespoon olive oil
1/2 teaspoon cayenne
1 teaspoon garlic powder
1/2 teaspoon ground cumin
Sea salt and ground black pepper, to taste
1 sheet puff pastry
8 ounces cream cheese
1 egg beaten

Directions

Start by preheating your oven to 420 degrees F.

Toss the asparagus with olive oil, cayenne pepper, garlic powder, cumin, salt, and ground black pepper.

Now, roll the puff pastry out to a large rectangle; cut the rectangle into 8 strips. Layer each strip generously with cream cheese.

Wrap one strip around one spear of asparagus and place them on a parchment-lined baking sheet. Brush with the beaten egg.

Bake in the preheated oven for about 13 to 16 minutes until your roll-ups are golden. Serve immediately.

Italian-Style Zucchini Boats

(Ready in about 25 minutes | Servings 3)

Per serving: Calories: 315; Fat: 18.4g; Carbs: 8.4g; Protein: 28.2g

Ingredients

3 medium-sized zucchinis, halved lengthwise, scoop out the center
3 teaspoons olive oil
1 small-sized red onion, chopped
1/2 teaspoon garlic, pressed
9 ounces tuna in water, canned and drained
1 large tomato, chopped
1 tablespoon Italian seasoning mix
Sea salt and ground black pepper, to taste
1 cup pecorino cheese, grated

Directions

Start by preheating your oven to 395 degrees F.

Drizzle the olive oil over them. Divide the onion, garlic, tuna, and tomato between the zucchini boats. Sprinkle the spices over them.

Top with the grated cheese and place in a lightly oiled baking pan.

Bake the zucchini boats in the preheated oven for about 23 minutes or until the cheese is bubbly. Bon appétit!

Quinoa with Swiss Chard and Feta Cheese

(Ready in about 20 minutes | Servings 3)

Per serving: Calories: 411; Fat: 18.1g; Carbs: 50.4g; Protein: 13.9g

Ingredients

2 tablespoons olive oil
1/2 cup leeks, sliced
2 Italian sweet peppers, deveined and sliced
2 cloves garlic, minced
1 cup quinoa
2 cups water
2 cups Swiss chard, chopped
1/4 teaspoon ground bay leaf
1/2 teaspoon dried oregano
Sea salt and ground black pepper, to taste
1/2 cup feta cheese, crumbled

Directions

Heat the olive oil in a frying pan over medium-high heat; now, sauté the leeks and peppers until just tender for about 3 minutes.

Stir in the garlic and continue to sauté until fragrant or about 30 seconds; reserve.

Now, cook your quinoa in the water over medium-low heat until it is tender and fluffy, for about 10 minutes.

Stir in the Swiss chard, ground bay leaf, oregano, salt, and black pepper and continue to simmer, covered, for 5 minutes more or until the chard has wilted.

Add in the sautéed vegetables and serve garnished with feta cheese. Bon appétit!

Roasted Eggplant with Herbs

(Ready in about 30 minutes | Servings 3)

Per serving: Calories: 209; Fat: 18.3g; Carbs: 11.6g; Protein: 2g

Ingredients

1 pound eggplant, sliced
1/4 cup extra virgin olive oil
2 cloves garlic, minced
Sea salt and ground black pepper, to taste
1/2 teaspoon paprika
1 tablespoon fresh oregano
1 tablespoon fresh basil
1 tablespoon fresh parsley
1 tablespoon lemon juice

Directions

Toss the eggplant slices with the remaining ingredients until well coated on all sides.

Roast the eggplant in the preheated oven at 390 degrees F for about 30 minutes. Serve warm or at room temperature.

Bon appétit!

Grilled Radicchio with Feta Cheese

(Ready in about 15 minutes | Servings 3)

Per serving: Calories: 189; Fat: 15g; Carbs: 8.4g; Protein: 5.8g

Ingredients

1 pound radicchio, cut into wedges
2 tablespoons extra-virgin olive oil
1/2 teaspoon dried oregano
1 teaspoon dried basil
1 teaspoon dried rosemary
Sea salt and freshly ground pepper, to taste
1 tablespoon fresh lemon juice
1/2 cup feta cheese, crumbled

Directions

Preheat an outdoor grill for medium heat; lightly oil the grate with the cooking spray.

Place the radicchio on the preheated grill, drizzle the olive oil over them and cook until lightly charred, 3 to 4 minutes per side.

Transfer the grilled radicchio to a platter and drizzle each piece with the lemon juice. Sprinkle with seasonings, garnish with feta cheese, and serve. Bon appétit!

Easy Garlicky Broccoli Rabe

(Ready in about 10 minutes | Servings 3)

Per serving: Calories: 119; Fat: 9.7g; Carbs: 5.6g; Protein: 5g

Ingredients

1 bunch broccoli rabe, trimmed and rinsed
2 tablespoons olive oil
3 cloves garlic, sliced
Sea salt and freshly ground black pepper, to taste
1 tablespoon lemon juice

Directions

Bring a large pot of salted water to a boil and cook the broccoli rabe for 1 minute. Place the broccoli rabe in a large colander to drain.

Heat the olive oil in a saucepan and sauté the broccoli rabe for about 7 minutes until al dente. Add in the garlic and continue to sauté for a minute or so until fragrant.

Stir in the salt, black pepper, and lemon juice and serve warm. Bon appétit!

Herb Millet Pilaf with Campari Tomatoes

(Ready in about 35 minutes | Servings 3)

Per serving: Calories: 469; Fat: 16.1g; Carbs: 62.4g; Protein: 20.9g

Ingredients

2 cups chicken stock
1 cup millet, rinsed and drained
1 tablespoon olive oil
1/2 red onion, chopped
4 cloves garlic, minced
8 ounces fresh kale, torn into smaller pieces
1/2 cup white wine
1 teaspoon fresh basil, chopped
1 teaspoon fresh oregano, chopped
1 cup Campari tomatoes, halved
Sea salt and ground black pepper, to taste
1/2 cup halloumi cheese, crumbled

Directions

Bring the chicken stock to a boil in a stockpot. Now, stir in the millet, turn the heat to medium-low, and let it simmer, covered, for about 20 minutes.

Heat the olive oil in a saucepan over a moderately high heat; then, sauté the onion and garlic until they are tender and fragrant, for about 5 minutes.

Stir in the kale, wine, herbs, and tomatoes. Continue to cook for a further 10 minutes or until everything is cooked through.

Afterwards, stir the kale mixture into the reserved millet. Season with salt and pepper to taste. Serve with crumbled cheese. Bon appétit!

Crunchy Chickpea Stuffed Zucchini

(Ready in about 25 minutes | Servings 6)

Per serving: Calories: 249; Fat: 15g; Carbs: 20.4g; Protein: 10.8g

Ingredients

3 large zucchinis, halved lengthwise, scoop out the center
1 (15-ounce) can chickpeas, drained
1 garlic clove
1 tomato
1 red onion
1/4 cup pine nuts
1 egg, whisked
1/2 cup kalamata olives, pitted and halved
1/2 teaspoon Greek oregano
1/2 teaspoon red pepper flakes
Sea salt and ground black pepper, to taste
1 tablespoon olive oil
1 cup feta cheese, crumbled

Directions

Start by preheating your oven to 395 degrees F.

Blend the chickpeas, garlic, tomato, onion, and, pine nuts in your food processor until you get the desired consistency.

Add in the egg and olives and stir to combine well.

Divide the mixture between the zucchini boats.

Sprinkle the spices over them and drizzle with the olive oil.

Now, place the stuffed zucchini in a lightly oiled baking pan.

Bake the stuffed zucchini in the preheated oven for about 23 minutes until they are tender. Top the warm zucchini with feta cheese and serve. Bon appétit!

Moroccan-Style Harissa Quinoa

(Ready in about 25 minutes | Servings 3)

Per serving: Calories: 509; Fat: 15g; Carbs: 81.4g; Protein: 15.7g

1 cup quinoa, rinsed
2 cups water
2 tablespoons olive oil
2 carrots, sliced
1/2 cup red onions, chopped
1 (15-ounce) can chickpeas, rinsed and drained
1/2 cup golden raisins
1 tablespoon fresh parsley, chopped
1 teaspoon fresh coriander, chopped
1/2 teaspoon turmeric powder
1/2 teaspoon cumin powder
 teaspoon Harissa chili paste
Sea salt and ground black pepper, to taste

Directions

Cook the rinsed quinoa in the water over medium-low heat until it is tender, for about 10 minutes; fluff with a fork and reserve.

Heat the olive oil in a frying pan over medium-high heat; now, sauté the carrots and onion until just tender for about 3 minutes.

Stir in the remaining ingredients and continue to simmer, covered, for 10 minutes more or until everything is cooked through.

Stir in the reserved quinoa, stir to combine well, and serve immediately. Bon appétit!

Arborio Rice with Sultanas and Pine Nuts

(Ready in about 20 minutes | Servings 3)
Per serving: Calories: 404; Fat: 18g; Carbs: 53.2g; Protein: 7.2g

Ingredients
2 tablespoons olive oil
1/2 cup red onions, chopped
1/2 teaspoon turmeric powder
1/2 teaspoon cinnamon
1 teaspoon garlic powder
1/2 teaspoon coriander seeds
Sea salt and ground black pepper, to taste
1 cup Arborio rice
2 cups water
1/4 cup sultanas
1/4 cup pine nuts, roughly chopped

Directions
Heat the olive oil in a Dutch oven over medium heat. Add in the onion, and sauté until it is tender and translucent, about 2 to 3 minutes.

Stir in the spices, Arborio rice, and water, bringing it to a rapid boil. Turn the heat to a medium-low and continue to cook for about 16 minutes.

Garnish with sultanas and pine nuts and serve immediately. Enjoy!

Wild Mushroom Cappuccino

(Ready in about 35 minutes | Servings 4)
Per serving: Calories: 389; Fat: 9.6g; Carbs: 65.4g; Protein: 13.2g

Ingredients
1 tablespoon olive oil, at room temperature
1 small-sized red onion, finely diced
1 garlic clove, pressed
2 cups wild mushrooms, thinly sliced
1 tablespoon plain flour
Sea salt and ground black pepper, to taste
3 cups vegetable broth
1/2 cup double cream
4 sprigs fresh chervil

Directions
Heat the olive oil in a soup pot. Once hot, sauté the onion and garlic until they've softened or about 5 minutes.

Fold in the mushrooms and continue to sauté until they release the liquid.

Stir in the flour, salt, and black pepper and continue to cook for about 3 minutes longer. Add in the vegetable broth and bring to a boil.

Immediately turn the heat to a simmer, and let it cook, covered, for 15 to 18 minutes more or until cooked through.

Add in the cream and continue to cook for 8 minutes more, stirring periodically.

Serve the soup in espresso cups garnished with fresh chervil. Bon appétit!

Easy Creamed Broccoli

(Ready in about 15 minutes | Servings 4)
Per serving: Calories: 129; Fat: 8g; Carbs: 12.7g; Protein: 4g

Ingredients
2 tablespoons olive oil
1 red onion, chopped
2 garlic cloves, minced
1 pound broccoli florets
1/4 cup cream of mushroom soup
Sea salt and ground black pepper, to taste
1/2 teaspoon red pepper flakes

Directions
Heat the olive oil in a saucepan over medium-high heat. Once hot, sauté the onion for about 3 minutes or until tender and fragrant.

Add in the garlic and continue to sauté for 30 seconds more until fragrant.

Stir in the broccoli, soup, salt, black pepper, and red pepper, and bring to a boil. Reduce the heat to a simmer

Now, continue to cook, covered, for about 9 minutes or until the broccoli florets are crisp-tender. Taste, adjust the seasonings, and serve warm with the grilled fish fillets, if desired. Bon appétit!

Classic Avocado and Campari Tomato Salad

(Ready in about 5 minutes | Servings 3)
Per serving: Calories: 254; Fat: 23.1g; Carbs: 11.3g; Protein: 2.7g

Ingredients
1 avocado, pitted, peeled and diced
1 cup Campari tomatoes, halved
1 red onion, thinly sliced
1 cup baby spinach
1 cup arugula
1 large Greek cucumber, sliced
3 tablespoons olive oil
1 tablespoon balsamic vinegar
Sea salt and pepper to taste

Directions
Toss the ingredients in a large salad bowl. Taste and adjust the seasonings.

Serve immediately with your favorite main course and enjoy!

Tzatziki Chickpea Bowl

(Ready in about 55 minutes | Servings 3)
Per serving: Calories: 334; Fat: 9.5g; Carbs: 49.3g; Protein: 15.7g

Ingredients

1 cup chickpeas, soaked overnight
1 cup grape tomatoes, halved
2 tablespoons fresh chervil, chopped
2 tablespoons parsley, chopped
1/2 cup fresh scallions, chopped
1 bell pepper, sliced
2 tablespoons extra-virgin olive oil
Sea salt and ground black pepper, to taste
3 tablespoons tzatziki

Directions

Drain the soaked chickpeas and tip them into a stockpot. Cover the chickpeas with water by 1 inch. Bring the water to a rolling boil over high heat. Immediately turn the heat to a simmer and cook for about 50 minutes. Transfer the cooked chickpeas to a serving salad bowl.

Stir in the tomatoes, chervil, parsley, scallions, and pepper; toss to combine well. Drizzle the olive oil over them and season with salt and pepper to taste Garnish with chilled tzatziki and serve. Bon appétit!

Moroccan-Style Millet with Roasted Carrots

(Ready in about 50 minutes | Servings 4)
Per serving: Calories: 309; Fat: 9.2g; Carbs: 48.4g; Protein: 8.3g

Ingredients
2 cups water
1 cup millet, rinsed and drained
2 tablespoons olive oil
1/2 pound carrots trimmed and cut into bite-sized pieces
1/2 teaspoon allspice
1/2 teaspoon turmeric powder
1 medium leek, chopped
1 teaspoon garlic, minced
1 Italia sweet pepper, deseeded and chopped
1 Serrano pepper, deseeded and chopped
Sea salt and cracked mixed peppercorns, to taste
2 ounces Greek-style yogurt
2 tablespoons fresh parsley leaves, roughly chopped

Directions
Bring the water to a boil in a stockpot. Now, stir in the millet, turn the heat to medium-low, and let it simmer, covered, for about 20 minutes.

Toss the carrots with 1 tablespoon of the olive oil, allspice, and turmeric powder. Roast the carrots at 395 degrees F for about 35 minutes, or until they're gently caramelized.

Heat the remaining tablespoon of the olive oil in a saucepan over a moderately high heat; then, sauté the leek and garlic until they are tender and fragrant, for about 5 minutes.

Stir in the peppers and continue to cook for a further 10 minutes or until everything is cooked through. Season with salt and pepper to taste. Stir the sautéed mixture into the reserved millet. Top with the roasted carrots.

Garnish with yogurt and parsley and serve immediately. Bon appétit!

Grilled Veggie Pita Pockets

(Ready in about 15 minutes | Servings 4)
Per serving: Calories: 348; Fat: 11.1g; Carbs: 56.7g; Protein: 12.4g

Ingredients
1 eggplant
4 ounces fresh portobello mushrooms, halved or quartered
2 sweet Italian peppers
1 zucchini
4 tablespoons tahini (sesame butter)
1 tablespoon soy sauce
1 tablespoon balsamic vinegar
1/2 teaspoon fresh garlic, minced
4 (6 1/2-inch) whole-wheat pita bread
1 cup cherry tomatoes, halved

Directions
Place the eggplant, mushrooms, peppers, and zucchini on the rack of your grill over medium heat. Grill the vegetables for about 10 minutes or until they are lightly charred, turning occasionally to promote even cooking. Chop the vegetables and set them aside.

Meanwhile, whisk the tahini with soy sauce, balsamic vinegar, ad minced garlic.

Break open your pita pockets and rub the inside of each pocket with the tahini sauce.

Fill your pita pockets with the grilled vegetables and fresh cherry tomatoes. Serve and enjoy!

Barbecue Cauliflower with Avocado Slaw

(Ready in about 25 minutes | Servings 3)
Per serving: Calories: 418; Fat: 20.6g; Carbs: 58.9g; Protein: 8.8g

Ingredients
Barbecue Cauliflower:
1 pound cauliflower florets
2 tablespoons olive oil
1 tablespoon soy sauce
1/2 teaspoon liquid smoke
1/2 cup tomato paste
1/4 cup honey
2 tablespoons balsamic vinegar
1 teaspoon hot sauce, or to taste
1 teaspoon garlic powder
1 teaspoon onion powder
Avocado Slaw:
1 medium avocado, peeled, pitted, and sliced
1 tablespoon fresh lemon juice
2 garlic cloves, pressed
Sea salt and ground black pepper, to taste
3 cups cabbage, shredded
2 tablespoons fresh scallions, chopped
2 tablespoons fresh basil, chopped
2 tablespoons fresh parsley, chopped

Directions
Toss the cauliflower florets with the olive oil and roast at 400 degrees F for about 12 minutes.

Add in the remaining ingredients for the Barbecue Cauliflower and toss to coat well. Roast the cauliflower for 8 to 10 minutes more until fork tender.

Make the Avocado Slaw: puree the avocado, lemon juice, garlic, salt, and black pepper in your food processor or blender, scraping down the sides of the bowl as needed.

Place the cabbage, fresh scallions, basil, and parsley in a salad bowl. Stir in the avocado dressing and toss to combine. Serve with the barbecue cauliflower and enjoy!

Italian-Style Stuffed Peppers with Couscous

(Ready in about 30 minutes | Servings 3)
Per serving: Calories: 358; Fat: 9.7g; Carbs: 53.3g; Protein: 15.1g
Ingredients
1 cup couscous
3 tablespoons walnuts, ground
Sea salt and ground black pepper, to taste
1 tablespoon Italian spice mix
1/2 cup parmesan cheese, grated
3 bell peppers, halved and deveined
Directions
Cover the couscous with the water and bring to boil; allow it to sit for about 15 minutes.
Fluff the couscous with a fork. Now, add in the walnuts, salt, black pepper, Italian spice mix, and parmesan cheese.
Divide the couscous stuffing between the pepper halves and bake in the preheated oven at 390 degrees F for 10 to 12 minutes. Bon appétit!

Stuffed Sweet Potatoes

(Ready in about 50 minutes | Servings 2)
Per serving: Calories: 358; Fat: 9.7g; Carbs: 53.3g; Protein: 15.1g
Ingredients
2 sweet potatoes
2 tablespoons olive oil
Sea salt and ground black pepper, to taste
1/2 cup red lentils, soaked overnight
1 small-sized red onion, chopped
1 clove garlic, minced
1 tomato, chopped
3 sun-dried tomatoes, chopped
Directions
Start by preheating your oven to 360 degrees F.
Brush the sweet potatoes with the olive oil and bake for about 40 minutes until they're fork-tender.
Meanwhile, bring the water and lentils to a boil and immediately turn the heat to a simmer. Let it simmer for about 20 minutes; drain and season with salt and ground black pepper.
Meanwhile, sauté the onion for about 4 minutes until it is tender and translucent. Add in the garlic and continue to sauté for a minute or so until aromatic. Now, add in the tomatoes, stir and remove from the heat. Add in the lentils and stir to combine. Divide the

filling between the sweet potatoes and bake in your oven for about 5 minutes. Enjoy!

Chickpea Pita Pockets

(Ready in about 40 minutes | Servings 2)
Per serving: Calories: 486; Fat: 18.8g; Carbs: 68.3g; Protein: 16.1g
Ingredients
1 cup canned chickpeas, drained
2 cloves garlic, minced
1 teaspoon ground coriander
Sea salt and ground black pepper
1/2 teaspoon turmeric powder
1/2 teaspoon hot paprika
2 tablespoons olive oil
2 (6 1/2-inch) whole-wheat pita bread
2 tablespoons aioli
1 large tomato, sliced
2 tablespoons scallions, chopped
Directions
Toss the chickpeas with the garlic, coriander, salt, black pepper, turmeric powder, hot paprika, and olive oil.
Place the chickpeas on a parchment-lined baking paper and roast them at 390 degrees F for about 35 minutes.
Break open your pita pockets and rub the inside of each pocket with the aioli.
Fill your pita pockets with the roasted chickpeas, fresh tomatoes, and scallions. Bon appétit!

Hummus Stuffed Yams

(Ready in about 45 minutes | Servings 3)
Per serving: Calories: 356; Fat: 12.8g; Carbs: 55.2g; Protein: 5.1g
Ingredients
1 pound yams, scrubbed and halved
2 tablespoons olive oil
1 large-sized red onion, thinly sliced
1/2 cup hummus
Sea salt and ground black pepper, to taste
Directions
Rub the yams with the olive oil; pierce the skin with a fork and transfer them to a baking pan.
Bake the yams until tender, about 35 minutes. Divide the remaining ingredients between your yams and continue to bake an additional 10 minutes.
Taste and adjust the seasonings. Bon appétit!

Lentil and Parmesan Stuffed Eggplant

(Ready in about 55 minutes | Servings 4)
Per serving: Calories: 484; Fat: 17.5g; Carbs: 62.2g; Protein: 24.5g
Ingredients
2 tablespoons olive oil
1 red onion, chopped
2 cloves garlic, finely chopped
2 medium eggplants, cut into halve and scoop out the center
1/4 cup fresh parsley, chopped

1/4 cup fresh tarragon leaves, chopped
1/2 pound canned red lentils, drained
1/2 cup black olives, pitted and sliced
1 teaspoon hot paprika
Sea salt and freshly ground black pepper, to taste
1/4 teaspoon ground cumin
1/2 cup bread crumbs
1 cup parmesan cheese, grated
Directions
In a saucepan, heat the olive oil over medium-high heat. Now, sauté the onion and garlic until they have softened or about 3 minutes.
Add in the eggplant flash that has been scooped out of the inside and continue to cook an additional 10 minutes.
Add in the parsley, tarragon, lentils, and black olives, stir, and remove from the heat. Stir in the paprika, salt, black pepper, ground cumin, and bread crumbs. Divide the filling between eggplant halves and transfer them to a lightly oiled baking dish. Bake the stuffed eggplant for about 40 minutes or until they are tender.
Lastly, top with the cheese and place under the preheated broiler for about 5 minutes or until the cheese is golden and bubbly. Bon appétit!

Traditional Italian Caponata

(Ready in about 30 minutes | Servings 3)
Per serving: Calories: 196; Fat: 10.7g; Carbs: 24.2g; Protein: 4.2g
Ingredients
2 tablespoons olive oil
1 medium-sized red onion, chopped
2 garlic cloves, minced
1 pound eggplants, peeled and diced
1/2 pound bell peppers, cut into strips
1 ripe tomato, chopped
1 tablespoon Italian seasoning mix
1/4 cup dry white wine
1/4 cup Italian olives, pitted and sliced
Directions
Heat the olive oil in a saucepan over medium-high heat. Then, sauté the onion for about 3 minutes until tender and translucent.
Add in the garlic and continue to sauté an additional 30 seconds until it is fragrant.
Add in the eggplant, peppers, tomato, seasoning mix, and wine. Continue to simmer, partially covered, for a further 20 to 25 minutes or until cooked through. Afterwards, stir in the olives and remove from the heat. Serve warm garnished with some extra fresh herbs if desired. Bon appétit!

Classic Tabbouleh Salad

(Ready in about 30 minutes + chilling time | Servings 2)
Per serving: Calories: 344; Fat: 15g; Carbs: 48.9g; Protein: 10.9g
Ingredients
1/2 cup dry bulgur wheat
1/2 cup hot water

1 Roma tomato, chopped
1/2 Greek cucumber, chopped
1 Italian sweet pepper, diced
1 small chili pepper, chopped
1/2 teaspoon garlic, minced
2 scallion stalks, sliced
1/4 cup fresh parsley, chopped
2 tablespoons olive oil
2 tablespoons fresh lemon juice
Sea salt and ground black pepper, to taste
Directions
Soak the bulgur in the hot water for about 1/2 hour or until most of the water has absorbed; drain any excess water.
Toss the prepared bulgur with the remaining ingredients and place in your refrigerator until ready to serve.
Bon appétit!

Roasted Beat Salad with Feta Cheese

(Ready in about 50 minutes + chilling time | Servings 4)
Per serving: Calories: 314; Fat: 21.6g; Carbs: 23.2g; Protein: 8.3g
Ingredients
1 pound beets
2 cups baby spinach, rinsed
2 cups arugula, rinsed
2 garlic cloves, minced
1/4 cup extra-virgin olive oil
2 tablespoons red wine vinegar
1 teaspoon stone-ground mustard
1/4 teaspoon ground cumin
1/2 teaspoon dried dill weed
1/2 teaspoon dried basil
Coarse sea salt and ground black pepper, to taste
5 ounces feta cheese, crumbled
1/4 cup packed sultanas
Directions
Pierce the beets with a fork and place them on a foil-lined roasting pan.
Bake the beets in the preheated oven at 395 degrees F for about 50 minutes; then, cool to room temperature and peel the skins.
Cut your beets into slices and add in the spinach, arugula, garlic, olive oil, vinegar, mustard, cumin, dill, basil, salt, and black pepper.
Serve garnished with crumbled feta cheese and sultanas. Bon appétit!

Pecorino and Vegetable Fritters

(Ready in about 15 minutes | Servings 4)
Per serving: Calories: 355; Fat: 17.8g; Carbs: 32.6g; Protein: 15.9g
Ingredients
3 ounces zucchini, shredded
1 ounce carrots, trimmed and shredded
3 ounces sweet potatoes, scrubbed and shredded
3 ounces Pecorino Romano cheese, grated
2 tablespoons scallions, chopped
1 teaspoon garlic, finely chopped

1 tablespoon fresh parsley, chopped
1/2 cup all-purpose flour
1/2 teaspoon baking powder
Sea salt and ground black pepper, to taste
1/2 teaspoon hot paprika
1/2 teaspoon Greek oregano
2 eggs, whisked
2 tablespoons olive oil
Directions
Thoroughly combine all ingredients, except for the olive oil, in a mixing bowl.
Heat the olive oil in a frying pan over medium-high heat.
Drop the vegetable mixture by heaping tablespoonfuls onto the hot oil; fry the patties for about 3 minutes per side or until golden.
Serve with chilled Greek yogurt if desired. Bon appétit!

Authentic Greek Lemoni Patatas

(Ready in about 1 hour 15 minutes | Servings 4)
Per serving: Calories: 317; Fat: 14.1g; Carbs: 43.2g; Protein: 6.2g
Ingredients
2 pounds gold potatoes, peeled and cut into bite-sized chunks
4 tablespoons extra-virgin olive oil
1/3 cup lemon juice, freshly squeezed
1 teaspoon lemon zest
1 cup vegetable broth
6 garlic cloves, chopped
1 teaspoon Greek seasoning mix
Directions
Toss the potatoes with the other ingredients until well coated. Arrange the potatoes on a foil, cover them, and place them in a baking pan.
Bake the potatoes at 350 degrees F for about 1 hour. Remove the foil and bake your potatoes an additional 15 minutes or until tender and cooked through.
Transfer the warm potatoes to a serving platter along with the cooking liquid and serve immediately. Enjoy!

Stuffed Tomatoes with Rice and Cheese

(Ready in about 35 minutes | Servings 4)
Per serving: Calories: 309; Fat: 14.2g; Carbs: 33.9g; Protein: 10.8g
Ingredients
4 large firm tomatoes, tops, seeds, and pulp removed
2 tablespoons olive oil
4 scallion stalks, chopped
2 garlic cloves, minced
1 cup cooked white rice
1 cup parmesan cheese, grated
Sea salt and ground black pepper, to taste
1 teaspoon cayenne pepper
1/3 cup seasoned breadcrumbs
Directions
Brush the tomatoes with the olive oil on all sides. Then, mix the scallions, garlic, rice, and cheese in a bowl.

Sprinkle the salt, black pepper, and cayenne pepper on them. Top them with the breadcrumbs.
Roast the stuffed tomatoes for about 30 minutes, rotating the pan halfway through the cooking time.
Top the warm tomatoes with grated parmesan cheese; serve warm or at room temperature.
Bon appétit!

Ultimate Avocado Crostini

(Ready in about 30 minutes | Servings 3)
Per serving: Calories: 275; Fat: 19.9g; Carbs: 23.2g; Protein: 4.6g
Ingredients
9 slices Italian baguette
2 garlic cloves, peeled and halved
1/2 teaspoon oregano
Flakes sea salt and ground black pepper, to taste
2 tablespoons extra-virgin olive oil
1 avocado, peeled, pitted and sliced
1 cup Campari tomatoes, halved
1/2 cup green olives, pitted and halved
Directions
Place the baguette slices in a single layer on a rimmed baking pan. Bake them at 370 degrees F for about 20 minutes.
Rub your crostini with the cut side of the garlic; sprinkle them with the oregano, salt, and pepper. Drizzle the olive oil over them.
Now, top each of them with the avocado, Campari tomatoes, and green olives. Place your crostini under the preheated broiler for about 5 minutes.
Bon appétit!

Sage and Parmesan Vegetable Cakes

(Ready in about 15 minutes | Servings 4)
Per serving: Calories: 257; Fat: 11.2g; Carbs: 32.8g; Protein: 7.9g
Ingredients
1/2 pound yams, peeled and grated
1/2 pound zucchini, grated
2 ounces, celery, peeled and grated
2 ounces sweet corn kernels, drained
1/2 cup leeks, chopped
1 teaspoon garlic, minced
1/4 cup all-purpose flour
1/2 cup parmesan cheese, grated
1 tablespoon fresh sage, roughly chopped
Sea salt and freshly ground black pepper, to taste
1/2 teaspoon cayenne pepper
1/2 cup breadcrumbs
2 tablespoons olive oil
Directions
Thoroughly combine all ingredients, except for the breadcrumbs and olive oil, in a mixing bowl.
Shape the mixture into the equal patties and roll each of them over the breadcrumbs.
Heat the olive oil in a frying pan over medium-high heat. Then, fry the vegetable cakes for about 3 minutes per side or until cooked through.
Bon appétit!

Twisted Sautéed Beets

(Ready in about 15 minutes + chilling time | Servings 2)
Per serving: Calories: 238; Fat: 13.1g; Carbs: 25.7g; Protein: 6.7g

Ingredients

1 tablespoon olive oil
1/2 small red onion, thinly sliced
2 cloves garlic, thinly sliced
1/2 pound beets, peeled and sliced into small chunks
1/2 cup water
1 cup baby spinach
1 cup Romaine lettuce
1 tablespoon roasted pepitas
1/2 teaspoon paprika
1 tablespoon fresh lemon juice
2 ounces Halloumi cheese, crumbled

Directions

Heat the olive oil in a frying pan over a moderately high heat. Now, sauté the onions and garlic until tender or about 3 minutes.

Add in the beets and water, and continue sautéing for about 12 minutes or until the beets are crisp-tender.

Let the sautéed mixture cool to room temperature.

Place the baby spinach and Romaine lettuce in a serving bowl; top with the sautéed mixture beet mixture, roasted pepitas, paprika, and lemon juice.

Garnish with crumbled Halloumi cheese and serve immediately. Enjoy!

FISH & SEAFOOD

Italian Shrimp Pasta

(Ready in about 25 minutes | Servings 4)
Per serving: Calories: 478; Fat: 8.7g; Carbs: 65.9g;
Protein: 34.7g
Ingredients
10 ounces spaghetti
2 tablespoons olive oil
1 red onion, chopped
1 garlic clove, minced
1/2 teaspoon cayenne pepper
1 teaspoon dried oregano
1/2 teaspoon dried basil
1/4 teaspoon mustard seeds
Sea salt and ground black pepper, to taste
2 cups marinara sauce
1 pound shrimp, peeled and deveined
Directions
Cook the spaghetti according to the manufacture's
directions; drain and reserve, keeping them warm.
Meanwhile, heat the olive oil in a saucepan over
medium-high heat. Now, sauté the onion and garlic
until tender and fragrant.
Stir in the spices and marinara sauce; immediately
turn the heat to a simmer.
Let it simmer for 18 to 20 minutes or until the sauce
has thickened. Stir in the shrimp and continue to
simmer for 5 minutes more or until cooked through.
Divide the cooked spaghetti between serving plates
and top them with the sauce. Bon appétit!

Provençal Striped Bass with Cherry Tomatoes

(Ready in about 20 minutes | Servings 4)
Per serving: Calories: 157; Fat: 6.2g; Carbs: 3.1g;
Protein: 20.7g
Ingredients
1 tablespoon olive oil
1/2 cup onion, thinly sliced
1 teaspoon garlic, minced
1 pound striped bass fillets
1 cup cherry tomatoes, halved
1 tablespoon Dijon mustard
Sea salt and ground black pepper, to taste
1 tablespoon Herbs de Provence
Directions
Start by preheating your oven to 420 degrees F.
Lightly oil a baking pan with a nonstick cooking
spray.
Heat the olive oil and sauté the onion and garlic until
they've softened.
Toss the fish fillets and cherry tomatoes with the
mustard and spices and arrange them on the baking
pan.
Bake in the preheated oven for about 18 minutes or
until the fish is cooked through and the tomatoes are
slightly caramelized.

Top the fish with the vegetables and serve
immediately. Bon appétit!

Couscous with Tuna and Basil

(Ready in about 15 minutes | Servings 4)
Per serving: Calories: 458; Fat: 13.1g; Carbs: 53.6g;
Protein: 29.6g
Ingredients
2 cups water
1 ½ cups pearl couscous
10 ounces canned tuna in oil, drained and flaked
2 medium-sized heirloom tomatoes, diced
1 Lebanese cucumber, sliced
1 medium-sized red onion, sliced
1 teaspoon fresh garlic, minced
1/4 cup fresh basil, chopped
2 tablespoons extra-virgin olive oil
2 tablespoons freshly squeezed lemon juice
Sea salt and freshly ground black pepper, to taste
Directions
Bring a lightly salted water to a boil over medium
heat. Add in the couscous; heat off; cover the pan and
allow your couscous to sit for about 10 minutes.
Fluff the couscous with a fork and transfer to a
serving bowl. Stir in the tuna, tomatoes, cucumber,
onion, garlic, and basil.
Drizzle the olive oil and lemon juice over the salad.
Season with salt and pepper to taste. Serve at room
temperature or well-chilled. Enjoy!

Baked Halibut with Cherry Tomatoes

(Ready in about 15 minutes | Servings 4)
Per serving: Calories: 178; Fat: 8.3g; Carbs: 2.8g;
Protein: 21.5g
Ingredients
1 pound halibut fillets
2 tablespoons olive oil
2 garlic cloves, minced
1/2 teaspoon Greek oregano
1/2 teaspoon dill
Sea salt and ground black pepper, to taste
1 cup cherry tomatoes, halved
1 red onion, sliced
1 lemon freshly squeezed
Directions
Brush the halibut with the olive oil; rub the garlic and
spices all over the fish.
Then, bake the halibut, cherry tomatoes, and onion in
the preheated oven at 395 degrees F for about 15
minutes, until the fish easily flakes with a fork and
vegetables are slightly caramelized.
Drizzle the halibut with the fresh lemon juice and
serve warm. Bon appétit!

Spaghetti alla Puttanesca

(Ready in about 20 minutes | Servings 4)
Per serving: Calories: 640; Fat: 28.1g; Carbs: 60.5g;
Protein: 36.5g

Ingredients
4 tablespoons olive oil
2 tablespoons onion, chopped
1 teaspoon garlic, minced
4 anchovy fillets, cut into chunks
2 cups marinara sauce
2 ounces green olives, pitted and halved
2 tablespoons capers, drained
Sea salt and ground black pepper, to taste
1 tablespoon Italian seasoning mix
8 ounces spaghetti
2 ounces parmesan, grated

Directions
Heat the olive oil in a saucepan over a moderate heat.
Now, cook the onion and garlic for about 2 minutes until tender and fragrant.
Add in the anchovy fillets and continue to cook for about 2 minutes per side. After that, str in the marinara sauce, olives, capers, and seasonings and bring to a boil.
Immediately turn the heat to a simmer; stir in the spaghetti and continue to cook for 15 minutes more or until everything is cooked through.
Ladle into serving bowls and top each serving with the grated parmesan cheese. Bon appétit!

Authentic Greek Calamari
(Ready in about 15 minutes | Servings 3)
Per serving: Calories: 406; Fat: 24.1g; Carbs: 21.1g; Protein: 25.5g
Ingredients
3/4 pound squid rings, rinsed
Sea salt and ground black pepper, to taste
1/2 teaspoon red pepper flakes, crushed
1/2 cup all-purpose flour
3 eggs
1/2 cup breadcrumbs
1/4 cup coconut oil

Directions
Pat the squid rings dry with kitchen towels. Season them with salt, black pepper, and red pepper.
Place the flour in a shallow dish. In another shallow dish, whisk the eggs until pale and frothy. Place the breadcrumbs in the third dish.
Now, dip the squid rings in the flour, then in the whisked eggs; afterwards, roll the squid rings over the breadcrumbs.
Heat the oil in a frying pan over medium-high heat. Once hot, fry the calamari until golden or about 3 minutes per side.
Serve with fresh lemon slices if desired and enjoy!

Baked Fish in Cheese-Tomato Sauce
(Ready in about 25 minutes | Servings 4)
Per serving: Calories: 350; Fat: 17.8g; Carbs: 16.9g; Protein: 32.2g
Ingredients
2 tablespoons olive oil
1 small-sized red onion, chopped
2 cloves garlic, sliced

2 Italian sweet peppers, sliced
1 peperoncino, sliced
2 Roma tomatoes, chopped
2 tablespoons tomato paste
1 tablespoon Italian seasoning mix
1 pound cod fillets
1/2 cup parmesan cheese, grated
4 ounces black olives, pitted and halved
1 tablespoon capers, drained

Directions
Start by preheating your oven to 370 degrees F.
Now, heat the olive oil in an oven-safe skillet over a moderately high heat. Once hot, sauté the onion, garlic, and peppers for about 2 minutes until tender and fragrant.
Add in the tomatoes and tomato paste and bring it to a rolling boil; heat off. Add in the fish, cheese, olives, and capers and transfer the skillet to the preheated oven.
Bake it in the center of your preheated oven for approximately 20 minutes, until everything is thoroughly cooked
Taste and adjust the seasonings. Bon appétit!

Old-Fashioned Cod Fish Stew
(Ready in about 30 minutes | Servings 4)
Per serving: Calories: 313; Fat: 13.7g; Carbs: 10.3g; Protein: 36.1g
Ingredients
2 tablespoons olive oil
1 red onion, chopped
2 garlic cloves, minced
1 carrot, chopped
1 celery stalk with leaves, chopped
Sea salt and ground black pepper, to taste
1/2 teaspoon cayenne pepper
4 cups vegetable broth
2 ripe tomatoes, chopped
1 ½ pounds cod fish, diced
1/2 cup dry white wine
2 tablespoons fresh basil, chopped
2 tablespoons fresh tarragon, chopped
2 tablespoons fresh parsley, chopped

Directions
Heat the olive oil in a soup pot over medium heat.
Now, sauté the onion, garlic, carrot, and celery until they've softened for 4 to 5 minutes.
Now, stir in the salt, black pepper, cayenne pepper, broth, and tomatoes and bring to a boil. Immediately turn the heat to a simmer and let it cook for about 15 minutes.
Then, add in the remaining ingredients and continue to simmer for a further 8 to 10 minutes, until the fish is cooked through.
Ladle the fish stew into individual bowls and serve with some extra fresh herbs, if desired. Enjoy!

Roasted Halibut with Aromatic Couscous
(Ready in about 15 minutes | Servings 3)

Per serving: Calories: 438; Fat: 29.6g; Carbs: 24.4g; Protein: 19.1g

Ingredients
3/4 pound halibut fillets
1 ½ cups water
1 cup couscous
Sea salt and freshly ground black pepper, to season
3 tablespoons extra-virgin olive oil
1 teaspoon stone-ground mustard
1 teaspoon lemon zest, grated
2 tablespoons freshly squeezed lemon juice,
1/4 cup fresh parsley, coarsely chopped
1/4 cup fresh dill, coarsely chopped
1/4 cup golden raisins

Directions
Brush the halibut with a nonstick cooking oil and roast it in the preheated oven at 395 degrees F for about 13 minutes until the fish is cooked through and easily flakes with a fork.

Meanwhile, bring a lightly salted water to a boil over medium heat. Add in the couscous; heat off; cover the pan and allow your couscous to sit for about 10 minutes.

Fluff the couscous with a fork and transfer to a serving bowl. Stir in the salt, black pepper, olive oil, mustard, lemon zest, lemon juice, parsley, and dill. Divide your couscous between serving bowls and top with the roasted halibut fillets and golden raisins. Bon appétit!

Sardinian-Style Calamari Fritti

(Ready in about 15 minutes | Servings 4)
Per serving: Calories: 498; Fat: 21.6g; Carbs: 35.6g; Protein: 37.3g

Ingredients
1 ½ pounds squid rings
Sea salt and black pepper, to taste
1/2 cup all-purpose flour
2 eggs
3 ounces semolina flour
1/2 cup Pecorino Sardo cheese, grated
1/4 cup olive oil

Directions
Pat the squid rings dry with kitchen towels. Season them with the sea salt and black pepper to taste.

Place the flour in a shallow dish. In another shallow dish, whisk the eggs until frothy. Place the semolina flour and Pecorino Sardo in the third dish.

Now, dip the squid rings in the flour, then in the whisked eggs; afterwards, roll the squid rings over the flour/cheese mixture.

Heat the oil in a frying pan over medium-high heat. Once hot, fry the calamari until golden or about 3 minutes per side.

Serve with fresh lemon slices, if desired. Bon appétit!

Traditional Zuppa di Pesce

(Ready in about 35 minutes | Servings 4)
Per serving: Calories: 318; Fat: 14.6g; Carbs: 12.6g; Protein: 28.6g

Ingredients
3 tablespoons olive oil
1 pound monkfish, diced
1/2 pound sea scallops
1 red onion, chopped
2 cloves garlic, minced
2 Roma tomatoes, pureed
2 tablespoons tomato paste
3 cups chicken bone broth
8 jumbo brown shrimp, cleaned
1 teaspoon red pepper flakes
1 teaspoon dried oregano
1/2 teaspoon dried rosemary
Sea salt and ground black pepper, to taste
1/2 cup dry white wine

Directions
Heat 2 tablespoons of the olive oil in a heavy-bottomed pot over medium-high heat. Once hot, sear the monkfish for about 7 minutes; reserve.

In the pan drippings, cook the scallops for about 2 minutes per side; reserve.

In the same pot, heat the remaining tablespoon of the olive oil and sauté the onions and garlic for about 3 minutes, until tender and translucent.

Deglaze the pan with a splash of the wine, scraping up all of the browned bits that are stuck to the bottom.

Next, add in the tomatoes, tomato paste, and broth, bringing to a boil. Immediately turn the heat to a simmer; let it simmer, partially covered, for about 15 minutes.

Add in the remaining ingredients and continue to simmer until the shrimp have almost cooked or about 10 minutes, depending on the size.

Add in the reserved fish and sea scallops. Stir and remove from the heat. Serve with crusty garlic-rubbed bread, if desired. Bon appétit!

Baked Fish Sandwiches

(Ready in about 25 minutes | Servings 4)
Per serving: Calories: 384; Fat: 15g; Carbs: 33.4g; Protein: 32.1g

Ingredients
1 pound salmon fillets
2 tablespoons olive oil
Sea salt and ground black pepper, to taste
1/2 teaspoon cayenne pepper
2 sprigs thyme, leaves chopped
1 sprig rosemary, leaves chopped
4 scallion stalks, sliced
4 garlic cloves, crushed
2 sweet Italian peppers, chopped
1 cup grape tomato, halved and sliced
4 hamburger buns

Directions
Start by preheating your oven to 395 degrees F. Toss the salmon fillets with the olive oil and seasonings and place each of them on a sheet of aluminum foil.

Top the salmon fillets with the scallions, garlic, peppers, and tomatoes. Fold the foil over the fish and veggies, sealing the packet closed.

Bake in the preheated oven for about 20 minutes, until cooked through.

Place the fish fillets on the cut side of the bottoms of the buns. Top with the vegetables. Place the top buns over the vegetables and serve.

Enjoy!

Parmesan Prawn Casserole

(Ready in about 25 minutes | Servings 4)
Per serving: Calories: 212; Fat: 7.7g; Carbs: 7.8g; Protein: 29.1g
Ingredients
1 pound prawns, cleaned and deveined
2 scallion stalks, chopped
2 garlic cloves, pressed
Sea salt and ground black pepper, to taste
1 bay laurel
1 teaspoon dried oregano
1/2 teaspoon dried marjoram
1 teaspoon dried parsley flakes
1/2 cup heavy cream
1/2 cup parmesan cheese, grated
Directions
Start by preheating your oven to 370 degrees F.
Arrange the prawns on the bottom of a lightly oiled baking pan. Top with the scallions and garlic. Add in the seasonings.
Pour the heavy cream over them and top with the cheese.
Bake in the preheated oven for about 20 minutes.
Discard the bay laurel and serve warm. Bon appétit!

Sicilian-Style Summer Squash and Fish Soup

(Ready in about 25 minutes | Servings 4)
Per serving: Calories: 413; Fat: 27.3g; Carbs: 20.8g; Protein: 22.5g
Ingredients
3 tablespoons olive oil
4 tablespoons spring onions, sliced
2 cloves garlic, minced
1 celery rib, chopped
2 carrots, chopped
1 cup bulb fennel, chopped
1 sweet Italian pepper, deseeded and chopped
1 Serrano pepper, deseeded and chopped
2 cups passata
1 tablespoon Italian herb mix
2 cups butternut squash, peeled and grated
3 cups chicken bone broth
1 pound halibut fillets
Directions
Heat the olive oil in a soup pot over medium heat.
Now, sauté the onion, garlic, celery, carrots, fennel, and peppers until they've softened for 4 to 5 minutes.
Now, stir in the passata, Italian herb mix, butternut squash, and broth, and bring to a rapid boil.

Immediately turn the heat to a simmer and let it cook for about 10 minutes.
Then, add in the halibut fillets; continue to simmer, partially covered, for a further 10 minutes, until the fish is cooked through.
Ladle the stew into individual bowls and serve hot.
Bon appétit!

Tuna and Asparagus Frittata

(Ready in about 35 minutes | Servings 4)
Per serving: Calories: 327; Fat: 21.1g; Carbs: 23.9g; Protein: 12.1g
Ingredients
2 tablespoons olive oil
1/2 cup green onions, chopped
1 teaspoon garlic, minced
2 sweet Italian peppers, chopped
1/2 pound asparagus spears, trimmed and chopped
5 ounces canned tuna, drained and chopped
5 eggs, whisked
1/2 cup soft cheese
Sea salt and ground pepper, to taste
1/2 cup parmesan cheese, grated
Directions
In an oven-proof skillet, heat the olive oil until sizzling. Once hot, sauté the onions, garlic, peppers, and asparagus until they've softened or about 3 minutes.
Add in the canned tuna and remove it from the heat.
In a mixing bowl, whisk the eggs, soft cheese, salt, and black pepper. Pour the mixture into the skillet.
Scatter the parmesan cheese over the top. Bake your frittata at 330 degrees F for about 30 minutes, until a tester inserted in the center comes out dry and clean.
Bon appétit!

Caprese Oven-Baked Portobellos

(Ready in about 25 minutes | Servings 3)
Per serving: Calories: 307; Fat: 15g; Carbs: 21.7g; Protein: 21.1g
Ingredients
3 tablespoons extra-virgin olive oil
6 large portabella mushrooms, cleaned and stalks removed
1/2 cup green onions, chopped
2 cloves garlic, minced
6 ounces tuna, canned and drained
1 cup cherry tomatoes, halved
Sea salt and ground black pepper, to taste
1 teaspoon cayenne pepper
1/2 cup parmesan, grated
4 tablespoon fresh seasoned breadcrumbs
1/2 cup fresh basil leaves, snipped
Directions
Begin by preheating your oven to 380 degrees F.
Brush the mushrooms with the olive oil and arrange them on a parchment-lined baking sheet.
Divide the onions, garlic, tuna, and tomatoes between the mushroom caps. Season them with salt, black pepper, and cayenne pepper.

In a mixing dish, combine the parmesan and breadcrumbs; top the mushrooms with the breadcrumb mixture.

Bake the stuffed mushrooms for about 20 minutes until the tomatoes have wilted and the cheese has melted.

Garnish with fresh basil leaves and serve. Bon appétit!

Lemon and Mustard-Crusted Salmon with Asparagus

(Ready in about 15 minutes | Servings 4)

Per serving: Calories: 330; Fat: 14.8g; Carbs: 11.3g; Protein: 39.5g

Ingredients

1 teaspoon lemon zest
1 teaspoon coriander seeds
1 teaspoon mustard seeds
1/2 teaspoon red pepper flakes
1 ½ pounds salmon filets
1 ½ pounds asparagus spears, trimmed
1/2 cup lemon juice
Sea salt and ground black pepper, to taste
2 tablespoons olive oil
2 garlic cloves, finely chopped
2 tablespoons fresh chives, roughly chopped
2 tablespoons fresh chervil, roughly chopped

Directions

Mix the lemon zest, coriander seeds, mustard seeds, and red pepper flakes in a spice grinder until finely ground.

Coat the salmon fillets with the spice mixture and transfer them to a parchment-lined baking pan.

Brush the salmon with 1 tablespoon of the olive oil.

Toss the asparagus spears with the lemon juice, salt, black pepper, the remaining tablespoon of the olive oil, and garlic.

Bake the asparagus and salmon at 440 degrees F for about 13 minutes, depending on thickness.

Garnish with fresh chives and chervil and serve immediately.

Tuscan Fish and Bean Soup

(Ready in about 25 minutes | Servings 4)

Per serving: Calories: 423; Fat: 10.8g; Carbs: 48.3g; Protein: 37.2g

Ingredients

2 tablespoons olive oil
1 onion diced
3 cloves garlic, minced
2 carrots, trimmed and thinly sliced
1 celery stalk, thinly sliced
1 zucchini, diced
2 cups fish broth
2 cups passata
2 bay leaves
1 pound sea bass, chopped
2 cups Great Northern beans, canned and drained
1/2 teaspoon red pepper flakes
Sea salt and ground black pepper, to taste

Directions

In a heavy-bottomed pot, heat the olive oil until sizzling. Once hot, sauté the onion, garlic, carrots, celery, and zucchini until they've softened.

After that, add in the broth and passata and bring to a boil. Immediately turn the heat to a simmer and add in the bay leaves and sea bass.

Continue to simmer, partially covered, for about 20 minutes. Add in the beans, red pepper, salt, and black pepper and continue to simmer for 5 minutes more or until cooked through.

Bon appétit!

Aromatic Halibut with Crostini

(Ready in about 20 minutes | Servings 4)

Per serving: Calories: 392; Fat: 23.7g; Carbs: 23.6g; Protein: 20.7g

Ingredients

1 pound halibut fillets
1 tablespoon olive oil
Sea salt and ground black pepper, to taste
8 slices French baguette
3 ounces black olives, pitted and sliced
1 large tomato, chopped
1 teaspoon garlic, minced

Directions

Brush the halibut with the olive oil and roast it in the preheated oven at 395 degrees F for about 13 minutes until the fish is cooked through and easily flakes with a fork.

Chop the fish into small chunks and season with salt and black pepper to taste.

Place the baguette slices in a single layer on a rimmed baking pan. Bake them at 370 degrees F for about 20 minutes.

Top each crostini with the olives, tomatoes, and garlic; top with the baked halibut and serve immediately. Bon appétit!

Provençal-Style Fish Bake

(Ready in about 25 minutes | Servings 4)

Per serving: Calories: 192; Fat: 9.2g; Carbs: 4.7g; Protein: 21.7g

Ingredients

2 tablespoons olive oil
1 medium-sized leek, sliced
2 garlic cloves, minced
1 celery stalk, peeled and chopped
2 ripe tomatoes, sliced
2 cups vegetable broth
1 pound orange roughy fillets
1 tablespoon Herbes de Provence
8 green olives, pitted and sliced
Sea salt and ground black pepper, to season

Directions

Start by preheating your oven to 390 degrees F.

Now, heat the olive oil in an oven-safe skillet over a moderately high heat. Once hot, sauté the leek, garlic, and celery for 2 to 3 minutes until tender and fragrant.

Add in the tomatoes and broth and bring it to a rolling boil; heat off. Add in the fish, Herbes de Provence, and olives.

Season with salt and pepper to taste and transfer the skillet to the preheated oven.

Bake it in the center of your preheated oven for approximately 20 minutes, until everything is thoroughly cooked

Taste and adjust the seasonings. Bon appétit!

Nonna's Halibut Stew

(Ready in about 35 minutes | Servings 3)

Per serving: Calories: 362; Fat: 26.2g; Carbs: 11.8g; Protein: 18.1g

Ingredients

3 tablespoons olive oil
1 red onion, chopped
2 cloves garlic, minced
1 Peperoncino, chopped
1 bell pepper, chopped
Sea salt and ground black pepper, to taste
1 tablespoon Italian herb mix
2 San Marzano tomatoes, pureed
2 cups fish broth
1/2 cup dry white wine
9 ounces halibut, cut into bite-sized pieces

Directions

Heat the olive oil in a soup pot over medium heat. Now, sauté the onion, garlic, and peppers until they've softened for 4 to 5 minutes.

Now, stir in the salt, black pepper, Italian herb mix, tomatoes, and fish broth, and bring to a boil. Immediately turn the heat to a simmer and let it cook for about 15 minutes.

Then, add in the wine and fish and stir to combine; continue to simmer, partially covered, for a further 10 minutes, until the fish is cooked through.

Ladle the halibut stew into individual bowls and serve with a slice of crusty Italian bread, if desired. Bon appétit!

Rustic Squid and Haddock Stew

(Ready in about 35 minutes | Servings 4)

Per serving: Calories: 264; Fat: 8.8g; Carbs: 16.8g; Protein: 28.1g

Ingredients

2 tablespoons olive oil
1 pound squid, cut into rings
1 red onion, chopped
2 cloves garlic, finely chopped
1 red chili pepper, deseeded and finely chopped
1 cup San Marzano tomatoes, pureed
1 cup clam juice
1 bay leaf
1 rosemary sprig
1 thyme sprig
1/2 pound haddock
Sea salt and ground black pepper, to taste

Directions

Heat the olive oil in a heavy-bottomed pot over medium-high heat. Once hot, sear the squid rings for about 5 minutes; reserve.

In the pan drippings, sauté the onions, garlic, and red chili pepper for about 3 minutes, until tender and translucent.

Deglaze the pan with a splash of the clam juice, scraping up all of the browned bits that are stuck to the bottom.

Next, add in the pureed tomatoes and clam juice, bringing to a boil. Immediately turn the heat to a simmer; let it simmer, partially covered, for about 15 minutes.

Add in the spices, haddock, and the reserved squid and continue to simmer until the seafood has almost cooked or about 10 minutes.

Serve with toasted garlic-rubbed bread, if desired. Bon appétit!

Grilled Mahi-Mahi Fish

(Ready in about 15 minutes | Servings 4)

Per serving: Calories: 297; Fat: 20.8g; Carbs: 4.9g; Protein: 21.9g

Ingredients

2 tablespoons olive oil
1 pound mahi-mahi fish, rinsed
Sea salt and ground black pepper, to taste
1/2 teaspoon hot paprika
1 tablespoon Greek seasoning mix
2 plum tomatoes, diced
3 ounces olives, pitted and sliced
2 cloves garlic, pressed

Directions

Preheat the grill to medium.

Pat the fish dry with a paper towel and brush it with the olive oil on all sides. Season the fish with salt, black pepper, paprika, and Greek seasoning mix.

Grill the fish for about 5 minutes. Top your fish with the tomatoes, olives, and garlic and continue to cook an additional 5 minutes until golden.

Serve warm and enjoy!

Striped Bass with Basil Pesto and Cheese

(Ready in about 15 minutes | Servings 4)

Per serving: Calories: 237; Fat: 14.1g; Carbs: 4.7g; Protein: 22.9g

Ingredients

1 pound striped bass fillets, rinsed
1 red onion, sliced
2 medium heirloom tomatoes, chopped
Sea salt and ground black pepper, to taste
1/3 cup Pecorino Romano cheese, freshly grated
1/3 cup basil pesto
1 tablespoon fresh lemon juice

Directions

Pat the striped bass fillets dry with a kitchen towel.

Place the fish on a foil-lined baking pan.

Top each fish fillet with the onion and tomatoes and season with salt and black pepper.

Place them under the preheated broiler for about 8 minutes. Top with the cheese and bake an additional 4 minutes or until the cheesy is bubbly.
Top with the basil pesto and lemon juice and serve. Bon appétit!

Moroccan-Style Cod with Swiss Chard

(Ready in about 15 minutes | Servings 4)
Per serving: Calories: 189; Fat: 7.5g; Carbs: 2.5g; Protein: 26.7g
Ingredients
1 ½ pounds cod fillets
1 tablespoon Moroccan spice mix
Salt and ground black pepper, to taste
2 tablespoons extra-virgin olive oil
1 red onion, sliced
2 cups Swiss chard, chopped
1/4 cup dry white wine
1/4 cup fresh basil, roughly chopped
1/4 cup fresh parsley, roughly chopped
Directions
Pat the fish dry and rub the seasonings all over both sides of the fish.
In a large frying pan, heat the olive oil over medium flame. Now, pan-fry the cod for about 4 minutes,
Turn them over and top with the red onion and Swiss chards; pour in the wine and continue to cook for 5 minutes more or until cooked through.
Garnish your cod with the basil and parsley and serve immediately. Bon appétit!

Saucy Shrimp with Italian Peppers

(Ready in about 10 minutes | Servings 4)
Per serving: Calories: 286; Fat: 10.9g; Carbs: 9.6g; Protein: 38.7g
Ingredients
1 ½ pounds shrimp, cleaned and deveined
2 tablespoons olive oil
Sea salt and cayenne pepper, to taste
1 teaspoon dried oregano
1/2 teaspoon dried basil
1/2 teaspoon dried rosemary
2 sweet Italian peppers, sliced
1 tablespoon Dijon mustard
1/2 cup dry white wine
1/4 cup oyster sauce
Directions
Pat the shrimp dry using a kitchen towel.
Then, heat the olive oil in a frying pan over medium-high heat. Add in the shrimp and sear them for about 2 minutes.
Add in the peppers and continue to cook for a further 3 minutes or until shrimp turn pink.
Stir in the remaining ingredients and continue to cook for about 3 minutes longer or until everything is cooked through. Bon appétit!

Creamed Shrimp with Linguine

(Ready in about 10 minutes | Servings 3)

Per serving: Calories: 530; Fat: 10.4g; Carbs: 72.6g; Protein: 34.8g
Ingredients
5 ounces linguine pasta, uncooked
6 ounces shrimp, cleaned and deveined
1/2 cup soft cheese
1/3 cup parmesan cheese, shredded
1/2 teaspoon dried oregano
1/2 teaspoon dried basil
1/2 teaspoon dried rosemary
1/2 teaspoon mustard seeds
1 teaspoon garlic powder
1/2 teaspoon onion powder
Sea salt and ground black pepper, to taste
Directions
Cook the linguine pasta according to the manufacturer's directions.
Add the shrimp during the last 3 minutes of cooking time. Cook until the shrimp turn pink and opaque. Drain.
Add the cheese and spices and serve warm. Bon appétit!

Baked Seafood Manicotti

(Ready in about 45 minutes | Servings 4)
Per serving: Calories: 576; Fat: 25.5g; Carbs: 56.6g; Protein: 32.8g
Ingredients
1 tablespoon olive oil
6 ounces manicotti pasta
10 ounces canned crabmeat, drained, flaked
1 cup soft cheese, room temperature
6 ounces parmesan cheese, grated
1 teaspoon dried basil
1/2 teaspoon dried oregano
1 teaspoon dried parsley
Sea salt and ground black pepper, to taste
12 ounces marinara sauce
Directions
Begin by preheating your oven to 350 degrees F. Then, brush the sides and bottom of a baking pan with the olive oil.
Cook the manicotti according to the manufacturer's directions. Place the manicotti in the prepared pan. Add in the canned crabmeat.
Mix the remaining ingredients until well combined. Pour the sauce over the crabmeat and transfer to the preheated oven.
Bake the manicotti for about 40 minutes, or until cooked through.

Halibut Stew with Arborio Rice and Herbs

(Ready in about 30 minutes | Servings 5)
Per serving: Calories: 576; Fat: 25.5g; Carbs: 56.6g; Protein: 32.8g
Ingredients
2 tablespoons olive oil
1 red onion, thinly sliced
2 sweet Italian peppers, deveined and thinly sliced
2 cloves garlic, minced

1 teaspoon fresh ginger, minced
Sea salt and ground black pepper, to taste
1 teaspoon smoked paprika
1 bay laurel
1 sprig thyme
1 sprig rosemary
1 cup water
2 cups fish broth
1 cup tomato puree
1 ½ cups Arborio rice
2 pounds halibut, cut into bite-sized chunks
1/4 cup fresh parsley leaves, chopped

Directions
Heat the olive oil in a heavy-bottomed pot over medium-high heat. Now, sauté the onion and peppers until just tender and fragrant or about 3 minutes.
Then, add in the garlic and ginger and continue to sauté for 30 seconds more or until just fragrant.
Add in the seasonings, water, broth, and tomato puree; bring it to a rolling boil. Turn the heat to a simmer and fold in the rice.
Let it simmer until the rice is al dente and liquid, about 15 minutes. Lastly, stir in the halibut and continue to cook for 10 minutes more or until the fish flakes easily when tested with a fork.
Ladle into individual bowls, garnish with fresh parsley and serve warm. Bon appétit!

Sole Fillets with Pomegranate Salsa

(Ready in about 15 minutes | Servings 4)
Per serving: Calories: 306; Fat: 11.5g; Carbs: 29.2g; Protein: 24.8g

Ingredients
2 tablespoons olive oil
1 ½ pound sole fillets
1 teaspoon shallot powder
1 garlic powder
1/2 teaspoon ground cumin
1/2 teaspoon dried basil
1/4 teaspoon ground bay leaf
1/4 teaspoon ground allspice
Flaked sea salt and ground black pepper, to taste
Pomegranate Salsa:
1/2 cup tomato paste
1/2 cup pomegranate arils
1/4 cup fresh cilantro, minced
1/4 cup red onion, minced
1 red chili pepper, deveined and minced

Directions
Heat the olive oil in a frying pan over medium-high heat. Now, pan-fry the sole fillets for about 4 minutes per side or until golden and thoroughly cooked.
Sprinkle the warm fish with the seasonings until coated on all sides.
Then, thoroughly combine the salsa ingredients until well blended.
Serve the fried fish with the pomegranate salsa on the side. Bon appétit!

Peppery Smoked Grouper Fillets

(Ready in about 15 minutes | Servings 5)
Per serving: Calories: 233; Fat: 7.4g; Carbs: 4.5g; Protein: 35.9g

Ingredients
2 pounds grouper fillets, rinsed
1 red onion, sliced
2 bell peppers, sliced
1 red chile pepper, sliced
4 cloves garlic, halved
Sea salt and ground black pepper, to taste
1 teaspoon smoked paprika
2 tablespoons olive oil
1 fresh lemon, sliced

Directions
Pat the fish fillets dry with a kitchen towel. Place the fish on a foil-lined baking pan.
Top each fish fillet with the onion, peppers, and garlic, and season them with salt, black pepper, and smoked paprika.
Drizzle the fish fillets with the olive oil.
Place the fish under the preheated broiler for about 6 minutes. Turn them over and cook an additional 5 to 6 minute or until golden and easily flakes with a fork.
Garnish with fresh lemon slices and serve warm. Bon appétit!

Sicilian Fish and Sweet Onions in Foil

(Ready in about 25 minutes | Servings 4)
Per serving: Calories: 314; Fat: 14.3g; Carbs: 27.1g; Protein: 21.1g

Ingredients
4 codfish fillets
4 sweet onions, cut into wedges
4 tablespoons olive oil
1 teaspoon red pepper flakes
Sea salt and ground black pepper, to taste
1 large handful fresh flat-leaf parsley, roughly chopped

Directions
Start by preheating your oven to 395 degrees F. Toss the codfish fillets and sweet onions with the olive oil, red pepper, salt, and black pepper
Now, divide the fish and sweet onions between four pieces of the aluminum foil.
Fold the foil over the fish and onions, sealing the packet closed. Bake in the preheated oven for about 20 minutes, until cooked through.
Garnish with fresh parsley and serve warm. Bon appétit!

Easy Pan-Fried Halibut

(Ready in about 15 minutes | Servings 4)
Per serving: Calories: 534; Fat: 38.3g; Carbs: 16.1g; Protein: 28.8g

Ingredients
1 ½ pounds halibut fillets, rinsed
Sea salt and ground black pepper, to taste
1 teaspoon Italian seasoning mix
1 egg
1/3 cup milk

1/4 cup all-purpose flour
1/4 cup semolina flour
4 tablespoons olive oil
Directions
Pat the fish dry using a kitchen towel. Then, sprinkle the fish with salt, black pepper, and Italian seasoning mix.

Beat the egg in a shallow bowl until pale and frothy. Stir in the milk and beat until well blended. In another shallow bowl, place both types of flour.

Dip your halibut in the egg/milk mixture; then, dip the halibut in the flour and press to adhere on all sides.

Heat the olive oil in a frying pan over medium-high heat. Once hot, cook the fish for about 6 minutes or until it flakes easily with a fork. Bon appétit!

Seafood and Spaghetti Casserole

(Ready in about 35 minutes | Servings 4)
Per serving: Calories: 385; Fat: 13.7g; Carbs: 41.3g; Protein: 22.1g
Ingredients
5 ounces spaghetti, uncooked
2 tablespoons olive oil
1 red onion, chopped
2 garlic cloves, minced
1/2 cup fish broth
1/2 cup sour cream
1/4 cup dry sherry
5 ounces prawns, deveined
5 ounces crabmeat
1/4 cup seasoned breadcrumbs
1/3 cup Pecorino Romano cheese, grated
Directions
Cook spaghetti according to the manufacturer's directions.

In the meantime, heat the olive oil in a saucepan over medium heat. Now, sauté the onion and garlic until just tender and fragrant or about 2 minutes.

Stir in the fish broth, sour cream, dry sherry, prawns, and crabmeat. Spoon the mixture into a lightly oiled baking pan.

Thoroughly combine the seasoned breadcrumbs and grated Pecorino Romano cheese. Sprinkle the topping mixture over the top.

Bake the casserole at 360 degrees F for about 30 minutes or until cooked through. Bon appétit!

Spicy Sea Bass and Couscous Mélange

(Ready in about 20 minutes | Servings 4)
Per serving: Calories: 455; Fat: 13.5g; Carbs: 39.3g; Protein: 42.5g
Ingredients
2 tablespoons olive oil
1 red onion, chopped
2 garlic cloves, minced
1/4 cup fresh tarragon, chopped
1/4 cup fresh parsley, chopped
2 Roma tomatoes, pureed
2 tablespoons passata

2 cups shellfish stock
1 cup water
1 cup couscous
1/3 cup dry white wine
1 ½ pounds sea bass, cubed
1/4 teaspoon hot sauce
Sea salt and freshly ground black pepper, to taste
Directions
Heat the olive oil in a heavy-bottomed pot over medium-high heat. Now, sauté the onion until just tender and fragrant or about 3 minutes.

Then, add in the garlic and continue to sauté for 30 seconds more or until just fragrant.

Add in the herbs, tomatoes, passata, shellfish stock, and water; bring it to a boil. Turn the heat to a simmer add in the remaining ingredients.

Let it simmer, partially covered, until the fish flakes easily when tested with a fork or about 10 minutes.

Ladle into individual bowls, garnish with some extra fresh herbs, and serve warm. Bon appétit!

Oven-Baked Salmon with Cauliflower

(Ready in about 20 minutes | Servings 4)
Per serving: Calories: 247; Fat: 12.1g; Carbs: 8.7g; Protein: 25.5g
Ingredients
1 pound cauliflower florets
1 pound salmon
2 tablespoons extra-virgin olive oil, for rubbing
2 cloves garlic, pressed
Sea salt and ground black pepper, to taste
1 teaspoon red pepper flakes
1 tablespoon Italian seasoning mix
1 red onion, sliced
Directions
Bring 2 cups of the water to a boil; add the cauliflower florets and gently boil for about 5 minutes.

Pat the salmon and cauliflower dry with a paper towel.

Brush the salmon and cauliflower with the olive oil; rub the garlic, salt, black pepper, red pepper, and Italian seasoning all over the fish.

Then, bake the salmon, cauliflower, and onion in the preheated oven at 395 degrees F for about 15 minutes, until the fish easily flakes with a fork. Bon appétit!

Rich Tuna and Chickpea Salad

(Ready in about 55 minutes | Servings 4)
Per serving: Calories: 427; Fat: 22.1g; Carbs: 47g; Protein: 15.5g
Ingredients
1 cup chickpeas, soaked overnight
1 small-sized red onion, sliced
1 Greek cucumber, sliced
2 Sweet Italian peppers, sliced
1 Serrano pepper, sliced
1 teaspoon garlic, pressed
1 cup cherry tomatoes, halved

10 ounces canned tuna in water, drained and chopped
 2 cups baby spinach
1/4 cup fresh parsley, chopped
1/4 cup fresh basil, chopped
3 ounces feta cheese, crumbled
4 tablespoons extra-virgin olive oil
2 tablespoon freshly squeezed lemon juice
Flaked sea salt and ground black pepper, to taste

Directions

Drain the soaked chickpeas and tip them into a saucepan. Cover the chickpeas with water by 1 inch. Bring the water to a rolling boil over high heat. Immediately turn the heat to a simmer and cook for about 50 minutes. Let your chickpeas cool completely. Transfer the cooked chickpeas to the salad bowl.

Stir in the remaining ingredients, toss to combine well, and serve. Bon appétit!

Greek-Style Seafood Frittata

(Ready in about 35 minutes | Servings 4)

Per serving: Calories: 434; Fat: 26.7g; Carbs: 41.6g; Protein: 5.3g

Ingredients

2 tablespoons olive oil
1 red onion, chopped
1 bell pepper, chopped
1/2 pound shrimp, cleaned, deveined, and chopped
1/2 pound crabmeat, chopped
9 eggs
1/4 cup Greek-style yogurt
1 teaspoon Old Bay seasoning
Sea salt and freshly ground black pepper, to taste
1/2 cup feta cheese, crumbled
2 tablespoons fresh parsley, chopped

Directions

In an oven-proof skillet, heat the olive oil until sizzling. Once hot, sauté the onions and peppers until they've softened or about 3 minutes.

Add in the shrimp and crabmeat and remove it from the heat.

In a mixing bowl, whisk the eggs, Greek-style yogurt and spices. Pour the mixture into the skillet.

Bake your frittata at 330 degrees F for about 30 minutes, until a tester inserted in the center comes out dry and clean.

Serve garnished with crumbled feta and fresh parsley leaves. Bon appétit!

Seafood Hash Brown Casserole

(Ready in about 25 minutes | Servings 3)

Per serving: Calories: 462; Fat: 19.7g; Carbs: 32.2g; Protein: 41.4g

Ingredients

1/2 cup soft cheese
1/2 cup Greek-style yogurt
1/2 teaspoon hot sauce
1 teaspoon stone-ground mustard
Sea salt and ground black pepper, to taste

1/2 pound tuna, chopped
1/2 pound shrimp, cleaned and deveined
2 cups Swiss chard, torn into pieces
2 cups frozen shredded hash browns

Directions

Thoroughly combine the cheese, yogurt, hot sauce, mustard, salt, and black pepper. Fold in the tuna, shrimp, and Swiss chard.

Spoon the mixture into a lightly oiled baking pan. Top with the hash browns and spritz with a cooking spray. Bake for about 20 minutes or until golden and thoroughly cooked. Bon appétit!

Tuna and Cauliflower Gnocchi Gratin

(Ready in about 25 minutes | Servings 4)

Per serving: Calories: 521; Fat: 28.7g; Carbs: 36.2g; Protein: 31.2g

Ingredients

2 tablespoons olive oil
1 large red onion, sliced
1 pound cauliflower, broken into small florets
2 garlic cloves, sliced
1/2 cup fish broth
1/4 cup white wine
1 pound potato gnocchi
1/2 pound tuna, chopped
1/3 cup Greek-style yogurt
Sea salt and freshly ground black pepper, to taste
1/4 teaspoon freshly grated nutmeg
2 cups parmesan cheese, grated

Directions

In a saucepan, heat the olive oil until sizzling. Once hot, sauté the onion and cauliflower until tender or about 3 minutes.

Now, stir in the garlic and continue sautéing for 1 minute more or until fragrant. Pour in the fish broth and continue to cook, covered, for about 10 minutes. Add the wine and continue to cook for 7 minutes more, uncovered.

Now, cook the potato gnocchi according to the manufacturer's instructions. Fold the cooked gnocchi into the cauliflower mixture.

Now, spoon the mixture into a lightly oiled casserole dish. Add in the chopped tuna, yogurt, salt, black pepper, and grated nutmeg.

Top with parmesan cheese and bake your casserole in the preheated oven at 390 degrees F for about 17 minutes until golden and bubbly. Bon appétit!

Smoked Salmon Stuffed Mushrooms

(Ready in about 25 minutes | Servings 4)

Per serving: Calories: 425; Fat: 32.2g; Carbs: 6.2g; Protein: 28.4g

Ingredients

10 button mushrooms, stalks removed
2 tablespoons olive oil
5 ounces smoked salmon, chopped
4 tablespoons scallions, chopped
2 garlic cloves, minced
5 tablespoons passata

9 ounces soft cheese, softened
Sea salt and ground black pepper, to taste
1/2 teaspoon onion powder
1/2 teaspoon garlic powder
1/2 teaspoon red pepper flakes
1/2 cup grated Parmesan cheese
Directions
Start by preheating your oven to 380 degrees F.
Brush the mushrooms with the olive oil and arrange them on a parchment-lined baking sheet.
Divide the salmon, scallions, garlic, passata, soft cheese between the mushroom caps. Season them with the spices.
Top the mushrooms with the grated parmesan cheese.
Bake the stuffed mushrooms for about 20 minutes until the cheese has melted. Bon appétit!

Tuna and Chickpea Bruschetta
(Ready in about 10 minutes | Servings 4)
Per serving: Calories: 325; Fat: 13.2g; Carbs: 33.6g; Protein: 20.2g
Ingredients
4 bread slices
2 cloves garlic, halved
1 ½ cups chickpeas
1 cup marinara sauce
6 ounces canned tuna, drained and chopped
2 tablespoons olive oil
1 teaspoon dried oregano
1 teaspoon dried basil
1/2 teaspoon dried rosemary
1/2 cup parmesan cheese, grated
Directions
Toast the bread to your desired doneness. Rub one side of each bread slice with the garlic halves.
Top the bread slices with the remaining ingredients.
Place the bread slices under the preheated broiler for about 4 minutes or until the cheese is melted and bubbly. Bon appétit!

Halibut Fillets Pomodoro
(Ready in about 10 minutes | Servings 4)
Per serving: Calories: 296; Fat: 22.2g; Carbs: 5.7g; Protein: 17.3g
Ingredients
1 pound halibut fillets
2 tablespoons olive oil
1 small-sized red onion, peeled and finely chopped
2 cloves garlic, minced
2 Roma tomatoes, pureed
1/2 teaspoon dried rosemary
1/2 teaspoon dried oregano
1/2 teaspoon dried basil
Sea salt and ground black pepper, to taste
Directions
Pat the halibut fillets dry with kitchen towels.
In a large saucepan, heat the olive oil over medium flame. Then, sear the fish fillets for about 4 minutes on each side; reserve.

Then, sauté the onion and garlic in the pan drippings for about 3 minutes or until they are tender and aromatic.
Stir in the remaining ingredients and turn the heat to a simmer. Let it simmer for about 5 minutes or until cooked through.
Str in the reserved halibut and serve warm. Bon appétit!

Greek-Style Fish Pitas
(Ready in about 15 minutes | Servings 4)
Per serving: Calories: 525; Fat: 29.2g; Carbs: 38.7g; Protein: 24.1g
Ingredients
1 pound catfish, cut into strips
1/3 cup cornmeal
2 tablespoons olive oil
4 tablespoons tzatziki sauce
4 (7-inch) pita flatbreads
1 red onion, chopped
1 large-sized tomato, sliced
1/3 cup aioli
2 tablespoons Kalamata olives, pitted and sliced
Directions
Pat the fish dry with kitchen towels. Coat the fish with the cornmeal and reserve.
Heat the olive oil in a frying pan over a moderately high heat. Now, fry the fish strips for about 3 minutes, until opaque. Work with batches, if needed.
Microwave your pita bread and place them on a working surface. Divide the fish strips between flatbreads.
Arrange your pitas: Top each pita bread with the remaining ingredients, roll them up and serve warm. Enjoy!

Salmon and Crab Hash Browns
(Ready in about 25 minutes | Servings 4)
Per serving: Calories: 502; Fat: 18.9g; Carbs: 37.2g; Protein: 44.4g
Ingredients
10 ounces Greek-style yogurt
1 teaspoon Dijon mustard
1/2 pound lump crab meat, chopped
1/2 pound salmon, chopped
1 tablespoon Cajun seasoning mix
Sea salt and ground black pepper, to taste
4 cups gold potatoes, shredded
6 ounces parmesan cheese, shredded
4 teaspoons extra-virgin olive oil
4 tablespoons fresh chives, roughly chopped
Directions
In a mixing bowl, combine the yogurt, mustard, lump crab meat, salmon, Cajun seasoning mix, salt, and black pepper.
Spoon the mixture into four lightly oiled ramekins.
Top each portion with the potatoes and parmesan cheese. Drizzle the olive oil over them.
Bake your hash browns for about 20 minutes or until bubbly and thoroughly cooked.

Serve garnished with fresh chopped chives. Bon appétit!

Smoked Salmon Frittata

(Ready in about 35 minutes | Servings 4)
Per serving: Calories: 434; Fat: 26.7g; Carbs: 41.6g; Protein: 5.3g

Ingredients
2 tablespoons olive oil
1 medium-sized leek, thinly sliced
1 cup broccoli, broken into small florets
1 teaspoon fresh garlic, minced
1 pound smoked salmon, chopped
9 eggs
1/4 cup soft cheese, at room temperature
1 teaspoon Old Bay seasoning
Sea salt and ground black pepper, to taste
1/2 cup feta cheese, crumbled
1 tablespoon fresh chervil, roughly chopped
1 tablespoon fresh parsley, roughly chopped

Directions
Begin by preheating your oven to 390 degrees F.
In an oven-proof skillet, heat the olive oil until sizzling. Once hot, sauté the leeks and broccoli until they've softened or about 3 minutes.
Add in the fresh garlic and continue to sauté an additional 30 seconds. Add in the smoked salmon; heat off.
In a mixing bowl, whisk the eggs, soft cheese, Old Bay seasoning, salt, and pepper. Pour the mixture into the skillet.
Bake your frittata at 330 degrees F for about 30 minutes, until a tester inserted in the center comes out dry and clean.
Serve garnished with crumbled feta, fresh chervil, and parsley. Bon appétit!

POULTRY

Chicken Wings with Kalamata Olives

(Ready in about 20 minutes | Servings 3)
Per serving: Calories: 393; Fat: 29.6g; Carbs: 7.5g; Protein: 24.3g

Ingredients
3 chicken wings, boneless and skinless
Sea salt and ground black pepper, to taste
1 tablespoon Italian seasoning mix
2 tablespoons olive oil
1/2 cup dry white wine
1/4 cup chicken broth
1 red onion, sliced
1 tomato, chopped
2 garlic cloves, minced
1/2 cup Kalamata olives, pitted and halved
2 tablespoons chives, roughly chopped

Directions
Pat the chicken wings dry with kitchen towels. Season the chicken with salt, black pepper, and Italian seasoning mix.
In a saucepan, heat the olive oil over medium-high flame. Then, sear the chicken for about 4 minutes per side.
Pour in the white wine and chicken broth to deglaze the pan. Add in the onion and tomato, and reduce the heat to medium.
Continue to cook, covered, for 12 minutes. Remove the lid, stir in the garlic and kalamata olives, and continue to cook an additional 2 to 3 minutes.
Serve garnished with freshly chopped chives and enjoy!

Tuscan-Style Turkey Stew

(Ready in about 40 minutes | Servings 4)
Per serving: Calories: 295; Fat: 11.2g; Carbs: 20.6g; Protein: 28.3g

Ingredients
2 tablespoons olive oil
1 pound turkey wings
1 medium-sized red onion, chopped
1 carrot, peeled and sliced
1 celery stalk, peeled and sliced
2 cloves garlic, pressed
2 sweet potatoes, peeled and diced
2 cups chicken stock
1 cup tomato puree
1 bay leaf
1 teaspoon mustard seeds
Sea salt and ground black pepper, to taste
1 teaspoon cayenne pepper
1 teaspoon dried basil
1/2 teaspoon dried oregano
2 tablespoons fresh parsley, roughly chopped

Directions
Heat 1 tablespoon of the olive oil in a Dutch oven over medium-high heat. Now, sear the turkey wings for about 4 minutes per side or until golden brown; reserve.
Then, heat the remaining tablespoon of olive oil and sauté the vegetables until they've softened.
Add in the chicken stock, tomato puree, and spices and turn the heat to a simmer. Let it simmer for 30 minutes more or until heated through.
Then, shred the turkey with two forks and add it back to the Dutch oven. Serve garnished with fresh parsley. Bon appétit!

Chicken and Penne Pasta Casserole

(Ready in about 30 minutes + marinating time | Servings 5)
Per serving: Calories: 555; Fat: 25.2g; Carbs: 51g; Protein: 33.1g

Ingredients
2 chicken breasts, boneless, cut into small pieces
1 teaspoon garlic, pressed
1 teaspoon dried oregano
1/2 teaspoon dried basil
2 tablespoon lemon juice
2 tablespoons wine vinegar
1 tablespoon brown mustard
10 ounces penne pasta
2 tablespoons olive oil
2 tomatoes, sliced
1 cup cannellini beans, rinsed
3 ounces black olives, roughly chopped
Sea salt and ground black pepper, to taste
1 teaspoon red pepper flakes
4 ounces Asiago cheese, shredded

Directions
In a ceramic bowl, place the chicken, garlic, oregano basil, lemon juice, vinegar, and mustard. Allow it to marinate for 2 hours in your refrigerator.
Meanwhile, cook the pasta according to the manufacturer's directions; drain your pasta and transfer it to a lightly oiled casserole dish.
Then, in a saucepan, heat the olive oil until sizzling. Now, sear the chicken until no longer pink on both sides. Add the chicken to the casserole dish.
Top the chicken with the sliced tomatoes, cannellini beans, olives, salt, black pepper, and red pepper. Bake in the preheated oven at 420 degrees F for about 18 minutes.
Top with the grated cheese and continue to cook for 6 to 8 minutes more or until the cheese is hot and bubbly. Bon appétit!

Classic Chicken Salad

(Ready in about 20 minutes | Servings 5)
Per serving: Calories: 355; Fat: 22.6g; Carbs: 7g; Protein: 29.4g

Ingredients
1 ½ pounds chicken breasts, boneless, skinless
1 red onion, thinly sliced
1 stalk celery, chopped

1 bell pepper, seeded and sliced
2 ounces Kalamata olives, pitted and sliced
1 Granny Smith apple, cored and chopped
2 cups baby spinach, torn into pieces
2 cups arugula, torn into pieces
3 tablespoons extra-virgin olive oil
1 tablespoon apple cider vinegar
2 teaspoons fresh lemon juice
1/4 teaspoon dried dill weed
Salt and black pepper, to taste

Directions

Bring a pot of the salted water to a boil. Add in the chicken breast and bring the water to a simmer. Cover the pot and allow your chicken to sit for about 15 minutes.

Cut the chicken into strips and transfer it to a salad bowl. Add in the onion, celery, bell pepper, olives, apple, baby spinach, and arugula.

Whisk the olive oil, vinegar, lemon juice, and dill. Dress your salad and season it with salt and black pepper to taste. Bon appétit!

Traditional Lebanese Chicken Fattoush

(Ready in about 20 minutes | Servings 4)
Per serving: Calories: 505; Fat: 28.3g; Carbs: 34.7g; Protein: 31.4g

Ingredients

5 tablespoons extra-virgin olive oil
1 pound chicken breasts
4 small pita breads, cut into triangles
1/2 head of iceberg lettuce, torn into pieces
1 Persian cucumber, sliced
1 cup grape tomatoes, halved
1 bell pepper, sliced
4 scallion stalks, sliced
Dressing:
1 tablespoon white vinegar
1 tablespoon lemon juice
1 teaspoon garlic, minced
1 teaspoon red chili pepper, minced
1 tablespoon plum preserves
Sea salt and ground black pepper, to taste

Directions

In a grill pan, heat 1 tablespoon of the olive oil over medium-high heat. Now, grill the chicken breasts for about 7 to 9 minutes per side or until the internal temperature reaches 165 degrees F.

Slice the chicken into strips and add it to a nice salad bowl.

In a grill pan, heat 2 tablespoons of the olive oil over medium-high heat. Grill the pita bread until crispy and golden.

In a salad bowl, place the vegetables and gently stir to combine. Mix the remaining ingredients to make the dressing; dress the salad and top with the grilled pita bread. Enjoy!

Cheesy Pesto Chicken

(Ready in about 40 minutes | Servings 4)

Per serving: Calories: 285; Fat: 15.4g; Carbs: 2.7g; Protein: 31.6g

Ingredients

4 chicken drumsticks, boneless and skinless
1/3 cup refrigerated basil pesto
1/2 cup parmesan cheese, shredded
1/2 cup mozzarella cheese, shredded
2 large tomatoes, sliced
Sea salt and ground black pepper, to taste

Directions

Start by preheating your oven to 390 degrees F. Spritz the sides and bottom of a baking pan with a nonstick cooking oil.

Place the chicken in the baking pan and top with the pesto sauce; bake for about 30 minutes or until golden brown.

Top with the cheese and tomatoes and bake for a further 6 minutes or until the cheese is bubbly. Season with salt and black pepper.

Bon appétit!

Hearty Chicken and Bulgur Soup

(Ready in about 55 minutes | Servings 5)
Per serving: Calories: 315; Fat: 12.7g; Carbs: 12.4g; Protein: 36g

Ingredients

2 tablespoons olive oil
1 ½ pounds chicken wings
1 medium-sized leek, chopped
2 celery ribs, chopped
2 carrots, chopped
5 cups roasted vegetable broth
4 ounces bulgur wheat
1 zucchini, diced
1 bay laurel
1 thyme sprig
1 rosemary sprig
1 tablespoon fresh parsley
Sea salt and ground black pepper, to taste
10 black olives, pitted and sliced

Directions

In a heavy-bottomed pot, heat the olive oil over medium-high heat. Now, sear the chicken for about 4 minutes until golden brown. Reserve.

In the pan drippings, sauté the leek, celery, and carrot for about 4 minutes until they've softened. Add in the roasted vegetable broth and bulgur wheat; bring to a rapid boil.

When the chicken is cool enough to handle, shred the meat, discarding the bones. Add the chicken back to the pot.

Turn the heat to a simmer and continue to cook for 30 minutes longer. Add in the zucchini and herbs. Continue to cook for a further 15 minutes or until cooked through.

Season with salt and ground black pepper to taste. Ladle into individual bowls and serve garnished with olives. Bon appétit!

Potato and Chicken Stew

(Ready in about 40 minutes | Servings 4)
Per serving: Calories: 405; Fat: 14.9g; Carbs: 27.9g; Protein: 38.8g

Ingredients

2 tablespoons olive oil
1/2 teaspoon cumin seeds
1 cup red onions, chopped
2 carrots, peeled and sliced
1 pound golden potatoes, diced
1 ½ pounds chicken legs
3 cloves garlic, peeled
1/2 teaspoon ginger, peeled and minced
Sea salt and freshly ground black pepper
2 bay leaves
1 thyme sprig
1 rosemary sprig
2 cups roasted vegetable broth
1/2 pound green beans, trimmed

Directions

Heat 1 tablespoon of the olive oil in a Dutch oven over medium-high heat. Now, cook the cumin seeds for 30 seconds or until fragrant.

Then, heat the remaining tablespoon of the olive oil and sauté the vegetables and chicken until the vegetables are tender and the chicken is no longer pink.

Add in the garlic, ginger, and spices and continue to cook an additional minute or so. Pour in the broth and stir to combine.

Next, turn the heat to a simmer. Let it simmer for 30 minutes more or until heated through.

Then, shred the chicken with two forks and add it back to the Dutch oven. Stir in the green beans and let it simmer for 4 minutes more until crisp-tender. Bon appétit!

Double Cheese Chicken Casserole

(Ready in about 30 minutes | Servings 4)
Per serving: Calories: 603; Fat: 23.1g; Carbs: 53g; Protein: 46.3g

Ingredients

1/2 pound rigatoni pasta
2 teaspoons olive oil
1 pound chicken breasts, boneless, skinless and cut into small chunks
1/2 teaspoon dried oregano
1/2 teaspoon dried rosemary
1/2 teaspoon dried basil
Sea salt, to taste
1/2 teaspoon freshly cracked black pepper
2 tomatoes, pureed
1 cup marinara sauce
2 ounces green olives, pitted and halved
2 cups loosely packed fresh kale leaves
3 ounces soft cheese
2 ounces parmesan cheese, freshly grated
2 tablespoons fresh parsley, chopped

Directions

Cook the pasta according to the manufacturer's directions; drain your pasta and transfer it to a lightly oiled casserole dish.

Then, in a saucepan, heat the olive oil until sizzling. Now, sear the chicken breasts until no longer pink. Add the chicken to the casserole dish.

Top the chicken with the oregano, rosemary, basil, salt, pepper, tomatoes, marinara sauce, olives, and kale. Bake in the preheated oven at 420 degrees F for about 18 minutes.

Top with both types of cheese and continue to cook for 6 to 8 minutes more or until the cheese is bubbly. Serve garnished with fresh parsley. Bon appétit!

Grilled Chicken Salad

(Ready in about 15 minutes | Servings 4)
Per serving: Calories: 431; Fat: 33.1g; Carbs: 4.8g; Protein: 24.8g

Ingredients

1 tablespoon olive oil
1 pound chicken breast
Sea salt and ground black pepper, to taste
1/2 cup aioli
1 tablespoon lemon juice
1 bell pepper, sliced
1 Serrano peppers, sliced
1 carrot, julienned
2 cups arugula

Directions

In a grill pan, heat the olive oil over medium-high heat. Now, grill the chicken for about 7 to 9 minutes per side or until the internal temperature reaches 165 degrees F.

Slice the chicken into strips and add it to a nice salad bowl. Now, add in the remaining ingredients and gently stir to combine.
Bon appétit!

Greek-Style Baked Chicken

(Ready in about 40 minutes | Servings 4)
Per serving: Calories: 291; Fat: 18.4g; Carbs: 2.8g; Protein: 27g

Ingredients

1 pound chicken breasts, boneless and skinless
2 garlic cloves, halved
1 tablespoon olive oil
Sea salt and ground black pepper
1 teaspoon Greek seasoning mix
3 ounces feta cheese, crumbled

Directions

Start by preheating your oven to 390 degrees F. Spritz the sides and bottom of a baking pan with a nonstick cooking oil.

Rub the garlic halves over the chicken. Toss the chicken with the olive oil and seasonings.

Place the chicken in the baking pan and bake for about 35 minutes or until golden brown.

Top with the cheese and bake for a further 4 minutes or until the cheese has melted. Season with salt and black pepper.

Bon appétit!

Saucy Turkey Wings

(Ready in about 2 hours | Servings 4)

Per serving: Calories: 541; Fat: 32.4g; Carbs: 6.8g; Protein: 54g

Ingredients

4 turkey wings
1 teaspoon garlic powder
1/2 teaspoon shallot powder
1 teaspoon dried oregano
1/2 teaspoon dried rosemary
Sea salt and ground black pepper, to taste
1 cup chicken broth
1 cup marinara sauce

Directions

Start by preheating your oven to 360 degrees F.
Place the turkey wings in a baking dish; season them with the spices and pour in the broth. Bake the turkey wings in the preheated oven for about 1 hour. Pour in the marinara sauce and continue to bake an additional 50 to 60 minutes until cooked through, checking and basting periodically.
Your instant thermometer should read at least 165 degrees F.
Bon appétit!

One-Pot Chicken Mélange

(Ready in about 40 minutes | Servings 5)

Per serving: Calories: 312; Fat: 12.9g; Carbs: 9g; Protein: 39.8g

Ingredients

2 teaspoons olive oil
1 teaspoon cumin seeds
2 pounds chicken legs, diced
1 celery stalk, sliced
2 red bell peppers, sliced
1 medium-sized leek, thinly sliced
2 garlic cloves, minced
Sea salt and ground black pepper, to season
1 teaspoon smoked paprika
1/2 cup dry white wine
1 cup chicken broth
1/2 cup tomato puree
2 cups loosely packed Swiss chard

Directions

Heat 1 teaspoon of the olive oil in a stockpot over medium-high heat. Now, cook the cumin seeds for 30 seconds or until fragrant.
Then, heat the remaining tablespoon of olive oil and sauté the vegetables and chicken until the vegetables are tender and the chicken is no longer pink.
Add in the garlic and spices and continue to cook an additional minute or so. Add a splash of wine to deglaze the pan.
Pour in the broth and tomato puree, and stir to combine. Next, turn the heat to a simmer. Let it simmer for 30 minutes more or until heated through. Stir in the Swiss chard and let it simmer for 4 minutes more until it has wilted. Bon appétit!

Turkey and Mushroom Casserole

(Ready in about 35 minutes | Servings 4)

Per serving: Calories: 601; Fat: 22.9g; Carbs: 62g; Protein: 38g

Ingredients

1/2 pound fusilli pasta
1 tablespoon olive oil
1 pound turkey breasts, boneless, skinless and diced
2 cups cremini mushrooms, sliced
2 bell peppers, sliced
1 red onion, chopped
1 cup cream of mushrooms soup
1/3 cup tomato puree
1 tablespoon Greek seasoning mix
Sea salt and ground black pepper, to taste
1 teaspoon garlic, minced
1 cup parmesan cheese, grated

Directions

Cook the pasta according to the manufacturer's directions; drain your pasta and transfer it to a lightly oiled baking dish.
Then, in a saucepan, heat the olive oil over medium-high heat. Once hot, sear the turkey breasts until no longer pink. Add the turkey breasts to the casserole dish.
In the pan drippings, sauté the mushrooms, peppers, and onion until just tender and aromatic. Add the sautéed mixture to the baking dish.
Top the turkey breasts and sautéed vegetables with the cream of the mushroom soup, tomato puree, Greek seasoning mix, salt, ground black pepper, and garlic.
Bake your casserole in the preheated oven at 400 degrees F for about 18 minutes.
Top your casserole with the parmesan cheese and continue to bake for a further 7 minutes or until the cheese has melted. Bon appétit!

Classic Chicken Parmigiana

(Ready in about 40 minutes | Servings 5)

Per serving: Calories: 601; Fat: 22.9g; Carbs: 62g; Protein: 38g

Ingredients

2 pounds chicken breast, boneless and skinless
2 garlic cloves, minced
2 tablespoons olive oil
1 tablespoon Italian seasoning
Sea salt and ground black pepper, to season
4 ounces parmesan cheese, sliced

Directions

Start by preheating your oven to 390 degrees F.
Spritz the sides and bottom of a baking dish with a nonstick cooking oil.
Rub the garlic halves over the chicken. Toss the chicken with the olive oil and seasonings.
Lower the chicken into the baking dish and bake for about 33 to 35 minutes or until golden brown.
Top with the cheese and bake for a further 6 minutes or until the cheese has melted. Bon appétit!

Turkey Wings with Horseradish Sauce

(Ready in about 2 hours | Servings 5)

Per serving: Calories: 483; Fat: 31.3g; Carbs: 7.8g; Protein: 40g

Ingredients

2 pounds turkey wings
1 tablespoon Italian seasoning mix
2 tablespoons olive oil
1 Italian pepper, quartered
1 red onion, quartered
2 cups roasted vegetable broth
Horseradish Sauce:
1/2 cup sour cream
2 tablespoons fresh horseradish, grated
1 tablespoon stone-ground mustard
Sea salt and ground black pepper, to taste

Directions

Start by preheating your oven to 360 degrees F.
Pat the turkey wings dry with paper towels. Toss the wings with the seasoning mix and olive oil, and transfer them to a lightly oiled baking dish.
Top the wings with the pepper and onion. Pour in the broth and transfer the baking dish to the preheated oven.
Bake the turkey in the preheated oven for about 2 hours, rotating the pan and basting the wings periodically to promote even cooking.
Meanwhile, whisk the sauce ingredients. Serve the warm turkey wings with the horseradish sauce on the side. Bon appétit!

Grilled Chicken Pitas

(Ready in about 15 minutes | Servings 2)

Per serving: Calories: 482; Fat: 26.2g; Carbs: 23.8g; Protein: 37g

Ingredients

1 tablespoon olive oil
1/2 pound chicken breasts
2 pita breads
1 cup baby spinach, torn into pieces
1 cup butterhead lettuce, torn into pieces
2 ounces Pecorino Romano cheese, sliced
1 medium-sized tomato, sliced
4 kalamata olives, pitted and sliced
1 small-sized red onion, sliced
Sea salt and ground black pepper, to taste
1/4 teaspoon red pepper flakes
1/4 teaspoon oregano
2 tablespoons fresh basil, roughly chopped

Directions

In a grill pan, heat the olive oil over medium-high heat. Now, grill the chicken for about 7 to 9 minutes per side or until the internal temperature reaches 165 degrees F.
Slice the chicken onto strips. Toast the pitas and place them on a flat surface.
Assemble the pitas with the grilled chicken and the other ingredients. Roll them up and serve warm. Enjoy!

Chicken with Cauliflower and Feta Cheese

(Ready in about 20 minutes | Servings 5)

Per serving: Calories: 458; Fat: 27.4g; Carbs: 8.6g; Protein: 43.5g

Ingredients

2 pounds chicken breasts, thinly sliced
1 tablespoon Italian seasoning mix
Sea salt and ground black pepper, to taste
2 tablespoons olive oil
1 pound cauliflower, cut into florets
8 ounces sun-dried tomatoes
1 cup chicken bone broth
4 ounces feta cheese, crumbled

Directions

Sprinkle the chicken with the Italian seasoning mix, sea salt, and black pepper.
Heat the olive oil in a frying pan over medium-high heat. Sear the chicken for about 5 minutes per side, adding a splash of broth periodically. Reserve.
Add in the cauliflower, sun-dried tomatoes, and the remaining chicken broth. Turn the heat to a simmer and add the chicken back to the pan.
Continue to cook for a further 8 minutes until thoroughly cooked. Serve with crumbled feta cheese. Bon appétit!

Chicken Kebabs with Greek Yogurt Sauce

(Ready in about 20 minutes | Servings 4)

Per serving: Calories: 318; Fat: 17.4g; Carbs: 8.6g; Protein: 29.1g

Ingredients

1 pound chicken breasts, cut into bite-sized pieces
2 bell peppers, cut into 1 1/4-inch pieces
1 red onion, cut into 1 1/4-inch pieces
1 teaspoon Italian seasoning mix
Sea salt and ground black pepper, to taste
2 tablespoons olive oil
Greek Yogurt Sauce:
1 cup Greek-style yogurt
2 cloves garlic, minced
1/2 teaspoon dried dill
1 tablespoon lime juice

Directions

Assemble bamboo skewers with the chicken, peppers, and onions. Toss them with the spices and olive oil.
Grill the skewers over a medium hot grill for 12 to 16 minutes, turning them periodically.
Meanwhile, whisk the ingredients for the sauce.
Serve your kabobs with the yogurt sauce on the side. Enjoy!

Chicken and Pasta Salad

(Ready in about 20 minutes | Servings 4)

Per serving: Calories: 572; Fat: 31.4g; Carbs: 43.1g; Protein: 31.5g

Ingredients

1 pound chicken breasts
6 ounces penne pasta
1/2 cup marinated artichoke hearts, drained and chopped

1/2 cup black olives, pitted and sliced
1 red bell pepper, sliced
1 green bell pepper, sliced
2 cups butterhead lettuce
1/2 cup feta cheese, crumbled
Dressing:
2 tablespoons lemon juice
2 tablespoons red wine vinegar
1 teaspoon stone-ground mustard
1/2 teaspoon dried oregano
1/2 teaspoon dried basil
1 tablespoon fresh parsley, chopped
2 garlic cloves, minced
4 tablespoons olive oil
Sea salt and ground black pepper, to taste
Directions
Bring a pot of the salted water to a boil. Add in the chicken breast and bring the water to a simmer. Cover the pot and allow your chicken to sit for about 15 minutes.
Meanwhile, cook the pasta according to the manufacturer's instructions; drain and reserve.
Cut the chicken into strips and transfer it to a salad bowl. Add in the marinated artichoke hearts, black olives, bell peppers, and butterhead lettuce. Add the reserved pasta and toss to combine.
Whisk the ingredients for the dressing. Dress your salad and serve garnished with crumbled feta cheese. Bon appétit!

Greek Pilaf with Chicken

(Ready in about 30 minutes | Servings 4)
Per serving: Calories: 562; Fat: 22.4g; Carbs: 59.1g; Protein: 28.1g
Ingredients
3 tablespoons extra-virgin olive oil
1 pound chicken drumsticks, boneless, skinless, and diced
2 garlic cloves, minced
Sea salt and ground black pepper, to taste
1/2 teaspoon cayenne pepper
1 teaspoon Greek seasoning mix
2 cups vegetable broth
1 ½ cups white rice, rinsed
1 teaspoon lemon juice
1 teaspoon lemon zest
2 tablespoons parsley, chopped
Directions
In a saucepan, heat the olive oil over medium-high heat. Now, sear the chicken for about 5 minutes per side until the meat is all the way cooked through.
Add in the garlic and continue to sauté an additional 30 seconds or until fragrant. Season the chicken with salt, black pepper, cayenne pepper, and Greek seasoning mix.
Bring the vegetable broth to a boil and add in the rice. Reduce the heat to a simmer, cover, and cook until your rice has absorbed all the liquid, for about 17 minutes.

Stir the chicken into the rice; add in the lemon zest and juice. Serve garnished with fresh parsley. Bon appétit!

Stracciatella alla Romana with Chicken

(Ready in about 15 minutes | Servings 3)
Per serving: Calories: 364; Fat: 20.8g; Carbs: 11.2g; Protein: 35.7g
Ingredients
1 tablespoon olive oil
1/2 pound chicken breasts, diced
3 cups chicken stock
3 eggs
1/4 cup parmesan cheese, grated
Sea salt and ground black pepper, to taste
2 bunches spinach, torn into pieces
2 tablespoons Italian parsley, roughly chopped
Directions
Heat the olive oil in a large stockpot over medium-high heat. Sear the chicken for about 5 minutes, stirring continuously to promote even cooking.
Pour in the chicken stock and bring to a boil. Turn the heat to a simmer.
In a mixing bowl, whisk the eggs, parmesan cheese, salt, and black pepper. Gradually pour the egg mixture into the hot stock, stirring with a wire whisk. Continue to stir for about 1 minute; heat off. Add in the baby spinach, cover, and let it wilt for about 5 minutes. Serve hot, garnished with fresh parsley and enjoy!

Roasted Provençal Turkey Drumettes

(Ready in about 2 hours | Servings 5)
Per serving: Calories: 423; Fat: 21.1g; Carbs: 7.9g; Protein: 46.1g
Ingredients
2 pounds turkey drumettes
2 garlic cloves, minced
1/2 teaspoon fresh ginger root, peeled and grated
1 tablespoon Herbes de Provence
1 tablespoon capers, drained
2 tablespoons olive oil
1/2 cup tomato sauce
1 cup chicken bone broth
1/2 cup dry white wine
Sea salt and ground black pepper, to taste
1/4 cup niçoise olives, pitted and sliced
1/4 cup fresh basil, sliced into ribbons
Directions
Start by preheating your oven to 360 degrees F.
Pat the turkey drumettes dry with paper towels. Toss the wings with the garlic, ginger, Herbes de Provence, capers, and olive oil; transfer them to a lightly oiled baking dish.
Pour the tomato sauce and broth into the baking dish. Bake the turkey in the preheated oven for about 1 hour 30 minutes, rotating the pan and basting the drumettes periodically to promote even cooking.
After that, pour in the wine and bake an additional 30 minutes. Season with salt and black pepper to taste.

Garnish with fresh olives and basil and serve immediately. Bon appétit!

Greek-Style Chicken Drumsticks

(Ready in about 20 minutes | Servings 4)
Per serving: Calories: 322; Fat: 19.4g; Carbs: 11.2g; Protein: 24.5g

Ingredients
1 pound chicken drumsticks, skinless and boneless
1 teaspoon Greek seasoning mix
1/2 teaspoon paprika
1/2 teaspoon mustard seed
1 teaspoon dried parsley flakes
1 teaspoon dried oregano
1 teaspoon dried basil
1 teaspoon dried rosemary
Sea salt and ground black pepper, to taste
1 tablespoon olive oil
1 cup cream of celery soup
1 medium-sized red onion, chopped
2 ripe tomatoes, chopped
1/3 cup Kalamata olives
2 ounces halloumi cheese, sliced

Directions
Sprinkle the chicken with the seasonings.
Heat the olive oil in a frying pan over medium-high heat. Sear the chicken for about 5 minutes per side, adding a splash of the soup periodically. Reserve.
Add in the onion, tomatoes, and the reserved soup. Turn the heat to a simmer and add the chicken back to the pan.
Continue to cook for a further 8 minutes until thoroughly cooked. Serve with Kalamata olives and cheese. Bon appétit!

Tuscan Chicken Ribollita

(Ready in about 35 minutes | Servings 6)
Per serving: Calories: 435; Fat: 30.4g; Carbs: 11.1g; Protein: 29.2g

Ingredients
2 tablespoons olive oil
2 pounds chicken thighs
2 carrots, sliced
2 stalks celery, sliced
1 teaspoon garlic powder
1 teaspoon onion powder
2 cups chicken bone broth
2 cups water
2 cups marinara sauce
4 cups Tuscan lacinato kale, torn into pieces
1 (15-ounce) can cannellini beans
Sea salt and ground black pepper, to taste

Directions
In a heavy-bottomed pot, heat the olive oil over medium-high heat. Now, sear the chicken thighs for about 4 minutes per side until golden brown. Reserve.
In the pan drippings, sauté the carrots and celery until they've softened. Add in the garlic powder, onion powder, chicken broth, and water; bring to a rolling boil.

When the chicken is cool enough to handle, shred the meat, discarding the bones. Add the chicken back to the pot.
Turn the heat to a simmer and continue to cook for 20 minutes longer. Add in the marinara sauce, kale, and beans. Continue to cook for a further 10 minutes or until cooked through.
Season with salt and ground black pepper to taste. Ladle into individual bowls and serve hot. Bon appétit!

Country-Style Chicken Traybake

(Ready in about 35 minutes | Servings 4)
Per serving: Calories: 297; Fat: 11.4g; Carbs: 22.4g; Protein: 31.2g

Ingredients
2 tablespoons olive oil
1 pound chicken drumettes
1 red onion, sliced
1 medium-sized zucchini, sliced lengthwise
1 teaspoon ginger-garlic paste
1 teaspoon Dijon mustard
1 pound canned white beans, drained
2 cups marinara sauce
1 tablespoon fresh mint leaves, chopped
1 tablespoon fresh parsley leaves, chopped

Directions
Start by preheating your oven to 390 degrees F. Then, spritz the sides and bottom of a casserole dish with a nonstick cooking oil.
Heat 1 tablespoon of the olive oil in a frying pan over medium-high heat; sear the chicken drumettes for about 4 minutes per side or until no longer pink.
Shred the meat, discarding the bones and transfer it to the prepared casserole dish. Add in the remaining ingredients. Drizzle with another tablespoon of the olive oil. Salt and pepper to taste.
Bake in the preheated oven for about 30 minutes until thoroughly cooked. Enjoy!

Chicken Drumsticks with Garlic-Yogurt Sauce

(Ready in about 25 minutes | Servings 4)
Per serving: Calories: 307; Fat: 17.4g; Carbs: 9.8g; Protein: 26g

Ingredients
2 tablespoons olive oil
1 pound chicken drumsticks, boneless and cut into bite-sized pieces
1 cup tomato purée
1 medium-sized leek, sliced
1 tablespoon Greek seasoning mix
2 cups fresh spinach
1 cup Greek-style yogurt
1 tablespoon cornstarch

Directions
Heat the olive oil in a saucepan over medium-high flame. Then, sear the chicken drumsticks for about 10 minutes until no longer pink.

Add in the tomato purée, leek, and Greek seasoning mix; continue to cook an additional 10 minutes.

Stir in the spinach, yogurt, and cornstarch; continue to cook for 4 to 5 minutes more or until cooked through.

Taste and adjust the seasonings. Serve with pita bread and enjoy!

Grilled Chicken with Peanut Sauce

(Ready in about 25 minutes | Servings 4)
Per serving: Calories: 365; Fat: 26.4g; Carbs: 5.1g; Protein: 25.5g

Ingredients
3 tablespoons olive oil
1 pound chicken breasts, skinless and boneless
1/2 cup chicken broth, homemade or low-sodium canned
1/4 cup peanut butter
2 tablespoons heavy cream
1/2 teaspoon hot sauce
1 tablespoon balsamic vinegar
Sea salt and black pepper, to taste

Directions
In a grill pan, heat 2 tablespoons of the olive oil over medium-high heat. Now, grill the chicken for about 7 to 9 minutes per side or until the internal temperature reaches 165 degrees F.

Heat the remaining tablespoon of the olive oil and chicken broth in a small saucepan over a moderate flame for about 3 minutes.

Whisk in the peanut butter, heavy cream, and hot sauce, bringing to a boil. Turn the heat to a simmer; continue to cook for a further 9 minutes until the sauce has thickened.

Stir in the balsamic vinegar and season with salt and pepper to taste. Spoon the sauce over the chicken breasts and serve. Bon appétit!

Saucy Chicken Creole

(Ready in about 20 minutes | Servings 4)
Per serving: Calories: 397; Fat: 24.5g; Carbs: 6.9g; Protein: 36.8g

Ingredients
1 ½ pounds chicken drumsticks, boneless and skinless
1 teaspoon Creole spice mix
Sea salt and ground black pepper, to taste
2 tablespoons olive oil
2 bell peppers, deseeded and sliced
1 red onion, thinly sliced
2 ripe tomatoes, pureed
1/2 cup Kalamata olives, pitted and sliced

Directions
Sprinkle the chicken breasts with the spices. Heat the olive oil in a frying pan over medium-high heat.

Sear the chicken for about 5 minutes per side until no longer pink; reserve.

Add in the peppers, onion, and tomatoes. Turn the heat to a simmer and add the chicken back to the pan.

Continue to cook for a further 8 minutes until thoroughly cooked. Serve with Kalamata olives. Enjoy!

Greek-Style Chicken and Pasta Salad

(Ready in about 20 minutes | Servings 4)
Per serving: Calories: 636; Fat: 33.5g; Carbs: 54.2g; Protein: 30.9g

Ingredients
1 pound chicken drumsticks
8 ounces bow tie pasta
1 cup cherry tomatoes, halved
1 orange bell pepper, deseeded and diced
4 scallion stalks, sliced
1 teaspoon oregano
1 tablespoon fresh parsley leaves, roughly chopped
1/2 cup mayonnaise
1/2 cup Greek-style yogurt
1 teaspoon fresh lemon juice
1/3 cup Kalamata olives, pitted and sliced

Directions
Bring a pot of the salted water to a boil. Add in the chicken and bring the water to a simmer. Cover the pot and allow your chicken to sit for about 15 minutes.

Meanwhile, cook the pasta according to the manufacturer's instructions; drain and reserve.

Cut the chicken into strips and transfer it to a salad bowl. Add in the tomatoes, pepper, scallions, oregano, parsley, mayonnaise, yogurt, and lemon juice.

Add the reserved pasta to the salad bowl and toss to combine.

Serve garnished with Kalamata olives. Bon appétit!

Turkish-Style Pilau

(Ready in about 30 minutes | Servings 4)
Per serving: Calories: 456; Fat: 15.5g; Carbs: 34.2g; Protein: 31.9g

Ingredients
2 tablespoons olive oil
1 pound turkey breast, skinless, boneless and diced
1/2 cup red onion, chopped
1 carrot, sliced
1 celery stalk, sliced
1 clove garlic, minced
1 teaspoon smoked paprika
Sea salt and ground black pepper
2 cups chicken broth
1 cup Calrose rice

Directions
In a saucepan, heat the olive oil over medium-high heat. Now, sear the turkey breasts for about 5 minutes per side until the meat is all the way cooked through.

Add in the onion, carrot, and celery and cook for 4 minutes more or until they are crisp-tender. Add in the garlic and continue to sauté an additional minute or until fragrant.

Season the chicken with the smoked paprika, salt, and black pepper.

Bring the chicken broth to a boil and add in the rice. Reduce the heat to a simmer, cover, and cook until your rice has absorbed all the liquid, for about 17 minutes.

Stir the turkey/vegetable mixture into the rice and serve warm. Bon appétit!

Old-Fashioned Turkey Orzo Soup

(Ready in about 35 minutes | Servings 5)
Per serving: Calories: 256; Fat: 11.8g; Carbs: 12.2g; Protein: 23.1g

Ingredients
2 tablespoons olive oil
1 pound turkey thighs
1 red bell pepper, deseeded and chopped
1 red onion, chopped
1 cup celery, chopped
1/2 cup carrots, chopped
1 cup zucchini, diced
5 cups chicken broth
1 bay laurel
1 teaspoon garlic powder
1/2 cup orzo pasta
1 cup green beans, trimmed
Sea salt and ground black pepper, to season

Directions
In a heavy-bottomed pot, heat the olive oil over medium-high heat. Now, sear the turkey for about 6 minutes until golden brown. Reserve.

In the pan drippings, sauté the vegetables, except for the green beans, for about 4 minutes until they've softened. Add in the broth, bay laurel, orzo pasta, and garlic powder; bring to a rapid boil.

When the turkey is cool enough to handle, shred the meat, discarding the bones. Add the meat back to the pot.

Turn the heat to a simmer, add in the pasta, and continue to cook for 20 minutes longer. Add in the green beans. Continue to cook for a further 5 minutes or until cooked through.

Season with salt and ground black pepper to taste. Ladle into individual bowls and serve hot. Bon appétit!

Caprese Chicken Fillets

(Ready in about 25 minutes | Servings 4)
Per serving: Calories: 238; Fat: 10g; Carbs: 3.7g; Protein: 32.7g

Ingredients
1 pound chicken fillets
1/2 teaspoon smoked paprika
Sea salt and freshly ground black pepper
1/2 teaspoon dried oregano
2 tablespoons olive oil
1/2 cup basil pesto
2 medium-sized tomatoes, sliced
4 ounces fresh mozzarella, sliced

Directions

Start by preheating your oven to 395 degrees F. Spritz the sides and bottom of a baking pan with a nonstick oil.

Pat the chicken fillets dry with paper towels; toss them with the smoked paprika, salt, black pepper, and oregano.

Drizzle the chicken with the olive oil. Top with the basil pesto and tomatoes.

Bake in the preheated oven for about 20 minutes. Top with the cheese and continue baking an additional 3 minutes or until the cheese is hot and bubbly. Bon appétit!

Classic Chicken Stroganoff

(Ready in about 40 minutes | Servings 4)
Per serving: Calories: 448; Fat: 19.1g; Carbs: 13.7g; Protein: 55.1g

Ingredients
2 tablespoons olive oil
1 teaspoon cumin seeds
1 large red onion, finely chopped
1 celery stalk, chopped
3 garlic cloves, sliced
1 pound cremini mushrooms, sliced
1 pound chicken drumettes, skinless, boneless and cut into bite-sized pieces
2 cups chicken broth
1 teaspoon paprika
1 sprig thyme
1 sprig rosemary
1 bay laurel
1 cup green peas

Directions
Heat 1 tablespoon of the olive oil in a Dutch oven over medium-high heat. Now, cook the cumin seeds for 30 seconds or until fragrant.

Then, heat the remaining tablespoon of the olive oil and sauté the vegetables and chicken until the vegetables are tender and the chicken is no longer pink.

Add in the broth and spices and turn the heat to a simmer. Let it simmer for 30 minutes more or until heated through.

Stir in the green peas and let it simmer for 5 minutes more until heated through. Bon appétit!

Italian Chicken and Tortellini Soup

(Ready in about 50 minutes | Servings 4)
Per serving: Calories: 558; Fat: 25.3g; Carbs: 53.5g; Protein: 31.2g

Ingredients
2 tablespoons olive oil
1/2 pound chicken breasts, skinless, boneless and diced
3 ounces chicken sausage, sliced
1 red onion, chopped
1 celery stalk, chopped
2 cups tomato puree
2 cups chicken bone broth
1 zucchini, sliced

Sea salt and ground black pepper, to taste
1 teaspoon poultry seasoning
10 ounces cheese tortellini, refrigerated
4 ounces cannellini beans, drained and rinsed
4 ounces kale, torn into pieces

Directions

In a heavy-bottomed pot, heat the olive oil over medium-high heat. Now, sear the chicken and sausage for about 4 minutes until no longer pink. Reserve.

In the pan drippings, sauté the onion and celery for about 4 minutes until they've softened. Add in the tomato puree and broth; bring to a rapid boil.

Add the chicken back to the pot.

Turn the heat to a simmer and continue to cook for 20 minutes longer. Add in the zucchini, spices, and tortellini. Continue to cook for a further 15 minutes or until cooked through.

Add in the beans and kale and continue to simmer for 5 minutes more until the kale has wilted. Bon appétit!

Traditional Chicken and Olive Soup

(Ready in about 35 minutes | Servings 4)

Per serving: Calories: 440; Fat: 33g; Carbs: 5.5g; Protein: 32.4g

Ingredients

1 tablespoon olive oil
1 pound chicken breasts, boneless and diced
1 cup black olives
1 bay laurel
1 teaspoon dried rosemary
1/2 teaspoon dried thyme
1/2 teaspoon dried oregano
2 tablespoons fresh parsley, roughly chopped
Sea salt and ground black pepper, to taste
4 cups roasted vegetable broth
2 eggs
1 cup heavy cream

Directions

In a heavy-bottomed pot, heat the olive oil over medium-high heat. Once hot, sear the chicken for about 7 minutes until no longer pink.

Add in the olives, seasonings, and vegetable broth and bring to a rapid boil.

Meanwhile, whisk the eggs and heavy cream.

Turn the heat to a simmer and continue to cook for 20 minutes longer. Gradually stir in the egg/cream mixture and continue to simmer until cooked through or about 6 minutes.

Ladle into individual bowls and serve hot. Bon appétit!

Herb Chicken with Orzo Pasta

(Ready in about 20 minutes | Servings 3)

Per serving: Calories: 509; Fat: 24.4g; Carbs: 45.5g; Protein: 27.4g

Ingredients

3/4 pound chicken drumsticks, boneless and skinless
1/4 cup all-purpose flour
2 tablespoons olive oil

2 garlic cloves, minced
Sea salt and ground black pepper, to taste
1 teaspoon dried oregano
1 teaspoon dried basil
1 cup cream of celery soup
1/2 cup tomato puree
1 cup orzo pasta
1/4 cup dry white wine
2 tablespoons fresh basil, chiffonade

Directions

Pat the chicken dry with pepper towels and toss them with the flour on all sides. Heat the olive oil in a frying pan over medium flame.

Sear the chicken for about 4 minutes per side until no longer pink. Add in the garlic and continue to sauté an additional 30 seconds or until aromatic.

Sprinkle the chicken with salt, black pepper, oregano, and basil. Pour in the soup and tomato puree, bringing to a rapid boil.

Add in the orzo pasta and wine and continue to simmer for about 10 minutes until thoroughly cooked. Serve garnished with fresh basil. Enjoy!

Chicken and Pecorino Soup

(Ready in about 20 minutes | Servings 4)

Per serving: Calories: 601; Fat: 26.4g; Carbs: 45.3g; Protein: 40.3g

Ingredients

2 tablespoons olive oil
1 pound chicken breasts, boneless and cut into bite-sized pieces
1 medium-sized red onion, finely chopped
4 cups chicken broth
1 large-sized tomato, pureed
Sea salt and ground black pepper, to taste
1/2 teaspoon cayenne pepper
7 ounces short-tubed pasta
1 cup Pecorino Romano cheese, grated
2 tablespoons chives, freshly chopped

Directions

Heat the olive oil in a large stockpot over medium-high heat. Cook the chicken and onion for about 5 minutes, stirring continuously to promote even cooking.

Pour in the broth and pureed tomatoes and bring to a boil. Turn the heat to a simmer.

Add in the salt, black pepper, cayenne pepper, and pasta; continue to simmer for about 10 minutes until tender and thoroughly cooked.

Afterwards, fold in the cheese and remove from the heat; stir the soup until the cheese has melted.

Serve hot, garnished with freshly chopped chives!

Traditional Chicken Cacciatore

(Ready in about 1 hour 5 minutes | Servings 4)

Per serving: Calories: 358; Fat: 17.5g; Carbs: 13.2g; Protein: 25.5g

Ingredients

4 chicken drumsticks
3 teaspoons olive oil

Sea salt and black pepper, to season
1 teaspoon red pepper flakes
1 red onion, chopped
3 garlic cloves, minced
2 bell peppers, deseeded and sliced
1 serrano pepper, deseeded and sliced
2 sprigs rosemary
2 sprigs thyme
2 bay leaves
1 cup red wine
2 Roma tomatoes, pureed
1/2 cup black olives, pitted and sliced
Directions
Pat the chicken dry with paper towels. Heat the olive oil in an oven-proof skillet over medium-high heat. Once hot, sear the chicken for about 4 minutes per side. Season the chicken with salt, black pepper, and red pepper.

Add in the onion, garlic, peppers, and herbs; continue sautéing for 4 to 5 minutes longer until your vegetables are crisp-tender.

Pour in the wine and pureed tomatoes and continue to simmer for 5 minutes more.

Lastly, fold in the olives and transfer the skillet to the oven. Bake your cacciatore at 370 degrees F for about 50 minutes. Bon appétit!

Chicken Drumsticks in Tuscan Sauce

(Ready in about 20 minutes | Servings 4)
Per serving: Calories: 514; Fat: 37.5g; Carbs: 13.4g; Protein: 31.4g
Ingredients
3 tablespoons olive oil
4 chicken drumsticks, boneless, skinless
Sea salt and ground black pepper, to taste
1 cup scallions, chopped
2 spring garlic stalks, chopped
1/2 cup chicken bone broth
1/2 cup tomato paste
2 tablespoons fresh parsley leaves, chopped
2 tablespoons fresh cilantro leaves, chopped
2 tablespoons fresh basil leaves, chopped
1 cup double cream
1/2 cup parmesan cheese, grated
Directions
Pat the chicken dry with paper towels. Heat 2 tablespoons of the olive oil in a frying pan over medium-high heat.

Once hot, sear the chicken for about 4 minutes per side. Season the chicken with salt and black pepper to taste. Reserve.

In the same pan, heat the remaining tablespoon of the olive oil. Then, sauté the scallions and garlic for 1 minute or so until aromatic.

Add in the broth and tomato paste and bring to a boil. Turn the heat to a simmer and add in the herbs; continue to simmer for a further 10 minutes.

Then, fold in the cream and cheese and continue to cook, covered, until the cheese has melted. Bon appétit!

Winter Hearty Chicken Pasta Casserole

(Ready in about 30 minutes | Servings 4)
Per serving: Calories: 674; Fat: 24g; Carbs: 80.2g; Protein: 36.3g
Ingredients
3 cups rigatoni
1 tablespoon olive oil
1 pound chicken drumsticks, skinless, boneless and diced
1 red onion, chopped
4 cloves garlic, minced
1 teaspoon dried oregano
1/2 teaspoon dried marjoram
1 teaspoon sweet paprika
Sea salt and ground black pepper, to taste
1 cup marinara sauce
2 tablespoons tomato paste
1 cup cream of onion soup
1 cup parmesan cheese, grated
Directions
Cook the pasta according to the manufacturer's directions; drain your pasta and transfer it to a lightly oiled casserole dish.

Then, in a saucepan, heat the olive oil until sizzling. Now, sear the chicken until no longer pink. Add the chicken to the casserole dish.

Top the chicken with the onion, garlic, oregano, marjoram, paprika, salt, black pepper, marinara sauce, and tomato paste.

Pour in the soup and bake in the preheated oven at 420 degrees F for about 18 minutes.

Top with the cheese and continue to cook for 6 to 8 minutes more or until the cheese is bubbly. Bon appétit!

Spicy Mozzarella and Tomato-Stuffed Chicken

(Ready in about 30 minutes | Servings 4)
Per serving: Calories: 356; Fat: 16g; Carbs: 10.3g; Protein: 40.3g
Ingredients
1 pound chicken fillets
1 teaspoon dried rosemary
1/2 teaspoon dried oregano
1/2 teaspoon ground bay leaf
Sea salt and ground black pepper, to taste
1 large-sized tomato, sliced
4 ounces mozzarella cheese, sliced
1 Serrano pepper, deseeded and sliced
2 tablespoons olive oil
1 cup marinara sauce
1 cup parmesan cheese, grated
Directions
Pat the chicken dry with paper towels. Toss the chicken with the spices until well coated on all sides.

Layer the slices of tomatoes, cheese, and pepper onto each chicken fillet. Roll them up and seal with toothpicks if needed.

Heat the olive oil in a frying pan over medium-high heat. Sear the stuffed chicken for about 4 minutes per side or until golden brown.

Transfer the chicken to a lightly oiled casserole dish. Pour in the marinara sauce and bake in the preheated oven at 395 degrees F for about 18 minutes.

Top with parmesan cheese and continue baking an additional 5 minutes or until the cheese is hot and bubbly. Enjoy!

Mediterranean Harvest Soup

(Ready in about 25 minutes | Servings 4)

Per serving: Calories: 347; Fat: 14.3g; Carbs: 26.3g; Protein: 27.7g

Ingredients

2 tablespoons olive oil
1 pound turkey thighs, boneless and cut into bite-sized pieces
1 red onion, finely chopped
2 carrots, chopped
2 Italian peppers, chopped
1 celery stalk, chopped
1 parsnip, chopped
1 yam, peeled and chopped
4 cups vegetable broth
1 teaspoon dried marjoram
1 teaspoon dried parsley flakes
Sea salt and ground black pepper, to taste

Directions

Heat the olive oil in a large stockpot over medium-high heat. Cook the turkey thighs for about 5 minutes, stirring continuously to promote even cooking.

Add in the onion, carrots, peppers, celery, parsnip, and yam, and continue to cook for 4 minutes more until they are crisp-tender.

Pour in the broth and bring to a boil. Turn the heat to a simmer.

Add in the spices and continue to simmer for about 10 minutes until thoroughly cooked.

Taste, adjust the seasonings and serve hot. Bon appétit!

Herb Mozzarella Chicken with Olives

(Ready in about 20 minutes | Servings 5)

Per serving: Calories: 364; Fat: 21.5g; Carbs: 5.4g; Protein: 36.4g

Ingredients

1 ½ pounds chicken breasts, boneless, skinless
2 tablespoons olive oil
Sea salt and ground black pepper, to taste

1 teaspoon Italian herb mix
1 teaspoon granulated garlic
1/2 cup tomato puree
4 ounces mozzarella cheese, sliced
4 ounces black olives, pitted and sliced
2 tablespoons fresh parsley leaves, roughly chopped

Directions

Pat the chicken dry with paper towels. Heat the olive oil in a frying pan over medium-high heat.

Once hot, sear the chicken for about 4 minutes per side. Season the chicken with salt and black pepper to taste.

Add in the Italian herb mix, granulated garlic, and tomato puree and bring to a boil. Turn the heat to a simmer; continue to simmer for a further 10 minutes.

Then, fold in the cheese and continue to cook, covered, until the cheese has melted. Serve garnished with olives and freshly chopped parsley.

Bon appétit!

Wine-Braised Chicken with Leeks

(Ready in about 30 minutes | Servings 4)

Per serving: Calories: 239; Fat: 10.4g; Carbs: 9.5g; Protein: 25.4g

Ingredients

2 tablespoons olive oil
1 pound chicken drumettes
1 red pepper, sliced
1 medium leek, sliced
2 garlic cloves, minced
1/2 cup chicken broth
4 tablespoons tomato paste
1/2 cup red wine
1/4 teaspoon ground allspice
1/2 teaspoon dried oregano
1/2 teaspoon dried marjoram
1/4 teaspoon ground bay leaf
1 teaspoon sweet paprika
Sea salt and ground black pepper, to taste

Directions

Pat the chicken dry with pepper towels. Heat the olive oil in a frying pan over medium flame.

Sear the chicken for about 4 minutes per side until no longer pink. Add in the vegetables and continue to sauté for about 2 minutes or until aromatic.

Pour in the chicken broth and tomato puree, bringing to a rapid boil.

Add in the wine and spices and continue to simmer for about 20 minutes until thoroughly cooked. Serve garnished with feta cheese, if desired. Enjoy!

BEEF

Classic Mediterranean Burritos

(Ready in about 2 hours 10 minutes | Servings 4)
Per serving: Calories: 499; Fat: 24.4g; Carbs: 42.5g; Protein: 25.7g

Ingredients
3/4 pound pot roast
1 tablespoon Creole seasoning mix
Sea salt and ground black pepper, to taste
1 cup beef bone broth
4 (8-inch) tortillas, warmed
4 tablespoons aioli
1 tablespoon Dijon mustard
1 tablespoon schug sauce
1 large-sized tomato, diced
1 Persian cucumber, sliced
1 cup arugula
1 cup Romaine lettuce
1 red onion, thinly sliced

Directions
Begin by preheating your oven to 350 degrees F.
Place the meat in a lightly oiled baking dish. Sprinkle with Creole seasoning mix, sea salt, and black pepper. Pour in the broth and cover with the foil. Bake the pot roast in the preheated oven for about 2 hours or until the beef is all the way cooked through.
Then, slice the beef across the grain.
Spread each tortilla with the aioli and mustard; drizzle with the schug sauce. Divide the tomato, cucumber, arugula, Romaine lettuce, and red onion between tortillas.
Top with the beef slices. Roll them up and serve immediately. Bon appétit!

Greek-Style Top Sirloin Steak

(Ready in about 1 hour 30 minutes | Servings 5)
Per serving: Calories: 454; Fat: 29g; Carbs: 6g; Protein: 40.5g

Ingredients
3 tablespoons olive oil
2 pounds top sirloin steak, sliced
1 teaspoon dried rosemary
1 teaspoon dried basil
1/2 cup red wine
1 cup tomato puree
4 cloves garlic, minced
2 cups beef bone broth
Sea salt and ground black pepper, to taste

Directions
Heat the olive oil in a saucepan.
Sear the beef for about 10 minutes until no longer pink.
Add in the remaining ingredients and bring to a boil. Immediately reduce the heat to a simmer. Let it simmer for about 80 minutes until the meat is tender and cooked through.
Serve with baked potatoes, if desired. Enjoy!

Moroccan Beef Koftas

(Ready in about 20 minutes | Servings 2)
Per serving: Calories: 308; Fat: 21.4g; Carbs: 6.9g; Protein: 23.1g

Ingredients
1/2 pound ground beef
1 small red onion, finely chopped
1 teaspoon garlic, minced
1 tablespoon olive oil
Sea salt and ground black pepper, to taste
1/4 teaspoon ground coriander
1/2 teaspoon paprika
1/2 teaspoon turmeric
1/4 teaspoon ground cumin
1/4 teaspoon allspice

Directions
Thoroughly combine all ingredients in a mixing bowl. Shape the meat into two thick sausages and thread a bamboo skewer through each sausage.
Preheat your grill for medium-high heat. Lower the koftas onto a lightly oiled grill. Grill for about 13 minutes, turning them over once or twice to promote even cooking.
An instant-read thermometer should register 160 degrees F. Serve with lemon slices or cold plain yogurt, if desired. Bon appétit!

Beef and Garden Vegetable Soup

(Ready in about 1 hour 5 minutes | Servings 4)
Per serving: Calories: 354; Fat: 16.4g; Carbs: 21.9g; Protein: 32.3g

Ingredients
2 tablespoons olive oil
1 pound beef stew meat, cut into cubes
Sea salt and ground black pepper, to taste
1 teaspoon red pepper flakes, crushed
1 red onion, sliced
1 parsnip, peeled and sliced
2 carrots, peeled and sliced
1 celery stalk, peeled and sliced
1 medium-sized zucchini, diced
2 Roma tomatoes, pureed
2 bay leaves
5 cups roasted vegetable broth
1 cup frozen sweet corn kernels
2 tablespoons parsley, roughly chopped

Directions
Heat the olive oil in a heavy-bottomed pot over medium-high flame. Once hot, sear the meat for about 4 minutes, until no longer pink; reserve.
Season the meat with salt, black pepper, and red pepper.
Add in the vegetables and continue sautéing for about 5 minutes or until they are crisp-tender.
Add the meat back to the pot along with the pureed tomatoes, bay leaves, and broth. Bring to a boil and immediately reduce the heat to a simmer.

Let it simmer, partially covered, for about 50 minutes or until everything is cooked through. Add in the corn kernels and continue to cook for 5 minutes longer.

Ladle into individual bowls and serve with fresh parsley. Bon appétit!

Beef Tenderloin Salad

(Ready in about 20 minutes | Servings 4)

Per serving: Calories: 485; Fat: 39.3g; Carbs: 13g; Protein: 23.3g

Ingredients

2 tablespoons olive oil
1 pound beef tenderloin, sliced
Sea salt and ground black pepper, to taste
1/2 teaspoon paprika
1 teaspoon oregano
1 red onion, sliced
2 Roma tomatoes, sliced
1 Persian cucumber, sliced
2 cups Romaine lettuce, torn into pieces
2 tablespoons red wine vinegar
1 avocado, peeled and sliced
4 ounces canned cannellini beans, drained
1 (6 ½-inch) pita, cut into wedges and toasted

Directions

Pat dry the beef tenderloin with paper towels. Season the meat with salt, black pepper, paprika, and oregano.

Then, cook the steaks on the preheated grill, turning them over once or twice. Cook for about 10 minutes until slightly charred.

Cut the beef into strips and place them in a salad bowl. Add in the remaining ingredients, except for the pita; toss to combine well.

Top your salad with the toasted pita and serve. Bon appétit!

Herb and Wine Beef Stew

(Ready in about 1 hour | Servings 4)

Per serving: Calories: 481; Fat: 16.8g; Carbs: 27.1g; Protein: 55.4g

Ingredients

2 tablespoons olive oil
Sea salt and freshly ground black pepper, to taste
1 teaspoon smoked paprika
2 pounds beef stew meat, boneless and cut into bite-sized cubes
1 red onion, chopped
1 pound Yukon Gold potatoes, peeled and diced
2 carrots, sliced
3 cloves garlic, minced
2 tomatoes, pureed
2 cups beef bone broth
1/2 cup dry red wine
2 bay leaves
2 thyme sprigs
2 rosemary sprigs

Directions

Heat the olive oil in a heavy-bottomed pot over medium-high flame. Once hot, sear the meat for about 4 minutes, until no longer pink; reserve. Season the meat with salt, black pepper, and smoked paprika.

Add in the vegetables and continue sautéing for about 5 minutes or until they are crisp-tender.

Add the meat back to the pot along with the pureed tomatoes, beef bone broth, red wine, bay leaves, thyme, and rosemary. Bring to a boil and immediately reduce the heat to a simmer.

Let it simmer, partially covered, for about 50 minutes or until everything is cooked through.

Ladle into individual bowls. Bon appétit!

Classic Italian Stir-Fry

(Ready in about 15 minutes | Servings 3)

Per serving: Calories: 369; Fat: 28.5g; Carbs: 10.1g; Protein: 19.4g

Ingredients

2 tablespoons olive oil
3/4 pound beef brisket, cut into bite-sized strips
2 Italian peppers, sliced
1 cup cauliflower florets
1 red onion, sliced
1 cup brown Italian mushrooms, sliced
1 medium zucchini, julienned
2 garlic cloves, sliced
1/2 teaspoon dried basil
1 teaspoon dried oregano
1/2 teaspoon crushed red pepper flakes
Salt and ground black pepper, to taste
1/2 cup Greek olives, pitted and sliced

Directions

In a large skillet, heat the olive oil until sizzling. Then, stir-fry the beef for about 5 minutes until no longer pink. Push the beef to one side of the skillet.

Add in the peppers, cauliflower, and onion and continue to cook for 3 minutes more.

Now, stir in the mushrooms, zucchini, garlic, basil, oregano, red pepper flakes, salt, and black pepper; stir-fry for a further 3 minutes or until the vegetables are just tender and fragrant.

Top with the olives and serve warm. Bon appétit!

Authentic Steak Gyros

(Ready in about 2 hours 10 minutes | Servings 4)

Per serving: Calories: 469; Fat: 12.4g; Carbs: 49.2g; Protein: 38.7g

Ingredients

1 pound flank steak
4 garlic cloves, sliced
2 rosemary sprigs
2 thyme sprigs
2 bay leaves
1 teaspoon dried oregano
1 cup beef bone broth
4 (6 ½ -inch) whole-wheat pitas, warmed
1/2 cup hummus
2 ounces black olives, pitted and sliced

1 red onion, sliced
1 large-sized tomato
Tzatziki Sauce:
1/2 medium cucumber, peeled and grated
1 cup cold Greek yogurt
2 teaspoons minced garlic
1/4 cup fresh dill, chopped
1 tablespoon lemon juice, freshly squeezed
Coarse sea salt and ground black pepper, to taste

Directions

Begin by preheating your oven to 350 degrees F.
Place the meat in a lightly oiled baking dish, along with the garlic, rosemary, thyme, bay leaves, and oregano.
Pour in the broth and cover with the foil. Roast the meat in the preheated oven for about 2 hours or until the beef is all the way cooked through.
Then, slice the beef across the grain.
Meanwhile, make the tzatziki sauce by whisking all of the ingredients.
Spread each pita with the hummus and tzatziki sauce.
Divide the olives, onion, and tomato slices between your pitas.
Top with the beef slices. Roll them up and serve warm with French fries, if desired. Enjoy!

Authentic Greek Brizoles

(Ready in about 1 hour 30 minutes | Servings 4)
Per serving: Calories: 544; Fat: 22.6g; Carbs: 42.2g; Protein: 42.2g

Ingredients

4 tablespoons olive oil
1 ½ pounds flank steak, sliced
1 tablespoon red wine vinegar
1 teaspoon dried Greek oregano
1 teaspoon dried basil
1 teaspoon cumin seeds
1/4 teaspoon nutmeg
1/2 tablespoon dried thyme
Sea salt and ground black pepper, to taste
1 tablespoon garlic, chopped
2 pounds potatoes, peeled and chopped into wedges
1/2 cup vegetable broth
2 tablespoons fresh parsley, roughly chopped

Directions

Heat the olive oil in a Dutch oven over medium-high heat. Sear the beef for about 10 minutes until no longer pink.
Add in the remaining ingredients and bring to a boil.
Immediately reduce the heat to a simmer.
Let it simmer for about 1 hour 20 minutes until the meat is tender and potatoes are cooked through.
Serve with the pan juices and enjoy!

Spicy Beef and Veggie Soup

(Ready in about 1 hour 5 minutes | Servings 3)
Per serving: Calories: 334; Fat: 15.3g; Carbs: 26.5g; Protein: 23.2g

Ingredients

1 tablespoon olive oil

1/2 pound chuck roast, cut into cubes
Sea salt and black pepper, to taste
1/2 teaspoon dried basil
1/2 teaspoon dried oregano
1 teaspoon garlic powder
1/2 teaspoon onion powder
2 celery stalks, chopped
2 carrots, peeled and chopped
1 potato, peeled and chopped
3 cups beef bone broth
1 teaspoon schug sauce
1 bay laurel
2 tablespoons olive oil
1/2 cup frozen sweet corn kernels
1/2 cup frozen green beans

Directions

Heat the olive oil in a heavy-bottomed pot over medium-high flame. Once hot, sear the meat for about 4 minutes, until no longer pink; reserve.
Sprinkle the meat with the seasonings.
Add in the vegetables and continue sautéing for about 5 minutes or until they are crisp-tender.
Add the meat back to the pot along with the broth, schug sauce, bay laurel, and olive oil. Bring to a boil and immediately reduce the heat to a simmer.
Let it simmer, partially covered, for about 50 minutes or until everything is cooked through. Add in the corn kernels and green beans; continue to cook for 5 minutes longer or until warmed through.
Ladle into individual bowls and serve hot. Bon appétit!

Beef Salad with Green Beans

(Ready in about 20 minutes | Servings 4)
Per serving: Calories: 434; Fat: 35.3g; Carbs: 10.5g; Protein: 18.4g

Ingredients

3/4 pound beef tenderloin, fat trimmed, sliced
Sea salt and ground black pepper, to taste
1/2 teaspoon red pepper flakes, crushed
1 tablespoon olive oil
1/2 teaspoon dried oregano
1/2 teaspoon dried rosemary
1/2 pound green beans
1 red onion, sliced
1 garlic clove, minced
1 Persian cucumber, sliced
1 tomato, sliced
2 roasted peppers, deseeded and sliced
1 green bell pepper, sliced
2 tablespoons fresh parsley, roughly chopped
2 tablespoons fresh basil, roughly chopped
2 tablespoons fresh mint leaves, roughly chopped
2 tablespoons red wine vinegar
1 tablespoon lemon juice
4 tablespoons extra-virgin olive oil
2 cups butterhead lettuce
2 cups baby spinach

Directions

Place the green bean in a saucepan and cover with the cold water (2 inches above them). Bring to a boil and turn the heat to a simmer.

Let it simmer for about 5 minutes or until they are crisp-tender; drain the green bean and place them in a bowl of the ice water; drain and reserve.

Sprinkle the salt, black pepper, and red pepper evenly over the steaks. Heat the olive oil in a cast-iron skillet over high flame.

Once hot, cook the steaks for 3 to 4 minutes per side or until browned. Reduce the heat to medium-low; add in the oregano and rosemary and continue to sauté an additional 30 seconds or until fragrant.

Cut the steaks into strips and transfer them to a salad bowl. Add in the remaining ingredients and toss to coat.

Top with the green beans. Bon appétit!

Rich Provençal Beef Stew

(Ready in about 1 hour 5 minutes | Servings 5)
Per serving: Calories: 385; Fat: 16.5g; Carbs: 18.5g; Protein: 40.4g
Ingredients
1 tablespoon extra-virgin olive oil
1/2 teaspoon cumin seeds
2 pounds brisket, cut into bite-sized pieces
Sea salt and freshly ground black pepper, to taste
1 red onion, chopped
1 sweet onion, sliced
2 carrots, trimmed and sliced
1 parsnip, trimmed and sliced
4 cloves garlic, pressed
2 cups beef broth
1 cup Provence wine
1 cup tomato puree
1 sprig thyme
1 sprig rosemary
1 bay laurel
Directions
Heat the olive oil in a heavy-bottomed pot over medium-high flame. Once hot, sauté the cumin seeds, stirring continuously, for 30 seconds until fragrant.

Now, sear the meat for about 6 minutes, until no longer pink. Season the meat with salt and black pepper; reserve.

Add in the vegetables and continue sautéing for about 5 minutes or until they are crisp-tender. Add in the garlic and continue to sauté an additional 30 seconds until aromatic.

Add the meat back to the pot along with the broth, wine, pureed tomatoes, thyme, rosemary, and bay laurel. Bring to a rolling boil and immediately turn the heat to a simmer.

Let it simmer, partially covered, for about 50 minutes or until everything is cooked through.

Ladle into individual bowls. Enjoy!

Beef and Vegetable Skillet with Cheese

(Ready in about 25 minutes | Servings 4)

Per serving: Calories: 335; Fat: 18.5g; Carbs: 5.5g; Protein: 35.4g
Ingredients
2 tablespoons olive oil
1 pound flank steak, sliced
1 red onion, sliced
1 red bell pepper, sliced
1 zucchini, sliced
2 cloves garlic, minced
Sea salt and ground black pepper, to taste
1 teaspoon dried oregano
1 teaspoon dried basil
1 teaspoon dried rosemary
1/2 cup chicken bone broth
2 ounces parmesan cheese, grated
Directions
In a large skillet, heat the olive oil until sizzling. Then, stir-fry the beef for about 5 minutes until no longer pink. Push the beef to one side of the skillet.

Add in the onion and peppers, and continue to cook for 3 minutes more.

Now, stir in the zucchini, garlic, salt, black pepper, basil, oregano, rosemary, and chicken bone broth; stir-fry for a further 3 minutes or until the vegetables are just tender and fragrant.

Top with the cheese and remove from the heat; allow it to sit, covered, for about 5 minutes until the cheese has melted. Bon appétit!

Chunky Beef and Cannellini Bean Casserole

(Ready in about 40 minutes | Servings 4)
Per serving: Calories: 675; Fat: 34.1g; Carbs: 38g; Protein: 54.4g
Ingredients
2 tablespoons olive oil
1 ¼ pounds ground chuck
1 red onion, chopped
2 garlic cloves, minced
1 Italian pepper, deseeded and sliced
8 ounces canned cannellini beans, rinsed
1 cup marinara sauce
1 cup chicken bone broth
3 ounces tortilla chips, crushed
1 cup parmesan cheese, grated
Directions
Heat the olive oil in a frying pan over medium-high heat. Now, brown the ground chuck until it is no longer pink, or about 5 minutes; crumble it with a fork.

Add in the onion, garlic, and peppers, and continue cooking for 2 minutes longer.

Transfer the cooked meat mixture to a lightly oiled casserole dish. Now, stir in the beans, marinara sauce, and chicken bone broth.

Top with the crushed tortilla chips and parmesan cheese.

Bake in the preheated oven at 350 degrees F for 30 minutes, or until the cheese is hot and bubbly. Bon appétit!

Crock Pot Beef Sandwiches

(Ready in about 8 hours | Servings 5)
Per serving: Calories: 552; Fat: 31.2g; Carbs: 32.9g; Protein: 33.4g
Ingredients
2 pounds beef brisket
2 garlic cloves, minced
1 tablespoon dried marjoram
1 teaspoon mustard seeds
1 teaspoon celery seeds
1/2 teaspoon red pepper flakes
1 sprig rosemary
2 sprigs thyme
Flaked sea salt and black peppercorns
10 ounces canned beef broth
10 dinner rolls, split
2 red onion, chopped
2 Italian peppers, deseeded and chopped
Directions
Place the beef, garlic, seasonings, and canned beef broth in your crock pot.
Seal with the lid and cook for about 8 hours on Low setting. Slice the meat against the grain.
Serve the beef on dinner rolls, garnished with onion and peppers. Bon appétit!

Beef and Mushroom Mélange

(Ready in about 45 minutes | Servings 4)
Per serving: Calories: 605; Fat: 22.5g; Carbs: 59.5g; Protein: 44.4g
Ingredients
2 tablespoons olive oil
1 ½ pounds lean chuck steak, cut into bite-sized chunks
Sea salt and ground black pepper, to taste
1 teaspoon hot paprika
1 red onion, chopped
1 red pepper, deseeded and sliced
3/4 pound brown Cremini mushrooms, sliced
3 cloves garlic, minced
2 cups roasted vegetable broth
1 cup cream of mushroom soup
1/2 cup dry red wine
1/2 pound penne pasta
1/4 cup scallions, roughly chopped
Directions
Heat the olive oil in a heavy-bottomed pot over medium-high flame. Once hot, sear the beef for about 6 minutes, until no longer pink. Season the meat with salt, black pepper, and paprika and reserve.
Add in the vegetables and continue sautéing for about 5 minutes or until they are crisp-tender. Add in the garlic and continue to sauté an additional 30 seconds until aromatic.
Add the meat back to the pot along with the broth, mushroom soup, wine, and penne pasta. Bring to a rolling boil and immediately turn the heat to a simmer.
Let it simmer, partially covered, for about 30 minutes or until everything is cooked through.

Ladle into individual bowls, garnish with freshly chopped scallions, and serve hot. Bon appétit!

Grilled Steak Salad with Cheese

(Ready in about 20 minutes | Servings 4)
Per serving: Calories: 330; Fat: 23.3g; Carbs: 7.4g; Protein: 22g
Ingredients
3/4 pound beef flank steak, sliced
Sea salt and ground black pepper, to taste
1/2 teaspoon cayenne pepper
2 tablespoons olive oil
1/4 cup radishes, thinly sliced
1/2 cup scallions, sliced
1 medium tomato, sliced
2 tablespoons extra-virgin olive oil
1/4 cup balsamic vinegar
1 teaspoon Greek seasoning mix
2 cups baby spinach
1/3 cup black olives, pitted and sliced
1/2 cup feta cheese, crumbled
Directions
Pat dry the beef tenderloin with paper towels. Season the meat with salt, black pepper, and cayenne pepper. Drizzle the steaks with the olive oil.
Then, cook the steaks on the preheated grill, turning them periodically to promote even cooking. Cook for about 10 minutes until slightly charred.
Cut the beef into strips and place them in a salad bowl. Add in the remaining ingredients, except for the cheese; toss to combine well.
Top your salad with the crumbled feta cheese and serve at room temperature. Bon appétit!

Beef Tenderloin with Harvest Vegetables

(Ready in about 1 hour 30 minutes | Servings 4)
Per serving: Calories: 624; Fat: 46.6g; Carbs: 15.7g; Protein: 36.1g
Ingredients
1 ½ pounds beef tenderloin
1 teaspoon dried oregano
1 teaspoon dried basil
1/2 teaspoon dried marjoram
1 teaspoon onion powder
1 teaspoon garlic powder
Sea salt and ground black pepper, to taste
1/2 pound potatoes, peeled and sliced into wedges
1/2 pound cauliflower florets
1 cup beef bone broth
2 tablespoons extra-virgin olive oil
1/4 cup feta cheese, crumbled
Directions
Heat the olive oil in a Dutch oven over medium-high heat. Sear the beef tenderloin for about 10 minutes until no longer pink.
Add in the remaining ingredients, except for the cheese; bring to a rolling boil. Immediately reduce the heat to a simmer.
Let it simmer for about 1 hour 20 minutes until the meat is tender and vegetables are cooked through.

Serve with crumbled feta cheese. Bon appétit!

Top Sirloin Steak with Halloumi Cheese

(Ready in about 1 hour 30 minutes | Servings 4)
Per serving: Calories: 481; Fat: 32g; Carbs: 3.5g;
Protein: 41g
Ingredients
2 tablespoons olive oil
1 ½ pounds top sirloin steak, sliced
1 cup beef bone broth
1/2 teaspoon onion powder
1 teaspoon garlic powder
1/4 teaspoon cumin seeds
1/2 teaspoon dried oregano
1 teaspoon dried basil
Sea salt and ground black pepper, to season
1/2 cup Halloumi cheese, sliced
1/2 cup Kalamata olives, pitted and sliced
Directions
Heat the olive oil in a Dutch oven over medium-high
heat. Once hot, sear the beef for about 10 minutes
until no longer pink.
Add in the broth and spices, and bring to a boil.
Immediately reduce the heat to a simmer.
Let it simmer for about 1 hour 20 minutes until the
meat is tender and thoroughly cooked.
Serve with sliced Halloumi cheese and Kalamata
olives. Enjoy!

Easy Zuppa Toscana

(Ready in about 1 hour 5 minutes | Servings 4)
Per serving: Calories: 282; Fat: 11.7g; Carbs: 16.1g;
Protein: 30.1g
Ingredients
1 tablespoon olive oil
1 pound chuck roast, cut into bite-sized cubes
Sea salt and ground black pepper, to taste
1/2 teaspoon sweet paprika
1 teaspoon Italian seasoning mix
1 onion, chopped
1 Italian pepper, chopped
1 zucchini, chopped
2 carrots, chopped
1 celery stalk, chopped
1 parsnip, chopped
4 cups beef bone broth
2 cups kale, torn into pieces
2 tablespoons Italian parsley, roughly chopped
Directions
Heat the olive oil in a heavy-bottomed pot over
medium-high flame. Once hot, sear the chuck roast
for about 4 minutes, until no longer pink; reserve.
Sprinkle the meat with the seasonings.
Add in the vegetables and continue sautéing for
about 5 minutes or until they are crisp-tender.
Add the meat back to the pot along with the broth.
Bring to a boil and immediately reduce the heat to a
simmer.
Let it simmer, partially covered, for about 50 minutes
or until everything is cooked through. Add in the kale

and continue to cook for 5 minutes longer or until it
has wilted.
Ladle your soup into individual bowls and serve
garnished with fresh parsley. Bon appétit!

Guinness Beef Stew with Greek Yogurt

(Ready in about 55 minutes | Servings 4)
Per serving: Calories: 532; Fat: 23.9g; Carbs: 44.4g;
Protein: 37.1g
Ingredients
2 tablespoons olive oil
1 pound beef brisket, cut into bite-sized pieces
Sea salt and ground black pepper, to taste
1 teaspoon smoked paprika
1/2 teaspoon dried oregano
1/2 teaspoon mustard seeds
1 teaspoon fennel seeds
1/2 teaspoon dried rosemary
1 medium leek, sliced
2 small potatoes, peeled and diced
1 celery stalk, peeled and diced
2 cloves garlic, minced
1 cup Guinness beer
3 cups chicken stock
1/2 cup tomato puree
1/2 cup Greek-style yogurt, well-chilled
Directions
Heat the olive oil in a soup pot over medium-high
flame. Once hot, sear the meat for about 4 minutes
until golden brown; reserve.
Add in the seasonings.
Add in the vegetables and continue sautéing for
about 5 minutes or until they are just tender.
Add the meat back to the pot along with the beer,
chicken, stock, and tomato puree. Bring to a boil;
then, turn the heat to a simmer.
Continue to simmer for about 45 minutes or until the
cooking juices have thickened and reduced. Ladle
into individual bowls and serve dolloped with the
well-chilled Greek yogurt. Bon appétit!

Beef with Portobello Mushrooms and Cheese

(Ready in about 25 minutes | Servings 4)
Per serving: Calories: 328; Fat: 16.9g; Carbs: 15.9g;
Protein: 29.5g
Ingredients
2 tablespoons olive oil
1 pound chuck roast, cut into bite-sized pieces
1 medium leek, sliced
1 carrot, julienned
1 small-sized eggplant, peeled and sliced
1 cup portobello mushrooms, sliced
2 garlic cloves, sliced
Seas salt and ground black pepper, to taste
1 tablespoon Greek seasoning mix
2 tablespoons dry red wine
1/2 cup Pecorino Romano cheese, grated
Directions

In a large skillet, heat the olive oil until sizzling. Then, cook the beef for about 5 minutes until no longer pink. Push the beef to one side of the skillet.

Add in the leek, carrot, and eggplant and continue to cook for 3 minutes more.

Now, stir in the mushrooms, garlic, salt, black pepper and Greek seasoning mix; cook for a further 3 minutes or until the vegetables are crisp-tender, adding the wine periodically.

Top with the cheese, cover, and allow it to melt for 4 to 5 minutes. Bon appétit!

Ground Beef, Vegetable and Cheese Bake

(Ready in about 40 minutes | Servings 4)
Per serving: Calories: 588; Fat: 29g; Carbs: 37.4g; Protein: 44.5g
Ingredients
1 tablespoon olive oil
1 ¼ pounds ground beef
1 red onion, chopped
2 garlic cloves, minced
1 eggplant, peeled and diced
8 ounces canned red kidney beans, drained and rinsed
1 cup tomato puree
1 cup cream of mushroom soup
1 cup breadcrumbs
1 cup Pecorino-Romano cheese, shredded
Directions
Heat the olive oil in a frying pan over medium-high heat. Once hot, brown the ground beef for about 5 minutes, crumbling it with a fork.

Add in the onion, garlic, and eggplant, and continue to cook for 2 minutes longer or until they are crisp-tender.

Transfer the cooked meat mixture to a lightly oiled casserole dish. Now, stir in the beans, tomato puree, and soup.

Top with the breadcrumbs and shredded cheese. Bake your casserole in the preheated oven at 350 degrees F for 30 minutes or until the cheese has melted. Bon appétit!

Pot Roast Sandwich

(Ready in about 8 hours | Servings 4)
Per serving: Calories: 554; Fat: 19.7g; Carbs: 30.5g; Protein: 61g
Ingredients
2 pounds chuck roast
1 tablespoon olive oil
2 garlic cloves, sliced
2 rosemary sprigs
2 thyme sprigs
1 bay laurel
1/2 teaspoon mixed peppercorns
Flakes sea salt, to taste
1 cup chicken bone broth
8 dinner rolls
1 tablespoon Dijon mustard
2 San Marzano tomatoes, sliced

1 cup butterhead lettuce
Directions
Place the beef, olive oil, garlic, seasonings, and broth in your slow cooker.

Seal with the lid and cook for about 8 hours on Low setting. Slice the meat against the grain.

Spread Dijon mustard over one piece of the dinner rolls. Top with the beef, tomatoes, and butterhead lettuce.

Bon appétit!

Chunky Hamburger Soup with Green Beans

(Ready in about 30 minutes | Servings 4)
Per serving: Calories: 254; Fat: 11.7g; Carbs: 12.1g; Protein: 23.4g
Ingredients
1 tablespoon olive oil
3/4 pound ground chuck
1 red onion, diced
2 carrots, chopped
1 celery stalk, chopped
1 red bell pepper, chopped
1 teaspoon ginger-garlic paste
4 cups beef bone broth
1 ripe tomato, pureed
1 teaspoon Italian seasoning mix
2 bay leaves
Sea salt and ground black pepper, to taste
1 cup green beans, trimmed
Directions
Heat the olive oil in a heavy-bottomed pot over medium-high heat. Once hot, brown the ground beef for about 4 minutes, crumbling with a fork.

Now, stir in the vegetables and continue to sauté for 3 to 4 minutes or until crisp-tender.

Add in the ginger-garlic paste, broth, tomato, and seasonings, bringing to a boil. Let it simmer, covered, for 10 to 15 minutes or until cooked through.

Stir in the green beans and continue to simmer for 5 minutes more until crisp-tender.

Ladle into individual bowls and serve hot. Bon appétit!

Classic Greek-Style Meatballs

(Ready in about 15 minutes | Servings 5)
Per serving: Calories: 305; Fat: 12.7g; Carbs: 14g; Protein: 31.4g
Ingredients
Meatballs:
1 ½ pounds ground chuck
1 red onion, chopped
2 garlic cloves, pressed
1 bell pepper, chopped
1 pepperoncino, minced
Sea salt and ground black pepper, to taste
1/2 teaspoon dried oregano
1/2 teaspoon dried basil
1/2 teaspoon dried rosemary
1 teaspoon dried parsley flakes

1 egg
1/2 cup seasoned breadcrumbs
Tzatziki Sauce:
1/2 cup Greek-style yogurt
1/2 cucumber, minced
1/2 teaspoon dried dill
2 cloves garlic, pressed
Sea salt and ground black pepper, to taste
Directions
Thoroughly combine the ingredients for the meatballs; mix to combine well and shape the mixture into small balls.

Preheat a large frying pan over medium-high heat; sear the meatballs for 5 to 6 minutes until nicely browned.

Then, make the tzatziki sauce by whisking the ingredients. Serve the meatballs with the sauce on the side. Enjoy!

Family Roast Beef

(Ready in about 2 hours | Servings 4)
Per serving: Calories: 445; Fat: 33.7g; Carbs: 6.4g; Protein: 27.1g
Ingredients
2 tablespoons olive oil
1 ½ pounds beef brisket
4 garlic cloves, peeled
1 cup cream of celery soup
1 cup beef bone broth
1 red onion, quartered
1 teaspoon mustard seeds
1 teaspoon fennel seeds
Sea salt and ground black pepper, to taste
1 thyme sprig
2 rosemary sprigs
1 bay laurel
Directions
Heat the olive oil in a large saucepan over medium-high heat. Brown the beef brisket until no longer pink. Transfer the meat to a lightly oiled baking dish. Add in the remaining ingredients.

Roast the beef brisket in the preheated oven at 330 degrees F for about 2 hours until the meat is cooked through and fork-tender. Bon appétit!

Beef Salad Niçoise

(Ready in about 35 minutes | Servings 4)
Per serving: Calories: 412; Fat: 24.7g; Carbs: 18.4g; Protein: 30.2g
Ingredients
2 small red potatoes
2 large eggs
1 pound flank steak, sliced
Sea salt and freshly ground black pepper, to taste
1/2 cup scallions, sliced
1/2 cup radishes, thinly sliced
1 Greek cucumber, sliced
1 Italian peppers, sliced
1 cup grape tomatoes, halved
4 tablespoons extra-virgin olive oil, divided

1 tablespoon champagne vinegar
1 teaspoon Dijon mustard
2 cups Romaine lettuce, torn into pieces
16 niçoise olives
Directions
Place the potatoes and eggs in a large saucepan; cover with cold water (2 inches above them). Bring to a boil; immediately, reduce heat to medium-low, and cook for 6 to 8 minutes.

Transfer the eggs to an ice water-filled bowl. Peel the eggs and cut into slices; reserve.

Continue to boil potatoes for a further 12 to 14 minutes or until fork-tender. Let them cool before cutting into thick slices; reserve.

Season the meat with salt and black pepper.

Then, cook the steaks on the preheated grill, turning them periodically to promote even cooking. Cook for about 10 minutes until slightly charred.

Cut the beef into strips and place them in a salad bowl. Add in the remaining ingredients and toss to combine well.

Top your salad with the hard-boiled eggs and potatoes. Bon appétit!

Marinated Steak with Feta Tzatziki

(Ready in about 35 minutes + marinating time | Servings 5)
Per serving: Calories: 429; Fat: 26.3g; Carbs: 4g; Protein: 44.1g
Ingredients
Marinated Steak:
2 pounds skirt steak, sliced
1 tablespoon stone-ground mustard
1/4 cup wine vinegar
2 cloves garlic, pressed
1 teaspoon dried basil
1 teaspoon dried oregano
Sea salt and freshly ground black pepper, to taste
1 tablespoon capers, drained
4 tablespoons olive oil
Feta Tzatziki:
3 ounces feta, at room temperature
6 ounces plain Greek yogurt
1 tablespoon lemon juice
1/4 cup loosely packed fresh dill, minced
1/2 medium Greek cucumber, peeled and grated
2 cloves garlic, peeled and pressed
Sea salt, to taste
Directions
Place the ingredients for the steak in a ceramic bowl. Cover and let it marinate at least 3 hours in the refrigerator.

Remove the steaks from the marinade and let them sit, covered, at room temperature for about 20 minutes.

Then, cook the steaks on the preheated grill, turning and basting them with the reserved marinade. Cook for about 10 minutes until slightly charred.

Meanwhile, make your feta tzatziki by whisking the ingredients. Serve the steak with the well-chilled feta tzatziki on the side. Bon appétit!

Greek-Style Steak Chowder

(Ready in about 1 hour 5 minutes | Servings 3)
Per serving: Calories: 329; Fat: 15.1g; Carbs: 17.4g; Protein: 28.4g

Ingredients
1 tablespoon olive oil
1/2 pound flank steak, cut into bite-sized pieces
1 tablespoon Greek herb mix
Sea salt and ground black pepper, to taste
1 teaspoon cayenne pepper
1 teaspoon Greek powder
1 onion, chopped
1 celery rib, chopped
1 carrot, peeled and chopped
1 cup broccoli florets
3 cups beef bone broth
1/2 cup parmesan cheese, grated
1/2 cup sweet corn kernels
2 tablespoons fresh chives, chopped

Directions
In a stockpot, heat the olive oil over medium-high flame. Once hot, sear the beef for about 4 minutes, until no longer pink; reserve.
Sprinkle the meat with the seasonings.
Add in the vegetables and continue sautéing for about 5 minutes or until they are crisp-tender.
Add the meat back to the pot along with the broth. Bring to a boil and immediately reduce the heat to a simmer.
Let it simmer, partially covered, for about 50 minutes or until everything is cooked through. Add in the parmesan cheese and corn; continue to cook for 5 minutes longer or until the cheese has melted.
Ladle your soup into individual bowls and serve garnished with fresh chives. Bon appétit!

Grilled Cheese and Beef Sandwiches

(Ready in about 8 hours | Servings 4)
Per serving: Calories: 590; Fat: 25.1g; Carbs: 27.4g; Protein: 62.1g

Ingredients
1 tablespoon olive oil
2 pounds chuck roast
2 garlic cloves, sliced lengthwise
Sea salt and black pepper, to taste
1 teaspoon smoked paprika
1 tablespoon Italian seasoning mix
1 cup vegetable broth
2 tablespoons horseradish sauce
2 San Marzano tomatoes, sliced
1 red onion, sliced
4 ciabatta rolls, split
4 ounces Pecorino-Romano cheese, sliced

Directions
Place the olive oil, beef, garlic, seasonings, and vegetable broth in your crock pot.

Seal with the lid and cook for about 8 hours on Low setting. Slice the meat against the grain.
Spread the horseradish sauce on the bottom of the ciabatta roll. Top with the beef, tomatoes, and onions. Top with cheese and grill the sandwiches until the cheese has melted. Bon appétit!

Ground Beef Soup with Sweet Corn

(Ready in about 40 minutes | Servings 3)
Per serving: Calories: 339; Fat: 11.5g; Carbs: 43g; Protein: 19.5g

Ingredients
1 tablespoon olive oil
1/2 pound ground chuck
2 carrots, sliced
1 Italian pepper, sliced
2 sweet potatoes, sliced
1 medium leek, chopped
1 parsnip, sliced
1 ripe tomato, pureed
2 ½ cups beef bone broth
Sea salt and ground black pepper, to taste
1 teaspoon poultry seasoning mix
1/2 teaspoon dried oregano
1/2 teaspoon dried basil
1/2 teaspoon dried rosemary
1 cup sweet corn kernels

Directions
Heat the olive oil in a heavy-bottomed pot over medium-high heat. Once hot, brown the ground chuck for about 4 minutes, crumbling with a fork.
Now, stir in the vegetables and continue to sauté for 3 to 4 minutes or until crisp-tender.
Add in the tomato, beef bone broth, and seasonings, bringing to a boil. Let it simmer, covered, for 25 minutes or until cooked through.
Stir in the corn kernels and continue to simmer for 5 minutes more until warmed through.
Ladle into individual bowls and serve hot. Bon appétit!

Braised London Broil with Herbs

(Ready in about 1 hour 25 minutes | Servings 5)
Per serving: Calories: 614; Fat: 54.3g; Carbs: 1.4g; Protein: 30.1g

Ingredients
2 pounds London broil, sliced
Sea salt and ground black pepper, to taste
1 sprig rosemary
1 sprig thyme
1 teaspoon dried basil
1 teaspoon dried oregano
1 bay laurel
2 tablespoons olive oil
2 cloves garlic, minced
1 cup water
1 teaspoon Dijon mustard
2 bouillon cubes
1/4 cup red wine
1 lemon, sliced

Directions

Heat the olive oil in a Dutch oven over medium-high heat. Once hot, sear the London broil for about 5 minutes per side until no longer pink.

Add in the spices, olive oil, garlic, water, Dijon mustard, and bouillon cubes, and bring to a boil. Immediately reduce the heat to a simmer.

Let it simmer for about 1 hour. Add in the wine and continue to cook for about 20 minutes until the meat is all the way cooked through.

Serve with sliced lemon. Bon appétit!

Sicilian Beef Ragoût

(Ready in about 1 hour 10 minutes | Servings 5)

Per serving: Calories: 364; Fat: 17.3g; Carbs: 14g; Protein: 39.6g

Ingredients

2 tablespoons olive oil
2 pounds beef chuck, cut into 2-inch chunks
1 medium leek, chopped
3 cloves garlic, minced
Sea salt and ground black pepper, to taste
1 teaspoon cayenne pepper
1 teaspoon red chile flakes
2 medium carrots, peeled and sliced
1 parsnip, peeled and sliced
1 cup marinara sauce
1/2 cup beef bone broth
1/4 cup robust red wine
10 Sicilian green olives, pitted and sliced

Directions

Heat 1 tablespoon of the oil in an ovenproof skillet over medium-high heat. Sear the beef for about 5 minutes until no longer pink; reserve.

In the same skillet, heat the remaining tablespoon of the olive oil. Once hot, sauté the leek and garlic for 2 minutes until just tender and fragrant.

Then, preheat your oven to 300 degrees F. Add the remaining ingredients to the skillet, along with the reserved beef.

Cover and bake in the preheated oven for 1 hour. Bon appétit!

Greek Steak Pitas

(Ready in about 20 minutes | Servings 4)

Per serving: Calories: 410; Fat: 15.5g; Carbs: 41.5g; Protein: 39.1g

Ingredients

1 pound ribeye steak, boneless and sliced
1 teaspoon Greek seasoning mix
Sea salt and ground black pepper, to taste
1/2 cup tzatziki dipping sauce
1 Greek cucumber, sliced
1 large tomato, sliced
1/4 cup Kalamata olives, pitted and chopped

4 (6 ½-inch) pitas

Directions

Season the steak with the Greek seasoning, salt, and black pepper.

Then, cook the steaks on the preheated grill, turning them over once or twice. Cook for about 10 minutes until slightly charred.

Arrange the pitas using the grilled steaks and the remaining ingredients.

Serve warm. Bon appétit!

London Broil with Herbs and Feta Cheese

(Ready in about 15 minutes | Servings 4)

Per serving: Calories: 350; Fat: 17.9g; Carbs: 9.3g; Protein: 39.1g

Ingredients

1 tablespoon olive oil
1 ½ pounds London broil, cut into bite-sized pieces
1 leek, sliced
2 carrots, julienned
3 garlic cloves, minced
1 teaspoon ginger, peeled and grated
Sea salt and ground black pepper, to taste
1/2 teaspoon hot paprika
1 teaspoon dried parsley flakes
1 teaspoon dried basil
1/2 teaspoon dried oregano
1/2 teaspoon mustard seeds
1/2 teaspoon coriander seeds
3 ounces feta cheese, crumbled

Directions

In a large frying pan, heat the olive oil over medium-high flame. Once hot, cook the beef for about 7 minutes until no longer pink; reserve.

Add in the leek and carrots and continue to cook for 3 minutes longer.

Now, stir in the garlic, ginger, and seasonings; continue to cook for a minute or so until fragrant. Serve immediately, garnished with feta cheese. Bon appétit!

Italian Meatballs in Marinara Sauce

(Ready in about 15 minutes | Servings 4)

Per serving: Calories: 388; Fat: 23g; Carbs: 14.9g; Protein: 27.9g

Ingredients

1/2 pound ground chuck
1/2 pound ground veal
2 garlic cloves, minced
2 tablespoons scallions, chopped
1/2 cup parmesan cheese, grated
1/3 cup breadcrumbs
1 tablespoon Italian seasoning mix
Sea salt and ground black pepper, to taste

1/2 teaspoon red pepper flakes
2 tablespoons olive oil
2 cups marinara sauce
Directions
Thoroughly combine the meat, garlic, scallions, cheese, breadcrumbs, and seasonings; mix to combine well and roll the mixture into small balls. Preheat the olive oil in a large skillet over medium-high heat; sear the meatballs for 5 to 6 minutes until nicely browned.

Then, heat the marinara sauce in a large saucepan over a moderate heat; add in the browned meatballs, turn the heat to a simmer, and continue to simmer for 5 minutes more or until thoroughly heated. Enjoy!

Classic Shoulder Roast with Herbs

(Ready in about 2 hours | Servings 5)
Per serving: Calories: 318; Fat: 13g; Carbs: 6.9g; Protein: 40.4g
Ingredients
2 tablespoons olive oil
2 pounds beef shoulder
1 cup cream of onion soup
1 red onion, cut into wedges
2 garlic cloves, sliced
2 bell peppers, sliced
1 teaspoon dried basil
1 teaspoon dried oregano
1 teaspoon dried rosemary
1 teaspoon dried marjoram
1/2 teaspoon dried dill weed
Directions
Heat the olive oil in a large frying pan over medium-high heat. Brown the beef shoulder until no longer pink.

Transfer the beef to a lightly oiled baking dish. Add in the remaining ingredients.

Roast the beef shoulder in the preheated oven at 330 degrees F for about 2 hours until the meat is fork-tender.

Allow the beef shoulder to cool slightly before cutting and serving. Bon appétit!

Oven-Roasted Steak with Parmesan Cheese

(Ready in about 25 minutes | Servings 4)
Per serving: Calories: 303; Fat: 13.5g; Carbs: 3.5g; Protein: 40.1g
Ingredients
1 ½ pounds flank steak, boneless, cut into slices (1-inch thickness)
1 garlic clove, halved
Sea salt and ground black pepper, to taste
1 teaspoon Italian seasoning mix

1/2 cup parmesan cheese, grated
10 black olives, pitted and sliced
Directions
Begin by preheating your oven to 330 degrees F. Place a rack over a rimmed baking sheet.
Rub the steaks on both sides with the garlic halves and season with salt, black pepper, and Italian seasoning mix.
Lower the steaks onto the rack and roast in the preheated oven for about 25 minutes.
Top with the cheese and olives and serve immediately. Bon appétit!

Spicy Beef Salad with Haricots and Potatoes

(Ready in about 35 minutes | Servings 4)
Per serving: Calories: 286; Fat: 6.5g; Carbs: 29.3g; Protein: 29.1g
Ingredients
2 small potatoes, peeled
8 ounces haricots (French green beans), trimmed
1 pound New York strip steak, sliced
Seas salt and ground black pepper, to taste
1 tablespoon butter, room temperature
1 teaspoon dried oregano
1/2 teaspoon dried rosemary
1/2 cup red onion, chopped
1 clove garlic, minced
1/4 cup fresh Italian parsley, chopped
2 tablespoons fresh mint leaves, chopped
2 tablespoons fresh basil leaves, chopped
4 tablespoons lemon juice
1 teaspoon schug sauce
1 tablespoon honey
1/2 Persian cucumber, sliced
1 Italian pepper, sliced
1 large plum tomato, sliced
Directions
Place the potatoes in a large saucepan; cover with cold water (2 inches above them).
Bring to a boil; immediately, reduce heat to medium-low, and cook for about 25 minutes.
Add in the haricots and continue cooking for 4 to 5 minutes or until they are crisp-tender and the potatoes are fork-tender; drain the haricots and place them in a bowl of the ice water; drain and reserve.
Let the potatoes cool before cutting into thick slices; reserve.
Sprinkle the salt and black pepper evenly over the steaks. Melt the butter in a cast-iron skillet over high flame.
Once hot, cook the steaks for 3 to 4 minutes per side or until browned. Reduce the heat to medium-low;

add in the oregano and rosemary and continue to sauté an additional 30 seconds or until fragrant.

Cut the steaks into strips and transfer them to a salad bowl. Add in the remaining ingredients and toss to coat.

Top with the potatoes and haricots. Bon appétit!

Flank Steak with Vegetables and Pasta

(Ready in about 20 minutes | Servings 4)

Per serving: Calories: 540; Fat: 18.5g; Carbs: 51.4g; Protein: 43.1g

Ingredients

2 tablespoons olive oil
1 ½ pounds flank steak, cut into bite-sized chunks
1 Spanish pepper, sliced
1/2 cup shallots, sliced
2 cups broccoli florets
2 cups cauliflower florets
1 cup cream of celery soup
8 ounces penne pasta

Directions

In a large frying pan, heat the olive oil over medium-high heat. Then, cook the beef for about 6 minutes until no longer pink; reserve.

Add in the peppers, shallots, broccoli, cauliflower florets, and soup; turn the heat to a medium and continue to cook for 5 minutes more or until they've softened.

Meanwhile, cook the pasta according to the manufacturer's instructions. Stir the pasta into the vegetables, along with the reserved beef.

Bon appétit!

Rich and Hearty Beef Chowder

(Ready in about 40 minutes | Servings 5)

Per serving: Calories: 240; Fat: 11.8g; Carbs: 12.8g; Protein: 20.4g

Ingredients

1 pound ground beef
2 cloves garlic, pressed
1 red onion, chopped
2 carrots, chopped
1 parsnip, chopped
2 Italian peppers, chopped
5 cups beef bone broth
2 tomatoes, pureed
1 tablespoon Italian seasoning mix
Sea salt and ground black pepper, to taste
1 cup green peas
1 cup Swiss chard, torn into pieces

Directions

Preheat a heavy-bottomed pot over medium-high heat. Once hot, brown the ground beef for about 4 minutes until no longer pink, crumbling with a fork.

Now, stir in the vegetables and continue to sauté for 3 to 4 minutes or until crisp-tender.

Add in the beef bone broth, tomato, Italian seasoning mix, salt, and black pepper; bring to a boil. Let it simmer, partially covered, for 25 minutes or until cooked through.

Stir in the green peas and Swiss chard; continue to simmer for 5 minutes more until they have wilted.

Ladle into individual bowls and serve hot. Bon appétit!

Favorite Greek Keftedes

(Ready in about 25 minutes | Servings 4)

Per serving: Calories: 436; Fat: 22.6g; Carbs: 26.4g; Protein: 33.2g

Ingredients

1 pound ground beef
1/4 cup red onion, chopped
2 cloves garlic, minced
1 cup Pecorino Romano cheese, grated
1/2 teaspoon ground coriander
1/2 teaspoon Greek oregano
1/2 teaspoon ground nutmeg
1/2 teaspoon fresh mint leaves, minced
2 tablespoons fresh parsley, chopped
Sea salt and ground black pepper, to taste
2 slices, day-old bread, cubed and soaked in milk
4 (4-inch) whole-wheat pitas

Directions

Mix all ingredients, except for the pitas, in a large bowl. Then, roll the mixture into small balls.

Place the meatballs in a lightly oiled baking pan.

Bake the meatballs in the preheated oven at 390 degrees F for about 20 minutes, rotating the pan halfway through the cooking time.

Serve hot keftedes with pita bread and enjoy!

Holiday Pot Roast

(Ready in about 2 hours | Servings 4)

Per serving: Calories: 329; Fat: 17.8g; Carbs: 5.5g; Protein: 37.1g

Ingredients

2 tablespoons olive oil
1 ½ pounds rump roast, boneless
Sea salt and ground black pepper, to taste
1/2 teaspoon red pepper flakes
1/2 teaspoon dried oregano
1/2 teaspoon dried basil
1/2 teaspoon dried thyme
2 bay leaves
1/2 teaspoon mustard seeds
1 medium-sized leek, sliced
3 cloves garlic, halved
1 cup chicken bone broth

Directions

Heat the olive oil in a large saucepan over medium-high heat. Brown the beef until no longer pink. Transfer the meat to a lightly oiled baking dish. Add in the seasonings, leek, garlic, and broth.

Roast in the preheated oven at 330 degrees F for about 2 hours until the meat is fork-tender. Bon appétit!

Marinated Oven-Roasted London Broil

(Ready in about 25 minutes + marinating time | Servings 4)

Per serving: Calories: 285; Fat: 14.5g; Carbs: 3.3g; Protein: 35.8g

Ingredients

1 ½ pounds London broil, cut into slices (1-inch thickness)
1/2 cup fresh lemon juice
1 tablespoon stone-ground mustard
2 cloves garlic, minced
Sea salt, and ground black pepper, to taste
1 teaspoon dried oregano
1 teaspoon dried basil
1/2 teaspoon dried thyme
1 tablespoon extra-virgin olive oil
1 heaping tablespoon fresh mint, chopped

Directions

Place the London broil steaks, lemon juice, mustard, garlic, and bay leaf in a ceramic dish. Cover and allow it to marinate for 2 hours in your refrigerator.

Preheat your oven to 330 degrees F. Place a rack over a rimmed baking sheet.

Season the steaks with salt, black pepper, oregano, basil, and thyme. Drizzle the olive oil all over the steaks.

Lower the steaks onto the rack and roast in the preheated oven for about 25 minutes.

Serve warm, garnished with fresh mint, and enjoy!

SNACKS & APPETIZERS

Creamy Hummus with Greek Yogurt

(Ready in about 1 hour | Servings 10)
Per serving: Calories: 145; Fat: 6.5g; Carbs: 16g;
Protein: 5.8g

Ingredients
8 ounces dried chickpeas, soaked for overnight,
rinsed
2 garlic cloves, green shoots removed
1/3 teaspoon ground cumin
1/2 teaspoon oregano
1/2 teaspoon dried basil
1 teaspoon onion powder
Sea salt and ground black, to taste
2 tablespoons lemon juice, freshly squeezed
2 tablespoons olive oil, to taste
2 tablespoons tahini (sesame butter)
2 ounces Greek-style yogurt
2ounces Kalamata olives, pitted and sliced

Directions
Drain the soaked chickpeas and tip them into a
stockpot. Cover the chickpeas with water by 1 inch.
Bring the water to a rolling boil over high heat.
Immediately turn the heat to a simmer and cook for
about 50 minutes. Transfer the cooked chickpeas to a
bowl of your food processor.
Add in the garlic, cumin, oregano, basil, onion
powder, salt, and black pepper. Add in the lemon
juice, olive oil, and tahini.
With the machine running, add the yogurt, and
process until creamy and smooth. Taste and adjust
the seasonings.
Serve garnished with Kalamata olives. Bon appétit!

Homemade Potato Chips

(Ready in about 25 minutes | Servings 4)
Per serving: Calories: 202; Fat: 6.9g; Carbs: 32.2g;
Protein: 3.8g

Ingredients
2 Idaho potatoes, peeled and sliced
2 tablespoons olive oil
Coarse sea salt and freshly ground black pepper, to
taste

Directions
Begin by preheating your oven to 395 degrees F.
Toss the potatoes with the oil, sea salt, and ground
black pepper. Now, arrange the potatoes in a single
layer on a parchment-lined baking sheet.
Bake in the preheated oven for about 15 minutes
until golden brown. Taste and adjust the seasonings.
For an Air Fryer: cook in two batches at 375 degrees
F for about 25 minutes until crispy. Bon appétit!

Cheesy Zucchini Sticks

(Ready in about 25 minutes | Servings 4)
Per serving: Calories: 138; Fat: 10.9g; Carbs: 5.2g;
Protein: 6.6g

Ingredients
1 pound zucchini, trimmed and cut into sticks
2 tablespoons extra-virgin olive oil
1/2 cup Pecorino-Romano, cheese
1 teaspoon dried thyme
1 teaspoon dried rosemary
1 teaspoon sweet paprika
Sea salt and black pepper

Directions
Start by preheating your oven to 350 degrees F. Toss
the zucchini sticks with the remaining ingredients.
Arrange the zucchini sticks on a parchment-lined
baking pan.
Bake in preheated oven for about 22 minutes or until
they are crisp-tender.
Serve with hummus, if desired. Bon appétit!

Grilled Street Corn

(Ready in about 30 minutes | Servings 4)
Per serving: Calories: 353; Fat: 25.4g; Carbs: 29g;
Protein: 7.3g

Ingredients
4 ears fresh corn, husked
2 cloves garlic, minced
2 tablespoons olive oil
2 tablespoons fresh lemon juice
1 teaspoon red chili powder
Flaky sea salt, to taste
4 tablespoons aioli
4 tablespoons feta cheese, crumbled

Directions
Preheat your grill to medium-high heat.
Clean the corn and set it aside. Mix the garlic, olive oil,
lemon juice, chili powder, and salt until well
combined.
Generously rub the corn with the topping mixture.
Place the corn on the aluminum foil; grill for around
20 minutes, flipping every 5 to 6 minutes.
Let them cool for 5 minutes before adding the aioli
and feta cheese. Serve immediately.

Balsamic-Roasted Brussels Sprouts

(Ready in about 35 minutes | Servings 4)
Per serving: Calories: 115; Fat: 7.4g; Carbs: 10.9g;
Protein: 3.8g

Ingredients
1 pound Brussels sprouts, brown ends and yellow
outer leaves removed
2 tablespoons extra-virgin olive oil
1/4 teaspoon cayenne pepper
Sea salt and freshly ground black pepper, to taste
1 tablespoon balsamic vinegar

Directions
Start by preheating your oven to 395 degrees F.
Toss the Brussels sprouts with the olive oil, cayenne
pepper, sea salt, black pepper, and balsamic vinegar.
Arrange the Brussels sprouts on a baking pan; roast
them for about 35 minutes, until crisp-tender. Bon
appétit!

Roasted Parmesan Carrots

(Ready in about 25 minutes | Servings 4)

Per serving: Calories: 205; Fat: 9.7g; Carbs: 24.8g; Protein: 5.3g

Ingredients
1 pound medium-sized carrots, halved lengthwise
2 tablespoons extra-virgin olive oil
Flaky sea salt and ground white pepper, to taste
2 tablespoons bread crumbs
1/4 cup parmesan cheese, grated
1 tablespoon fresh dill, minced
1 tablespoon fresh mint, minced

Directions
Begin by preheating your oven to 395 degrees F. Spritz a baking sheet with a nonstick cooking oil spray.
Place the carrots on the baking sheet; toss them with the olive oil, salt, pepper, bread crumbs, and cheese.
Roast the carrots for about 25 minutes or until crisp-tender, turning them over halfway through the cooking time.
Top with the fresh parsley and mint leaves. Bon appétit!

Easy Three Layer Dip

(Ready in about 10 minutes | Servings 6)

Per serving: Calories: 235; Fat: 16.3g; Carbs: 11.8g; Protein: 11.3g

Ingredients
6 ounces soft cheese
2 tablespoons fresh scallions, chopped
2 cloves garlic, minced
1 tablespoon lime juice
1/2 teaspoon dried basil
1/2 teaspoon dried rosemary
1/2 teaspoon dried oregano
1 cup hummus
2 tablespoons tahini
1 ripe large tomato, chopped
1/3 cup black olives, pitted and chopped
1/2 cup Halloumi cheese, crumbled

Directions
Mix the soft cheese, scallions, garlic, lime juice, basil, rosemary, and oregano. Layer the mixture onto the bottom of a baking dish. Spread the hummus on top.
Mix the tahini, tomatoes, and olives and layer the mixture over the hummus. Scatter Halloumi cheese over the top.
Serve well-chilled with crackers, if desired. Bon appétit!

Aromatic Party Mushrooms

(Ready in about 15 minutes | Servings 4)

Per serving: Calories: 115; Fat: 7.3g; Carbs: 10.8g; Protein: 4.2g

Ingredients
2 tablespoons olive oil
1 small onion, chopped
1 pound small white mushrooms
3 cloves garlic, pressed
4 tablespoons dry sherry
Sea salt and ground black pepper, to taste
1/2 teaspoon cayenne pepper
1 tablespoon fresh basil, chopped
1 tablespoon fresh parsley, chopped

Directions
Heat the olive oil in a saucepan over medium-high heat.
Sauté the onion for about 3 minutes until tender and translucent.
Stir in the mushrooms and garlic, and continue to sauté for about 4 minutes until golden. Add in the wine and continue to sauté for 2 to 3 minutes, until the liquid has reduced.
Stir in the salt, black pepper, and cayenne pepper; continue to sauté an additional minute or so. Garnish with basil and parsley and serve with toothpicks. Bon appétit!

Herb Potato Wedges

(Ready in about 30 minutes | Servings 4)

Per serving: Calories: 185; Fat: 7g; Carbs: 28g; Protein: 3.4g

Ingredients
1 ½ pounds baby red potatoes, scrubbed and cut into wedges
2 tablespoons olive oil
1 teaspoon shallot powder
1 teaspoon garlic powder
1 teaspoon dried parsley flakes
1/2 teaspoon cayenne pepper
1/2 teaspoon dried oregano
1/2 teaspoon dried dill
Sea salt and freshly ground black pepper, to taste

Directions
Toss the potato wedges with the remaining ingredients.
Spread the potato wedges in a single layer on a parchment-lined baking sheet.
Bake the potatoes for about 15 minutes; flip the potato wedges and bake for another 15 minutes until golden and crisp.
Bon appétit!

Garlic Marinated Cherry Tomatoes

(Ready in about 10 minutes + marinating time | Servings 4)

Per serving: Calories: 185; Fat: 17g; Carbs: 6g; Protein: 1.4g

Ingredients
1 pound cherry tomatoes, cut into strips
2 cloves garlic, pressed
1/4 cup parsley, finely chopped
1 teaspoon sea salt
1/2 teaspoon freshly ground black pepper
1/3 cup extra-virgin olive oil
2 tablespoons red wine vinegar
2 tablespoons fresh lemon juice

Directions

Place the cherry tomatoes, garlic, and parsley in jars and set it aside.

Mix the salt, black pepper, olive oil, vinegar, and lemon juice; add the mixture to jars.

Let them sit at room temperature for about 2 hours, stirring periodically. Serve with toasted bread and enjoy!

Layered Hummus and Turkey Dip

(Ready in about 1 hour | Servings 10)

Per serving: Calories: 232; Fat: 12.5g; Carbs: 19g; Protein: 11.8g

Ingredients
8 ounces dried chickpeas, soaked for overnight, rinsed
2 garlic cloves, green shoots removed
1/3 teaspoon ground cumin
Sea salt and ground black, to taste
2 tablespoons tahini (sesame butter)
2 tablespoons lemon juice, freshly squeezed
4 tablespoons olive oil, to taste
8 ounces ground turkey
2 red onions, chopped
2 garlic cloves, minced
1 teaspoon cayenne pepper
Sea salt and black pepper
2 bell peppers, chopped
4 ounces feta cheese, crumbled

Directions
Drain the soaked chickpeas and tip them into a stockpot. Cover the chickpeas with water by 1 inch. Bring the water to a rolling boil over high heat. Immediately turn the heat to a simmer and cook for about 50 minutes. Transfer the cooked chickpeas to a bowl of your food processor.

Add in the garlic, cumin, salt, black pepper, and tahini. With the machine running, add the lemon juice and olive oil, and process until creamy and smooth. Taste and adjust the seasonings.

Preheat a nonstick skillet over medium-high heat; now, sauté the turkey, onions, and garlic for about 4 minutes.

Preheat the oven to 350 degrees F. Spread the hummus onto the bottom of a lightly oiled casserole dish.

Scatter the sautéed meat mixture; top with the peppers and feta cheese. Bake your dip for about 18 minutes or until thoroughly cooked.

Season with cayenne pepper, salt, and black pepper. Serve with crackers. Bon appétit!

Classic Pizza Dip

(Ready in about 20 minutes | Servings 8)

Per serving: Calories: 143; Fat: 9.5g; Carbs: 6.7g; Protein: 9.4g

Ingredients
6 ounces soft goat cheese
1/2 cup Greek-style yogurt
1 clove garlic, pressed
1 red bell pepper, sliced

Sea salt and ground black pepper, to taste
1 tablespoon Italian seasoning mix
1 teaspoon red pepper flakes, crushed
1/2 teaspoon smoked paprika
1 cup pasta sauce
1/2 cup black olives, sliced
1 cup parmesan cheese, grated

Directions
Begin by preheating your oven to 360 degrees F. Thoroughly combine the goat cheese, yogurt, garlic, pepper in a bowl. Spread the mixture onto the bottom of a lightly oiled baking dish.

Sprinkle with salt, black pepper, Italian seasoning mix, red pepper, and smoked paprika. Then, top with the pasta sauce and bake for about 11 minutes.

Lastly, top with the black olives and cheese and bake an additional 7 minutes, or until the cheese is hot and bubbly. Bon appétit!

Zucchini Chips with Pine Nuts

(Ready in about 25 minutes | Servings 3)

Per serving: Calories: 92; Fat: 9.2g; Carbs: 2.4g; Protein: 0.8g

Ingredients
3 medium-sized zucchinis, trimmed and sliced
2 tablespoons olive oil
Sea salt and ground black pepper, to taste
1/2 teaspoon smoked paprika
1/2 teaspoon granulated garlic
1/2 teaspoon dried rosemary
1/2 teaspoon dried basil
1/2 teaspoon dried thyme
8 mint leaves, roughly chopped
2 tablespoons pine nuts, lightly toasted

Directions
Start by preheating your oven to 350 degrees F. Toss the zucchini slices with the olive oil and seasonings. Arrange the zucchini slices on a parchment-lined baking pan.

Bake in preheated oven for about 22 minutes or until they are crisp-tender.

Garnish with mint leaves and pine nuts. Bon appétit!

Lebanese-Style Aromatic Corn on the Cob

(Ready in about 30 minutes | Servings 4)

Per serving: Calories: 246; Fat: 14.2g; Carbs: 30g; Protein: 4.2g

Ingredients
4 ears corn, husked
4 tablespoons olive oil
Flaky sea salt, to taste
Grated zest from 1/2 lemon
1 teaspoon cinnamon
1/2 teaspoon cumin
1 tablespoon cilantro, minced
1 tablespoon parsley, minced

Directions
Preheat your grill to medium-high heat.

Clean the corn and set it aside. Mix the remaining ingredients until well combined.

Generously rub the corn with the topping mixture. Place the corn on the aluminum foil; grill for around 20 minutes, flipping every 5 to 6 minutes. Bon appétit!

Garlicky Roasted Brussels Sprouts

(Ready in about 35 minutes | Servings 5)
Per serving: Calories: 136; Fat: 5.9g; Carbs: 17.4g; Protein: 6.3g
Ingredients
2 pounds Brussels sprouts, brown ends and yellow outer leaves removed
5 cloves garlic, roughly chopped
1 tablespoon fresh lemon juice
2 tablespoons extra-virgin olive oil
1/4 teaspoon cayenne pepper
Sea salt and freshly ground black pepper, to taste
Directions
Start by preheating your oven to 395 degrees F.
Toss the Brussels sprouts with the remaining ingredients.
Arrange the Brussels sprouts on a baking pan; roast them for about 35 minutes, until crisp-tender. Bon appétit!

Cheese Balsamic Roasted Asparagus

(Ready in about 20 minutes | Servings 4)
Per serving: Calories: 175; Fat: 12.1g; Carbs: 13.3g; Protein: 8.1g
Ingredients
1 pound asparagus spears, trimmed
2 tablespoons olive oil
Sea salt and ground black pepper, to season
1 teaspoon garlic powder
1 teaspoon shallot powder
1/2 cup cayenne pepper
1 tablespoon balsamic vinegar
1/2 cup Pecorino Romano cheese, grated
Directions
Toss the asparagus with the olive oil, salt, black pepper, garlic powder, shallot powder, cayenne pepper, and balsamic vinegar.
Bake in the preheated oven at 420 degrees F for about 10 minutes.
Top with cheese and bake an additional 5 minutes or until the cheese has melted. Bon appétit!

Greek-Style Potato Bites

(Ready in about 30 minutes | Servings 4)
Per serving: Calories: 175; Fat: 12.1g; Carbs: 13.3g; Protein: 8.1g
Ingredients
1 ½ pounds potatoes, peeled and cut into wedges
3 tablespoons olive oil
Sea salt and freshly cracked black pepper, to taste
1/2 teaspoon onion powder
1 teaspoon garlic powder
1/4 cup fresh dill, chopped
Grated zest of 1 lemon
Directions

Toss the potato wedges with the olive oil, salt, black pepper, onion powder, and garlic powder.
Spread the potato wedges in a single layer on a parchment-lined baking sheet.
Bake the potatoes for about 15 minutes; flip the potato wedges and bake for another 15 minutes until golden and crisp.
Gently toss the potatoes with the fresh dill and lemon zest. Bon appétit!

Garlic Carrots with Yogurt Dip

(Ready in about 30 minutes | Servings 6)
Per serving: Calories: 156; Fat: 11.7g; Carbs: 10.7g; Protein: 2.6g
Ingredients
1 ½ pounds carrots, peeled and halved lengthwise
2 tablespoons olive oil
Sea salt and freshly ground black pepper, to taste
3 garlic cloves, minced
1/2 cup Greek-style yogurt
1/4 cup mayonnaise
1 tablespoon Dijon mustard
1 teaspoon dried dill
Directions
Start by preheating your oven to 400 degrees F. Spritz a baking sheet with a nonstick cooking oil spray.
Place the carrots on the baking sheet; toss them with the olive oil, salt, pepper, and garlic.
Roast the carrots for about 25 minutes or until crisp-tender, turning them over halfway through the cooking time.
Meanwhile, whisk the remaining ingredients for your dip. Serve the roasted carrots with the yogurt dip on the side.
Bon appétit!

Double Cheese Stuffed Mushrooms

(Ready in about 20 minutes | Servings 6)
Per serving: Calories: 146; Fat: 9.7g; Carbs: 6.9g; Protein: 9.1g
Ingredients
2 pounds Portobella mushrooms, stems removed
2 tablespoons olive oil
2 cloves garlic, minced
1/3 cup breadcrumbs
Sea salt and freshly ground black pepper, to taste
1/3 cup Pecorino Romano, grated
3 ounces soft cheese
2 tablespoons basil leaves, freshly chopped
Directions
Begin by preheating an oven to 395 degrees F. Spritz the mushrooms with olive oil.
Mix the garlic, breadcrumbs, salt, black pepper, and cheese.
Place the mushroom caps on the roasting pan. Divide the garlic mixture between the mushroom caps.
Bake the mushrooms for about 18 minutes or until tender. Top with the basil leaves. Bon appétit!

Roasted Cauliflower with Feta Cheese

(Ready in about 45 minutes | Servings 4)
Per serving: Calories: 206; Fat: 17.7g; Carbs: 7g;
Protein: 4.9g
Ingredients
1 pound cauliflower florets
1 teaspoon dried rosemary
1 teaspoon dried thyme
1 teaspoon dried parsley flakes
1/2 teaspoon garlic powder
1/2 teaspoon onion powder
Sea salt and freshly ground black pepper, to taste
4 tablespoons olive oil
1/2 cup feta cheese, crumbled
Directions
Begin by preheating your oven to 420 degrees F.
Gently toss the cauliflower florets with the
seasonings and olive oil.
Arrange the cauliflower florets on a parchment-lined
baking pan.
Roast the cauliflower florets for about 45 minutes.
Serve with crumbled feta cheese. Bon appétit!

Easy Zucchini Croquettes

(Ready in about 25 minutes | Servings 3)
Per serving: Calories: 322; Fat: 25g; Carbs: 14.7g;
Protein: 11.3g
Ingredients
1/2 pound zucchini, trimmed and grated
1 egg
1 small red onion, finely chopped
1 tablespoon fresh dill, finely chopped
1/2 cup parmesan cheese, grated
1 garlic clove, minced
Sea salt and ground black pepper
1 teaspoon Italian seasoning mix
4 tablespoons chickpea flour
1/2 teaspoon baking powder
4 tablespoons olive oil
Directions
Place the grated zucchini in a fine-mesh strainer and
set over a bowl. Toss the zucchini with 1/2 teaspoon
of the sea salt and allow it to sit for about 15 minutes.
Drain the excess liquid out of the zucchini and
reserve.
Then, in a mixing bowl, whisk the egg until frothy.
Add in the onion, fresh dill, parmesan cheese, garlic,
salt, black pepper, Italian seasoning mix, chickpea
flour, and baking powder.
Add in the grated zucchini and mix to combine well.
Heat the olive oil in a frying pan over a moderately
high heat. Shape the mixture into tablespoon-sized
balls and cook for about 5 minutes or until light
brown. Drain on paper towels and serve hot. Bon
appétit!

Whipped Feta Dip with Mint

(Ready in about 5 minutes | Servings 5)
Per serving: Calories: 292; Fat: 25g; Carbs: 5.4g;
Protein: 12.3g

Ingredients
10 ounces feta cheese, room temperature
6 ounces ricotta cheese, room temperature
3/4 cup Greek-style yogurt
3 tablespoons extra-virgin olive oil
Juice and zest of 1/2 lemon
Sea salt and ground black pepper, to taste
1 bell pepper, chopped
1 tablespoon fresh mint, chopped
Directions
In a food processor or a blender, process all the
ingredients, except for the mint, until creamy and
uniform.
Top with the mint leaves and serve well-chilled. Bon
appétit!

Herb and Garlic Shrimp Skewers

*(Ready in about 10 minutes + marinating time |
Servings 5)*
Per serving: Calories: 232; Fat: 12.5g; Carbs: 1.4g;
Protein: 28g
Ingredients
1 ½ pounds shrimp, peeled and deveined
4 tablespoons olive oil
1 tablespoon lemon juice
Sea salt and black pepper
1/2 teaspoon dried oregano
1/2 teaspoon dried rosemary
1 teaspoon garlic, pressed
1 tablespoon basil, chopped
1 tablespoon parsley, chopped
Directions
Toss the shrimp with the olive oil, lemon juice, salt,
black pepper, oregano, rosemary, and garlic.
Allow it to marinate for about 1 hour.
Carefully thread the shrimp onto skewers. Heat your
grill over a moderately high heat.
Cook the shrimp for about 6 minutes, turning them
once or twice, until they are opaque.
Sprinkle with fresh basil and parsley. Enjoy!

Greek-Style Corn on the Cob

(Ready in about 35 minutes | Servings 5)
Per serving: Calories: 223; Fat: 12.2g; Carbs: 27.8g;
Protein: 4.8g
Ingredients
5 ears of corn, husked
4 tablespoons butter
Sea salt, to taste
1 tablespoon fresh oregano, chopped
2 tablespoons fresh basil, chopped
1 heaping teaspoon garlic, pressed
2 ounces Kalamata olives, pitted and sliced
Directions
Start by preheating your oven to 395 degrees F. Coat
a baking sheet with aluminum foil.
Place the ears of corn on the baking sheet. Divide 2
tablespoons of the butter between the ears of corn.
Sprinkle them with salt, oregano, and basil.

Roast the corn in the preheated oven for about 35 minutes, turning them occasionally to ensure even cooking.

Spread the remaining butter, garlic, and Kalamata olives over each ear of corn. Serve warm.

Garlicky Pita Triangles

(Ready in about 15 minutes | Servings 6)

Per serving: Calories: 83; Fat: 4.8g; Carbs: 8g; Protein: 1.5g

Ingredients
3 (6 ½-inch) pita bread
2 tablespoons extra-virgin olive oil
4 cloves garlic, pressed
Flaky sea salt, to taste
1 teaspoon cayenne pepper

Directions
Begin by preheating your oven to 360 degrees F. Toss the pita triangles with the remaining ingredients until well coated.

Place the pita triangles in a single layer on a parchment-lined baking pan.

Bake for about 12 minutes, turning them over halfway through the cooking time, until crisp and golden brown. Bon appétit!

Roasted Asparagus with Peanuts

(Ready in about 20 minutes | Servings 5)

Per serving: Calories: 173; Fat: 12.8g; Carbs: 10.8g; Protein: 8g

Ingredients
2 pounds asparagus spears, trimmed
2 tablespoons olive oil
Flaky sea salt and ground black pepper, to taste
1 tablespoon Greek herb mix
1 teaspoon garlic powder
1/2 cup peanuts, roughly chopped, dry-roasted

Directions
Toss the asparagus with the olive oil, salt, black pepper, Greek herb mix, and garlic powder.

Roast in the preheated oven at 420 degrees F for about 15 minutes.

Top with the roasted peanuts. Bon appétit!

Parmesan Potato Wedges

(Ready in about 35 minutes | Servings 4)

Per serving: Calories: 447; Fat: 16.8g; Carbs: 66g; Protein: 9g

Ingredients
4 Yukon Gold potatoes, peeled and cut into wedges
4 tablespoons extra virgin olive oil
Sea salt, to taste
1/4 teaspoon mixed peppercorns, freshly cracked
1/2 teaspoon garlic powder
1 teaspoon onion powder
1/2 teaspoon cayenne pepper
1/3 cup Parmesan cheese

Directions
Toss the potato wedges with the olive oil, salt, mixed peppercorns, onion powder, garlic powder, and cayenne pepper.

Spread the potato wedges in a single layer on a parchment-lined baking pan.

Bake the potatoes for about 15 minutes; flip the potato wedges and bake for another 15 minutes until golden and crisp.

Next, toss the potatoes with the Parmesan cheese and bake for a further 5 minutes until the cheese has melted. Bon appétit!

Mushroom and Parmesan Eggplant Cannelloni

(Ready in about 35 minutes | Servings 4)

Per serving: Calories: 217; Fat: 10.8g; Carbs: 20.8g; Protein: 10g

Ingredients
1 tablespoon olive oil
1 red onion, chopped
1 cup button mushrooms, sliced
2 cloves garlic, minced
1/4 cup fresh basil, chopped
1/4 cup fresh parsley, chopped
1 teaspoon capers, chopped
Sea salt and ground black pepper, to taste
1 cup parmesan cheese, grated
1 large eggplant, thinly sliced
1 cup marinara sauce

Directions
Heat the olive oil in a frying pan over a moderately high heat. Cook the onion and mushrooms until just soft, about 3 minutes.

Reduce the heat and sauté the garlic until tender and fragrant or about 1 minute or so.

Ad in the basil, parsley, capers, salt, and black pepper. Add in the parmesan cheese and gently stir to combine.

Meanwhile, spritz the eggplant slices with a nonstick cooking spray and broil for about 15 minutes.

Preheat your oven to 395 degrees F. Divide the filling between the eggplant slices and roll them up. Place the eggplant cannelloni in a casserole dish. Pour in the marinara sauce.

Bake the eggplant cannelloni for about 15 minutes. Bon appétit!

Avocado and Ricotta Bruschetta

(Ready in about 15 minutes | Servings 4)

Per serving: Calories: 437; Fat: 22.2g; Carbs: 48g; Protein: 12g

Ingredients
1 Italian ciabatta, cut into slices
2 garlic cloves, peeled and halved
2 tablespoons olive oil
1 large ripe avocado, pitted, peeled and sliced
1/2 lemon, freshly juiced
4 ounces ricotta cheese
1/2 cup black olives, pitted and sliced
8 fresh basil leaves

1 tablespoon Everything bagel seasoning
Directions
Rub one side of each bread slice with the garlic and drizzle the other side with the olive oil using a pastry brush. Then, place the olive oil-side down on a roasting pan.
Toast the bread slices at 400 degrees F for 5 to 6 minutes until lightly browned around the edges.
Divide the avocado slices between the bread slices and drizzle the avocado with the fresh lemon juice.
Top with ricotta salata and black olives. Garnish with basil leaves, sprinkle with Everything bagel seasoning and serve. Bon appétit!

Stuffed Mushrooms with Halloumi Cheese
(Ready in about 20 minutes | Servings 6)
Per serving: Calories: 156; Fat: 8.7g; Carbs: 6.9g; Protein: 13.5g
Ingredients
1 ½ pounds white mushrooms caps
2 tablespoons olive oil
8 ounces crabmeat
1 red onion, chopped
2 garlic cloves, minced
1/2 teaspoon fennel seeds
1/2 teaspoon mustard seeds
1/2 teaspoon dried oregano
Sea salt and ground black pepper, to taste
1/2 teaspoon smoked paprika
1/2 cup Halloumi cheese, crumbled
Directions
Begin by preheating an oven to 395 degrees F. Spritz the mushroom caps with the olive oil.
Mix the crabmeat, onion, garlic, seasonings, and cheese.
Place the mushroom caps on the roasting pan. Divide the crabmeat mixture between the mushroom caps.
Bake the mushrooms for about 18 minutes or until tender. Bon appétit!

Zucchini Cakes with Feta and Dill
(Ready in about 20 minutes | Servings 4)
Per serving: Calories: 186; Fat: 15.7g; Carbs: 5g; Protein: 5.5g
Ingredients
2 medium-sized zucchinis, grated
1 egg
1/2 cup breadcrumbs
2 scallions, chopped
2 ounces feta cheese
1/2 teaspoon lemon zest
1/2 teaspoon dried dill
1/2 teaspoon dried thyme
1/2 teaspoon cayenne pepper
Sea salt and ground black pepper, to taste
3 tablespoons olive oil
Directions
Place the grated zucchini in a fine-mesh strainer and set over a bowl. Toss the zucchini with 1/2 teaspoon of the sea salt and allow it to sit for about 15 minutes.

Drain the excess liquid out of the zucchini and reserve.
Then, in a mixing bowl, whisk the egg until frothy.
Add in the remaining ingredients, except for the olive oil.
Add in the grated zucchini and mix to combine well.
Heat the olive oil in a frying pan over a moderately high heat. Drop heaping tablespoons of the mixture into the frying pan; cook for about 5 minutes or until light brown.
Drain on paper towels and serve hot. Bon appétit!

Tomato and Feta Dip
(Ready in about 10 minutes | Servings 5)
Per serving: Calories: 206; Fat: 18.3g; Carbs: 5.6g; Protein: 6.6g
Ingredients
2 ripe tomatoes, chopped
2 scallions stalks, sliced thinly
6 ounces feta cheese, crumbled
1 teaspoon Greek seasoning
Sea salt and crushed red pepper flakes, to taste
1/4 cup olive oil
Directions
Gently stir all ingredients until well combined.
Serve well-chilled. Bon appétit!

Broiled Prawn Skewers
(Ready in about 10 minutes | Servings 5)
Per serving: Calories: 136; Fat: 9.3g; Carbs: 4.2g; Protein: 8.7g
Ingredients
1/2 pound king prawns, peeled and deveined
3 tablespoons olive oil
3 tablespoons lemon juice
1 tablespoon stone-ground mustard
3 garlic cloves, minced
1/2 red onion, chopped
1 teaspoon red pepper flakes, crushed
1/2 teaspoon ground cumin
Sea salt and black pepper, to taste
1 teaspoon dried oregano
Directions
Toss the prawns with the olive oil, lemon juice, mustard, onion, and garlic. Allow it to marinate for about 1 hour.
Carefully thread the prawns onto soaked bamboo skewers.
Preheat the broiler. Place the prawn skewers on a lightly oiled baking pan. Broil your prawns for about 3 minutes or until opaque. Bon appétit!

Italian Tortini di Melanzane
(Ready in about 1 hour | Servings 5)
Per serving: Calories: 149; Fat: 3.6g; Carbs: 18.7g; Protein: 13.3g
Ingredients
2 medium-sized eggplants, sliced lengthwise
4 ounces mozzarella cheese, sliced
2 ounces parmesan cheese, grated

1 cup pasta sauce
1 teaspoon Italian seasoning mix
Sea salt and ground black pepper, to taste
Directions
Place the eggplant and 1 teaspoon of sea salt in a ceramic bowl; let it sit for about 30 minutes and drain it using a colander.
Pat the eggplant slices dry using kitchen towels. Next, spritz the eggplant slices with a nonstick cooking spray and broil for about 15 minutes.
Preheat your oven to 395 degrees F. Divide the cheese, pasta sauce, and spices between the eggplant slices.
Bake the eggplant slices for about 15 minutes. Bon appétit!

Beetroot and Ricotta Tater Tots

(Ready in about 15 minutes | Servings 4)
Per serving: Calories: 319; Fat: 20.6g; Carbs: 20.4g; Protein: 11.3g
Ingredients
1/2 pound beetroots
1/2 pound ricotta cheese
2 eggs, beaten
1 cup tortilla chips, crumbled
1/4 cup corn flour
1 teaspoon cayenne pepper
1/2 teaspoon dried oregano
1/2 teaspoon dried basil
1/2 teaspoon dried rosemary
Sea salt and ground black pepper, to taste
3 tablespoons olive oil
Directions
Thoroughly combine the beetroots, cheese, eggs, tortilla chips, corn flour, and spices in a bowl.
Now, using oiled hands, shape the mixture into equal balls and flatten them lightly.
Heat the olive oil in a frying pan over medium-high heat. Cook the croquettes for 4 to 5 minutes until they're nicely browned on all sides, turning them over to ensure even cooking.
Garnish with olives, if desired. Bon appétit!

Roasted Tomatoes with Feta Cheese

(Ready in about 2 hours | Servings 4)
Per serving: Calories: 189; Fat: 17.3g; Carbs: 6.7g; Protein: 3.3g
Ingredients
1 pound small tomatoes, cut into halves
4 tablespoons extra virgin olive oil
1 teaspoon dried basil
1 teaspoon dried oregano
1/2 teaspoon paprika
Sea salt and ground black pepper, to taste
1 teaspoon garlic, minced
2 ounces feta cheese, crumbled
Directions
Start by preheating your oven to 280 degrees F. Arrange the tomato halves in a single layer on a parchment-lined roasting pan.

Drizzle the olive oil over them and sprinkle with basil, oregano, paprika, salt, black pepper, and garlic.
Roast the tomatoes for about 2 hours; top the warm tomatoes with the crumbled feta cheese and serve. Bon appétit!

Veggie Kabobs with Garlic-Yogurt Sauce

(Ready in about 20 minutes | Servings 6)
Per serving: Calories: 139; Fat: 10.1g; Carbs: 11.3g; Protein: 2.5g
Ingredients
3 medium red onion, cut into wedges
3 bell peppers, quartered
3 medium zucchinis, cut into thick rounds
2 green bell pepper
3 tablespoons extra-virgin olive oil
1/2 teaspoon red pepper flakes, crushed
1 teaspoon hot paprika
Sea salt and ground black pepper, to taste
Yogurt Garlic Sauce:
1/2 cup Greek yogurt
1 tablespoon olive oil
3 cloves garlic, pressed
2 tablespoons fresh parsley, minced
Directions
Toss the vegetable with the olive oil and spices until well coated on all sides.
Tread your veggies onto bamboo skewers and place them on the preheated grill.
Grill the vegetable kabobs over medium heat for about 14 minutes, turning them every few minutes to promote even cooking.
Meanwhile, whisk the ingredients for the sauce until well combined.
Serve the vegetable skewers with the yogurt sauce on the side. Bon appétit!

Cheesy Potato Wedges

(Ready in about 35 minutes | Servings 4)
Per serving: Calories: 156; Fat: 8.7g; Carbs: 6.9g; Protein: 13.5g
Ingredients
1 ½ pounds baby potatoes, scrubbed and cut into wedges
4 tablespoons olive oil
1/2 teaspoon onion powder
1 teaspoon garlic powder
1 teaspoon cayenne pepper
Sea salt and ground black pepper, to taste
1/2 cup Pecorino Romano cheese, finely grated
Directions
Toss the potato wedges with the olive oil, onion powder, garlic powder, cayenne pepper, sea salt, black pepper, and cayenne pepper.
Spread the potato wedges in a single layer on a parchment-lined roasting pan.
Roast the potato wedges for about 15 minutes; flip the potato wedges and bake for another 15 minutes until golden and crisp.

Next, toss the potatoes with the Pecorino Romano cheese and bake for a further 5 minutes until the cheese has melted. Bon appétit!

Greek Lemon-Cheese Dip

(Ready in about 5 minutes | Servings 8)

Per serving: Calories: 140; Fat: 12.7g; Carbs: 0.7g; Protein: 5.5g

Ingredients

1/4 cup olive oil
8 ounces soft cheese, room temperature
1/4 cup Greek-style yogurt
2 tablespoons fresh lemon juice
1 teaspoon cayenne pepper
1 small garlic clove, minced
Flaky sea salt and freshly ground black pepper

Directions

Gently stir all ingredients until well combined. Serve well-chilled with vegetable sticks or crostini. Bon appétit!

Green Avocado and Hummus Dip

(Ready in about 55 minutes | Servings 8)

Per serving: Calories: 104; Fat: 8.7g; Carbs: 7g; Protein: 1.8g

Ingredients

8 ounces garbanzo beans, soaked overnight
2 avocados, pitted and peeled
4 garlic cloves
1/4 cup parsley
1/4 cup fresh chives
1/4 cup fresh basil
1 cup baby spinach
1/4 cup lemon juice
Sea salt and ground black pepper, to taste
1/2 teaspoon smoked paprika
3 tablespoons pine nuts
1 tablespoon extra-virgin olive oil

Directions

Drain the soaked chickpeas and tip them into a stockpot. Cover the chickpeas with water by 1 inch. Bring the water to a rolling boil over high heat. Immediately turn the heat to a simmer and cook for about 50 minutes. Transfer the cooked chickpeas to a bowl of your food processor.

Add in the remaining ingredients, except the olive oil. Process until creamy and uniform; transfer to a serving bowl.

Drizzle the olive oil over the top and serve. Bon appétit!

Easy Shrimp Kabobs

(Ready in about 10 minutes + marinating time | Servings 5)

Per serving: Calories: 219; Fat: 9g; Carbs: 7.2g; Protein: 28g

Ingredients

1 ½ pounds shrimp
3 tablespoons olive oil
3 garlic cloves, pressed
3 tablespoons lemon juice
1 tablespoon brown mustard
1 bay laurel
2 red onions, cut into wedges
2 bell peppers, deseeded and quartered
1 teaspoon red pepper flakes, crushed
Sea salt and black pepper, to taste

Directions

Toss the shrimp with the olive oil, garlic, lemon juice, mustard, and bay laurel. Allow it to marinate for about 1 hour.

Now, thread the shrimp, onions, and pepper onto soaked bamboo skewers. Heat your grill over a moderately high heat.

Cook your kabobs for about 6 minutes, turning them once or twice, until they are opaque.

Season your kabobs with the red peppers, salt, and black pepper and serve hot. Bon appétit!

Classic Italian Bruschetta

(Ready in about 55 minutes | Servings 4)

Per serving: Calories: 304; Fat: 9.1g; Carbs: 47g; Protein: 9.8g

Ingredients

1 French baguette
2 cloves garlic
2 tablespoons extra-virgin olive oil
2 ripe tomatoes, chopped
1 teaspoon dried oregano
1 teaspoon dried basil

Directions

Rub one side of each bread slice with the garlic and drizzle the other side with the olive oil using a pastry brush. Then, place the olive oil-side down on a roasting pan.

Toast the bread slices at 400 degrees F for 5 to 6 minutes until lightly browned around the edges.

Top with the tomatoes, oregano, and basil and serve immediately. Bon appétit!

Toasted Pita Wedges

(Ready in about 15 minutes | Servings 6)

Per serving: Calories: 95; Fat: 4.7g; Carbs: 11.1g; Protein: 1.8g

Ingredients

2 (6 ½-inch) pita bread, cut into triangles
2 tablespoons olive oil
1 teaspoon dried oregano
Sea salt and red pepper, to taste

Directions

Begin by preheating your oven to 370 degrees F. Toss the pita triangles with the remaining ingredients until well coated.

Place the pita triangles in a single layer on a parchment-lined baking pan.

Bake for 10 to 11 minutes, turning them over halfway through the cooking time, until crisp. Bon appétit!

Famous Moroccan Yogurt Dip

Per serving: Calories: 116; Fat: 7.7g; Carbs: 3.6g; Protein: 8.1g

Ingredients

1 small Lebanese cucumber, minced
1 teaspoon garlic, minced
1 teaspoon chili pepper, minced
10 ounces feta, crumbled
8 ounces Greek yogurt
1 teaspoon freshly squeezed lemon juice
1 teaspoon lemon zest

Directions

Thoroughly combine all ingredients until well combined.

Serve with toasted pita wedges, if desired. Bon appétit!

Greek Kolokithokeftedes with Yogurt Sauce

(Ready in about 20 minutes | Servings 5)
Per serving: Calories: 205; Fat: 15.6g; Carbs: 7.2g; Protein: 9.5g

Ingredients

3 medium-sized zucchinis, grated
2 eggs
2 garlic cloves, minced
1 Italian pepper, deseeded and chopped
1 Serrano pepper, deseeded and chopped
1/2 cup pecorino Romano cheese, grated
1/2 cup bread crumbs
1/2 teaspoon baking powder
Sea salt and ground black pepper, to taste
4 tablespoons olive oil
6 ounces Greek-style yogurt
2 dill pickle spears, finely chopped
1/2 teaspoon dried parsley flakes

Directions

Place the grated zucchini in a fine-mesh strainer and set over a bowl. Toss the zucchini with 1 teaspoon of the sea salt and allow it to sit for about 15 minutes. Drain the excess liquid out of the zucchini and reserve.

Then, in a mixing bowl, whisk the egg until frothy. Add in the garlic, peppers, cheese, bread crumbs, baking powder, salt, and black pepper.

Add in the grated zucchini and mix to combine well. Heat the olive oil in a frying pan over a moderately high heat. Drop heaping tablespoons of the mixture into the frying pan; cook for about 5 minutes or until light brown.

Meanwhile, whisk the Greek-style yogurt, dill pickle spears, and parsley flakes until well combined. Serve your kolokithokeftedes with the sauce on the side. Bon appétit!

RICE, BEANS & GRAINS

Greek-Style Tangy Rice Bowl

(Ready in about 25 minutes | Servings 3)
Per serving: Calories: 355; Fat: 10.6g; Carbs: 56g; Protein: 8.5g
Ingredients
2 cups roasted vegetable broth
1 cup Arborio rice, rinsed
2 tablespoons olive oil
1 small-sized red onion, chopped
1 garlic clove, pressed
1 lemon, freshly squeezed
Sea salt and ground black pepper, to taste
1 teaspoon dried oregano
1 heaping tablespoon fresh parsley, chopped
Directions
In a heavy-bottomed pot, bring the vegetable broth and Arborio rice to a boil over medium-high heat. Turn the heat to medium-low and let it simmer until the liquid is fully absorbed or about 20 minutes. Drain your rice and reserve.
In a saucepan, heat the olive oil over a moderately high heat. Now, sauté the onions for about 3 minutes until tender and translucent.
Stir in the garlic and continue to sauté for 30 seconds more until aromatic. Str in the rice along with the lemon juice, salt, black pepper, and oregano. Serve warm garnished with fresh parsley. Bon appétit!

Fennel Quinoa Salad

(Ready in about 20 minutes | Servings 4)
Per serving: Calories: 375; Fat: 14g; Carbs: 48.1g; Protein: 13.7g
Ingredients
1 ½ cups quinoa
3 cups vegetable broth
2 tablespoons olive oil
1 red onion, chopped
1 cup fennel, chopped
2 cloves garlic, minced
1 red bell pepper, sliced
1 large tomato, sliced
1 small Lebanese cucumber, sliced
2 ounces black olives, pitted and sliced
2 tablespoons fresh parsley, roughly chopped
Directions
Cook the quinoa and vegetable broth for about 15 minutes until it has absorbed all of the liquid. Remove from the heat and let the quinoa steam for about 5 minutes.
Toss the remaining ingredients in a salad bowl; add in the cooked quinoa.
Gently stir to combine and serve at room temperature. Bon appétit!

Colorful Cannellini Bean and Pea Soup

(Ready in about 20 minutes | Servings 4)

Per serving: Calories: 295; Fat: 4g; Carbs: 49.1g; Protein: 15.6g
Ingredients
1 teaspoon olive oil
1 red onion, chopped
1 carrot, chopped
1 parsnip, chopped
4 cups vegetable broth
1 teaspoon granulated garlic
1/2 teaspoon ground cumin
1/2 teaspoon fennel seeds
1/2 teaspoon oregano
Sea salt and ground black pepper, to season
20 ounces canned cannellini beans, drained
2 cups green peas
Sea salt and ground black pepper, to taste
1 cup whole-wheat croutons
Directions
Heat the oil in a large soup pot over medium-high heat. Now, sauté the onion, carrot, and parsnip for 2 to 3 minutes until they've softened.
Add in the broth and seasonings and bring to a boil. Turn the heat to a simmer and let it cook for 5 minutes more.
Add in the beans and green peas; continue to cook for 10 minutes more or until thoroughly cooked. Season with salt and black pepper to taste.
Ladle your soup into individual bowls and serve garnished with croutons. Bon appétit!

Classic Black-Eyed Peas with Herbs

(Ready in about 35 minutes | Servings 4)
Per serving: Calories: 195; Fat: 4.9g; Carbs: 24.5g; Protein: 9.7g
Ingredients
1 tablespoon extra virgin olive oil
1 large red onion, chopped
1 carrot, trimmed and sliced
1 celery rib, sliced
20 ounces canned black-eyed peas, drained and rinsed
1/4 cup fresh parsley, chopped
1/4 cup fresh basil, chopped
1 bay laurel
1 thyme sprig
1 rosemary sprig
2 cups vegetable broth
1/4 cup tomato puree
Sea salt and pepper, to taste
Directions
In a heavy-bottomed pot, heat the olive oil over medium-high heat. Once hot, sauté the onion, carrot, and celery for about 4 minutes or until just tender.
Add in the remaining ingredients and turn the heat to a simmer. Let it simmer, partially covered, for about 27 minutes.
Taste and adjust the seasonings. Bon appétit!

Cremini Mushroom Risotto

(Ready in about 50 minutes | Servings 3)
Per serving: Calories: 375; Fat: 11.4g; Carbs: 60g; Protein: 10.3g

Ingredients
2 tablespoons olive oil
4 scallion stalks, sliced
2 cups Cremini mushrooms, sliced
4 cloves garlic, sliced
1 cup medium grain brown rice, rinsed
2 cups water
1 tablespoon bullion powder
1 teaspoon Greek seasoning mix
1 bay laurel
Sea salt and ground black pepper, to taste

Directions
Heat the olive oil in a saucepan over a moderately high heat. Add in the scallions and mushrooms, and cook for 3 minutes until just tender.
Add in the garlic and continue to sauté, stirring constantly, until fragrant or about 30 seconds.
Add the rice, water, bullion powder, Greek seasoning, mix bay laurel, salt, and ground black pepper to the saucepan.
Turn the heat to a simmer.
Continue to simmer, covered, for about 45 minutes.
Use a fork to fluff the rice. Serve with some extra fresh herbs, if desired. Enjoy!

Provençal Couscous with Peppers and Corn

(Ready in about 20 minutes | Servings 4)
Per serving: Calories: 385; Fat: 7.8g; Carbs: 68g; Protein: 11.3g

Ingredients
2 tablespoons olive oil
1 red onion, chopped
2 Italian peppers, sliced
1 Sucette de Provence chili pepper, sliced
1 celery, chopped
2 cloves garlic, pressed
2 ½ cups water
Sea salt and ground black pepper, to taste
1/2 teaspoon turmeric
1/2 teaspoon fennel seeds
1/2 teaspoon mustard seeds
1 tablespoon capers, drained
1 ½ cups couscous
1 cup frozen sweet corn kernels

Directions
In a saucepan, heat the oil over a moderately high flame. Once hot, sauté the onion, peppers and celery until just tender and fragrant or about 3 minutes. Now, sauté the garlic for 30 seconds more until fragrant.
Add in the water and bring to a boil. Immediately reduce the heat to a simmer and add in the seasonings.

Continue to cook for 5 to 6 minutes. Stir the couscous and sweet corn kernels into the saucepan. Remove from the heat and let the couscous and corn steam for 5 to 6 minutes. Serve and enjoy!

Traditional Pita Bread

(Ready in about 1 hour 25 minutes | Servings 4)
Per serving: Calories: 265; Fat: 4.1g; Carbs: 48g; Protein: 6.8g

Ingredients
1/2 cup warm water
1 teaspoon active dry yeast
A pinch of brown sugar
2 cups plain flour
1/2 teaspoon sea salt
1 tablespoon olive oil

Directions
Mix the water, yeast, and sugar until well combined. Stir in the 1 ½ cups of flour, salt and olive oil and mix until the dough starts to come together; knead the dough, adding a small amount of flour, until it starts to form a ball.
Then, knead the dough for 2 minutes and let it sit, covered for 10 to 15 minutes; knead again for 2 more minutes.
Now, cover the dough with the plastic wrap and let it sit for 1 hour until it has doubled.
Divide the dough into four pieces and roll them into the equal balls. Then, pat each dough ball flat, forming a round bread about 1/4-inch thick.
Brush a cast-iron skillet with a nonstick cooking spray. Cook the pita bread for about 3 minutes. Flip and cook for a further 2 minutes until it begins to puff up. Serve and enjoy!

Cornbread with Feta and Sun-Dried Tomatoes

(Ready in about 25 minutes | Servings 6)
Per serving: Calories: 277; Fat: 13.6g; Carbs: 31.8g; Protein: 7g

Ingredients
3/4 cup plain flour
3/4 cup cornmeal
1/2 teaspoon baking soda
1/2 teaspoon baking powder
1/4 teaspoon brown sugar
1/4 teaspoon coarse sea salt
1 egg
1/4 cup olive oil
1/2 cup milk
1/2 cup feta cheese, crumbled
1/2 teaspoon dried oregano
1 teaspoon dried basil
1/2 cup sun-dried tomatoes, chopped

Directions
Start by preheating your oven to 370 degrees F. Spritz a square baking pan with a nonstick cooking oil.

In a mixing bowl, thoroughly combine the flour, the cornmeal, baking soda, baking powder, sugar, and salt.

In a separate bowl, whisk the egg, olive oil, and milk until everything is well combined. Add the wet mixture to the dry ingredients and mix again to combine well.

Fold in the cheese, oregano, basil, and sun-dried tomatoes. Gently stir again to combine and do not over-mix the batter.

Spoon the batter into the prepared baking pan. Bake in the preheated oven for about 20 minutes until the cornbread is crisp around the edges and a toothpick comes out dry and clean. Bon appétit!

Farro Bowl with Herbs and Cheese

(Ready in about 30 minutes | Servings 5)
Per serving: Calories: 417; Fat: 17g; Carbs: 51.8g; Protein: 13.2g

Ingredients
1 ½ cups farro
3 cups vegetable broth
Sea salt and ground black pepper, to taste
1/2 teaspoon cayenne pepper
1/2 teaspoon dried oregano
1/2 teaspoon dried basil
1/2 teaspoon dried thyme
1 red onion, chopped
2 ounces black olives, pitted and sliced
2 cups Romaine lettuce, torn into pieces
4 tablespoons extra-virgin olive oil
1 tablespoon fresh lime juice
2 tablespoons balsamic vinegar
1 tablespoon honey
1/2 cup Pecorino-Romano cheese, grated

Directions
In a saucepan, bring the farro and vegetable broth to a boil. Immediately turn the heat to a simmer and let it cook for about 30 minutes until the farro is tender. Place the farro in a salad bowl.

Sprinkle with salt, black pepper, cayenne pepper, oregano, basil, and thyme. Add in the onion, olives, and lettuce and toss to combine.

Then, stir in the lime juice, vinegar, and honey and stir to combine. Garnish with cheese and serve at room temperature.

Saucy Bulgur with Tomato and Herbs

(Ready in about 20 minutes | Servings 4)
Per serving: Calories: 217; Fat: 7g; Carbs: 34g; Protein: 5.7g

Ingredients
2 tablespoons olive oil
1 red onion, chopped
1 red bell pepper, chopped
1 green bell pepper, chopped
2 garlic cloves, minced
1/2 cup tomato puree
1 cup medium bulgur wheat, soaked in 1 cup of water
1 tablespoon cilantro, chopped

2 tablespoons parsley, chopped
1/2 teaspoon cayenne pepper
1/2 teaspoon dried oregano
Sea salt and ground black pepper, to taste

Directions
Heat the olive oil in a saucepan. Sauté the onion and peppers until just tender and fragrant. Now, add in the garlic and continue to sauté for about 30 seconds. Add in the remaining ingredients and stir to combine. Let it simmer for about 8 minutes.

Cover the saucepan and let the bulgur stand for about 5 minutes. Taste, adjust the seasonings and serve warm. Bon appétit!

Polenta with Creamy Tomato Beans

(Ready in about 45 minutes | Servings 4)
Per serving: Calories: 419; Fat: 4.8g; Carbs: 75.5g; Protein: 19.7g

Ingredients
1 tablespoon olive oil
1 teaspoon fresh garlic, pressed
1/2 teaspoon dried oregano
1/2 teaspoon dried basil
1/2 teaspoon smoked paprika
2 ripe tomatoes, chopped
Sea salt and freshly ground black pepper, to taste
1 bay leaf
1½ cups cannellini beans, soaked overnight
5 cups water
1 cup polenta

Directions
In a large saucepan, heat the oil over medium-high heat. Now, sauté the garlic, oregano, and basil for about 30 seconds until fragrant.

Add in the paprika, tomatoes, salt, black pepper, bay leaf, beans, and water.

Reduce the heat to a simmer. Let it simmer gently until beans are creamy all the way through about 40 minutes.

Cook the polenta according to the manufacturer's instructions. Ladle the polenta into individual bowls, top with the tomato/bean mixture and serve warm. Bon appétit!

Spicy Colorful Pilaf

(Ready in about 50 minutes | Servings 4)
Per serving: Calories: 385; Fat: 8.9g; Carbs: 68g; Protein: 6.6g

Ingredients
2 tablespoons olive oil
1 carrot, peeled and diced
1 celery stalk, peeled and diced
1 red onion, chopped
4 cloves garlic, sliced
1 ½ cups short-grain brown rice, rinsed
2 cups water
1 cup cream of onion soup
1 ripe tomato, chopped
1 teaspoon hot paprika
1/2 teaspoon dried oregano

1/2 teaspoon dried basil
Sea salt and freshly ground black pepper, to taste
2 tablespoons fresh parsley, chopped
Directions
Heat the olive oil in a saucepan over a moderately high heat. Add in the carrots, celery, and red onion; cook for 3 minutes until just tender.
Add in the garlic and continue to sauté, stirring constantly, until fragrant or about 30 seconds.
Add the rice, water, soup, tomato, paprika, oregano, basil, salt, and black pepper to the saucepan.
Turn the heat to a simmer.
Continue to simmer, covered, for about 45 minutes.
Use a fork to fluff the rice. Serve with fresh parsley. Bon appétit!

Italian-Style Rice with Olives

(Ready in about 25 minutes | Servings 4)
Per serving: Calories: 375; Fat: 11g; Carbs: 61.8g; Protein: 6.5g
Ingredients
3 cups water
1 ½ cups Arborio rice
2 tablespoons olive oil
1 medium leek, chopped
2 garlic cloves, crushed
1 tablespoon lemon rind, grated
1 tablespoon bullion powder
1 tablespoon Italian seasoning mix
Sea salt and ground black pepper, to taste
2 tablespoons Italian parsley, chopped
2 ounces black olives, pitted and sliced
Directions
In a heavy-bottomed pot, bring the water and Arborio rice to a boil over medium-high heat.
Turn the heat to medium-low and let it simmer until the liquid is fully absorbed or about 20 minutes. Drain your rice and reserve.
In a saucepan, heat the olive oil over a moderately high heat. Now, sauté the leeks for about 3 minutes until tender and translucent.
Stir in the garlic and continue to sauté for 30 seconds more until aromatic. Str in the rice along with the lemon rind, bullion powder, Italian seasoning mix, salt, and black pepper.
Serve warm garnished with fresh parsley and black olives. Bon appétit!

Spicy Quinoa and Cannellini Bean Salad

(Ready in about 20 minutes | Servings 4)
Per serving: Calories: 357; Fat: 17.9g; Carbs: 39.2g; Protein: 11.5g
Ingredients
1 cup quinoa, rinsed
2 cups vegetable broth
4 tablespoons extra-virgin olive oil
2 tablespoons fresh lime juice
2 tablespoons balsamic vinegar
Sea salt and freshly ground black pepper, to taste
10 ounces canned cannellini beans, drained

1 cup grape tomatoes, halved
2 bell peppers, sliced
1 jalapeno pepper, sliced
2 scallion stalks, sliced
2 green garlic stalks, sliced
1 cup radishes, sliced
1 tablespoon fresh parsley, chopped
1 tablespoon fresh basil, chopped
1 tablespoon fresh chives, chopped
Directions
Cook the quinoa and vegetable broth for 13 to 15 minutes until it has absorbed all of the liquid.
Remove from the heat and fluff with a fork.
In a small mixing bowl, whisk the olive oil, lime juice, vinegar, salt, and black pepper.
Toss the beans and vegetables in a salad bowl; add in the cooked quinoa. Dress the salad.
Top with fresh herbs and serve well-chilled. Bon appétit!

Mushroom Pilaf with Pecorino Cheese

(Ready in about 25 minutes | Servings 6)
Per serving: Calories: 417; Fat: 8.9g; Carbs: 72.2g; Protein: 12.5g
Ingredients
2 tablespoons olive oil
1 medium-sized leek, sliced
1 pound king oyster mushrooms, sliced
2 garlic cloves, sliced
2 cups white rice
4 cups roasted vegetable broth
1/2 cup tomato puree
1/2 teaspoon cayenne pepper
1/2 teaspoon dried oregano
1/2 teaspoon dried basil
1/2 teaspoon dried rosemary
Sea salt and freshly ground black pepper, to taste
1/2 cup Pecorino Romano cheese, grated
Directions
Heat the olive oil in a saucepan over a moderately high heat. Add in the leek and mushrooms; continue to cook for 3 minutes until the mushrooms release the liquid and the onions are crisp-tender.
Add in the garlic and continue to sauté, stirring constantly, until fragrant or about 30 seconds.
Add the rice, broth, tomato puree, and spices to the saucepan. Turn the heat to a simmer.
Continue to simmer, covered, for about 20 minutes. Use a fork to fluff the rice. Serve with grated Pecorino Romano cheese. Enjoy!

Traditional Greek Fasolada

(Ready in about 20 minutes | Servings 5)
Per serving: Calories: 287; Fat: 8.2g; Carbs: 34.7g; Protein: 17.7g
Ingredients
2 teaspoons olive oil
1 medium-sized leek, chopped
1 carrot, sliced
2 celery stalks, chopped

5 cups roasted vegetable broth
1 teaspoon Greek seasoning mix
1/2 teaspoon cayenne pepper
1/2 lemon, zested and juiced
25 ounces canned white beans, drained
Sea salt and ground black pepper, to taste
3 ounces feta cheese, crumbled

Directions

Heat the oil in a large soup pot over medium-high heat. Once hot, sauté the leek, carrot, and celery for 2 to 3 minutes until they've softened.

Add in the broth, Greek seasoning mix, and cayenne pepper and bring to a boil. Turn the heat to a simmer and let it cook for 5 minutes more.

Add in the lemon, beans, salt, and black pepper; continue to cook for 10 minutes more or until thoroughly cooked.

Ladle your soup into individual bowls and serve garnished with crumbled feta cheese. Bon appétit!

Classic Tomato-Braised Beans

(Ready in about 45 minutes | Servings 4)

Per serving: Calories: 286; Fat: 9.1g; Carbs: 41.6g; Protein: 12.3g

Ingredients

2 tablespoons olive oil
1 red onion, chopped
1 large carrot, chopped
3 garlic cloves, very thinly sliced
1 cup cannellini beans, soaked overnight
2 bay leaves
Sea salt and ground black pepper
4 medium-sized ripe tomatoes, chopped
1 cup cream of celery soup

Directions

In a large saucepan, heat the oil over medium-high heat. Now, sauté the onion and carrot for about 3 minutes or until they are crisp-tender.

Add in the remaining ingredients and gently stir to combine.

Reduce the heat to a simmer. Let it simmer, partially covered, until the beans are creamy all the way through, about 40 minutes.

Ladle into individual bowls and serve hot! Bon appétit!

Moroccan Couscous Salad

(Ready in about 10 minutes | Servings 4)

Per serving: Calories: 473; Fat: 29.1g; Carbs: 42.6g; Protein: 10.3g

Ingredients

Salad:
1 ½ cups water
1 cup couscous
2 tablespoons olive oil
1 ripe tomato, sliced
1 Lebanese cucumber, sliced
2 bell peppers, sliced
1 chili peppers, sliced
1 small red onion, thinly sliced

14 ounces red kidney beans, drained
2 ounces black olives, pitted and sliced
2 ounces feta cheese, crumbled
1 tablespoon fresh basil, roughly chopped
1 tablespoon fresh parsley, roughly chopped
Dressing:
4 tablespoons extra-virgin olive oil
2 tablespoons lemon juice
1/2 teaspoon paprika
1/4 teaspoon allspice
1/4 teaspoon turmeric powder
Sea salt and ground black pepper, to taste

Directions

Bring the water to a boil. Immediately reduce the heat to a simmer and add in the couscous; heat off. Let the couscous steam for 5 to 6 minutes.

Add in the remaining salad ingredients and toss to combine.

Whisk the dressing ingredients; dress your salad and toss to coat. Serve and enjoy!

Polenta with Cheese and Beef Ragout

(Ready in about 15 minutes | Servings 5)

Per serving: Calories: 475; Fat: 22.4g; Carbs: 43g; Protein: 24.7g

Ingredients

2 tablespoons olive oil
1 red onion, chopped
2 garlic cloves, finely chopped
1 pound ground beef
2 ripe tomatoes, chopped
1 teaspoon dried basil
1/2 teaspoon dried oregano
1 thyme sprig, chopped
2 rosemary sprigs, chopped
1 ½ cups polenta
Sea salt, to taste
2 ounces Kalamata olives, pitted and sliced
1/2 cup Parmigiano-Reggiano cheese, freshly grated

Directions

Heat the oil in a cast-iron skillet over a moderately high heat. Once hot, cook the onion, garlic, and ground beef for about 4 minutes.

Stir in the tomatoes and herbs. Turn the heat to a simmer and continue to cook for another 9 minutes until cooked through.

Meanwhile, cook the polenta according to the manufacturer's instructions. Remove from the heat. Salt to taste.

Spoon the warm polenta into the individual bowls; top with the ragout, olives, and cheese. Bon appétit!

Farro with Roasted Veggies and Feta Cheese

(Ready in about 40 minutes | Servings 4)

Per serving: Calories: 345; Fat: 11.9g; Carbs: 47g; Protein: 12.3g

Ingredients

1 cup farro
2 cups vegetable broth

1 red onion, cut into wedges
2 bell peppers, quartered
5 cloves garlic, peeled
1 cup cherry tomatoes
2 tablespoons olive oil
Sea salt and ground black pepper, to taste
1 teaspoon Italian herb mix
1/2 cup feta cheese, crumbled
Directions
In a saucepan, bring the farro and vegetable broth to a boil. Immediately turn the heat to a simmer and let it cook for about 30 minutes until the farro is tender. Place the farro in a serving bowl.

In the meantime, toss your veggies with the olive oil, salt, black pepper, and Italian herb mix.

Roast your veggies in the preheated oven at 400 degrees F for about 40 minutes, tossing every 10 minutes to ensure even cooking.

Garnish with crumbled feta cheese and serve at room temperature. Bon appétit!

Bulgur and Cannellini Bean Salad

(Ready in about 35 minutes | Servings 4)
Per serving: Calories: 375; Fat: 14g; Carbs: 51g; Protein: 11.3g
Ingredients
1 cup light bulgur
1 red onion
2 bell peppers, sliced
1 Lebanese cucumber, seeded and diced
1/4 cup fresh basil leaves, finely chopped
10 ounces canned cannellini beans, drained
2 tablespoons fresh lemon juice
1 tablespoon red wine vinegar
4 tablespoons extra-virgin olive oil
1 garlic clove, minced
1/2 teaspoon dried oregano
1/2 teaspoon cayenne pepper
Sea salt and ground black pepper, to taste
Directions
Place the bulgur in 1 ¼ cups of boiling water. Cover and let it stand for about 30 minutes until all of the liquid has been absorbed.

Then, add in the remaining ingredients and gently toss to combine. Bon appétit!

Pearl Barley with Sautéed Vegetables

(Ready in about 45 minutes | Servings 3)
Per serving: Calories: 431; Fat: 16.3g; Carbs: 61.2g; Protein: 14g
Ingredients
1 cup pearl barley, rinsed
2 tablespoons olive oil
1/2 pound zucchini, diced
2 Italian peppers, deseeded and sliced
3 scallions, sliced
1 teaspoon garlic, minced
Sea salt and ground black pepper, to taste
1/2 teaspoon hot paprika
1 tablespoon fresh parsley leaves, roughly chopped

1 tablespoon fresh basil leaves, roughly chopped
3 ounces feta cheese, crumbled
Directions
Bring 2 ½ cups of water to a boil over medium-high heat; now, turn the heat to a simmer and cook for about 45 minutes or until the barley is thoroughly cooked.

Meanwhile, heat the olive oil in a saucepan over a moderate flame; sauté the zucchini, peppers, and scallions until just tender or about 4 minutes.

Add in the garlic and continue to cook for about 30 seconds or until aromatic. Stir the cooked barley into the vegetables. Sprinkle the salt, black pepper, and hot paprika over everything.

Serve garnished with crumbled feta cheese. Bon appétit!

Brown Rice with Green Peas and Feta

(Ready in about 50 minutes | Servings 4)
Per serving: Calories: 475; Fat: 18.1g; Carbs: 65g; Protein: 13g
Ingredients
2 tablespoons olive oil
1 carrot, trimmed and diced
1 red onion, chopped
1 teaspoon ginger-garlic powder, pressed
1 teaspoon dried oregano
1/2 teaspoon dried basil
1/2 teaspoon turmeric powder
Sea salt and ground black pepper, to taste
1 ½ cups medium-grain brown rice, rinsed
2 cups water
1 cup cream of celery soup
1 cup frozen peas
1 cup feta cheese, crumbled
Directions
Heat the olive oil in a saucepan over a moderately high heat. Add in the carrots and red onion; cook for 3 minutes until just tender.

Add in the ginger-garlic paste and continue to sauté, stirring constantly, until fragrant or about 30 seconds.

Add the oregano, basil, turmeric, salt, black pepper, rice, water, and soup to the saucepan. Turn the heat to a simmer.

Continue to simmer, covered, for about 40 minutes. Stir in the green peas and let it simmer for 5 to 6 minutes more until warmed through.

Serve garnished with feta cheese. Bon appétit!

Quinoa and Swiss Chard Bowl

(Ready in about 25 minutes | Servings 3)
Per serving: Calories: 336; Fat: 13.5g; Carbs: 41.8g; Protein: 12.3g
Ingredients
2 tablespoons olive oil
1 red onion, chopped
1/2 teaspoon ginger-garlic paste
1 cup rinsed quinoa
2 cups vegetable broth

3 cups Swiss chard, cleaned and torn into pieces
1 teaspoon dried basil
1/2 teaspoon dried oregano
1 teaspoon cayenne pepper
1/4 teaspoon celery seeds
1/2 teaspoon fennel seeds
Sea salt and ground black pepper, to taste
Directions
Heat the olive oil in a saucepan over medium-high heat.
Now, sauté the onion for about 3 minutes until tender and translucent. Stir in the ginger-garlic paste and continue to cook for 30 seconds more. Turn the heat to a simmer.
Add in the quinoa and vegetable broth for about 10 minutes until it has absorbed all of the liquid.
Add in the remaining ingredients and continue to simmer for 10 minutes more until the chard has wilted. Bon appétit!

Rice and White Bean Buddha Bowl

(Ready in about 30 minutes | Servings 4)
Per serving: Calories: 533; Fat: 16.7g; Carbs: 78g; Protein: 20.3g
Ingredients
1 cup brown rice
20 ounces canned white beans, drained and rinsed
2 tomatoes, diced
1 Italian pepper, sliced
1 Serrano pepper, sliced
2 Greek cucumbers, sliced
1 small-sized red onion thinly sliced
1/2 cup Kalamata olives, pitted and halved
1/2 cup feta cheese, crumbled
1 heaping tablespoon fresh basil
1 heaping tablespoon fresh parsley
Sauce:
2 tablespoons fresh lime juice
2 tablespoons balsamic vinegar
1 teaspoon Dijon mustard
1/4 cup tahini
1 garlic clove, pressed
Sea salt and ground black pepper, to taste
Directions
Bring the rice, 2 cups of water, and 1/4 teaspoon of sea salt to a boil. Cover, and reduce the temperature to a simmer; let it simmer for 30 minutes and remove from the heat.
Fluff your rice and transfer it to a nice salad bowl.
Add in the salad ingredients and toss to combine well.
Mix the ingredients for the sauce.
Toss your salad with the prepared sauce and serve immediately. Bon appétit!

Couscous with Dried Fruits

(Ready in about 10 minutes | Servings 3)
Per serving: Calories: 393; Fat: 9.7g; Carbs: 71.4g; Protein: 8.6g
Ingredients
1 ½ cups water

1 cup couscous
2 tablespoons olive oil
1/2 cup dried figs, chopped
1/4 cup Sultanas
1/4 teaspoon ground cloves
1/4 teaspoon ground allspice
1/2 teaspoon ground cinnamon
Directions
Bring the water to a boil. Immediately reduce the heat to a simmer and add in the couscous; heat off. Let the couscous steam for 5 to 6 minutes.
Stir in the remaining ingredients and serve warm. Bon appétit!

Italian Corn Muffins

(Ready in about 25 minutes | Servings 6)
Per serving: Calories: 363; Fat: 20g; Carbs: 33.1g; Protein: 11.6g
Ingredients
1/2 cup all-purpose flour
1 cup cornmeal
1 teaspoon baking powder
1/2 teaspoon coarse sea salt
2 eggs
6 tablespoons olive oil
1/2 cup water
1/2 cup Greek-style yogurt
1 tablespoon honey
1 cup Pecorino-Romano cheese, grated
1 teaspoon Italian seasoning mix
Directions
Start by preheating your oven to 370 degrees F. Spritz a muffin tin with a nonstick cooking oil.
In a mixing bowl, thoroughly combine the flour, the cornmeal, baking powder, and salt.
In a separate bowl, whisk the egg, olive oil, water, yogurt, and honey until everything is well combined.
Add the wet mixture to the dry ingredients and mix again to combine well.
Fold in the cheese and Italian seasoning mix. Gently stir to combine.
Spoon the batter into the prepared muffin tin. Bake in the preheated oven for about 20 minutes until a toothpick comes out dry and clean.
Bon appétit!

Farro with Portabellas and Cheese

(Ready in about 30 minutes | Servings 4)
Per serving: Calories: 325; Fat: 11.6g; Carbs: 44.1g; Protein: 11.6g
Ingredients
1 cup farro
2 cups water
2 tablespoons olive oil
1 red onion, chopped
2 garlic cloves, minced
1 pound portabella mushrooms, sliced
1/2 cup tomato puree
1 teaspoon dried basil
1/2 teaspoon dried oregano

1/2 teaspoon dried marjoram
1/2 teaspoon mustard seeds
1/2 teaspoon smoked paprika
Sea salt and freshly ground black pepper, to taste
1/2 cup feta cheese, crumbled
Directions
In a saucepan, bring the farro and water to a boil.
Immediately turn the heat to a simmer and let it cook for about 30 minutes until the farro is tender.
Place the farro in a serving bowl.
Meanwhile, heat the olive oil in a saucepan over medium-high heat. Now, sauté the onion, garlic, and mushrooms until just tender and fragrant.
Stir in the tomato puree and seasonings, and continue to simmer, partially covered, for about 10 minutes.
Garnish with crumbled feta cheese and serve immediately. Bon appétit!

Bulgur and Bean Soup

(Ready in about 40 minutes | Servings 5)
Per serving: Calories: 282; Fat: 7.6g; Carbs: 41.2g; Protein: 13.9g
Ingredients
2 tablespoons olive oil
1 red onion, chopped
1 medium carrot, chopped
1 celery stalk, chopped
5 cups vegetable broth
1 tomato, pureed
1 thyme sprig
1 rosemary sprig
1 bay laurel
Sea salt and ground black pepper, to taste
1 cup bulgur
10 ounces canned white beans, drained
Directions
Heat the olive oil in a heavy-bottomed pot over medium-high heat. Now, sauté the onion, carrot, and celery for about 4 minutes until just tender.
Add in the vegetable broth and tomato puree and bring to a boil.
Immediately reduce the heat to a simmer and stir in the seasonings and bulgur. Continue to cook for 30 minutes more or until cooked through.
Add in the canned beans and continue to simmer for 4 to 5 minutes more until thoroughly cooked. Bon appétit!

Traditional Greek Paximadia

(Ready in about 7 hours 30 minutes | Servings 6)
Per serving: Calories: 334; Fat: 10.2g; Carbs: 55.2g; Protein: 7.9g
Ingredients
1 cup warm water
2 tablespoons honey
1 ½ teaspoons active dry yeast
1/2 cup whole-grain wheat flour
12 ounces barley flour, hulled
4 tablespoons olive oil

4 tablespoons red wine
1/2 teaspoon salt
Directions
Whisk 1/4 cup of water with the honey and active dry yeast; add in half of the wheat flour. Let it stand for about 15 minutes until it gets foamy.
Mix the flour and create a well in the center; now, pour the olive oil, wine and fermented yeast mixture in the well.
Mix the ingredients at medium speed, gradually adding the remaining water. Add in the salt and mix at low speed until they start to come together as a dough.
Now, knead the dough on a work surface until elastic, adding some extra flour if needed.
Cover the dough and let it rise until doubled, 1 ½ to 2 hours. Knead the dough again and place it in a lightly oiled baking pan.
Allow it to rise for 1 hour more. Bake in the preheated oven at 360 degrees F for about 1 hour.
Slice the bread and arrange the slices on a baking sheet. Dry the bread slices at 150 F for 5 to 5 ½ hours. Store in a sealed container. Enjoy!

Barley Soup with Vegetables and Crostini

(Ready in about 50 minutes | Servings 4)
Per serving: Calories: 222; Fat: 6g; Carbs: 34.6g; Protein: 9g
Ingredients
1 tablespoon olive oil
1 medium leek, chopped
1 large zucchini, diced
2 carrots, trimmed and diced
1 celery stalk, diced
4 cups vegetable broth
2 Roma tomatoes, pureed
1/2 cup pearl barley
1/2 teaspoon dried oregano
1/2 teaspoon cayenne pepper
1 cup sweet corn kernels, frozen
2 teaspoons lemon juice
1/4 cup fresh basil, roughly chopped
1 cup crostini
Directions
In a heavy-bottomed pot, heat the olive oil until sizzling. Then, sauté the leek, zucchini, carrot, and celery until crisp-tender, about 5 minutes.
Pour in the vegetable broth and pureed tomatoes. Once boiling, turn the heat to a simmer.
Add in the barley, oregano, and cayenne pepper; continue to simmer for about 35 minutes.
Stir in the corn kernels and continue to simmer for 8 to 10 minutes more until cooked through.
Ladle your soup into individual bowls and garnish with lemon juice and basil. Serve with crostini and enjoy!

Polenta and Mushroom Tart

(Ready in about 25 minutes | Servings 4)

Per serving: Calories: 325; Fat: 13.7g; Carbs: 41.5g; Protein: 10.6g

Ingredients

2 tablespoons olive oil
12 ounces Cremini mushrooms, sliced
1 red onion, chopped
1 teaspoon fresh garlic, minced
1/2 cup tomato puree
1/2 teaspoon cayenne pepper
1/2 teaspoon dried oregano
1/2 teaspoon dried basil
Sea salt and ground black pepper, to taste
1 cup polenta
1/4 cup black olives, pitted and sliced
1/2 cup Halloumi cheese, grated

Directions

Heat the oil in a cast-iron skillet over a moderately high heat. Once hot, sauté the mushrooms, onion, and garlic, stirring periodically, for about 4 minutes.

Stir in the tomato puree, turn the heat to a simmer and continue to cook for another 8 minutes until cooked through. Sprinkle with seasonings and stir to combine.

Meanwhile, cook the polenta according to the manufacturer's instructions. Remove from the heat.

Spoon the warm polenta into a lightly oiled baking pan; top with the sautéed mixture, black olives, and Halloumi cheese.

Place under the preheated broiler until the cheese is hot and bubbly, for 3 to 4 minutes. Bon appétit!

Cheesy Mushroom Risotto with Green Beans

(Ready in about 25 minutes | Servings 4)

Per serving: Calories: 376; Fat: 22.3g; Carbs: 32g; Protein: 16.7g

Ingredients

2 tablespoons olive oil
1 small-sized red onion, finely chopped
1/2 pound button mushrooms, cleaned and sliced
1 teaspoon ginger-garlic paste
1 1/2 cups Carnaroli rice
4 cups vegetable broth
1 saffron tread
1 cup Sauvignon Blanc
Sea salt and freshly ground pepper, to taste
1 cup green beans
3 ounces Halloumi cheese, crumbled

Directions

Heat the olive oil in a saucepan over a moderately high heat. Add in the onion and mushrooms; continue to cook for 3 minutes until the mushrooms release the liquid and the onions are crisp-tender.

Add in the ginger-garlic paste and continue to sauté, stirring constantly, until fragrant or about 30 seconds.

Add the rice, broth, saffron tread, wine, salt, and black pepper to the saucepan. Turn the heat to a simmer and stir in the green beans.

Continue to simmer, covered, for about 20 minutes; fluff the rice with a fork.

Top with the crumbled cheese and serve. Bon appétit!

Saucy Quinoa with Prawns

(Ready in about 25 minutes | Servings 3)

Per serving: Calories: 366; Fat: 13.7g; Carbs: 48.2g; Protein: 13.3g

Ingredients

1 cup quinoa
2 cups fish broth
2 tablespoons olive oil
1 red onion, chopped
2 garlic cloves, sliced
6 ounces prawns, peeled and deveined
Sea salt and ground black pepper, to taste
1/2 teaspoon smoked paprika
1/2 teaspoon dried oregano
1/2 teaspoon dried basil
1/4 teaspoon cayenne pepper
1/2 cup tomato puree
2 tablespoons fresh basil, chopped

Directions

Cook the quinoa with broth for about 15 minutes until it has absorbed all of the liquid. Remove from the heat and let the quinoa steam for about 5 minutes; reserve.

In a saucepan, heat the olive oil until sizzling. Once hot, cook the onion until tender and translucent or about 2 minutes.

Add in the garlic and continue to sauté an additional minute or so.

Add in the prawns, seasonings, and tomato puree and continue to cook until your prawns are pink and opaque.

Stir the quinoa into the prawn mixture and serve garnished with fresh basil leaves. Bon appétit!

Bulgur Pilaf with Cremini Mushrooms

(Ready in about 25 minutes | Servings 3)

Per serving: Calories: 256; Fat: 5.7g; Carbs: 44.4g; Protein: 10.9g

Ingredients

1 cup coarse bulgur
1 1/2 cups boiling water
1 tablespoon olive oil
1 red onion, chopped
1 pound Cremini mushrooms, sliced
2 cloves garlic, minced
1 thyme sprig
1 rosemary sprig
Sea salt and ground black pepper, to taste
1 teaspoon smoked paprika
1/2 teaspoon dried oregano
1/2 teaspoon dried basil

Directions

Cook the bulgur, covered, for 20 minutes; fluff with a fork and set aside.

Meanwhile, in a saucepan, heat the olive oil over medium-high heat. Sauté the onion and mushrooms until tender and fragrant, about 4 minutes.

Add in the garlic, thyme, and rosemary, and continue to cook for 1 minute more until fragrant.

Stir in the reserved bulgur and add in the salt, black pepper, paprika, oregano, and basil. Remove from the heat and serve immediately. Bon appétit!

Classic Freekeh Salad

(Ready in about 20 minutes | Servings 3)
Per serving: Calories: 201; Fat: 9.7g; Carbs: 26.4g; Protein: 3.9g
Ingredients
1/2 cup cracked freekeh
1 ½ cups water
A pinch of sea salt
1 red onion, chopped
1/2 teaspoon garlic, minced
1 red bell peppers, deseeded and sliced
1 Greek cucumber, sliced
2 tablespoons extra-virgin olive oil
1 tablespoon red wine vinegar
1 tablespoon fresh lemon juice
2 tablespoons pine nuts
Directions
In a medium saucepan, place the freekeh, water, and salt; bring to a boil. Immediately turn the heat to a simmer and continue to simmer for about 15 minutes, until all the liquid has been absorbed.

Add in the onion, garlic, peppers, cucumber, olive oil, wine, and lemon juice; toss to combine well.

Garnish with pine nuts and serve at room temperature. Bon appétit!

Authentic Farro Pilaf

(Ready in about 35 minutes | Servings 3)
Per serving: Calories: 427; Fat: 17g; Carbs: 60.4g; Protein: 13.5g
Ingredients
2 tablespoons olive oil
1 red onion, chopped
1 red bell pepper, deseeded and chopped
4 ounces cremini mushroom, sliced
1 teaspoon fresh garlic, minced
1 cup farro
1 cup cream of mushroom soup
1 cup vegetable broth
Sea salt and ground black pepper, to taste
1/2 teaspoon hot paprika
1 teaspoon lemon zest, grated
1/4 cup fresh basil leaves, roughly chopped
1/4 cup Kalamata olives, pitted and sliced
Directions
In a Dutch oven, heat the olive oil over medium-high heat. Now, sauté the onion, pepper, and mushrooms for about 4 minutes until tender and fragrant.

Then, add in the garlic and continue to sauté for 1 minute more or until fragrant.

Stir in the farro, soup, and broth, bringing to a rapid boil. Immediately reduce the heat to a simmer and season with salt, black pepper, and paprika.

Let it simmer for 30 minutes or until the farro is tender. Add in the lemon zest, stir, and remove from the heat.

Ladle into individual bowls, garnish with basil and olives and enjoy!

Easy Kamut with Sautéed Vegetables

(Ready in about 40 minutes | Servings 4)
Per serving: Calories: 327; Fat: 9.4g; Carbs: 48.9g; Protein: 14.5g
Ingredients
3 ½ cups vegetable broth
1 ¼ cups kamut, soaked overnight and drained
2 tablespoons olive oil
1 red onion, chopped
2 bell peppers, deseeded and chopped
2 cloves garlic, finely chopped
1 tomato, chopped
2 cups Swiss chard, torn into pieces
Directions
Bring the vegetable broth to a boil over medium-high heat. Now, add in the kamut and reduce the heat to a simmer.

Let it simmer, covered, for about 35 minutes. Meanwhile, heat the olive oil in a saucepan over medium-high heat. Once hot, cook the onion and peppers until they are just tender or about 5 minutes. Then, add in the garlic and continue to sauté for 30 seconds longer until aromatic. Turn the heat to a simmer.

Add in the tomato and let it simmer for about 5 minutes, stirring periodically. Add in the cooked kamut along with the Swiss chard.

Cover and let it simmer for 5 minutes longer or until the chard has wilted. Bon appétit!

Brown Rice Salad

(Ready in about 35 minutes | Servings 3)
Per serving: Calories: 433; Fat: 21.7g; Carbs: 54g; Protein: 6.5g
Ingredients
1 cup brown rice
2 cups water
1/2 teaspoon salt
2 roasted peppers, sliced
1 Greek cucumber, sliced
1 teaspoon fresh garlic, pressed
1 cup rocket lettuce
1 cup Romaine lettuce
1/2 cup scallions, chopped
1/4 cup extra-virgin olive oil
2 tablespoons red wine vinegar
Sea salt and freshly ground black pepper, to taste
1 teaspoon paprika
1/3 cup black olives, chopped
2 tablespoons pine nuts, chopped
Directions

Bring the rice, 2 cups of water, and 1/2 teaspoon of sea salt to a boil. Cover, and reduce the temperature to a simmer; let it simmer for 30 minutes and remove from the heat.

Fluff your rice and transfer it to a nice salad bowl. Add in the roasted peppers, cucumber, garlic, lettuce, and scallions. Toss the ingredients with the olive oil, vinegar, salt, black pepper, and paprika. Toss to combine well.

Serve with black olives and pine nuts and enjoy!

Kamut, Cannellini Bean and Corn Soup

(Ready in about 45 minutes | Servings 4)
Per serving: Calories: 430; Fat: 10.4g; Carbs: 64.2g; Protein: 24g

Ingredients
1 tablespoon olive oil
1 large carrot, trimmed and sliced
1 large zucchini, diced
1/2 teaspoon garlic, minced
3 cups vegetable broth
2 ripe tomatoes, pureed
1 cup kamut
1 tablespoon fresh parsley
1 tablespoon fresh basil
1 tablespoon fresh cilantro
Sea salt and ground black pepper, to taste
12 ounces canned cannellini beans, drained
1 cup sweet corn kernels
2 ounces Pecorino-Romano cheese, grated

Directions
In a heavy-bottomed pot, heat the olive oil over medium-high heat. Now, sauté the carrots, zucchini, and garlic for about 2 minutes or until they are just tender and aromatic.

Add in the broth and tomatoes and bring to a boil. Immediately reduce the heat to a simmer and add in the kamut. Let it cook, partially covered, for about 35 minutes.

After that, add in the herbs, salt, black pepper, beans, and corn kernels. Let it simmer for 4 to 5 minutes more until thoroughly cooked.

Ladle the soup into individual bowls and garnish each serving with Pecorino-Romano cheese. Bon appétit!

Freekeh Bowl with Roasted Peppers

(Ready in about 55 minutes | Servings 4)
Per serving: Calories: 512; Fat: 20.6g; Carbs: 75.4g; Protein: 16.1g

Ingredients
4 red bell peppers
1 cup freekeh
4 cups water
2 cup grape tomatoes, halved
4 scallion stalks, sliced
1/2 teaspoon fresh garlic, minced
1 tablespoon fresh parsley, roughly chopped
1 tablespoon fresh basil, roughly chopped
1 teaspoon fresh oregano, roughly chopped

1/2 lemon, freshly juiced
4 tablespoons extra-virgin olive oil
Sea salt and ground black pepper, to taste
2 tablespoons pomegranate seeds
2 ounces feta cheese, crumbled

Directions
Place the peppers on a parchment-lined baking pan. Bake the peppers at 420 degrees F for about 25 minutes.

Allow the peppers to sit for 30 minutes, then, peel them and remove the seeds and membranes. Slice them into strips and reserve.

Meanwhile, in a saucepan, place the freekeh and water; bring to a boil. Immediately turn the heat to a simmer and continue to simmer for about 15 minutes, until all the liquid has been absorbed.

Stir in the tomatoes, scallion, garlic, parsley, basil, and oregano. Add in the reserved roasted peppers.

In a small mixing dish, whisk the lemon juice, olive oil, salt, and pepper; dress the salad and toss to combine well.

Garnish with pomegranate seeds and feta cheese; serve at room temperature. Bon appétit!

Old-Fashioned Barley Pilaf with Vegetables

(Ready in about 45 minutes | Servings 3)
Per serving: Calories: 376; Fat: 9.7g; Carbs: 64g; Protein: 14.4g

Ingredients
1 cup pearl barley
1 teaspoon olive oil
1 medium-sized red onion, chopped
1 cup king oyster mushrooms, sliced
2 zucchinis, diced
2 garlic cloves, sliced
2 Roma tomatoes, chopped
Sea salt and freshly ground black pepper, to taste
1/2 teaspoon cayenne pepper
1/2 teaspoon dried oregano
1 teaspoon dried parsley flakes
1/2 cup Halloumi cheese, crumbled

Directions
Bring 2 ½ cups of water to a boil over medium-high heat; now, turn the heat to a simmer and cook for about 45 minutes or until the barley is thoroughly cooked.

Meanwhile, heat the olive oil in a saucepan over a moderate flame; sauté the onion, mushrooms, and zucchini until just tender or about 4 minutes.

Add in the garlic and continue to cook for about 30 seconds or until aromatic. Stir the tomatoes and cooked barley into the vegetables. Sprinkle with seasonings.

Top with the crumbled cheese and place under the preheated broiler for about 4 minutes or until the cheese is hot and bubbly. Enjoy!

Italian-Style Polenta Pie

(Ready in about 25 minutes | Servings 4)

Per serving: Calories: 266; Fat: 7.7g; Carbs: 40.2g; Protein: 10.2g

Ingredients

1 cup polenta
2 tablespoons olive oil
2 scallion stalks, chopped
4 garlic cloves, minced
1 cup marinara sauce
1 teaspoon dried oregano
1/2 cup mozzarella cheese, sliced
5-6 basil leaves

Directions

Cook the polenta according to the manufacturer's instructions. Remove from the heat.

Spoon the warm polenta into a lightly oiled baking pan; spread the olive oil, scallions, garlic, marinara sauce, and oregano over the top of your polenta.

Top with the cheese and bake in the preheated oven at 390 degrees F for about 15 minutes.

Let it sit for 5 to 6 minutes before cutting and serving. Garnish with fresh basil leaves. Bon appétit!

Grandma's Sweet Cornbread

(Ready in about 25 minutes | Servings 8)

Per serving: Calories: 342; Fat: 12.7g; Carbs: 53.2g; Protein: 5.4g

Ingredients

1 ¼ cups all-purpose flour
1 ¼ cups cornmeal
1 teaspoon baking powder
1/2 teaspoon baking soda
A pinch of sea salt
1/2 teaspoon ground cloves
1/2 teaspoon ground cinnamon
1/2 cup honey
1 egg
1 cup Greek yogurt
2 tablespoons coconut oil, room temperature
1/4 cup olive oil

Directions

Start by preheating your oven to 370 degrees F. Spritz a baking pan with a nonstick cooking oil.

In a mixing bowl, thoroughly combine the flour, cornmeal, baking powder, baking soda, sea salt, ground cloves, and cinnamon.

In a separate bowl, whisk the honey, egg, yogurt, coconut oil, and olive oil until everything is well combined. Add the wet mixture to the dry ingredients and mix again to combine well.

Spoon the batter into the prepared muffin pan. Bake in the preheated oven for about 20 minutes until a toothpick comes out dry and clean.

Bon appétit!

Quinoa with Garden Vegetables

(Ready in about 25 minutes | Servings 4)

Per serving: Calories: 316; Fat: 4.7g; Carbs: 55.2g; Protein: 14.6g

Ingredients

3 tablespoons olive oil
1 small-sized leek, sliced
1 carrot, trimmed and sliced
1/2 pound zucchini, sliced
1 bell pepper, sliced
1 Serrano pepper, sliced
2 cups brown mushrooms, sliced
4 cloves garlic, peeled
1 ½ cups quinoa
1 cup water
1 cup vegetable broth
1 cup tomato puree
Sea salt and ground black pepper, to taste

Directions

Heat the olive oil in a saucepan over medium-high heat.

Now, sauté the leeks, carrot, zucchini, and peppers for about 3 minutes until they are crisp-tender.

Stir in the garlic and mushrooms, and continue to cook for 1 minute more. Turn the heat to a simmer.

Add in the quinoa, water, vegetable broth, and tomato puree; continue to cook for about 20 minutes until it has absorbed all of the liquid.

Season with salt and black pepper to taste. Bon appétit!

Italian Rice with Mushrooms and Ricotta Salata

(Ready in about 50 minutes | Servings 4)

Per serving: Calories: 436; Fat: 13.3g; Carbs: 68.2g; Protein: 13.2g

Ingredients

2 tablespoons olive oil
1 red onion, minced
1 Italian peppers, sliced
1 small red chile pepper, sliced
1 pound Portobella mushroom, sliced
1 teaspoon garlic, minced
1 ½ cups medium-grain brown rice, rinsed
2 cups water
1 cup marinara sauce
1 tablespoon Italian herb mix
Sea salt and ground black pepper, to taste
1/2 cup Ricotta salata cheese, crumbled

Directions

Heat the olive oil in a saucepan over a moderately high heat. Add in the onion and peppers, and cook for 3 minutes until they are crisp-tender.

Add in the mushrooms and garlic and continue to sauté, stirring constantly, until fragrant about 1 minute or so.

Add the rice, water, marinara sauce, Italian herbs, salt, and black pepper to the saucepan. Turn the heat to a simmer.

Continue to simmer, covered, for about 45 minutes; fluff with a fork and ladle into individual bowls.

Serve garnished with crumbled cheese. Bon appétit!

VEGETARIAN

Roasted Baby Potatoes with Herbs and Cheese

(Ready in about 30 minutes | Servings 4)

Per serving: Calories: 248; Fat: 10.7g; Carbs: 30.8g; Protein: 8.1g

Ingredients

1 ½ pounds baby potatoes, quartered
2 tablespoons olive oil
1 teaspoon garlic, minced
1 tablespoon fresh parsley, chopped
1 teaspoon fresh oregano, chopped
1 teaspoon fresh basil, chopped
1/2 teaspoon coarse sea salt
1/4 teaspoon black pepper, or more to taste
2 ounces Pecorino-Romano cheese, grated

Directions

Start by preheating your oven to 390 degrees F.
Toss the potatoes with the olive oil, garlic, parsley, oregano, basil, salt, and black pepper.
Transfer them to a lightly oiled baking pan and bake for about 25 minutes or until the potatoes are fork-tender.
Top with cheese and continue baking an additional 4 to 5 minutes until the cheese is hot and bubbly. Enjoy!

Fluffy Golden Cornbread

(Ready in about 35 minutes | Servings 3)

Per serving: Calories: 338; Fat: 13.1g; Carbs: 50.8g; Protein: 6.5g

Ingredients

1/2 cup cornmeal
1/2 teaspoon baking soda
1/2 cup creamed corn
1/2 cup Greek yogurt
1/4 cup almond milk
2 tablespoons extra-virgin olive oil
A pinch of grated nutmeg
1/4 teaspoon ground allspice
1 tablespoon honey

Directions

Start by preheating your oven to 380 degrees F.
In a mixing bowl, thoroughly combine the cornmeal with baking soda. Gradually, stir in the other ingredients and mix to combine well.
Spoon the mixture into a lightly greased baking dish.
Bake your cornbread in the preheated oven for about 35 minutes, until a tester comes out dry and clean.
Bon appétit!

Buddha Bowl with Crispy Tofu

(Ready in about 15 minutes | Servings 3)

Per serving: Calories: 478; Fat: 34.9g; Carbs: 29.2g; Protein: 19.7g

Ingredients

2 tablespoons olive oil
12 ounces extra-firm tofu, pressed and cut into cubes
1 garlic clove, minced
1/2 teaspoon dried oregano
1/2 teaspoon dried basil
1/2 teaspoon dried rosemary
1 teaspoon smoked paprika
1 cup baby spinach
1 cup arugula
1/2 cup canned chickpeas, drained
2 Italian peppers, seeded and sliced
1 small avocado, pitted, peeled and sliced
Coarse sea salt and ground black pepper, to taste
3 tablespoons balsamic vinegar
3 tablespoons tahini

Directions

Heat the olive oil in a cast-iron over medium-high heat. Now, fry the tofu until crisp or 5 to 6 minutes, stirring to promote even cooking.
Sprinkle your tofu with the garlic, oregano, basil, rosemary, and paprika; continue to cook for a minute or so or until fragrant.
Place the spinach, arugula, chickpeas, peppers, and avocado in a serving bowl. Sprinkle salt and pepper over everything.
In a small dish, whisk the vinegar and tahini butter. Drizzle the sauce over the vegetables, top with the reserved tofu and serve at room temperature. Bon appétit!

Green Beans with Feta Cheese

(Ready in about 15 minutes | Servings 2)

Per serving: Calories: 248; Fat: 19.9g; Carbs: 12.2g; Protein: 6.7g

Ingredients

1/2 pound green beans, trimmed and cut in half
2 tablespoons olive oil
2 cloves garlic, minced
Sea salt and ground black pepper, to taste
1/4 teaspoon dried dill weed
2 ounces feta cheese, crumbled
1 tablespoon pine nuts, lightly toasted

Directions

Place green beans in a saucepan and cover with the water; bring to a rapid boil. Immediately turn the heat to a simmer and continue to cook for 4 to 5 minutes until green beans are crisp-tender. Drain well.
Next, add in the olive oil and continue to stir for a further 2 minutes.
Add in the garlic, salt, black pepper, and dill.
Continue to simmer, stirring occasionally, for a further 4 minutes.
Taste and adjust the seasonings. Garnish with cheese and pine nuts. Bon appétit!

White Beans with Spinach

(Ready in about 1 hour | Servings 3)

Per serving: Calories: 328; Fat: 5g; Carbs: 51.2g; Protein: 19.1g

Ingredients

1/2 pound white beans, soaked overnight
1 bay leaf
1 tablespoon olive oil
1 onion, chopped
1 bell pepper, seeded and diced
2 garlic cloves, finely chopped
2 cups spinach, torn into pieces
1 teaspoon Greek seasoning mix
1/2 teaspoon cayenne pepper
Salt and freshly ground black pepper, to taste

Directions

Drain the beans and transfer to a stock pot. Cover by 2 inches with cold water, add bay leaf, and bring to a boil.

Reduce the heat to a simmer and cook for about 1 hour; reserve.

Meanwhile, heat the olive oil in a large saucepan. Cook the onion and pepper until just tender and fragrant or about 4 minutes.

Then, sauté the garlic for a further 30 seconds.

Add in the remaining ingredients, along with the reserved beans; stir and let it simmer for 4 to 5 minutes more or until warmed through. Bon appétit!

Roasted Broccoli with Peppers and Cheese

(Ready in about 40 minutes | Servings 4)

Per serving: Calories: 248; Fat: 16g; Carbs: 16.2g; Protein: 11.6g

Ingredients

1 pound broccoli florets
1 medium leek, cut into thick slices
2 Italian peppers, seeded and halved
1 Serrano pepper, seeded
2 garlic cloves, peeled
1 large ripe tomato, quartered
2 tablespoons olive oil
1/2 teaspoon dried rosemary
1/2 teaspoon dried thyme
1/2 teaspoon dried oregano
1/2 teaspoon red pepper flakes, crushed
Sea salt and ground black pepper, to season
4 ounces Halloumi cheese, crumbled

Directions

Start by preheating your oven to 390 degrees F. Arrange the broccoli, leek, peppers, garlic, and tomato on a lightly oiled baking pan. Drizzle the olive oil over the vegetables. Sprinkle the vegetables with the seasonings.

Roast the vegetables in the preheated oven for 35 minutes.

Top with cheese and continue to cook an additional 5 to 6 minutes or until the cheese softens. Bon appétit!

Oven-Roasted Cauliflower with Tahini Sauce

(Ready in about 40 minutes | Servings 4)

Per serving: Calories: 216; Fat: 18.3g; Carbs: 10.8g; Protein: 6g

Ingredients

1 pound cauliflower florets
2 tablespoons olive oil
1/2 teaspoon red pepper flakes, crushed
1/2 teaspoon dried oregano
1/2 teaspoon dried basil
Sea salt and ground black pepper, to taste
4 tablespoons tahini
2 tablespoons soy sauce
1 teaspoon Dijon mustard
1 tablespoon fresh lemon juice
1 tablespoon balsamic vinegar
2 tablespoons pine nuts, lightly toasted

Directions

Begin by preheating your oven to 450 degrees F. Toss the cauliflower florets with the olive oil, red pepper, oregano, basil, salt, and black pepper.

Arrange the cauliflower florets on a parchment-lined baking sheet.

Roast the cauliflower for about 35 minutes, rotating the baking sheet occasionally to promote even cooking.

In the meantime, prepare the sauce by whisking tahini, soy sauce, mustard, lemon juice, and balsamic vinegar.

Spoon the sauce over the roasted cauliflower and serve garnished with pine nuts. Bon appétit!

Refried Beans with Goat Cheese

(Ready in about 1 hour | Servings 4)

Per serving: Calories: 502; Fat: 17.7g; Carbs: 58g; Protein: 29.6g

Ingredients

3/4 pound cannellini beans, soaked overnight and drained
2 tablespoons olive oil
1 red onion, finely diced
2 cloves garlic, sliced
2 Roma tomatoes, chopped
1 tablespoon fresh cilantro, chopped
1 tablespoon fresh parsley, chopped
1/2 teaspoon dried oregano
1 bay leaf
1/2 teaspoon dried basil
1/2 teaspoon cayenne pepper
Sea salt and ground black pepper, to taste
4 ounces goat cheese, crumbled

Directions

Place the beans in a stockpot. Cover by 2 inches with cold water, add bay leaf, and bring to a boil.

Reduce the heat to a simmer and cook for about 1 hour; reserve.

Meanwhile, heat the olive oil in a large saucepan. Cook the onion and garlic for 2 minutes until tender and aromatic.

Add in the tomatoes, cilantro, parsley, oregano, bay leaf, basil, cayenne pepper, salt, and black pepper. Turn the heat to a simmer and let it cook, partially covered, for 5 to 6 minutes.

Stir in the beans. Smash the bean mixture with a potato masher to desired texture. Top with the cheese and place under the preheated broiler for about 5 to 6 minutes until the cheese is hot and bubbly. Bon appétit!

Sautéed Mushrooms with Black Olives
(Ready in about 10 minutes | Servings 3)
Per serving: Calories: 197; Fat: 16.7g; Carbs: 10.1g; Protein: 4.6g
Ingredients
3 tablespoons olive oil
1 red onion, chopped
3/4 pound button mushroom, sliced
2 garlic cloves, minced
Sea salt and ground black pepper, to taste
1/2 teaspoon cayenne pepper
1/2 teaspoon dried dill weed
2 ounces black olives, pitted and sliced
Directions
Heat the olive oil in a saucepan over medium-high heat. Now, sauté the onion and mushrooms until the mushrooms release the liquid or about 6 minutes.
Add in the garlic and continue to sauté an additional minute or so.
Season the mushrooms with salt, black pepper, cayenne pepper, and dill. Let it simmer for about 2 minutes more.
Serve with olives and enjoy!

Chickpea Salad with Cheese
(Ready in about 55 minutes | Servings 4)
Per serving: Calories: 457; Fat: 25.3g; Carbs: 44.2g; Protein: 17.1g
Ingredients
1/2 pound chickpeas, soaked overnight
2 San Marzano tomatoes, sliced
1 Persian cucumber, thinly sliced
2 Italian peppers, deseeded and sliced
2 tablespoons sun-dried tomatoes in olive oil, chopped
2 garlic cloves, minced
4 tablespoons extra-virgin olive oil
2 tablespoons lemon juice
1 teaspoon stone-ground mustard
1/2 teaspoon red pepper flakes
Sea salt and fresh ground black pepper, to taste
2 ounces black olives, pitted and sliced
2 ounces feta cheese, crumbled
2 ounces ricotta salata, crumbled
Directions
Drain the soaked chickpeas and tip them into a stockpot. Cover the chickpeas with water by 1 inch. Bring the water to a rolling boil over high heat.
Immediately turn the heat to a simmer and cook for about 50 minutes. Transfer the cooked chickpeas to the salad bowl.
Stir in the tomatoes, cucumber, peppers, sun-dried tomatoes, and garlic.
In a mixing bowl, whisk the olive oil, lemon juice, mustard, red pepper, salt, and black pepper. Dress your salad and toss to combine well.

Top with the olives and cheese and serve well-chilled. Bon appétit!

Garlicky and Lemony Greek Potatoes
(Ready in about 30 minutes | Servings 4)
Per serving: Calories: 275; Fat: 15.7g; Carbs: 31.3g; Protein: 4.4g
Ingredients
1 ½ pounds baby potatoes, cut into wedges
4 tablespoons olive oil
Coarse sea salt and ground black pepper, to taste
1 teaspoon dried rosemary
1 teaspoon dried thyme
1 teaspoon dried oregano
4 garlic cloves, sliced
Fresh juice of 1 lemon
1/2 cup vegetable broth
1/2 cup Kalamata olives, pitted and sliced
Directions
Start by preheating your oven to 390 degrees F.
Toss the potatoes with the olive oil, salt, black pepper, rosemary, thyme, oregano, garlic, and lemon juice. Pour in the vegetable broth.
Transfer the potatoes to a lightly oiled baking pan and bake for about 25 minutes or until the potatoes are fork-tender.
Garnish with Kalamata olives. Enjoy!

Grilled Tofu with Swiss Chard
(Ready in about 15 minutes + marinating time | Servings 4)
Per serving: Calories: 257; Fat: 22.7g; Carbs: 5.1g; Protein: 12.4g
Ingredients
16 ounces extra-firm tofu, cut into slices
2 garlic cloves, minced
1 tablespoon stone-ground mustard
2 tablespoons wine vinegar
1 tablespoon lime juice
4 tablespoons olive oil
1 teaspoon salt
1/4 teaspoon ground black pepper, or more to taste
1 cup Swiss chard, torn into pieces
1 teaspoon Greek herb mix
1/2 cup Kalamata olives, chopped
2 tablespoons pine nuts, lightly toasted
Directions
Place your tofu, garlic, mustard, vinegar, lime juice, olive oil, sea salt, and ground black pepper in a ceramic bowl. Let it marinate for about 1 hour.
Transfer your tofu to the preheated grill, reserving the marinade.
Now, grill your tofu for about 5 minutes, basting with the reserved marinade. Turn it over and cook on the other side for a further 5 minutes.
Meanwhile, cook the chard in the boiling water for about 4 minutes. Drain and reserve.
Top the cooked chard with the grilled tofu. Sprinkle the Greek herb mix over everything. Serve garnished with olives and pine nuts. Enjoy!

Green Beans with Halloumi Cheese

(Ready in about 20 minutes | Servings 3)
Per serving: Calories: 266; Fat: 16.9g; Carbs: 20.7g; Protein: 8.9g
Ingredients
2 tablespoons olive oil
1/2 teaspoon ground cumin
1/4 teaspoon ground bay leaf
1 small red onion, chopped
1 teaspoon garlic, minced
1 pound green beans, trimmed and cut into halves
Sea salt and ground black pepper, to taste
1 teaspoon paprika
3/4 cup cream of onion soup
3 ounces Halloumi cheese, crumbled
Directions
Heat the olive oil over medium-high heat.
Sauté the cumin and ground bay leaf for 30 to 40 seconds until aromatic.
Add in the onion and garlic and continue to sauté an additional 4 minutes until tender and aromatic.
Add in the green beans, salt, black pepper, paprika, and cream of onion soup. Let it cook for 13 to 15 minutes until green beans are tender.
Serve with crumbled Halloumi cheese and enjoy!

White Bean Soup with Kale and Cheese

(Ready in about 20 minutes | Servings 4)
Per serving: Calories: 383; Fat: 12.9g; Carbs: 46g; Protein: 22.1g
Ingredients
2 tablespoons olive oil
1 medium red onion, chopped
1 carrot, sliced
1 celery, sliced
4 cloves garlic, finely chopped
4 cups vegetable broth
1 medium ripe tomato, chopped
Sea salt and ground black pepper, to taste
1 teaspoon fennel seeds
1/4 teaspoon ground allspice
1 tablespoon Greek herb mix
20 ounces canned white beans, drained
2 cups kale, torn into pieces
1/2 cup Pecorino-Romano cheese, grated
2 tablespoons fresh parsley, chopped
Directions
In a heavy-bottomed pot, heat the olive over medium-high heat. Now, sauté the onion, carrot, and celery for about 3 minutes until they have softened.
Add in the garlic and continue to sauté for 30 seconds more until fragrant. Add in the vegetable broth and tomato and bring to a boil.
Add in the salt, black pepper, fennel seeds, ground allspice, and Greek herb mix. Immediately turn the heat to a simmer and continue to cook for about 8 minutes.
Now, fold in the beans and kale. Continue to simmer for about 4 minutes until the kale has wilted.

Ladle into individual bowls and garnish with cheese and fresh parsley. Bon appétit!

Easy Oven-Roasted Broccoli

(Ready in about 25 minutes | Servings 3)
Per serving: Calories: 134; Fat: 9g; Carbs: 10.6g; Protein: 4.3g
Ingredients
1 pound broccoli florets
2 tablespoons olive oil
2 cloves garlic, sliced
1/2 teaspoon dried basil
1/2 teaspoon dried oregano
1/2 teaspoon cayenne pepper
Sea salt and freshly ground black pepper, to taste
Directions
Start by preheating your oven to 420 degrees F.
Toss the broccoli florets with the remaining ingredients. Arrange your broccoli on a lightly oiled baking pan.
Roast the broccoli florets for about 25 minutes. Taste and adjust the seasonings. Bon appétit!

Giant Bean in Tomato Sauce

(Ready in about 2 hours | Servings 4)
Per serving: Calories: 504; Fat: 14.9g; Carbs: 74g; Protein: 23.3g
Ingredients
3/4 pound giant beans, soaked overnight
1 bay leaf
4 tablespoons olive oil olive oil
2 medium carrots, chopped
1 medium parsnip, chopped
1 large bell pepper, chopped
2 medium red onions, chopped
4 garlic cloves, sliced
1 teaspoon dried parsley flakes
1 tablespoon fresh sage
1 ½ cups tomato puree
2 bay leaves
1 teaspoon cayenne pepper
Sea salt and ground black pepper, to taste
Directions
Cover the beans with the water and boil over high heat for a few minutes. Turn to a simmer and let it cook for about 1 hour, adding the cooking liquid if needed.
In the meantime, sauté the onion, carrot, and parsnip in 1 tablespoon of the olive oil for about 2 minutes. Place the cooked beans in a lightly oiled casserole dish.
Add 2 cups of the cooking liquid to the casserole dish. Add in the remaining ingredients and stir to combine.
Preheat the oven to 390 degrees F. Bake your beans approximately for 1 hour until thoroughly cooked. Serve warm or at room temperature. Bon appétit!

Stuffed Portabella Mushrooms

(Ready in about 20 minutes | Servings 4)

Per serving: Calories: 146; Fat: 9g; Carbs: 5.3g; Protein: 10.2g

Ingredients
4 large portabella mushroom caps
1/2 cup soft cheese
1 bell peppers, seeded and chopped
1 Roma tomato, chopped
1 teaspoon garlic, finely chopped
1/2 teaspoon dried oregano
1/2 teaspoon dried basil
1/2 teaspoon red pepper flakes, crushed
Flaky sea salt and ground black pepper, to taste
4 tablespoons Pecorino-Romano cheese, grated
8 Kalamata olives, pitted and sliced

Directions
Begin by preheating your oven to 395 degrees F. Line a baking pan with a parchment-lined baking paper.
Bake the mushrooms, covered, for about 10 minutes.
In a mixing bowl, thoroughly combine the soft cheese, peppers, tomato, garlic, oregano, basil, red pepper, salt, black pepper, and pecorino cheese.
Divide the filling between the mushroom caps.
Continue to bake until the cheese is hot and bubbly or about 7 minutes.
Serve garnished with Kalamata olives. Bon appétit!

Spicy and Cheesy Zucchini Fritters

(Ready in about 25 minutes | Servings 4)
Per serving: Calories: 266; Fat: 17.3g; Carbs: 18.3g; Protein: 12.2g

Ingredients
1 pound zucchini, grated
4 scallion stalks, chopped
2 garlic cloves, minced
1 teaspoon jalapeno peppers, deseeded and minced
1/2 cup crackers, crushed
1/2 cup chickpea flour
1/2 cup Pecorino-Romano cheese, grated
2 eggs, whisked
Sea salt and ground black pepper, to taste
1/4 cup olive oil

Directions
Place the grated zucchini in a fine-mesh strainer and set over a bowl. Toss the zucchini with 1/2 teaspoon of the sea salt and allow it to sit for about 15 minutes.
Drain the excess liquid out of the zucchini and place in a mixing bowl.
Add in the scallions, garlic, jalapeno pepper, crushed crackers, chickpea flour, cheese, eggs, salt, and black pepper; mix to combine well.
Heat the olive oil in a frying pan over a moderately high heat. Shape the mixture into tablespoon-sized balls and cook for 5 to 6 minutes or until light brown.
Drain the zucchini fritters on paper towels and serve warm. Bon appétit!

Authentic Carrot Soup with Yogurt

(Ready in about 25 minutes | Servings 4)
Per serving: Calories: 190; Fat: 9.6g; Carbs: 19.2g; Protein: 7.7g

Ingredients
2 tablespoons olive oil
1 red onion
1 pound carrots, trimmed and sliced
2 cloves garlic, minced
4 cups vegetable broth
1 teaspoon molasses
1/2 teaspoon cumin seeds
1/2 teaspoon ground allspice
1/2 teaspoon ginger
1/4 teaspoon cinnamon
1/2 teaspoon red pepper flakes, crushed
Sea salt and white pepper, to taste
1/2 cup Greek-style full-fat yogurt

Directions
In a heavy-bottomed pot, heat the olive oil over medium-high heat.
Once hot, cook the onion and carrots until they've softened, about 4 minutes. Add in the garlic and continue to sauté an additional 30 seconds.
Pour in the vegetable broth and bring to a boil. Immediately turn the heat to a simmer, cover, and continue to cook for approximately 18 minutes.
Add the molasses and spices to the warm soup, remove from the heat and let it sit for a few minutes.
Puree the soup in your blender until creamy and smooth. You can reheat the soup, if desire.
Ladle the soup into individual bowls and serve dolloped with the chilled yogurt. Bon appétit!

Classic Egg Salad with Herbs

(Ready in about 20 minutes | Servings 5)
Per serving: Calories: 169; Fat: 15.3g; Carbs: 1.2g; Protein: 5.9g

Ingredients
5 eggs
1 red onion, sliced
1 Greek cucumber, sliced
1 teaspoon deli mustard
1/3 cup mayonnaise
2 tablespoons yogurt
1 tablespoon fresh parsley, roughly chopped
1 tablespoon fresh basil, roughly chopped
1 tablespoon fresh oregano, roughly chopped
1 tablespoon fresh lemon juice
Sea salt and ground black pepper, to taste

Directions
In a saucepan, bring the water to a boil. Then, boil the eggs for 12 to 13 minutes. Place the eggs in a bowl of ice water.
Peel the eggs and cut them into slices.
Toss the eggs with the remaining ingredients and serve well chilled. Bon appétit!

Old-Fashioned Baby Potato Salad

(Ready in about 20 minutes | Servings 4)
Per serving: Calories: 278; Fat: 14.1g; Carbs: 35.3g; Protein: 4.2g

Ingredients
1 ½ pounds red baby potatoes

1 small red onion, thinly sliced
1 small sweet onion, thinly sliced
2 tablespoons fresh basil, chopped
2 tablespoons fresh parsley, chopped
1/4 cup extra-virgin olive oil
2 tablespoons red wine vinegar
1 teaspoon Dijon mustard
1/4 teaspoon black pepper
1/4 teaspoon cumin seeds
Coarse sea salt, to taste

Directions
Place the potatoes in a stockpot and add the water to cover by 1 inch. Bring to a rolling boil and then, turn to a simmer.

Let it simmer until your potatoes are tender for about 15 minutes. Peel the skins from your potatoes and transfer them to a serving bowl. Cut the potatoes into slices.

Toss the potatoes with the remaining ingredients and keep your salad in the refrigerator until ready to serve.

Bon appétit!

Spicy BBQ Tofu Steaks

(Ready in about 10 minutes + marinating time | Servings 4)

Per serving: Calories: 298; Fat: 22.3g; Carbs: 10.7g; Protein: 19g

Ingredients
16 ounces firm tofu, pressed and cut into steak sized pieces
4 tablespoons fresh lemon juice
1 teaspoon schug sauce
1 tablespoon tamari sauce
4 tablespoons dry white wine
4 tablespoons garlic, pressed
3 tablespoons olive oil
1 teaspoon dried oregano
1 teaspoon dried basil
1 teaspoon dried rosemary
Sea salt and freshly ground pepper, to taste
1/2 teaspoon smoked paprika
2 ounces black olives, sliced
2 Roma tomatoes, sliced
1 red onion, thinly sliced

Directions
Place your tofu, fresh lemon juice, schug sauce, tamari sauce, wine, garlic, olive oil, oregano, basil, rosemary, sea salt, black pepper, and paprika in a ceramic bowl. Let it marinate for about 1 hour.

Transfer your tofu to the preheated grill, reserving the marinade.

Now, grill your tofu for about 5 minutes, basting with the reserved marinade. Turn it over and cook on the other side for a further 5 minutes.

Serve the grilled tofu steaks with the olives, tomatoes, and onion. Bon appétit!

Old-Fashioned Green Beans

(Ready in about 20 minutes | Servings 3)

Per serving: Calories: 218; Fat: 9.7g; Carbs: 28.1g; Protein: 7.3g

Ingredients
1 tablespoon olive oil
1 red onion, chopped
1 carrot, trimmed and chopped
7 ounces king oyster mushrooms, sliced
2 cloves garlic, minced
1 pound green beans
Sea salt and freshly ground black pepper, to taste
1 bay laurel
1 cup cream of mushroom soup
2 large San Marzano tomatoes, pureed
2 tablespoons parsley, roughly chopped

Directions
Heat the olive oil over medium-high heat. Sauté the onion, carrot, and mushrooms for about 4 minutes until tender and aromatic.

Then, sauté the garlic for about 30 seconds or until aromatic.

Add in the green beans, salt, black pepper, bay laurel, soup, and pureed tomatoes. Let it cook for 13 to 15 minutes until green beans are tender.

Ladle into individual bowls and serve garnished with fresh parsley. Bon appétit!

Roasted Broccoli Salad

(Ready in about 25 minutes | Servings 3)

Per serving: Calories: 248; Fat: 18.2g; Carbs: 15.7g; Protein: 7.9g

Ingredients
1 pound broccoli florets
3 tablespoons extra-virgin olive oil
1 ½ tablespoons fresh lemon juice
Sea salt and ground black pepper, to taste
1 teaspoon garlic, pressed
1 cup grape tomatoes, halved
1 Persian cucumber, sliced
1/2 bell pepper, sliced
2 ounces feta cheese, crumbled

Directions
Start by preheating your oven to 420 degrees F.

Toss the broccoli florets with 1 tablespoon of the olive oil and place them on a lightly oiled baking pan.

Roast the broccoli florets for about 25 minutes. Toss the broccoli with the lemon juice, salt, black pepper, garlic, tomatoes, cucumber, bell pepper and the remaining 2 tablespoons of the olive oil.

Top with feta cheese and serve immediately. Bon appétit!

Black-Eyed Bean Salad

(Ready in about 1 hour | Servings 4)

Per serving: Calories: 508; Fat: 21.2g; Carbs: 60.7g; Protein: 22g

Ingredients
3/4 pound black-eyed beans, soaked overnight and drained
3 cups water
1 red onion, chopped

2 San Marzano tomatoes, diced
1/4 cup fresh basil, roughly chopped
1/4 cup fresh parsley, roughly chopped
1 large avocado, pitted, peeled and sliced
2 tablespoons lime juice
1/2 teaspoon hot paprika
1/2 teaspoon dried oregano
1/4 cup extra-virgin olive oil
Sea salt and ground black pepper, to taste
Directions
Bring the water to a boil and add in the black-eyed beans; turn the heat to a simmer and continue to cook until the beans are tender or about 1 hour.
Drain your beans and transfer to a serving bowl. Toss the beans with the remaining ingredients. Taste and adjust the seasonings. Bon appétit!

Oyster Mushroom and Kale Orecchiette

(Ready in about 10 minutes | Servings 4)
Per serving: Calories: 438; Fat: 9.4g; Carbs: 82g; Protein: 13.2g
Ingredients
3/4 pound orecchiette pasta
2 tablespoons olive oil
3 scallion stalks, chopped
1 pound king oyster mushrooms, sliced
2 cloves garlic, sliced
1/2 teaspoon paprika
1/2 teaspoon dried oregano
1/2 teaspoon dried basil
Sea salt and ground black pepper, to taste
Zest of 1 lemon, grated
2 cups kale, torn into pieces
Directions
Cook the orecchiette pasta according to the package directions.
Heat the olive oil in a saucepan over medium-high heat. Now, sauté the scallions and mushrooms until the mushrooms release the liquid or about 5 minutes. Add in the garlic and continue to sauté an additional minute or so.
Season the mushrooms with the paprika, oregano, basil, salt, and black pepper. Add in the lemon zest and kale; let it simmer for about 4 minutes, until the kale has wilted. Bon appétit!

Zucchini Polpette with Greek Sauce

(Ready in about 25 minutes | Servings 4)
Per serving: Calories: 355; Fat: 27g; Carbs: 16.2g; Protein: 11.5g
Ingredients
1 pound zucchini, grated
1/2 cup chickpea flour
1/2 cup tortilla chips, crushed
2 eggs, whisked
1/2 cup red onion, chopped
1/4 cup olive oil
1/2 cup Greek-style yogurt
1 teaspoon Dijon mustard
4 tablespoons mayonnaise

1/2 teaspoon dried dill weed
2 garlic cloves, minced
Directions
Place the grated zucchini in a fine-mesh strainer and set over a bowl. Toss the zucchini with 1 teaspoon of the sea salt and allow it to sit for about 15 minutes. Drain the excess liquid out of the zucchini and place in a mixing bowl.
Add in the chickpea flour, crushed tortilla chips, eggs, and red onion; stir to combine well.
Heat the olive oil in a frying pan over a moderately high heat. Shape the mixture into tablespoon-sized balls and cook for 5 to 6 minutes or until light brown. Meanwhile, whisk the remaining ingredients for the sauce.
Drain the zucchini fritters on paper towels and serve with the sauce on the side. Bon appétit!

Mint and Green Pea Soup

(Ready in about 20 minutes | Servings 3)
Per serving: Calories: 229; Fat: 5.3g; Carbs: 30g; Protein: 15.9g
Ingredients
2 teaspoons olive oil
1 small leek, chopped
2 garlic cloves, minced
3 cups vegetable broth
1 teaspoon dried oregano
1/2 teaspoon dried parsley flakes
1/2 teaspoon dried dill
Sea salt and ground black pepper, to taste
1 pound green peas, fresh or frozen
2 ounces Greek yogurt
1 tablespoon fresh mint leaves, chopped
Directions
In a heavy-bottomed pot, heat the olive oil over a moderate flame. Now, sauté the leek for about 4 minutes until tender and fragrant.
Then, sauté the garlic for about 30 seconds or until aromatic.
Now, add in the broth and spices; bring to a rolling boil and immediately turn the heat to a simmer. Fold in the green peas and continue to simmer for 10 minutes more.
Now, puree the soup in your blender or food processor until creamy and uniform.
Ladle the soup into serving bowls, garnish with yogurt and mint and serve. Enjoy!

New Potato and Green Bean Salad

(Ready in about 15 minutes | Servings 4)
Per serving: Calories: 279; Fat: 14.5g; Carbs: 33.9g; Protein: 4.4g
Ingredients
1 ½ pounds new potatoes
8 ounces green beans
1 tablespoon white vinegar
2 tablespoons lemon juice
4 tablespoons extra-virgin olive oil
1 teaspoons deli mustard

1 teaspoon garlic, minced
1/2 cup scallions, sliced
1/4 teaspoon cumin seeds
Sea salt and ground black pepper, to taste

Directions
Add new potatoes to a deep saucepan and cover them with the cold water. Boil them for about 10 minutes.
Add in the green beans and continue to cook for a further 2 to 3 minutes. Drain the potatoes and green beans and transfer them to a large salad bowl.
Stir in the remaining ingredients and toss to combine well. Taste and adjust the seasonings. Bon appétit!

Authentic Sicilian Caponata

(Ready in about 25 minutes | Servings 4)
Per serving: Calories: 199; Fat: 13.5g; Carbs: 16g; Protein: 5.7g

Ingredients
3 tablespoons olive oil
1 large-sized onion, chopped
4 garlic cloves, minced
1 pound eggplant, unpeeled and cut into bite-sized cubes
2 bell peppers, sliced
2 ripe tomatoes, chopped
1/2 cup dry white wine
2 tablespoons fresh oregano, chopped
2 tablespoons fresh parsley, chopped
2 tablespoons fresh basil, chopped

Directions
Heat the olive oil in a saucepan over medium-high heat. Then, sauté the onion for about 3 minutes until tender and translucent.
Add in the garlic and continue to sauté an additional 30 seconds until it is fragrant.
Add in the eggplant, peppers, tomato, wine, and seasoning mix. Continue to simmer, partially covered, for a further 20 to 25 minutes or until cooked through.
Bon appétit!

Hummus, Feta and Vegetable Dip

(Ready in about 10 minutes | Servings 8)
Per serving: Calories: 157; Fat: 10.3g; Carbs: 11.6g; Protein: 5.8g

Ingredients
8 ounces hummus
1/2 cup Greek-style yogurt
4 tablespoons tahini
2 bell peppers, chopped
1 cup grape tomatoes, chopped
3 ounces sweet corn kernels, thawed and drained
3 ounces Kalamata olives, pitted and sliced
1/2 cup feta cheese, crumbled
1/2 teaspoon dried oregano
1/2 teaspoon dried rosemary
1/2 teaspoon dried basil
Sea salt and ground black pepper, to taste

Directions

Layer the hummus in a serving bowl. In a mixing dish, thoroughly combine the yogurt and tahini.
Place the yogurt over the hummus.
Then, layer the other ingredients in the order listed above. Sprinkle with seasonings and serve with your favorite dippers. Bon appétit!

Oven-Roasted Tofu with Red Onion

(Ready in about 30 minutes | Servings 4)
Per serving: Calories: 218; Fat: 15.4g; Carbs: 10g; Protein: 12g

Ingredients
16 ounces extra-firm tofu, pressed and cubed
2 tablespoons olive oil
1 red onion, cut into wedges
2 cloves garlic, minced
1 teaspoon lemon zest, grated
1 teaspoon dried rosemary
1 teaspoon dried thyme
1 teaspoon dried oregano
Sea salt and ground black pepper, to taste
2 ounces sun-dried tomatoes in olive oil, chopped

Directions
Start by pretreating your oven to 425 degrees F. Toss the tofu cubes with the other ingredients until well coated on all sides. Arrange them on a lightly oiled baking pan.
Bake your tofu in the preheated oven for about 30 minutes. Bon appétit!

Chickpea and Rice Stuffed Peppers

(Ready in about 1 hour | Servings 4)
Per serving: Calories: 498; Fat: 16.3g; Carbs: 71.1g; Protein: 18.2g

Ingredients
1 cup Arborio rice, rinsed
2 tablespoons olive oil
1 medium-sized red onion, chopped
2 cloves garlic, minced
1 large tomato, chopped
12 ounces canned chickpeas, drained and mashed with a fork
Sea salt and ground black pepper, to taste
1/2 teaspoon ground bay leaf
1/2 teaspoon coriander seeds
1 cup pasta sauce
1 cup Pecorino-Romano cheese, shredded

Directions
In a saucepan, bring 2 cups of water and Arborio rice to a boil over medium-high heat. Turn the heat to medium-low and let it simmer until the liquid is fully absorbed or about 20 minutes. Drain your rice and reserve.
In a saucepan, heat the olive oil over a moderately high heat. Now, sauté the onions for about 3 minutes until tender and translucent.
Stir in the garlic and tomato; continue to sauté for 1 to 2 minutes more until aromatic. Str in the reserved rice along with the chickpeas, salt, black pepper, bay leaf, and coriander seeds.

Stuff the peppers and place them in a lightly oiled casserole dish. Pour the pasta sauce into the casserole dish.

Preheat your oven to 360 degrees F.

Bake in the preheated oven for about 20 minutes. Top with the shredded Pecorino-Romano cheese and continue baking an additional 5 to 7 minutes until the cheese has melted. Bon appétit!

Double-Cheese Broccoli Casserole

(Ready in about 40 minutes | Servings 4)
Per serving: Calories: 468; Fat: 26.4g; Carbs: 33.1g; Protein: 25.9g
Ingredients
1 pound broccoli florets
1/2 cup ricotta cheese, room temperature
1 cup cream of celery soup
2 eggs, whisked
1 cup breadcrumbs
1 ½ tablespoons olive oil
1 cup Pecorino-Romano cheese, grated
Directions
Begin by preheating your oven to 360 degrees F. Place the broccoli florets in a lightly oiled casserole dish.

In a mixing bowl, combine the ricotta cheese, celery soup, and eggs. Spoon the mixture over the broccoli florets.

Mix the breadcrumbs with olive oil. Top the casserole with the breadcrumb mixture. Bake for about 30 minutes or until cooked through.

Top with the cheese and continue to bake for 5 to 6 minutes or until the cheese is hot and bubbly. Bon appétit!

Creamed Lima Bean Salad

(Ready in about 1 hour 45 minutes | Servings 4)
Per serving: Calories: 504; Fat: 21.4g; Carbs: 60.3g; Protein: 20.2g
Ingredients
2 cups lima beans, drained and rinsed
1 large tomato, sliced
2 Italian peppers, sliced
1 medium Greek cucumber, sliced
1 medium red onion, thinly sliced
1/4 cup fresh parsley, chopped
2 tablespoons fresh scallions, chopped
2 garlic cloves, sliced
1 tablespoon lemon juice
1 tablespoon red wine vinegar
1/2 cup mayonnaise
1 teaspoon Dijon mustard
Sea salt and freshly ground black pepper, to taste
Directions
Bring 4 cups of water to a boil. Add in the beans and let it boil for 2 to 3 minutes. Let it stand, covered, for approximately 1 hour. Drain, add in the 4 cups of hot water and bring to a rolling boil.

Turn the heat to a simmer; let it cook for 40 to 45 minutes until the beans are tender. Transfer the beans to a salad bowl.

Add in the tomato, peppers, cucumber, onion, parsley, scallion, and garlic.

In a small mixing bowl, thoroughly combine the lemon juice, vinegar, mayonnaise, mustard, salt, and black pepper; whisk to combine well and dress your salad.

Place the salad in the refrigerator until ready to serve. Bon appétit!

Cream of Cauliflower Soup with Yogurt

(Ready in about 25 minutes | Servings 4)
Per serving: Calories: 184; Fat: 9.8g; Carbs: 15.5g; Protein: 12.2g
Ingredients
2 tablespoons olive oil
1/2 teaspoon cumin seeds
4 scallion stalks, chopped
2 cloves garlic, sliced
1 pound cauliflower, cut into florets
3 ½ cups vegetable broth
2 rosemary sprigs
1 bay leaf
Sea salt and ground white pepper, to taste
1/2 cup Greek yogurt
Directions
In a heavy-bottomed pot, heat the olive oil over medium-high heat. Once hot, sauté the cumin seeds for about 30 seconds until aromatic.

Then, cook the scallions and garlic for about 2 minutes or until aromatic.

Add in the cauliflower, vegetable broth, rosemary sprigs, bay leaf, salt, and white pepper, and bring to a rolling boil.

Immediately turn the heat to a simmer, cover, and continue to cook for approximately 18 minutes. Puree the soup in your blender until creamy and uniform. Ladle the soup into individual bowls and garnish with chilled yogurt. Bon appétit!

Egg Salad Niçoise

(Ready in about 15 minutes | Servings 5)
Per serving: Calories: 167; Fat: 9.2g; Carbs: 12.8g; Protein: 10.7g
Ingredients
1 pound green beans, trimmed and cut in halves
5 eggs
Sea salt and ground black pepper, to taste
1 red bell pepper, sliced
1 green bell pepper, sliced
1/4 cup mayonnaise
1/4 cup Greek-style yogurt
1 teaspoon Dijon mustard
1 teaspoon lime zest
1/4 cup drained capers, patted dry
2 scallion stalks, chopped
1/2 teaspoon garlic, minced
1/4 cup Niçoise olives, pitted and halved

Directions

In a saucepan, place the green beans and eggs. Cover them with cool water by 1 inch, and cook over medium heat. Let it cook for about 10 minutes.

Drain and transfer the green bean to a salad bowl. Peel the eggs, slice them into quarters, and reserve. Season your beans and eggs with salt and black pepper.

Add in the peppers, mayonnaise, Greek yogurt, mustard, lime zest, capers, scallions, and garlic; toss to combine well.

Garnish your salad with the hard-boiled eggs and Niçoise olives; serve well-chilled. Bon appétit!

Italian-Style Zucchini Lasagna with Mushrooms

(Ready in about 50 minutes | Servings 4)

Per serving: Calories: 487; Fat: 31.2g; Carbs: 23g; Protein: 33.5g

Ingredients

2 tablespoons olive oil
1 ½ pounds Cremini mushrooms, sliced
1 medium red onion, chopped
1 teaspoon garlic, minced
2 cups marinara sauce
1/2 teaspoon cayenne pepper
1/2 teaspoon dried oregano
1/2 teaspoon dried basil
1/2 teaspoon dried rosemary
1/4 teaspoon ground bay leaf
Sea salt and ground black pepper, to taste
1 pound zucchini, thinly sliced
10 ounces soft cheese
1 cup Pecorino-Romano cheese, grated
2 eggs, whisked

Directions

Start by preheating your oven to 395 degrees F.

In a frying pan, heat the olive oil over a moderately high heat. Cook the mushrooms, onion, and garlic for about 3 minutes or until they've softened.

Pour 1/2 of the marinara sauce into the pan and stir to combine. Add in the seasonings.

Then, in a mixing bowl, thoroughly combine the cheese and eggs.

Spread 1/2 of the marinara sauce onto the bottom of a lightly oiled baking dish.

Place 1/2 of the zucchini slices on top of the marinara sauce.

Top with 1/2 of the mushrooms sauce and 1/2 of the cheese mixture. Repeat these layers, ending with the cheese layer.

Bake your lasagna in the preheated oven for about 45 minutes. Bon appétit!

Delicious Cucumber Rounds

(Ready in about 10 minutes | Servings 4)

Per serving: Calories: 217; Fat: 16g; Carbs: 9.1g; Protein: 8.6g

Ingredients

2 Greek cucumbers, cut into 1/2-inch thick rounds

2 medium-sized tomatoes, chopped
1 Italian pepper, chopped
7 ounces feta cheese, crumbled
2 tablespoons mayonnaise
1 tablespoon Italian seasoning mix
2 heaping tablespoon fresh parsley leaves, roughly chopped

Directions

Place the cucumber rounds on a serving platter.

In a mixing bowl, thoroughly combine the tomatoes, pepper, cheese, mayo, and seasoning mix until well combined.

Pipe or spoon the tomato/cheese mixture onto the cucumber rounds. Garish with the fresh Italian parsley and enjoy!

Bruschetta with Hummus and Basil

(Ready in about 10 minutes | Servings 4)

Per serving: Calories: 422; Fat: 19g; Carbs: 52.6g; Protein: 10.6g

Ingredients

12 ounces baguette, cut into thin slices
2 garlic cloves, peeled and halved
4 tablespoons extra-virgin olive oil
2 tablespoons deli mustard
2 ripe tomatoes, chopped
1/2 cup hummus, preferably homemade
Sea salt and ground black pepper, to taste

Directions

Toast the bread slices at 400 degrees F for 5 to 6 minutes until lightly browned around the edges.

Rub one side of each bread slice with the garlic and drizzle the other side with the olive oil and mustard using a pastry brush.

Divide the tomatoes and hummus between the bread slices. Now, sprinkle each bruschetta with salt and black pepper to taste and serve. Bon appétit!

Tangy Cheese Dipping Sauce

(Ready in about 10 minutes | Servings 8)

Per serving: Calories: 224; Fat: 18g; Carbs: 2.9g; Protein: 11.6g

Ingredients

4 ounces feta cheese, crumbled
6 ounces goat cheese
8 ounces Greek-style yogurt
2 ounces mayonnaise
1 teaspoon dill, chopped
1 teaspoon lemon zest
Sea salt and black pepper, to taste
1 tablespoon olive oil
2 ounces green olives, pitted and sliced

Directions

Thoroughly combine the cheese, yogurt, mayonnaise, dill, lemon zest, salt, and black pepper in a mixing bowl.

Place your dip in a serving bowl. Drizzle with the olive oil and garnish with olives.

Serve with pita chips or veggies sticks, if desired. Enjoy!

Creamed Broccoli Soup with Pecorino-Romano

(Ready in about 25 minutes | Servings 4)
Per serving: Calories: 274; Fat: 16.8g; Carbs: 12.5g; Protein: 21.2g
Ingredients
2 tablespoons olive oil, plus more for drizzling
4 scallion stalks, chopped
4 green garlic stalks, chopped
1 pound broccoli florets
4 cups vegetable broth
Sea salt and ground black pepper, to taste
1 teaspoon dried basil
1/2 teaspoon dried oregano
1 teaspoon dried sage
4 ounces Pecorino-Romano cheese, grated
Directions
In a heavy-bottomed pot, heat the olive oil over medium-high heat. Once hot, sauté the scallions and garlic for about 2 minutes or until aromatic.
Add in the broccoli, vegetable broth, salt, black pepper, basil, oregano, and sage; bring to a rolling boil.
Immediately turn the heat to a simmer, cover, and continue to cook for approximately 18 minutes.
Puree the soup in your blender until creamy and uniform. Reheat the soup, stir in the cheese and let it simmer for 2 to 3 minutes more or until everything is well incorporated.
Ladle the soup into individual bowls and enjoy!

Butter Bean Mash

(Ready in about 1 hour 45 minutes | Servings 8)
Per serving: Calories: 187; Fat: 3.7g; Carbs: 29.7g; Protein: 9.7g
Ingredients
2 cups dry butterbeans, presoaked overnight
2 tablespoons olive oil
1 red onion, finely chopped
2 cloves garlic, chopped
1/2 teaspoon cumin seeds
1/2 teaspoon turmeric
1/2 teaspoon dried basil
1/2 teaspoon dried oregano
1/2 teaspoon dried marjoram
1 teaspoon cayenne pepper
1/4 teaspoon mustard seeds
Sea salt and ground black pepper, to taste
Directions
Bring 4 cups of water to a boil. Add in the beans and let it boil for 2 to 3 minutes. Let it stand, covered, for approximately 1 hour. Drain, add in the 4 cups of hot water and bring to a rolling boil.
Turn the heat to a simmer; let it cook for 40 to 45 minutes until the beans are tender. Transfer the beans to a mixing bowl.
Heat the olive oil over medium-high flame. Once hot, sauté the onion for 2 to minutes until aromatic and

translucent. Add in the garlic and seasonings and continue to sauté for 1 minute more until aromatic. Add the sautéed mixture to the mixing bowl with the beans. Mash the ingredients or process them in your blender to desired texture. Enjoy!

Parmesan, Penne and Broccoli Bake

(Ready in about 35 minutes | Servings 4)
Per serving: Calories: 551; Fat: 27.4g; Carbs: 48.1g; Protein: 31g
Ingredients
8 ounces penne pasta
1 pound small broccoli florets
1 cup cream of celery soup
2 eggs, whisked
1 cup soft cheese
1/2 cup crackers, crashed
1 ½ tablespoons olive oil
1 cup parmesan cheese, grated
Directions
Cook the pasta according to the manufacturer's instructions; drain and transfer to a lightly oiled baking dish.
Place the broccoli florets in the boiling water and cook for 2 to 3 minutes. Drain the broccoli florets and transfer them to the baking dish.
Preheat your oven to 360 degrees F.
In a mixing bowl, combine the soup, eggs, cheese. Spoon the mixture over the broccoli florets.
Mix the crackers with olive oil and parmesan cheese. Top the casserole with the parmesan cheese mixture. Bake for about 30 minutes or until cooked through. Bon appétit!

Grilled Green Bean Salad

(Ready in about 10 minutes | Servings 3)
Per serving: Calories: 261; Fat: 16.5g; Carbs: 25.1g; Protein: 9g
Ingredients
2 tablespoons extra-virgin olive oil
3/4 pound green beans, trimmed and cut into halves
Sea salt and ground black pepper, to taste
1/2 teaspoon cayenne pepper
3 scallion stalks, sliced
1 San Marzano tomato, diced
2 Italian peppers, sliced
1 garlic clove, minced
2 tablespoons tahini
2 tablespoons balsamic vinegar
1 teaspoon Dijon mustard
1 tablespoon soy sauce
Directions
Heat the olive oil in a grill pan over a moderately high heat. Now, grill your beans for about 8 minutes. Toss grilled beans with salt, black pepper, cayenne pepper, scallion, tomato, and peppers.
In a small mixing dish, whisk the garlic, tahini, vinegar, mustard, and soy sauce. Drizzle the vinaigrette over the salad and toss to combine. Bon appétit!

Grilled Tofu Vegetable Kabobs

(Ready in about 20 minutes + marinating time | Servings 4)

Per serving: Calories: 428; Fat: 20.7g; Carbs: 52.2g; Protein: 14.7g

Ingredients

16 ounces extra-firm tofu, pressed and cubed
1 cup tomato puree
2 tablespoons wine vinegar
4 tablespoons olive oil
1 tablespoon honey
2 garlic cloves, minced
1 teaspoon onion powder
1 teaspoon Dijon mustard
Sea salt and black pepper, to taste
1/2 teaspoon cayenne pepper

For the kebabs:
1 red onion, cut into wedges
1 zucchini, diced
1 cup cherry tomatoes
1 small pineapple, diced

Directions

Place your tofu, tomato puree, vinegar, olive oil, honey, garlic, onion powder, mustard, salt, black pepper, and cayenne pepper in a ceramic bowl.

Allow it to marinate for about 30 minutes; reserve the marinade.

Tread your tofu, veggies, and pineapple onto soaked bamboo skewers; transfer them to the preheated grill.

Grill your kabobs over medium heat for about 14 minutes, basting with the reserved marinade and turning them every few minutes. Bon appétit!

PIZZA & PASTA

Basic Homemade Pizza

(Ready in about 1 hour 30 minutes | Servings 3)
Per serving: Calories: 660; Fat: 11.4g; Carbs: 98g;
Protein: 29.2g
Ingredients
3/4 cups warm water
1/2 package active dry yeast
1 teaspoon honey
3 cups all-purpose flour
1/2 teaspoon flaky sea salt
2 tablespoons olive oil
8 ounces pizza sauce
1/2 teaspoon dried rosemary
1 teaspoon dried parsley flakes
1 teaspoon dried oregano
1 teaspoon dried basil
Sea salt, to taste
1/2 pound cremini mushrooms, chopped
1 Italian pepper, chopped
1 cup mozzarella cheese, shredded
Directions
Mix the water, yeast, and honey and let it rest for
approximately 5 minutes. Stir in the flour, salt and oil,
and beat on low speed for 2 minutes.
Turn the dough out onto a lightly floured surface.
Knead the dough with lightly floured hands for 3 to 4
minutes or until elastic. If your dough slowly bounces
back when you poke it with your finger, it is ready.
Cover with a plastic wrap and let it rise in a warm
place until doubled, about 1 hour.
On a lightly floured work surface, gently flatten the
dough into a disc using a rolling pin.
Press the crust into a parchment-lined pizza pan.
Spread the pizza sauce, rosemary, parsley, oregano,
and basil over the crust.
Top with the mushrooms, peppers, and cheese.
Sprinkle with salt to taste.
Preheat your oven to 425 degrees F.
Bake in the preheated oven for 20 to 25 minutes or
until the crust is lightly browned and cheese is hot
and bubbly.
Slice your pizza and serve immediately. Bon appétit!

Tuna Pasta Salad

(Ready in about 15 minutes | Servings 4)
Per serving: Calories: 366; Fat: 8.9g; Carbs: 55.8g;
Protein: 19.3g
Ingredients
8 ounces bow tie pasta
8 ounces canned tuna in oil, drained
1 medium-sized red onion, chopped
1/2 teaspoon garlic, minced
2 bell peppers, deseeded and diced
1/4 cup fresh basil, chopped
1 small Greek cucumber, sliced
2 cups rocket lettuce
2 cups baby spinach

1 tablespoon fresh lime juice
1/4 cup mayonnaise
1/4 cup Greek-style yogurt
1 teaspoon honey
1/2 teaspoon chili pepper flakes
Sea salt and ground black pepper, to taste
2 ounces Niçoises olives, pitted and sliced
Directions
Cook the pasta according to the package directions.
Drain and transfer to a salad bowl. Add in the canned
tuna, onion, garlic, peppers, basil, cucumber, rocket
lettuce, and spinach.
Make the dressing by whisking the lime juice,
mayonnaise, Greek-style yogurt, honey, chili pepper
flakes, salt, and black pepper.
Dress your salad and toss to coat well. Garnish with
olives and serve well-chilled. Bon appétit!

Spaghetti with Mushrooms and Cheese

(Ready in about 30 minutes | Servings 4)
Per serving: Calories: 269; Fat: 16.4g; Carbs: 23.1g;
Protein: 8.8g
Ingredients
8 ounces whole-wheat spaghetti
2 tablespoons olive oil
1 red onion, sliced
1 cup button mushrooms, sliced
1 cup cremini mushrooms, sliced
3 cloves garlic
2 ripe tomatoes, chopped
4 ounces Kalamata olives, pitted and sliced
Sea salt and ground black pepper, to taste
1/2 teaspoon cayenne pepper
1/2 teaspoon dried oregano
1/2 teaspoon dried basil
1/2 cup parmesan cheese, grated
Directions
Cook the spaghetti according to the package
directions; drain and reserve.
Meanwhile, heat the olive oil in a frying pan over
medium-high flame. Once hot, sauté the onion and
mushrooms until they've softened or about 4
minutes.
Add in the garlic and continue to sauté an additional
30 seconds until aromatic.
Now, stir in the tomatoes, olives, and spices. Now, stir
the reserved pasta into the pan and toss to combine
well.
Spoon into individual bowls and serve garnished
with parmesan cheese. Bon appétit!

Old-Fashioned Pizza Sandwiches with Turkey

(Ready in about 30 minutes | Servings 4)
Per serving: Calories: 603; Fat: 26.2g; Carbs: 61.1g;
Protein: 30g
Ingredients

1 pound pizza dough, divide into four pieces
1/2 pound turkey breasts, sliced into strips
1 cup grape tomatoes, halved
4 (1-inch) slices Halloumi cheese
1 small-sized red onion, sliced
1 tablespoon mustard
2 ounces black olives, pitted and sliced
Directions
Flatten the dough into mini pizzas using a rolling pin. Then, preheat a lightly oiled nonstick skillet. Cook mini pizzas for 7 to 8 minutes or until golden-brown; reserve.
Heat the olive oil in the skillet. Then, sear the meat for about 5 minutes, stirring periodically to promote even cooking.
Top each mini pizza crust with the browned meat, tomatoes, cheese, onion, mustard, and olives. Fold the crust in half over filling and serve warm. Bon appétit!

Vegetarian Skillet Pizza

(Ready in about 25 minutes | Servings 4)
Per serving: Calories: 613; Fat: 37.2g; Carbs: 58.8g; Protein: 16.8g
Ingredients
3/4 pound pizza dough
1 teaspoon olive oil
1/2 marinara sauce
1 cup Provolone cheese, shredded
1 Italian pepper, sliced
1 small red onion, sliced
5-6 fresh basil leaves, for garnish
Directions
Stretch and roll out the pizza dough; divide the dough into two pieces. Using a rolling pin, roll each piece of the dough into a round to fit your nonstick skillet.
Brush the nonstick skillet with a cooking oil; preheat the skillet over medium-high heat.
Cook the pizza crust for about 2 minutes until large bubbles form on top. Now, spread the toppings and reduce the heat to medium.
Cook the pizza, covered, for about 5 minutes or until the cheese has melted. Repeat with the other pizza and the remaining toppings.
Garnish with fresh basil leaves and serve hot. Bon appétit!

Breakfast Pizza Waffles

(Ready in about 15 minutes | Servings 4)
Per serving: Calories: 344; Fat: 15.3g; Carbs: 32.2g; Protein: 16g
Ingredients
8 ounces refrigerated crescent rolls
6 ounces tomato sauce
1/2 teaspoon dried oregano
3 ounces prosciutto, sliced
1 cup Mizithra cheese, shredded
Directions

Unroll the crescent rolls and separate them into rectangles.
Divide the dough between rectangles.
Then, broil your pizza waffles for about 4 minutes until the cheese has melted. Bon appétit!

Traditional Spaghetti Bolognese

(Ready in about 25 minutes | Servings 4)
Per serving: Calories: 717; Fat: 13.4g; Carbs: 101.2g; Protein: 31.3g
Ingredients
9 ounces spaghetti
1 tablespoon olive oil
1 red onion, chopped
1 carrot, trimmed and grated
3/4 pound ground chuck
1/2 cup dry white wine
26 ounces tomato passata
2 sprigs thyme
2 bay leaves
2 beef bouillon cubes
1 cup water
Sea salt and ground black pepper, to taste
3 ounces parmesan cheese, preferably freshly grated
Directions
Cook the spaghetti according to the package directions; drain and reserve.
Meanwhile, heat the olive oil in a frying pan over medium-high flame. Once hot, sauté the onion and carrot until they've softened or about 4 minutes.
Add in the ground chuck and continue to cook, breaking it up with a fork, until browned.
Add a splash of wine and bring to a simmer, scraping the bottom of the pan, until the alcohol smell is gone. Now, stir in the tomato passata, thyme, bay leaves, bouillon cubes, and water. Continue to cook for 15 minutes more until cooked through.
Season with salt and pepper to taste. Spoon the Bolognese sauce over warm spaghetti and garnish with parmesan cheese. Bon appétit!

Kid-Friendly Pizza Bites

(Ready in about 15 minutes | Servings 3)
Per serving: Calories: 297; Fat: 9.4g; Carbs: 41.2g; Protein: 11.3g
Ingredients
6 ounces refrigerated buttermilk biscuits
1/2 cup tomato sauce
1 teaspoon granulated garlic
1/2 teaspoon onion powder
1/2 teaspoon dried oregano
1/2 teaspoon dried basil
6 ounces button mushrooms, sliced
8 Kalamata olives, pitted and sliced
1/2 cup Pecorino-Romano cheese, grated
Directions
Start by preheating your oven to 395 degrees F. Then, line a baking sheet with a piece of parchment paper.
Separate each biscuit into four layers and arrange them on the prepared baking sheet.

Divide the topping ingredients between your biscuits. Bake in the preheated oven for about 8 minutes or until the cheese has melted. Bon appétit!

Old-Fashioned Lasagna

(Ready in about 1 hour 40 minutes | Servings 8)
Per serving: Calories: 537; Fat: 23.7g; Carbs: 43.3g; Protein: 37.8g

Ingredients
1 tablespoon olive oil
1 red onion, minced
1 ½ pounds ground chuck
4 cloves garlic, crushed
2 ripe tomatoes, chopped
2 cups pasta sauce
2 cups beef bone broth
1/2 teaspoon dried oregano
1 teaspoon dried parsley flakes
1/2 teaspoon dried rosemary
1 teaspoon dried basil
Sea salt and ground black pepper, to taste
3/4 pound lasagna noodles
1 large egg
12 ounces whole-milk ricotta
2 cups parmesan cheese, grated

Directions
Heat the olive oil in a frying pan over medium-high heat; now, cook the onion and ground beef for about 4 minutes.
Add in the garlic and continue to cook an additional 30 seconds or until aromatic. Stir in the tomatoes, pasta sauce, and beef bone broth.
Add in the seasonings and bring to a boil.
Immediately turn the heat to a simmer; let it simmer for 1 hour, stirring periodically.
Meanwhile, cook the lasagna noodles in a large pot of salted boiling water according to the package instructions. Drain the noodles and toss with a bit of olive oil to prevent them from sticking together.
In a mixing bowl, whisk the egg until pale and frothy; add in thericotta cheese and mix to combine well.
Now, spoon 1/3 of the beef sauce into the bottom of a lightly oiled casserole dish. Top the sauce layer with a single layer of lasagna noodles, a layer of egg/ricotta mixture, and a single layer of parmesan cheese.
Repeat the layers, ending with the parmesan cheese layer.
Cover your lasagna with a piece of aluminum foil and bake in the preheated oven at 375 degrees F for 15 minutes. Increase the temperature to 390 degrees F, remove the foil, and continue baking for about 20 minutes more.
Garnish with some extra herbs and serve warm. Bon appétit!

Old-Fashioned Pasta Bake

(Ready in about 50 minutes | Servings 6)
Per serving: Calories: 487; Fat: 16.9g; Carbs: 53.6g; Protein: 33.7g

Ingredients
10 ounces tagliatelle pasta
1 tablespoon olive oil
1 ½ pounds ground chuck
1 red onion, chopped
1 red bell pepper, seeded and chopped
2 garlic cloves, minced
20 ounces marinara sauce
2 ripe San Marzano tomatoes, crushed
6 ounces canned artichoke hearts
1 teaspoon Italian seasoning mix
1 cup Pecorino-Romano cheese, grated

Directions
Cook your pasta according to the package directions.
Heat the olive oil in a frying pan over medium-high heat. Now, cook the ground chuck until no longer pink, crumbling it with a fork.
Add in the onion and garlic and continue to cook for 1 minute more. Stir in the marinara sauce, tomatoes, artichoke hearts, and seasoning. Bring to a boil and immediately reduce the heat to a simmer.
Let it simmer for 18 to 20 minutes or until cooked through. Stir in the cooked pasta and transfer the mixture to a lightly oiled casserole dish.
Sprinkle the cheese on top. Bake in the preheated oven at 350 degrees F for about 30 minutes or until the cheese is hot and bubbly. Bon appétit!

Pasta and Mushroom Stroganoff

(Ready in about 25 minutes | Servings 4)
Per serving: Calories: 621; Fat: 24.2g; Carbs: 78.2g; Protein: 24.8g

Ingredients
12 ounces spaghetti
2 tablespoons olive oil
1 red onion, chopped
1 bell pepper, sliced
1 pound button mushrooms, sliced
3 cloves garlic, minced
1 teaspoon stone-ground mustard
1/2 teaspoon cayenne pepper
1 rosemary sprig, chopped
1 bay leaf
Sea salt and ground black pepper, to taste
1/4 cup white wine
1 cup cream of mushrooms soup
2 ounces Kalamata olives, sliced
1 cup manouri cheese, crumbled

Directions
Cook the spaghetti according to the package directions; drain and reserve.
Meanwhile, heat the olive oil in a frying pan over medium-high flame. Once hot, sauté the onion and pepper until they've softened or about 4 minutes.
Add in the mushrooms and continue to cook until they release the liquid.
Add a splash of wine and bring to a simmer, scraping the bottom of the pan, until the alcohol smell is gone.
Add in the garlic and continue to cook, stirring frequently, for about 30 seconds.

Now, stir in the mustard, cayenne pepper, rosemary, bay leaf, salt, black pepper, remaining wine, and mushrooms soup. Continue to cook for 15 minutes more until cooked through.

Stir in the reserved spaghetti, Kalamata olives, and cheese. Let it simmer for a few minutes more or until the cheese has melted. Bon appétit!

Old-Fashioned Margherita Pizza

(Ready in about 1 hour 30 minutes | Servings 5)
Per serving: Calories: 549; Fat: 14.4g; Carbs: 85g; Protein: 18.7g
Ingredients
1 ¼ cups warm water
1 package active dry yeast
1 teaspoon brown sugar
4 cups all-purpose flour
1/2 teaspoon sea salt
2 tablespoons olive oil
14 ounces pizza sauce
1 teaspoon Italian herb mix
1 cup Provolone cheese, shredded cheese
5-6 fresh basil leaves
Directions
Mix the water, yeast, and sugar and let it rest for approximately 5 minutes. Stir in the flour, salt, and oil, and beat on low speed for 2 minutes.

Turn the dough out onto a lightly floured surface. Knead the dough with lightly floured hands for 3 to 4 minutes or until elastic. If your dough slowly bounces back when you poke it with your finger, it is ready to rise.

Cover with a plastic wrap and let it rise in a warm place until doubled in size, about 1 hour.

On a lightly floured work surface, gently flatten the dough into a disc using your floured hands or a rolling pin.

Preheat your oven to 425 degrees F.

Press the crust into a parchment-lined pizza pan. Spread the pizza sauce and Italian herb mix over the crust.

Top your pizza with the cheese and bake in the preheated oven for 20 to 25 minutes or until the crust is lightly browned and cheese is hot and bubbly. Serve hot, garnished with fresh basil leaves and enjoy!

Penne with Cheese and Swiss Chard

(Ready in about 20 minutes | Servings 4)
Per serving: Calories: 439; Fat: 17.2g; Carbs: 58.6g; Protein: 13.5g
Ingredients
8 ounces penne pasta
2 tablespoons olive oil
1 red onion, chopped
2 garlic cloves, minced
10 ounces pasta sauce
1/2 teaspoon dried oregano
1/2 teaspoon dried basil
 Sea salt and ground black pepper, to taste
2 ounces green olives, sliced

2 cups Swiss chard
1 cup Pecorino-Romano cheese, grated
Directions
Cook the pasta according to the package directions; drain and reserve.

Meanwhile, heat the olive oil in a frying pan over medium-high flame. Once hot, sauté the onion until tender and translucent or about 4 minutes.

Add in the garlic and continue to sauté an additional 30 seconds until aromatic.

Now, stir in the pasta sauce, oregano, basil, salt, black pepper, olives, and chard. Now, stir the reserved pasta into the pan and toss to combine well.

Spoon into individual bowls and serve garnished with Pecorino-Romano cheese. Bon appétit!

Puff Pastry Pizza

(Ready in about 20 minutes | Servings 4)
Per serving: Calories: 541; Fat: 36.2g; Carbs: 38.6g; Protein: 16.5g
Ingredients
10 ounces puff pastry, ready-rolled
1/2 cup passata sauce
1/2 teaspoon dried oregano
1/2 teaspoon dried rosemary
1/2 teaspoon dried basil
1/2 teaspoon granulated garlic
3 ounces Parma ham slices
1 cup parmesan cheese, shaved
2 ounces green olives, pitted and sliced
1 handful rocket lettuce
Directions
Begin by preheating your oven to 370 degrees F.

Unroll the crescent dough sheet and press it into the bottom of a parchment-lined cookie sheet.

Bake for about 10 minutes or until golden brown. Let it cool completely.

Thoroughly combine the passata sauce and spices. Spread the mixture over the crust.

Top with the Parma ham, cheese, and olives; bake for 5 minutes more or until the cheese has melted.

Garnish with fresh rocket lettuce and enjoy!

Easy Stovetop Pepperoni Pizza

(Ready in about 2 hours 20 minutes | Servings 4)
Per serving: Calories: 510; Fat: 21.2g; Carbs: 51.6g; Protein: 27g
Ingredients
2 cups all-purpose flour
3/4 teaspoon active dry yeast
1/2 sea salt
2/3 cup warm water
1 tablespoon olive oil
1/2 cup tomato sauce
1/2 teaspoon dried oregano
1/2 teaspoon granulated garlic
1/2 teaspoon granulated onion
12 slices pepperoni
8 ounces mozzarella cheese, grated
5-6 Kalamata olives, sliced

A few fresh basil leaves, for garnish
Directions
Thoroughly combine the flour, yeast, and salt. Slowly pour in the water and olive oil and mix to combine. Knead the dough on a lightly floured surface until it becomes elastic and smooth. Allow the dough to rise for about 2 hours in a warm place.

Then, stretch the dough into a thin round to fit your skillet. Heat a lightly oiled nonstick skillet over medium flame.

Cook the crust for about 2 minutes. Turn it over, turn the heat to low, and arrange the toppings. Continue to cook for 3 to 4 minutes longer, until the cheese has melted.

Garnish with fresh basil leaves and serve hot. Bon appétit!

Ground Turkey and Pasta Casserole

(Ready in about 50 minutes | Servings 6)
Per serving: Calories: 551; Fat: 22.7g; Carbs: 56g; Protein: 32.4g
Ingredients
3/4 pound ziti pasta
1 tablespoon olive oil
3/4 pound ground turkey
1 medium leek, sliced
4 garlic cloves, chopped
1 tablespoon Italian seasoning mix
2 large tomatoes, crushed
1 cup pizza sauce
1 cup ricotta cheese
2 cups Pecorino-Romano cheese, grated
Directions
Cook your pasta according to the package directions. Heat the olive oil in a frying pan over medium-high heat. Now, cook the ground turkey until no longer pink, crumbling it with a fork.

Add in the leek and garlic and continue to cook for 1 minute more. Stir in the Italian seasoning mix, tomatoes, and pizza sauce. Bring to a boil and immediately reduce the heat to a simmer.

Let it simmer for 18 to 20 minutes or until cooked through. Stir in the cooked pasta and ricotta cheese; transfer the mixture to a lightly oiled casserole dish. Sprinkle the Pecorino-Romano cheese on the top.

Bake in the preheated oven at 350 degrees F for about 30 minutes or until the cheese is hot and bubbly. Bon appétit!

Keto Pizza Waffles

(Ready in about 20 minutes | Servings 2)
Per serving: Calories: 346; Fat: 24.6g; Carbs: 13.6g; Protein: 17g
Ingredients
3 eggs
3 tablespoons Pecorino-Romano cheese, grated
3 tablespoons almond flour
1 teaspoon psyllium husk powder
1/2 teaspoon baking powder
1 tablespoon olive oil

1/3 cup tomato sauce
1/2 teaspoon dried oregano
1/2 teaspoon dried basil
1/2 teaspoon dried parsley
1/2 teaspoon granulated garlic
1/2 teaspoon onion powder
12 black olives, pitted and sliced
2 ounces feta cheese, crumbled
Directions
In your blender or food processor, thoroughly combine the eggs, Pecorino-Romano cheese, almond flour, psyllium husk powder, baking powder, and olive oil. Process until everything is well incorporated.

Then, preheat your waffle iron; spoon 1/2 of the batter into the waffle iron; repeat with the remaining ingredients.

Spread the tomato sauce and spices on the top of each waffle. Top with the olives and feta cheese. Place under the preheated broiler for about 5 minutes or until the cheese has melted. Bon appétit!

Individual Egg Pizzas with Onion

(Ready in about 1 hour 30 minutes | Servings 4)
Per serving: Calories: 680; Fat: 15.4g; Carbs: 95g; Protein: 29g
Ingredients
1 ¼ cups warm water
1 package active dry yeast
1 teaspoon brown sugar
4 cups all-purpose flour
1/2 teaspoon sea salt
2 tablespoons olive oil
10 ounces pizza sauce
1 red onion, thinly sliced
1 cup mozzarella cheese, shredded
4 eggs
1 teaspoon dried oregano
2 ounces Kalamata olives, pitted
Directions
Mix the water, yeast, and sugar and let it rest for approximately 5 minutes. Stir in the flour, salt, and oil, and beat on low speed for 2 minutes.

Turn the dough out onto a lightly floured surface. Knead the dough with lightly floured hands for 3 to 4 minutes or until elastic. If your dough slowly bounces back when you poke it with your finger, it is ready to rise.

Cover with a plastic wrap and let it rise in a warm place until doubled in size, about 1 hour. Divide the dough into four balls.

On a lightly floured work surface, gently flatten each ball into a disc using your floured hands or a rolling pin.

Preheat your oven to 425 degrees F.

Lower the crust into parchment-lined pizza pans. Spread the pizza sauce over the crust. Top your pizza with the onion and cheese; crack an egg on the top of each pizza. Scatter the oregano and olives over the top.

Bake in the preheated oven for 20 to 25 minutes or until the crust is lightly browned and cheese is hot and bubbly.
Bon appétit!

One-Pot Chicken Pasta

(Ready in about 25 minutes | Servings 4)
Per serving: Calories: 620; Fat: 18.4g; Carbs: 79g; Protein: 37.7g
Ingredients
1 tablespoon olive oil
1 pound chicken fillets, cut into small pieces
1 medium leek, chopped
2 cloves garlic, minced
1 cup marinara sauce
1 cup chicken bone broth
Sea salt and ground black pepper, to taste
1 teaspoon poultry seasoning mix
12 ounces bow tie pasta
1 cup feta cheese, crumbled
2 ounces Kalamata olives, pitted and sliced
1 tablespoon fresh basil leaves
Directions
Heat the olive oil in a saucepan over medium-high flame. Once hot, sear the chicken until no longer pink or about 4 minutes.
Add in the leek and garlic and continue to sauté an additional 2 minutes until aromatic.
Now, stir in the marinara sauce, chicken broth, salt, pepper, poultry seasoning mix, and pasta; bring to a boil. Immediately reduce the heat to a simmer and continue to cook for about 15 minutes.
Spoon into individual bowls and serve garnished with feta cheese, olives, and basil leaves. Bon appétit!

Rich and Easy Vegetarian Lasagna

(Ready in about 1 hour 50 minutes | Servings 6)
Per serving: Calories: 492; Fat: 19.7g; Carbs: 59.1g; Protein: 21.5g
Ingredients
1 tablespoon olive oil
1 celery, chopped
1 carrot, chopped
1 Italian pepper, chopped
1 cup button mushrooms, sliced
1 zucchini, diced
1 red onion, chopped
2 garlic cloves, minced
2 ounces green olives, pitted and sliced
2 cups pasta sauce
Sea salt and ground black pepper, to taste
1/2 teaspoon paprika
1/2 teaspoon dried oregano
1/2 teaspoon dried basil
1/2 teaspoon dried rosemary
1 teaspoon dried parsley flakes
1 cup cream of mushroom soup
15 lasagna noodles
1 ½ cups ricotta cheese, divided
1 ½ cups Pecorino-Romano cheese, freshly grated

Directions
Heat the olive oil in a frying pan over medium-high heat; now, cook the celery, carrot, pepper, mushrooms, zucchini, and onion for about 4 minutes or until they've softened.
Add in the garlic and green olives, and continue to cook an additional 30 seconds or until aromatic. Stir in the pasta sauce, seasonings, and mushroom soup. Bring to a boil. Immediately turn the heat to a simmer; let it simmer for 1 hour, stirring periodically. Meanwhile, cook the lasagna noodles in a large pot of salted boiling water according to the package instructions. Drain the noodles and toss with a bit of olive oil to prevent them from sticking together.
Now, spoon 1/3 of the vegetable mixture into the bottom of a lightly oiled casserole dish. Top the vegetable layer with a single layer of lasagna noodles, a layer of ricotta cheese, and a single layer of the grated Pecorino-Romano cheese.
Repeat the layers, ending with the grated Pecorino-Romano cheese.
Cover your lasagna with a piece of aluminum foil and bake in the preheated oven at 375 degrees F for 15 minutes. Increase the temperature to 390 degrees F, remove the foil, and continue baking for about 20 minutes more.
Allow your lasagna to cool for 10 minutes before slicing and serving. Bon appétit!

Roasted Veggie Rotini Salad

(Ready in about 35 minutes | Servings 4)
Per serving: Calories: 359; Fat: 17.7g; Carbs: 45.2g; Protein: 7.5g
Ingredients
7 ounces rotini pasta
3 tablespoons extra-virgin olive oil
1 small zucchini, diced
2 bell peppers, seeded and sliced
1 cup cherry tomatoes, sliced
1 red onion, thinly sliced
1 Persian cucumber, sliced
1/2 teaspoon garlic, minced
Sea salt and ground black pepper, to taste
2 tablespoons fresh basil leaves, roughly chopped
2 tablespoons fresh parsley leaves, roughly chopped
2 tablespoons fresh scallions, roughly chopped
1 tablespoon sun-dried tomatoes in olive oil, chopped
2 ounces Niçoise olives, pitted and sliced
1/2 cup feta cheese, crumbled
Directions
Cook the pasta according to the package directions
In the meantime, toss the zucchini, peppers, and tomatoes with 1 tablespoon of the olive oil. Roast the vegetables in the preheated oven at 390 degrees F for about 35 minutes or until tender and slightly charred.
Toss the pasta with the roasted vegetables; add in the remaining olive oil, onion, cucumber, garlic, salt, pepper, basil, parsley, scallions, and sun-dried tomatoes. Toss to combine well.

Top with the olives and feta cheese and serve at room temperature. Enjoy!

Shrimp Stuffed Rigatoni

(Ready in about 15 minutes | Servings 5)

Per serving: Calories: 522; Fat: 20.6g; Carbs: 57.9g; Protein: 28.2g

Ingredients
9 ounces rigatoni pasta
2 tablespoons olive oil
1 carrot, trimmed and chopped
1 zucchini, diced
1 large onion, chopped
3 cloves garlic, minced
1 cup pasta sauce
1/4 cup dry white wine
1/2 cup cream of onion soup
1/4 cup milk
2 cups spinach, torn into pieces
Sea salt and ground black pepper, to taste
1/2 teaspoon smoked paprika
1/2 teaspoon dried oregano
1/2 teaspoon dried thyme
1/2 teaspoon dried rosemary
1/4 teaspoon cumin seeds, ground
1/2 teaspoon dried basil
3/4 pound medium shrimp, peeled and deveined
2 cups Pecorino-Romano cheese, grated

Directions
Cook your rigatoni according to the package instructions.

In a frying pan, heat the olive oil over medium-high heat. Sauté the carrot, zucchini, and onion for about 4 minutes or until they are tender.

Now, sauté the garlic for 1 minute or so. Add in the pasta sauce, wine, soup, milk, spinach, and seasonings. Spoon the mixture into a lightly greased baking pan.

Fold in the shrimp and sprinkle the cheese on the top. Bake for about 8 minutes or until everything is cooked through. Bon appétit!

Orzo Pasta with Veggies and Cheese

(Ready in about 20 minutes | Servings 4)

Per serving: Calories: 412; Fat: 14.9g; Carbs: 62.9g; Protein: 9.2g

Ingredients
8 ounces orzo pasta
1/2 cup sweet corn kernels
1/2 cup green peas
1 large tomato, diced
1/2 cup pineapple, sliced
1 red chili pepper, deseeded and finely chopped
4 tablespoons scallions, chopped
1/2 teaspoon fresh garlic, minced
1 teaspoon Greek seasoning mix
Sea salt and ground black pepper, to taste
1 tablespoon white vinegar
1 tablespoon fresh lemon juice
3 tablespoons extra-virgin olive oil
1 teaspoon honey
2 ounces Halloumi cheese, crumbled

Directions
Cook the orzo pasta in a large saucepan according to the package directions; drain and let it cool completely.

Meanwhile, in another saucepan, gently simmer the corn and green peas for about 7 to 8 minutes; let them cool completely and transfer to a salad bowl.

Transfer the pasta to the salad bowl. Add in the tomatoes, pineapple, chili pepper, scallions, garlic, and spices.

Make the dressing by whisking the vinegar, lemon juice, olive oil, and honey.

Dress your salad and toss to combine well. Top with Halloumi cheese and serve immediately. Bon appétit!

Classic Baked Spaghetti

(Ready in about 55 minutes | Servings 7)

Per serving: Calories: 555; Fat: 25.3g; Carbs: 58.8g; Protein: 25.4g

Ingredients
1 pound spaghetti
1 tablespoon olive oil
1/2 pound Italian sausage
1 carrot, grated
1/2 pound mushrooms, thinly sliced
1 red onion, chopped
1 teaspoon garlic, minced
1/2 teaspoon dried basil
1/2 teaspoon dried oregano
1/2 teaspoon dried marjoram
Sea salt and ground black pepper, to taste
1/2 teaspoon red chili flakes
30 ounces tomato sauce
2 large ripe tomatoes, chopped
2 tablespoons Kalamata olives, pitted and sliced
2 cups Myzithra cheese, grated

Directions
Cook the spaghetti according to the package directions.

Heat the olive oil in a frying pan over medium-high heat. Now, cook the Italian sausage until no longer pink, crumbling it with a fork.

Add in the carrot, mushrooms, and onion and continue cooking for 3 minutes more or until they have softened.

Add in the garlic and herbs, continue to sauté for 30 seconds more until fragrant. Stir in the salt, black pepper, red chili flakes, tomato sauce, and tomatoes. Bring to a boil and immediately reduce the heat to a simmer.

Let it simmer for 18 to 20 minutes or until cooked through. Stir in the cooked spaghetti and olives; transfer the mixture to a lightly oiled casserole dish. Scatter the cheese over the top. Bake in the preheated oven at 350 degrees F for about 30 minutes or until the cheese is hot and bubbly. Bon appétit!

Greek Yogurt Fettuccine Alfredo

(Ready in about 25 minutes | Servings 4)

Per serving: Calories: 445; Fat: 15.2g; Carbs: 65.2g; Protein: 13.2g

Ingredients

10 ounces fettuccine pasta
1 tablespoon olive oil
1 tablespoon butter
2 cloves garlic, minced
1 cup milk
1 cup plain Greek yogurt
1/2 cup Parmesan cheese, shredded
Sea salt and ground black pepper, to taste
2 tablespoons fresh basil leaves, roughly chopped

Directions

Start by preparing the fettuccine pasta according to the package instructions.

In a saucepan, heat the olive oil and butter over medium flame. Stir in the garlic and sauté until aromatic. Heat off.

Gradually whisk in the milk and yogurt. Stir to combine, add in the cheese and continue to simmer over medium-low heat until everything is well incorporated.

Season with salt and black pepper to taste; garnish with basil leaves and enjoy!

Nonna's Pizza Rustica

(Ready in about 1 hour 30 minutes | Servings 4)

Per serving: Calories: 675; Fat: 14.4g; Carbs: 101g; Protein: 22g

Ingredients

1 ¼ cups warm water
1 package active dry yeast
1 teaspoon brown sugar
4 cups all-purpose flour
1/2 teaspoon sea salt
2 tablespoons olive oil
8 ounces pizza sauce
1 teaspoon Italian herb mix
8 ounces canned artichoke hearts
1 red onion, thinly sliced
1 bell pepper, thinly sliced
1/2 cup black olives, pitted
1/2 cup part-skim ricotta cheese, crumbled
1/4 cup Parmesan cheese, grated
8 cherry tomatoes, halved

Directions

Mix the water, yeast, and sugar and let it rest for approximately 5 minutes. Stir in the flour, salt, and oil, and beat on low speed for 2 minutes.

Turn the dough out onto a lightly floured surface. Knead the dough with lightly floured hands for 3 to 4 minutes or until elastic. If your dough slowly bounces back when you poke it with your finger, it is ready to rise.

Cover with a plastic wrap and let it rise in a warm place until doubled in size, about 1 hour.

On a lightly floured work surface, gently flatten the dough into a disc using your floured hands or a rolling pin.

Preheat your oven to 425 degrees F.

Press the crust into a lightly floured and oiled baking pan. Spread the pizza sauce and Italian herb mix over the crust.

Top your pizza with the artichoke hearts, onion, peppers, olives, cheese and tomatoes. Bake in the preheated oven for 20 to 25 minutes or until the cheese has melted. Bon appétit!

Greek Pasta Spetsofai

(Ready in about 25 minutes | Servings 4)

Per serving: Calories: 665; Fat: 30.4g; Carbs: 80.3g; Protein: 21.2g

Ingredients

2 tablespoons olive oil
8 ounces spicy Greek sausage, sliced
1 red onion, sliced
1 Florina pepper, sliced
2 pickled pepperoncini peppers, minced
2 cloves garlic, sliced
1 cup pasta sauce
1/2 cup dry white wine
12 ounces rotini pasta
1 teaspoon Greek oregano
Sea salt and ground black pepper, to taste
2 ounces Kalamata olives, pitted and sliced
4 ounces feta cheese, crumbled

Directions

Heat the olive oil in a saucepan over medium-high flame. Once hot, sear the sausage until no longer pink or about 4 minutes.

Add in the onion, peppers, and garlic and continue to sauté an additional 2 minutes until aromatic.

Now, stir in the pasta sauce, wine, pasta, and seasonings; bring to a boil. Immediately reduce the heat to a simmer and continue to cook for about 15 minutes.

Spoon into individual bowls and serve garnished with Kalamata olives and feta cheese. Bon appétit!

Vegetarian Pizza Sandwich

(Ready in about 15 minutes | Servings 1)

Per serving: Calories: 383; Fat: 25.1g; Carbs: 28.2g; Protein: 13g

Ingredients

1 (2-ounces) pizza dough
1 small-sized tomato, sliced
1 ounce parmesan cheese, shredded
3 olives, pitted and sliced
1/4 teaspoon dried basil
1/4 teaspoon dried oregano

Directions

Flatten the dough into a mini pizza crust using a rolling pin.

Then, preheat a lightly oiled nonstick skillet. Cook the crust for about 4 minutes per side or until golden-brown; reserve.

Top the pizza crust with the tomato, cheese, and olives; sprinkle the basil and oregano over the top. Fold the crust in half over filling and serve warm. Bon appétit!

Easy Greek Pizza

(Ready in about 25 minutes | Servings 3)
Per serving: Calories: 497; Fat: 22.3g; Carbs: 58.2g; Protein: 17g
Ingredients
1 ½ cups all-purpose flour
1/2 teaspoon sea salt
1 teaspoon baking powder
1/2 cup warm water
1 egg, whisked
2 tablespoons olive oil
1/2 cup tomato sauce
2 tablespoons ketchup
1 teaspoon deli mustard
2 ounces canned tuna in oil, drained
1/2 cup button mushrooms, sliced
1 red bell peppers, sliced
1 cup feta cheese, crumbled
Directions
Thoroughly combine the flour, salt, and baking powder. Slowly pour in the water, whisked egg, and olive oil; mix to combine well.
Heat a lightly oiled nonstick skillet over medium flame. Spread the dough on the oiled skillet.
Cook the crust for about 3 minutes. Turn it over, turn the heat to low, and arrange the toppings. Continue to cook for 5 to 6 minutes longer, until the cheese is hot and bubbly.
Bon appétit!

Flaky Mini Pizza Rolls with Sardines

(Ready in about 20 minutes | Servings 4)
Per serving: Calories: 427; Fat: 20.8g; Carbs: 40.3g; Protein: 19.1g
Ingredients
1 tablespoon olive oil
2 tablespoons scallions, chopped
1 teaspoon garlic, pressed
1 cup tomato puree
1/2 teaspoon dried oregano
1/2 teaspoon dried rosemary
1/2 teaspoon dried basil
Sea salt and cayenne pepper, to season
8 ounces refrigerated crescent rolls
4 ounces sardine, deboned and flaked
2 ounces black olives, pitted and sliced
4 ounces Halloumi cheese, crumbled
1 egg, whisked
Directions
Heat the olive oil in a nonstick skillet over medium-high heat. Now, sauté the scallions and garlic for 1 minute until tender and fragrant.
Now, add in the tomato puree and spices and turn the heat to a simmer; let it simmer for 5 to 6 minutes more until slightly thickened.

Unroll the crescent rolls into a rectangle. Spread the prepared tomato sauce evenly over the dough. Spread the chopped sardines over the crust, followed by the olives and Halloumi cheese. Now, roll up the rectangle and cut it into 8 slices.
Brush with the egg and bake at 375 degrees F for about 11 minutes or until edges are golden brown. Serve warm and enjoy!

Greek Makaronia me Kima

(Ready in about 25 minutes | Servings 4)
Per serving: Calories: 609; Fat: 21.1g; Carbs: 64.3g; Protein: 40.2g
Ingredients
10 ounces elbow pasta
1 tablespoon olive oil
1 pound lean ground beef
1 medium red onion, chopped
2 cloves garlic, crushed
1/2 cup red wine
2 ripe tomatoes, pureed
1 cup chicken stock
Sea salt and ground black pepper, to taste
1 teaspoon cayenne pepper
1/2 teaspoon dried oregano
1 teaspoon dried basil
1 teaspoon dried rosemary
2 ounces Mizithra cheese, grated
Directions
Cook the pasta according to the package directions; drain and reserve.
Meanwhile, heat the olive oil in a frying pan over medium-high flame. Once hot, sear the beef until no longer pink or about 4 minutes.
Then, cook the onion and garlic for about 2 minutes until aromatic, adding a splash of wine to deglaze the pan.
Now, stir in the remaining wine, tomatoes, chicken stock, and spices. Afterwards, stir the reserved pasta into the pan and toss to combine well.
Spoon into individual bowls and serve garnished with Mizithra cheese. Enjoy!

Greek-Style Mushroom Lasagna

(Ready in about 1 hour 50 minutes | Servings 8)
Per serving: Calories: 591; Fat: 26.5g; Carbs: 62.1g; Protein: 26.2g
Ingredients
2 tablespoons olive oil
1 pound Portobello mushrooms, sliced
1 red onion, chopped
1 teaspoon garlic, minced
2 ounces Kalamata olives, pitted and sliced
1 ½ cups tomato sauce
1 ½ cups cream of mushroom soup
20 ounces canned tomatoes, crushed
Sea salt and ground black pepper, to taste
1 teaspoon red pepper flakes
1 teaspoon Italian herb mix
1 pound lasagna noodles

1 large egg
1 cup soft cheese
1 cup Greek yogurt
2 cups Graviera cheese, shaved

Directions

Heat the olive oil in a frying pan over medium-high heat; now, cook the mushrooms and onion for about 3 minutes or until the mushrooms release the liquid. Add in the garlic and olives, and continue to cook an additional 30 seconds or until aromatic. Stir in the tomato sauce, cream of mushroom soup, canned tomatoes, and seasonings.

Bring to a boil, and then, turn the heat to a simmer; let it simmer for 1 hour, stirring periodically.

Meanwhile, cook the lasagna noodles in a large pot of salted boiling water according to the package instructions. Drain the noodles and toss with a bit of olive oil to prevent them from sticking together.

In a mixing bowl, whisk the egg until pale and frothy; add in the soft cheese and Greek yogurt, and mix to combine well.

Now, spoon 1/3 of the mushrooms sauce into the bottom of a lightly oiled casserole dish. Top the sauce layer with a single layer of lasagna noodles, a layer of egg/cheese mixture, and a single layer of Graviera cheese.

Repeat the layers, ending with the Graviera cheese. Cover your lasagna with a piece of aluminum foil and bake in the preheated oven at 375 degrees F for 15 minutes. Increase the temperature to 390 degrees F, remove the foil, and continue baking for about 20 minutes more.

Allow your lasagna to cool on a wire rack for about 10 minutes before slicing. Bon appétit!

Green Bean Pasta Salad

(Ready in about 20 minutes | Servings 4)

Per serving: Calories: 591; Fat: 26.5g; Carbs: 62.1g; Protein: 26.2g

Ingredients

8 ounces whole-wheat pasta
3/4 pound green beans, trimmed and snipped in half
2 ounces Kalamata olives, pitted and sliced
1 cup cherry tomatoes, halved
3 tablespoons extra-virgin olive oil
2 tablespoons fresh lemon juice
1/2 tablespoon deli mustard
1/2 teaspoon garlic, minced
Sea salt and ground black pepper, to taste
1 teaspoon paprika
1 teaspoon fresh rosemary, chopped
1 teaspoon fresh dill, chopped
2 ounces feta cheese, crumbled

Directions

Cook the pasta according to the package directions. Bring a large saucepan of water to a boil. Throw the green beans into the boiling water and bring to a full boil. Let it cook until the beans are crisp- tender, for about 5 to 6 minutes.

Drain the boiled green beans into a colander and transfer them to a salad bowl. Add in the olives and tomatoes.

Make the dressing by whisking the olive oil, lemon juice, mustard, garlic, salt, black pepper, paprika, rosemary, and dill.

Dress your salad and toss to coat well. Garnish with crumbled feta cheese and serve well-chilled. Bon appétit!

Authentic Socca Pizza

(Ready in about 1 hour 20 minutes | Servings 5)

Per serving: Calories: 356; Fat: 22.1g; Carbs: 27.2g; Protein: 12g

Ingredients

1 ½ cups chickpea flour
1 ½ cups water
1/3 cup olive oil, divided
1 teaspoon granulated garlic
1/2 teaspoon paprika
1/2 teaspoon turmeric powder
Flaky sea salt, to taste
1 cup tomato paste
1 teaspoon dried oregano
1 teaspoon dried basil
1/2 teaspoon dried rosemary
1 medium zucchini, diced
2 ounces Kalamata olives, pitted and sliced
1/2 cup Halloumi cheese, shredded

Directions

Thoroughly combine the chickpea flour, water, 3 tablespoons of the olive oil, granulated garlic, paprika, turmeric, and sea salt. Let it stand for approximately 1 hour.

Heat 1 teaspoon of the olive oil in an oven-safe skillet and pour in the chickpea batter. Cook for about 7 minutes, until the edges are browning. Repeat with the remaining olive oil and batter.

Place the topping ingredients on each socca and bake in the preheated oven at 425 degrees F for about 9 minutes, until the cheese is hot and bubbly. Bon appétit!

Old-Fashioned Cheese Ravioli with Tuna

(Ready in about 1 hour 5 minutes | Servings 5)

Per serving: Calories: 622; Fat: 36.5g; Carbs: 24.4g; Protein: 48.9g

Ingredients

1 tablespoon olive oil
3/4 pound tuna fillets, diced
1 medium red onion, chopped
1 teaspoon garlic, minced
Sea salt and freshly ground black pepper, to taste
1 teaspoon Cajun seasoning mix
1/2 cup dry white wine
30 ounces tomato sauce
2 ounces Kalamata olives, pitted and sliced
10 ounces frozen cheese ravioli
1 egg
2 ounces Greek yogurt

12 ounces soft cheese
2 cups Pecorino-Romano cheese, grated
Directions
Heat the olive oil in a frying pan over medium-high heat. Now, cook tuna fillets for about 3 minutes.
Add in the onion and garlic and continue to cook for 2 minutes more, adding a splash of wine to deglaze the pan.
Add in the salt, black pepper, Cajun seasoning mix, remaining wine, and tomato sauce and bring to a boil; immediately reduce the heat to a simmer.
Let it simmer for about 15 minutes or until cooked through. Stir in the olives and ravioli; transfer the mixture to a lightly oiled baking dish.
Beat the egg with the yogurt and cheese and top your casserole with this mixture. Bake in the preheated oven at 350 degrees F for about 45 minutes or until the top is golden.
Serve garnished with fresh mint or basil leaves if desired. Bon appétit!

Pizza with Ground Chicken

(Ready in about 1 hour 30 minutes | Servings 5)
Per serving: Calories: 675; Fat: 22.4g; Carbs: 88.1g; Protein: 27g
Ingredients
1 package active dry yeast
1 ¼ cups warm water
1 teaspoon honey
4 cups all-purpose flour
1/2 teaspoon sea salt
2 tablespoons olive oil
3/4 pound ground chicken
1 red onion, chopped
1 teaspoon Greek seasoning mix
1 cup pizza sauce
1 cup Swiss chard
2 bell peppers, sliced
2 ounces Kalamata olives, pitted and halved
3 ounces Halloumi cheese, crumbled
Directions
Mix the water, yeast, and honey and let it rest for approximately 5 minutes. Stir in the flour, salt, and oil, and beat on low speed for 2 minutes.
Turn the dough out onto a lightly floured surface. Knead the dough with lightly floured hands for 3 to 4 minutes or until elastic. If your dough slowly bounces back when you poke it with your finger, it is ready to rise.
Cover the dough and let it rise in a warm place until doubled in size, about 1 hour.
Meanwhile, brown the ground chicken and onion in a lightly greased skillet. Cook for about 5 minutes, stirring and crumbling with a fork. Sprinkle with Greek seasoning mix.
On a lightly floured work surface, gently flatten the dough into a disc **using your floured hands or a** rolling pin.
Preheat your oven to 425 degrees F.

Press the crust into a lightly floured and oiled baking pan. Spread the pizza sauce over the crust.
Top your pizza with the Swiss chard, bell peppers, olives, and cheese. Bake in the preheated oven for 20 to 25 minutes or until the cheese has melted. Bon appétit!

Puff Pastry Veggie Pizza

(Ready in about 20 minutes | Servings 4)
Per serving: Calories: 325; Fat: 12.4g; Carbs: 41.8g; Protein: 11.1g
Ingredients
10 ounces refrigerated crescent dough sheet
1 cup feta cheese
1/2 teaspoon granulated garlic
1/2 teaspoon dried oregano
1/2 teaspoon dried basil
1/2 teaspoon dried dill weed
1 bell pepper, diced
1 red onion, thinly sliced
1 cup grape tomatoes
Directions
Begin by preheating your oven to 370 degrees F.
Unroll the crescent dough sheet and press it in the bottom of a parchment-lined cookie sheet.
Bake for about 10 minutes or until golden brown. Let it cool completely.
Thoroughly combine the feta and spices. Spread the cheese mixture over the crust. Top with the prepared veggies and bake for 5 minutes more or until the cheese has melted. Enjoy!

Penne alla Vodka

(Ready in about 20 minutes | Servings 4)
Per serving: Calories: 579; Fat: 24.7g; Carbs: 77.3g; Protein: 13.3g
Ingredients
12 ounces penne pasta
2 tablespoons olive oil
1 red onion, chopped
1 teaspoon garlic, minced
1/2 teaspoon red pepper flakes plus more for garnish if desired
Sea salt and black pepper, to taste
2 ripe tomatoes, chopped
1/4 cup vodka
1 cup double cream
1/2 cup Pecorino-Romano cheese, grated
Directions
Cook the pasta according to the package directions; drain and reserve.
Meanwhile, heat the olive oil in a frying pan over medium-high flame. Once hot, sauté the onion and garlic for about 2 minutes until aromatic, adding a splash of wine to deglaze the pan.
Now, stir in the red pepper, salt, black pepper, tomatoes, vodka.
Afterwards, stir the reserved pasta, double cream, and cheese; toss to combine well. Fold in the cheese and continue to simmer for a further 5 to 6 minutes.

Spoon into individual bowls and serve hot. Bon appétit!

Pasta with Traditional Greek Kokkinisto

(Ready in about 1 hour 40 minutes | Servings 4)
Per serving: Calories: 641; Fat: 21.7g; Carbs: 73g; Protein: 34.3g
Ingredients
8 ounces fettuccine
4 tablespoons olive oil
1 pound lean beef, cut into bite-sized pieces
1 red onion, chopped
4 garlic cloves, minced
1/2 cup red wine
2 cups tomato sauce
1 teaspoon red pepper flakes
1/2 teaspoon dried oregano
1/2 teaspoon dried oregano
Sea salt and freshly ground black pepper, to taste
2 bay leaves
Directions
Cook the pasta in a large pot of a salted water according to the package directions.
In a saucepan, heat 1 tablespoon of the olive oil; sauté the onion over medium heat for about 3 minutes until translucent.
Add in the another tablespoon of the olive oil and brown the meat for about 5 minutes. Add a splash of wine to deglaze the pan.
Add in the remaining ingredients and turn the heat to a simmer. Let it simmer for about 1 hour 30 minutes until thoroughly cooked.
Discard the bay leaves and serve with the warm fettuccine pasta. Bon appétit!

Father's Day Pizza with Fefferoni

(Ready in about 1 hour 25 minutes | Servings 4)
Per serving: Calories: 648; Fat: 29.3g; Carbs: 60.3g; Protein: 32.2g
Ingredients
14 ounces pizza dough
1/2 cup tomato sauce
1/2 teaspoon red pepper flakes, crushed
1/2 teaspoon dried rosemary
1/2 teaspoon dried oregano
1/2 teaspoon dried basil
1/2 teaspoon granulated garlic
8 slices pepperoni
6 slices prosciutto
8 ounces Pecorino-Romano cheese, shredded
2 fefferoni peppers
Directions
Knead the dough out onto a lightly floured surface until smooth and elastic.
Cover the dough and let it rise in a warm place until doubled, about 1 hour. Divide the dough into two pieces and roll them into balls.
Next, gently flatten the dough into a disc using a rolling pin.

Press the crust into a parchment-lined pizza pan. Spread the tomato sauce, spices, pepperoni, prosciutto, and cheese over the crust. Repeat with the other pizza.
Preheat your oven to 425 degrees F.
Bake your pizza in the preheated oven for 20 to 25 minutes or until the crust is lightly browned and cheese is hot and bubbly.
Slice your pizza, garnish with fefferoni peppers, and serve hot. Bon appétit!

Linguine with Chicken and Kefalograviera Cheese

(Ready in about 20 minutes | Servings 4)
Per serving: Calories: 534; Fat: 20.4g; Carbs: 57.7g; Protein: 31g
Ingredients
9 ounces linguine pasta
1 tablespoon olive oil
3/4 pound chicken breast half, boneless and diced into bite-sized pieces
Sea salt and ground black pepper, to taste
1 cup tomatoes, pureed
1/4 cup chicken broth
1 teaspoon Greek herb mix
1 tablespoon capers, drained
4 ounces canned artichoke hearts, drained
1/2 cup Kefalograviera cheese, crumbled
1/2 cup Kalamata olives, pitted and halved
Directions
Cook the pasta according to the package instructions; drain and reserve,
Heat the olive oil in a saucepan over medium-high flame. Once hot, sear the chicken until no longer pink or about 4 minutes. Season with salt and pepper to taste.
Now, stir in the pureed tomatoes, chicken broth, Greek herb mix, capers, and artichoke hearts; Reduce the heat to a simmer and continue to cook for about 10 minutes.
Add in the reserved pasta and cheese and stir to combine well.
Spoon into individual bowls and serve garnished with Kalamata olives. Bon appétit!

Chicken and Mostaccioli Bake

(Ready in about 1 hour | Servings 6)
Per serving: Calories: 524; Fat: 18.8g; Carbs: 57.3g; Protein: 32.6g
Ingredients
3/4 pound mostaccioli
2 tablespoons olive oil
1/2 pound chicken breasts, diced
1/2 pound chicken sausage, sliced
1 small red onion, chopped
1 teaspoon garlic, minced
1 teaspoon Italian seasoning mix
2 cups pasta sauce
2 ounces Kalamata olives, pitted and sliced
Sea salt and ground black pepper, to taste

2 cups spinach, torn into pieces
2 cups Greek yogurt
1 cup parmesan cheese, grated
1 tablespoon fresh basil, roughly chopped
1 tablespoon fresh parsley, roughly chopped
Directions
Cook your pasta according to the package directions.
Heat the olive oil in a frying pan over medium-high heat. Now, cook the chicken until no longer pink or about 4 minutes.
Add in the sausage and onion and continue to cook for 2 to 3 minutes more. Stir in the garlic and Italian seasoning mix, and continue sautéing for 30 seconds more.
Add in the pasta sauce and bring to a boil; immediately reduce the heat to a simmer.
Let it simmer for 18 to 20 minutes or until cooked through. Stir in the cooked pasta, olives, salt, black pepper, and spinach; transfer the mixture to a lightly oiled baking dish.
Combine the yogurt and cheese and top your casserole with this mixture. Bake in the preheated oven at 350 degrees F for 25 to 30 minutes or until the top is golden.
Serve garnished with fresh basil and parsley leaves. Bon appétit!

Avocado, Poppy Seed and Farfalle Salad

(Ready in about 15 minutes | Servings 4)
Per serving: Calories: 488; Fat: 19.8g; Carbs: 63g; Protein: 17.1g
Ingredients
8 ounces farfalle pasta
1 cup rotisserie chicken, diced
1 cup grape tomatoes, halved
4 tablespoons scallions, sliced
1/2 cup full-fat mayonnaise
1/4 cup Greek yogurt
1 teaspoon Dijon mustard
1 tablespoon poppy seeds
1 tablespoon fresh lime juice
1 tablespoon honey
1/2 teaspoon red chili pepper flakes
Sea salt and ground black pepper, to taste
2 ounces pomegranate seeds
2 ounces feta cheese, crumbled
Directions
Cook the pasta according to the package directions. Drain your pasta and toss with the chicken, tomatoes, and scallions.
In a mixing bowl, thoroughly combine the mayonnaise, Greek yogurt, Dijon mustard, poppy seeds, lime juice, honey, chili pepper, salt, and black pepper. Toss to combine well.
Top with the pomegranate seeds and crumbled feta cheese. Enjoy!

The Best Vegan Lasagna

(Ready in about 1 hour 45 minutes | Servings 6)

Per serving: Calories: 444; Fat: 18.4g; Carbs: 55.7g; Protein: 16g
Ingredients
2 tablespoons olive oil
1 red onion, chopped
2 carrots, chopped
1 cup broccoli florets
2 cups Cremini mushrooms, chopped
2 garlic cloves, minced
1 teaspoon Greek herb mix
Sea salt and ground black pepper, to taste
2 cups pizza sauce
2 ounces Kalamata olives, pitted and sliced
2 cups Swiss chard, torn into pieces
10 ounces lasagna noodles
Cashew Cream:
1 cup raw cashews, soaked overnight
1/4 cup soy milk
1/4 cup water
1 tablespoon lime juice
1 teaspoon white vinegar
1/2 teaspoon sea salt
2 tablespoons nutritional yeast
Directions
Heat the olive oil in a frying pan over medium-high heat; now, cook the onion, carrots, broccoli, and mushrooms for about 3 minutes or until the vegetables are tender and the mushrooms release the liquid.
Add in the garlic and herbs, and continue to cook an additional 30 seconds or until aromatic. Stir in the salt, black pepper, and pizza sauce.
Bring to a boil, and then, turn the heat to a simmer; let it simmer for 1 hour, stirring periodically. Add in the olives and Swiss chard.
Meanwhile, cook the lasagna noodles in a large pot of salted boiling water according to the package instructions. Drain the noodles and toss with a bit of olive oil to prevent them from sticking together.
Process all ingredients for the cashew cream in your blender until creamy and soft.
Now, spoon 1/3 of the mushroom/tomato sauce into the bottom of a lightly oiled casserole dish. Top the sauce layer with a single layer of lasagna noodles, and a layer of cashew cream.
Repeat the layers, ending with the mushroom/tomato sauce.
Cover your lasagna with a piece of aluminum foil and bake in the preheated oven at 375 degrees F for 15 minutes. Increase the temperature to 390 degrees F, remove the foil, and continue baking for about 20 minutes more.
Allow your lasagna to cool on a wire rack for about 10 minutes before slicing and serving. Bon appétit!

Easy Pizza with Goat Cheese and Veggies

(Ready in about 20 minutes | Servings 4)
Per serving: Calories: 404; Fat: 16.2g; Carbs: 48.4g; Protein: 15.3g
Ingredients

12 ounces refrigerated crescent dough sheet
1 cup goat cheese
1 teaspoon Italian herb mix
Sea salt and red pepper, to taste
1/2 teaspoon granulated garlic
1 Italian peppers, sliced
1 cup button mushrooms, sliced
1 zucchini, sliced
10 Kalamata olives, pitted and sliced
1 cup cherry tomatoes, halved

Directions

Begin by preheating your oven to 370 degrees F.
Unroll the crescent dough sheet and press it into the bottom of a parchment-lined cookie sheet.
Bake for about 10 minutes or until golden brown. Let it cool completely.
Thoroughly combine the goat cheese and spices.
Spread the goat cheese mixture over the crust.
Top with the other topping ingredients and bake for 5 minutes more or until the cheese has melted. Bon appétit!

Traditional Cacio e Pepe

(Ready in about 20 minutes | Servings 4)

Per serving: Calories: 458; Fat: 14.4g; Carbs: 62.7g; Protein: 20.1g

Ingredients

8 ounces angel hair pasta
1 tablespoon olive oil
1 teaspoon black pepper, freshly cracked
1 cup Pecorino **cheese**, grated
Sea salt, to taste

Directions

Cook the pasta according to the package instructions; drain and reserve.
Heat the olive oil in a saucepan over medium-high flame. Once hot, cook the pepper for about 1 minute or until fragrant.
Add 1/2 cup of the cooking liquid to the saucepan.
Add in the cooked pasta and cheese; let it simmer for a few minutes more until the cheese has melted.
Season with salt to taste and serve hot. Bon appétit!

DESSERTS

Classic Fig Clafoutis

(Ready in about 45 minutes | Servings 4)
Per serving: Calories: 328; Fat: 10.4g; Carbs: 45.3g; Protein: 6.3g

Ingredients
2 large eggs
1/4 cup granulated sugar
2 tablespoons honey
A pinch of grated nutmeg
A pinch of flaky salt
1/3 cup all-purpose flour
1 tablespoon unsalted butter, at room temperature
1/4 cup whole milk
1/2 cup double cream
1/4 cup cognac
1 teaspoon orange zest, finely grated
8 figs, halved

Directions
Begin by preheating your oven to 350 degrees F.
In a mixing dish, thoroughly combine the eggs, sugar, honey, nutmeg, and salt.
Gradually stir in the flour and beat until creamy and smooth. Whisk in the butter, milk, double cream, cognac, and orange zest. Mix again to combine well.
Divide the batter into four lightly greased ramekins. Top with the fresh figs and bake in the preheated oven for about 40 minutes until the clafoutis is golden at the edges. Bon appétit!

Semolina Cake with Almonds

(Ready in about 2 hours 10 minutes | Servings 8)
Per serving: Calories: 404; Fat: 16.4g; Carbs: 54.8g; Protein: 8.3g

Ingredients
2 cups Greek yogurt
1 cup full-fat milk
1/2 cup coconut oil
1 ½ cups powdered sugar
2 cups semolina
1 cup shredded coconut
1 teaspoon baking soda
1 teaspoon baking powder
1 tablespoon pure vanilla extract
1/4 teaspoon ground cinnamon
1/2 cup almonds, slivered

Directions
Thoroughly combine the yogurt, milk, coconut oil, and sugar. Add in the semolina, shredded coconut, baking soda, baking powder, vanilla, and cinnamon. Let it rest for 1 ½ hour.
Bake in the preheated oven at 350 degrees F for approximately 40 minutes or until a tester inserted in the center of the cake comes out dry and clean. Transfer to a wire rack to cool completely before slicing and serving. Garnish with almonds and serve. Bon appétit!

Romantic Mug Cakes

(Ready in about 5 minutes | Servings 2)
Per serving: Calories: 264; Fat: 14.4g; Carbs: 25.5g; Protein: 10.1g

Ingredients
2 eggs
1 ½ tablespoons butter, melted
4 tablespoons full-fat milk
1 tablespoon rose water
1/4 teaspoon ground cinnamon
1/8 teaspoon grated nutmeg
A pinch of coarse sea salt
4 tablespoons all-purpose flour
1/2 teaspoon baking powder
2 tablespoons cocoa powder
2 tablespoons powdered sugar
1 teaspoon grated orange zest

Directions
Whisk the eggs, melted butter, milk, rose water, cinnamon, nutmeg, and salt.
Add in the flour, baking powder, cocoa powder, and sugar. Spoon the batter into two mugs.
Microwave for 1 minute 30 seconds and top with the grated orange zest. Bon appétit!

Pistachio and Tahini Halva

(Ready in about 15 minutes + chilling time | Servings 6)
Per serving: Calories: 464; Fat: 28.4g; Carbs: 49.5g; Protein: 9.4g

Ingredients
1/2 cup water
1/2 pound sugar
10 ounces tahini, at room temperature
A ping of sea salt
1/2 teaspoon vanilla paste
1/2 teaspoon crystal citric acid
1/3 cup shelled pistachios, chopped

Directions
Bring the water to a full boil in a small saucepan. Add in the sugar and stir. Let it cook, stirring occasionally, until a candy thermometer registers 250 degrees F. Heat off.
Stir in the tahini. Continue to stir with a wooden spoon just until halva comes together in a smooth mass; do not overmix your halva.
Add in the remaining ingredients and stir again to combine well. Now, scrape your halva into a parchment-lined square pan and smooth the top.
Let it cool to room temperature; cover tightly with a plastic wrap and place in your refrigerator for at least 2 hours.

Authentic Greek Rizogalo

(Ready in about 40 minutes | Servings 3)
Per serving: Calories: 247; Fat: 10.4g; Carbs: 29.1g; Protein: 8g

Ingredients

1 ½ cups water
1/4 cup rice
2 cups whole milk
1/4 cup sugar
A pinch of sea salt
A pinch of grated nutmeg
1 egg, whisked
1 tablespoon butter
1/2 teaspoon vanilla extract
1/4 teaspoon ground cloves
1 teaspoon orange zest, grated
1/2 ground cinnamon

Directions

Bring the water and rice to a boil in a saucepan. Immediately turn the heat to a simmer. Let it simmer, stirring occasionally, until most of the water has been absorbed, about 30 minutes.

Add in the milk, sugar, salt, and nutmeg, and bring to a boil again.

Add about 1 cup of the warm mixture to the beaten egg and whisk to combine well.

Turn the heat to low; add in the egg mixture and continue simmering, stirring constantly, until the pudding has thickened.

Stir in the butter, vanilla, cloves, orange zest, and cinnamon and serve at room temperature. Enjoy!

Greek Frozen Yogurt Dessert

(Ready in about 10 minutes | Servings 3)
Per serving: Calories: 307; Fat: 14.4g; Carbs: 29.1g; Protein: 18g

Ingredients

1/2 pineapple, diced
2 cups Greek-style yogurt, frozen
3 ounces almonds, slivered

Directions

Divide the pineapple between two dessert bowls.
Spoon the yogurt over it.
Top with the slivered almonds.
Cover and place in your refrigerator until you're ready to serve. Bon appétit!

Salted Pistachio and Tahini Truffles

(Ready in about 5 minutes + chilling time | Servings 8)
Per serving: Calories: 224; Fat: 9.5g; Carbs: 38.7g; Protein: 7.4g

Ingredients

1/2 cup pure agave syrup
1/2 cup dates, pitted and soaked
1/3 cup tahini
1/3 cup shelled pistachios, roasted and salted
1 teaspoon pure vanilla extract
1/2 teaspoon ground cinnamon
A pinch of sea salt
2 tablespoons carob powder
2 tablespoons cocoa powder
2 cups rolled oats

Directions

In your food processor, mix all of the above ingredients, except for the oats, until well combined.

Add in the rolled oats and stir with a wooden spoon. Roll the mixture into small balls and place in your refrigerator until ready to serve. Bon appétit!

Traditional Olive Oil Cake with Figs

(Ready in about 45 minutes | Servings 9)
Per serving: Calories: 339; Fat: 15.6g; Carbs: 44.7g; Protein: 6.4g

Ingredients

1/2 pound cooking apples, peeled, cored, and chopped
2 tablespoons fresh lemon juice
2 ½ cups all-purpose flour
1 teaspoon baking powder
1/4 teaspoon sea salt
1/2 teaspoon ground cinnamon
A pinch of grated nutmeg
3/4 cup granulated sugar
1/2 cup extra-virgin olive oil
2 eggs
1/2 cup dried figs, chopped
2 tablespoons walnuts, chopped

Directions

Begin by preheating your oven to 350 degrees F.
Toss the chopped apples with lemon juice and set them aside.
Then, thoroughly combine the flour, baking powder, sea salt, cinnamon, and nutmeg.
Then, beat the sugar and olive oil using your mixer at low speed.
Gradually fold in the eggs, one at a time, and continue to mix for a few minutes more until it has thickened.
Add the wet mixture to the dry ingredients and stir until you get a thick batter. Fold in the figs and walnuts and stir to combine well.
Spoon the batter into a parchment-lined baking pan and level the top using a wooden spoon.
Bake in the preheated oven for about 40 minutes or until tester comes out dry and clean. Let it cool on a wire rack before slicing and serving. Bon appétit!

Traditional Mediterranean Lokum

(Ready in about 25 minutes + chilling time | Servings 10)
Per serving: Calories: 208; Fat: 0.5g; Carbs: 54.4g; Protein: 0.2g

Ingredients

1 ounce confectioners' sugar
3 ½ ounces cornstarch
20 ounces caster sugar
4 ounces pomegranate juice
16 ounces cold water
3 tablespoons gelatin, powdered

Directions

Line a baking sheet with a parchment paper.
Mix the confectioners' sugar and 2 ounces of cornstarch until well combined.
In a saucepan, heat the caster sugar, pomegranate juice and water over low heat.

In a mixing bowl, combine 4 ounces of cold water with the remaining cornstarch. Stir the mixture into the sugar syrup.

Slowly and gradually, add in the powdered gelatin and whisk until smooth and uniform.

Bring the mixture to a boil, turn the heat to medium and continue to cook for another 18 minutes, whisking constantly, until the mixture has thickened. Scrape the mixture into the baking sheet and allow it to set in your refrigerator.

Cut your lokum into cubes and coat with the confectioners' sugar mixture. Bon appétit!

Mixed Berry and Fig Compote

(Ready in about 20 minutes + chilling time | Servings 5)
Per serving: Calories: 150; Fat: 0.5g; Carbs: 36.4g; Protein: 1.4g
Ingredients
2 cups mixed berries
1 cup figs, chopped
4 tablespoons pomegranate juice
1/2 teaspoon ground cinnamon
1/2 teaspoon crystalized ginger
1/2 teaspoon vanilla extract
2 tablespoons honey
Directions
Place the fruit, pomegranate juice, ground cinnamon, crystalized ginger, vanilla extract in a saucepan; bring to medium heat.

Turn the heat to a simmer and continue to cook for about 11 minutes, stirring occasionally to combine well. Add in the honey and stir to combine.

Remove from the heat and keep in your refrigerator. Bon appétit!

Creamed Fruit Salad

(Ready in about 10 minutes + chilling time | Servings 3)
Per serving: Calories: 250; Fat: 0.7g; Carbs: 60g; Protein: 6.4g
Ingredients
1 orange, peeled and sliced
2 apples, pitted and diced
2 peaches, pitted and diced
1 cup seedless grapes
3/4 cup Greek-style yogurt, well-chilled
3 tablespoons honey
Directions
Divide the fruits between dessert bowls.

Top with the yogurt. Add a few drizzles of honey to each serving and serve well-chilled. Bon appétit!

Mini Orange Tarts

(Ready in about 45 minutes | Servings 6)
Per serving: Calories: 398; Fat: 28.5g; Carbs: 24.9g; Protein: 11.9g
Ingredients
1 cup coconut flour
1/2 cup almond flour
A pinch of grated nutmeg

A pinch of sea salt
1/4 teaspoon ground cloves
1/4 teaspoon ground anise
1 cup brown sugar
6 eggs
2 cups heavy cream
2 oranges, peeled and sliced
Directions
Begin by preheating your oven to 350 degrees F. Thoroughly combine the flour with spices. Stir in the sugar, eggs, and heavy cream. Mix again to combine well.

Divide the batter into six lightly greased ramekins. Top with the oranges and bake in the preheated oven for about 40 minutes until the clafoutis is just set. Bon appétit!

Traditional Kalo Prama

(Ready in about 1 hour 45 minutes + chilling time | Servings 6)
Per serving: Calories: 478; Fat: 22.5g; Carbs: 62.4g; Protein: 8.2g
Ingredients
2 large eggs
1/2 cup Greek yogurt
1/2 cup coconut oil
1/2 cup sugar
8 ounces semolina
1 teaspoon baking soda
2 tablespoons walnuts, chopped
1/4 teaspoon ground nutmeg
1/4 teaspoon ground anise
1/2 teaspoon ground cinnamon
1 cup water
1 ½ cups caster sugar
1 teaspoon lemon zest
1 teaspoon lemon juice
Directions
Thoroughly combine the eggs, yogurt, coconut oil, and sugar. Add in the semolina, baking soda, walnuts, nutmeg, anise, and cinnamon.

Let it rest for 1 ½ hour.

Bake in the preheated oven at 350 degrees F for approximately 40 minutes or until a tester inserted in the center of the cake comes out dry and clean. Transfer to a wire rack to cool completely before slicing.

Meanwhile, bring the water and caster sugar to a full boil; add in the lemon zest and lemon juice, and turn the heat to a simmer; let it simmer for about 8 minutes or until the sauce has thickened slightly.

Cut the cake into diamonds and pour the syrup over the top; allow it to soak for about 2 hours. Bon appétit!

Turkish-Style Chocolate Halva

(Ready in about 20 minutes + chilling time | Servings 12)
Per serving: Calories: 388; Fat: 27.5g; Carbs: 31.6g; Protein: 7.9g

Ingredients
1/2 cup water
2 cups sugar
2 cups tahini
1/4 teaspoon cardamom
1/4 teaspoon cinnamon
A pinch of sea salt
6 ounces dark chocolate, broken into chunks
Directions
Bring the water to a full boil in a small saucepan. Add in the sugar and stir. Let it cook, stirring occasionally, until a candy thermometer registers 250 degrees F. Heat off.
Stir in the tahini. Continue to stir with a wooden spoon just until halva comes together in a smooth mass; do not overmix your halva.
Add in the cardamom, cinnamon, and salt; stir again to combine well. Now, scrape your halva into a parchment-lined square pan.
Microwave the chocolate until melted; pour the melted chocolate over your halva and smooth the top.
Let it cool to room temperature; cover tightly with a plastic wrap and place in your refrigerator for at least 2 hours. Bon appétit!

Rice Pudding with Dried Figs

(Ready in about 45 minutes | Servings 4)
Per serving: Calories: 228; Fat: 6.1g; Carbs: 35.1g; Protein: 7.1g
Ingredients
3 cups milk
1 cup water
2 tablespoons sugar
1/3 cup white rice, rinsed
1 tablespoon honey
4 dried figs, chopped
1/2 teaspoon cinnamon
1/2 teaspoon rose water
Directions
In a deep saucepan, bring the milk, water and sugar to a boil until the sugar has dissolved.
Stir in the rice, honey, figs, raisins, cinnamon, and turn the heat to a simmer; let it simmer for about 40 minutes, stirring periodically to prevent your pudding from sticking.
Afterwards, stir in the rose water. Divide the pudding between individual bowls and serve. Bon appétit!

Fruit Kabobs with Yogurt Deep

(Ready in about 10 minutes | Servings 4)
Per serving: Calories: 98; Fat: 0.2g; Carbs: 20.7g; Protein: 2.8g
Ingredients
8 clementine orange segments
8 medium-sized strawberries
8 pineapple cubes
8 seedless grapes
1/2 cup Greek-style yogurt
1/2 teaspoon vanilla extract
2 tablespoons honey

Directions
Thread the fruits onto 4 skewers.
In a mixing dish, thoroughly combine the yogurt, vanilla, and honey.
Serve alongside your fruit kabobs for dipping. Bon appétit!

No-Bake Chocolate Squares

(Ready in about 10 minutes + chilling time | Servings 12)
Per serving: Calories: 198; Fat: 13g; Carbs: 17.3g; Protein: 4.6g
Ingredients
8 ounces bittersweet chocolate
1 cup tahini paste
1/4 cup almonds, chopped
1/4 cup walnuts, chopped
Directions
Microwave the chocolate for about 30 seconds or until melted. Stir in the tahini, almonds, and walnuts.
Spread the batter into a parchment-lined baking pan.
Place in your refrigerator until set, for about 3 hours. Cut into squares and serve well-chilled. Bon appétit!

Greek Parfait with Mixed Berries

(Ready in about 10 minutes | Servings 2)
Per serving: Calories: 238; Fat: 16.7g; Carbs: 53g; Protein: 21.6g
Ingredients
2 cups Greek yogurt
2 cups mixed berries
1/2 cup granola
Directions
Alternate layers of mixed berries, granola, and yogurt until two dessert bowls are filled completely.
Cover and place in your refrigerator until you're ready to serve. Bon appétit!

Greek-Style Chocolate Semifreddo

(Ready in about 15 minutes + chilling time | Servings 3)
Per serving: Calories: 517; Fat: 27.7g; Carbs: 61g; Protein: 6.8g
Ingredients
3 ounces dark chocolate, broken into chunks
1 teaspoon vanilla extract
A pinch of grated nutmeg
A pinch of sea salt
1 cup heavy cream, divided
2 egg whites, at room temperature
1/2 cup caster sugar
4 tablespoons water
1/2 cup plain Greek yogurt
1 tablespoon brandy
2 tablespoons dark chocolate curls, to decorate
Directions
In a glass bowl, thoroughly combine the chocolate, vanilla, nutmeg, and sea salt.
In a small saucepan, bring the cream to a simmer. Pour the hot cream over the chocolate mixture and stir until everything is well incorporated.

Place in your refrigerator for about 1 hour.
Now, mix the egg whites on high speed until soft peaks form.
Dissolve the sugar in water over medium-low heat until a candy thermometer registers 250 degrees F or until the syrup has thickened.
Now, pour the syrup into the beaten egg whites and continue to beat until glossy. Fold in the chilled chocolate mixture, Greek yogurt, and brandy; mix again until everything is well combined.
Freeze your dessert for at least 3 hours. Then, let it sit at room temperature for about 15 minutes before slicing and serving. Top with the chocolate curls. Bon appétit!

Traditional Italian Cake with Almonds

(Ready in about 45 minutes | Servings 9)
Per serving: Calories: 407; Fat: 14.7g; Carbs: 61.4g; Protein: 6.6g
Ingredients
4 ripe peaches, peeled, pitted, and sliced
1 tablespoon fresh lemon juice
2 ¼ cups all-purpose flour
1 teaspoon baking soda
1/2 teaspoon baking powder
A pinch of grated nutmeg
A pinch of sea salt
1/2 teaspoon ground cloves
1/2 teaspoon ground cinnamon
1/2 cup olive oil
1 1/3 cups sugar
3 eggs, at room temperature
1 cup Greek yogurt
1 teaspoon pure vanilla extract
1/2 cup almonds, chopped
Directions
Begin by preheating your oven to 350 degrees F. Toss the peaches with lemon juice and set them aside.
Then, thoroughly combine the dry ingredients.
Then, beat the olive oil and sugar using your mixer at low speed.
Gradually fold in the eggs, one at a time, and continue to mix for a few minutes more until it has thickened.
Add in the yogurt and vanilla, and mix again.
Add the wet mixture to the dry ingredients and stir until you get a thick batter. Fold in the almonds and stir to combine well.
Spoon the batter into a parchment-lined baking pan and level the top using a wooden spoon.
Bake in the preheated oven for about 40 minutes or until a tester comes out dry and clean. Let it cool on a wire rack before slicing and serving. Bon appétit!

Date, Walnut and Tahini Balls

(Ready in about 10 minutes | Servings 8)
Per serving: Calories: 233; Fat: 9.7g; Carbs: 34.9g; Protein: 6g
Ingredients
1 ½ cups dates, pitted and soaked for 15 minutes
1/4 cup tahini

1/4 cup peanut butter
1/4 cup raw cacao powder
2 tablespoons chocolate chunks
4 tablespoons walnuts, chopped
Directions
Mix all ingredients in your food processor or blender until it forms a thick dough.
Using oiled hands, roll it into bite-sized balls.
Transfer to your refrigerator and serve well-chilled. Enjoy!

Classic Mixed Berry Cake

(Ready in about 40 minutes | Servings 9)
Per serving: Calories: 409; Fat: 16.1g; Carbs: 63.2g; Protein: 4g
Ingredients
2 ½ cups mixed berries, fresh or frozen
6 ounces all-purpose flour)
7 ounces granulated sugar
1 tablespoon baking powder
A pinch of sea salt
A pinch of grated nutmeg
1/2 teaspoon ground cinnamon
1 teaspoon vanilla paste
8 tablespoons olive oil
1/2 cup Greek yogurt
Directions
Begin by preheating your oven to 330 degrees F.
Arrange the mixed berries on the bottom of a parchment -ined baking pan.
Thoroughly combine all the dry ingredients. In another bowl, thoroughly combine the wet ingredients.
Stir the wet mixture into the dry ingredients and mix to combine well. Spoon the batter over the berries.
Bake in the preheated oven for approximately 36 minutes or until lightly golden.
Serve at room temperature and enjoy!

The Best Chocolate Quinoa Cake Ever

(Ready in about 15 minutes | Servings 9)
Per serving: Calories: 299; Fat: 14.1g; Carbs: 39.8g; Protein: 6.1g
Ingredients
3/4 cup dry quinoa
1/2 cup butter, melted
3 eggs
1/2 cup Greek yogurt
1 teaspoon vanilla extract
1 cup granulated sugar
2 tablespoons honey
3/4 cup cocoa powder
1 teaspoon baking powder
A pinch of sea salt
1/2 cup chocolate chips
Directions
Bring 1 2/3 cups of water to a boil over medium-high heat; add the quinoa and lower the heat. Let it simmer until the quinoa has absorbed all of the water, about 15 minutes.

Then, preheat your oven to 350 degrees F.

Now, mix the quinoa, butter, eggs, Greek yogurt, and vanilla extract in a blender until well combined.

Combine the sugar, honey, cocoa powder, baking powder, and salt in a large bowl. Add the quinoa mixture to the sugar/cocoa mixture and mix to combine well.

Fold in the chocolate chips; scrape the batter into a parchment-lined cake pan.

Bake in the preheated oven for about 40 minutes. Bon appétit!

Creamy Apricot and Almond Dessert

(Ready in about 5 minutes | Servings 4)

Per serving: Calories: 139; Fat: 8.2g; Carbs: 6g; Protein: 8.2g

Ingredients

1/4 cup Greek-style yogurt
1 cup ricotta
1/4 cup raisins
1/4 cup almonds, slivered
1/2 teaspoon almond extract
2 teaspoons agave syrup
1 cup apricots, pitted and sliced

Directions

Thoroughly combine the yogurt, ricotta, raisins, almonds, almond extract, and agave syrup.

Divide the mixture between dessert bowls and top with the sliced apricots.

Bon appétit!

Ravani Cake with Mango

(Ready in about 1 hour 40 minutes + chilling time | Servings 7)

Per serving: Calories: 348; Fat: 16.4g; Carbs: 44.4g; Protein: 5.4g

Ingredients

1/2 cup full-fat milk
1/2 cup coconut oil
1 cup granulated sugar
1 ½ cups semolina
1 teaspoon baking powder
1/2 teaspoon ground anise
1/4 teaspoon ground cinnamon
1/4 teaspoon ground cloves
1 teaspoon vanilla paste
1 cup mango pulp, chopped

Directions

Thoroughly combine the milk, coconut oil, and granulated sugar. Add in the semolina, baking powder, and aromatics.

Fold in the mango pulp and allow the batter to rest for about 1 hour.

Bake in the preheated oven at 350 degrees F for approximately 40 minutes or until a tester inserted in the center of the cake comes out dry and clean.

Transfer to a wire rack to cool completely before slicing and serving. Enjoy!

Traditional Greek Prune Compote

(Ready in about 20 minutes + chilling time | Servings 4)

Per serving: Calories: 238; Fat: 0.4g; Carbs: 60.4g; Protein: 3.4g

Ingredients

1/3 cup water
1/2 cup orange juice
1/3 pound dried prunes, soaked
1 ounce raisins, soaked
4 tablespoons honey
1/2 teaspoon cloves
1/2 vanilla bean
1 cinnamon stick
2 tablespoon Metaxa
2 ounces Greek yogurt, well-chilled

Directions

In a saucepan, place the water, orange juice, prunes, raisins, honey, and spices. Bring to a boil and immediately reduce the heat to a simmer.

Let it simmer for about 18 minutes. Let it cool completely and add in the Metaxa brandy.

Serve in individual bowls, garnished with a dollop of well-chilled Greek yogurt. Enjoy!

Greek-Style Fruit Salad

(Ready in about 10 minutes + chilling time | Servings 5)

Per serving: Calories: 259; Fat: 5.7g; Carbs: 51.7g; Protein: 6g

Ingredients

1 cup blueberries
1 cup seedless grapes
1 cup apples, peeled, cored and diced
1 cup prunes, soaked and diced
2 tablespoons orange juice
2 tablespoons lemon juice
1/2 cup walnuts, roughly chopped
1 cup Greek-style yogurt
5 tablespoons honey

Directions

Toss the fruits with the orange juice and lemon juice. Add in the walnuts and gently stir to combine.

Top with the Greek-style yogurt. Drizzle each serving with the honey.

Serve well-chilled and enjoy!

Authentic Greek Yogurt and Walnut Dessert

(Ready in about 10 minutes | Servings 2)

Per serving: Calories: 251; Fat: 5.2g; Carbs: 39.7g; Protein: 14.6g

Ingredients

1 ½ cups Greek yogurt
4 tablespoons honey
2 tablespoons walnuts, roughly chopped

Directions

Add half of the yogurt to a dessert bowl. Drizzle with half of the honey; top with half of the walnuts.

Repeat with the remaining ingredients and serve well chilled.

Bon appétit!

Coffee and Nougat Semifrío

(Ready in about 1 hour 15 minutes + chilling time | Servings 7)
Per serving: Calories: 308; Fat: 14g; Carbs: 42.3g; Protein: 3.6g

Ingredients
3 ounces bittersweet chocolate
1 teaspoon instant coffee
A pinch of grated nutmeg
A pinch of sea salt
2 cups heavy cream
4 eggs whites
3/4 cup caster sugar
3 ounces nougat, chopped into small chunks

Directions
In a glass bowl, thoroughly combine the chocolate, instant coffee, nutmeg, and sea salt.
In a small saucepan, bring the cream to a simmer.
Pour the hot cream over the chocolate mixture and stir until everything is well incorporated.
Place in your refrigerator for about 1 hour.
Now, mix the egg whites on high speed until soft peaks form.
Dissolve the sugar in 1/6 cup of water over medium-low heat until a candy thermometer registers 250 degrees F or until the syrup has thickened.
Now, pour the syrup into the beaten egg whites and continue to beat until glossy. Fold in the nougat chunks and mix again until everything is well combined.
Freeze your dessert for at least 3 hours. Allow it to sit at room temperature for about 15 minutes before slicing and serving. Bon appétit!

The Best Family Baklava Ever

(Ready in about 35 minutes + chilling time | Servings 8)
Per serving: Calories: 338; Fat: 21.4g; Carbs: 32.9g; Protein: 5.2g

Ingredients
1 can (8-ounces) refrigerated crescent rolls
2 cups walnuts, chopped
1/2 cup sugar
1/2 teaspoon ground cloves
1 teaspoon vanilla extract
1/2 teaspoon ground cinnamon
1/4 cup honey
4 tablespoons olive oil
2 teaspoons fresh lemon juice

Directions
Start by preheating your oven to 350 degrees F.
Unroll the dough and separate into 2 rectangles.
Place 1 rectangle in a lightly greased pie pan to form a crust.
In a mixing bowl, thoroughly combine the walnuts, 1/4 cup of the sugar and the spices.
Spread the walnut mixture evenly over the crust. Top with the other dough rectangle. Using a sharp knife, cut into diamond shapes all the way to the bottom of the pie pan.

In a saucepan, bring the remaining 1/4 cup sugar, honey, olive oil, and lemon juice to a rapid boil. Heat off; spoon half of the sugar syrup over the pie.
Bake in the preheated oven for approximately 30 minutes or until golden brown on the top. Spoon the remaining sugar syrup evenly over the hot baklava.
Allow it to cool completely, and then, refrigerate for at least 1 hour. Bon appétit!

Easy Chocolate Cream Pie

(Ready in about 15 minutes + chilling time | Servings 8)
Per serving: Calories: 528; Fat: 35.6g; Carbs: 46g; Protein: 7.9g

Ingredients
25 Oreos, crushed
4 tablespoons butter, melted
5 ounces dark chocolate, chopped
9 ounces ounce condensed milk, sweetened
1/4 teaspoon ground cinnamon
A pinch of sea salt
2 cups double cream
2 tablespoons honey
1/4 cup caster sugar
1 teaspoon vanilla extract
3 ounces Greek-style yogurt

Directions
Mix the Oreo cookies and melted butter to form a crust; press the crust into a pie pan.
Microwave the chocolate until melted and smooth.
Stir the milk, cinnamon, and salt into the chocolate.
Mix the cream with the honey, sugar, and vanilla until stiff peaks form.
Slowly add the chocolate mixture to 1/2 of the cream mixture; add in the yogurt and stir again to combine well. Spoon the mixture into the pie pan.
Top with the remaining cream mixture. Place in your refrigerator until ready to serve. Serve well-chilled and enjoy!

Koufeto with Walnuts

(Ready in about 15 minutes | Servings 12)
Per serving: Calories: 316; Fat: 6.6g; Carbs: 67g; Protein: 2.3g

Ingredients
2 pounds pumpkin, peeled and cut into chunks
1 pound sugar
1 cup honey
1 teaspoon whole cloves
1 cinnamon stick
1 cup walnuts, chopped

Directions
Bring the pumpkin, sugar, and honey to a boil; add in the cloves and cinnamon.
Stir continuously to prevent from sticking.
Cook until your Koufeto has thickened; fold in the walnuts and let it cool completely. Bon appétit!

Fudge with Almonds

(Ready in about 15 minutes + chilling time | Servings 12)

Per serving: Calories: 176; Fat: 11.6g; Carbs: 13.8g; Protein: 3.7g

Ingredients

1 cup milk chocolate, cut into chunks
1 cup dark chocolate, cut into chunks
8 ounces chocolate almond milk
1/4 cup peanut butter
1/2 cup almonds, chopped
1/4 teaspoon ground cloves
1/2 teaspoon ground cinnamon

Directions

Microwave the chocolate until melted.
In a saucepan, heat the milk and add the warm milk to the melted chocolate.
Add in the peanut butter, chopped almonds, cloves, and cinnamon. Mix to combine well.
Pour the mixture into a well-greased pan and place it in your refrigerator until set. Bon appétit!

Italian Berry Composta

(Ready in about 20 minutes + chilling time | Servings 4)
Per serving: Calories: 405; Fat: 5.8g; Carbs: 75.3g; Protein: 6.29g

Ingredients

1 cup semi-sweet red wine
1/2 cup water
4 tablespoons brown sugar
1 cup cranberries
1 cup sweet cherries
1 cup golden raisins
4 tablespoons almonds, slivered
Juice from 1 orange
1 cinnamon stick
1 vanilla bean, split into halves
3 ounces mascarpone cheese
1/2 cup dark chocolate, shaved
1/2 cup candied orange peel

Directions

Add the wine, water, and sugar to a large saucepan. Bring to a boil, stirring continuously to dissolve the sugar.
Ad in the fruits, almonds, orange juice, cinnamon, and vanilla. Let it simmer for about 18 minutes longer.
Allow the mixture to cool completely and then, refrigerate for at least 1 hour.
Alternate layers of the compote and mascarpone cheese; top with the chocolate and candied orange peel. Serve well-chilled. Bon appétit!

Turkish Irmik Helvasi

(Ready in about 1 hour 40 minutes + chilling time | Servings 9)
Per serving: Calories: 344; Fat: 16.9g; Carbs: 36.6g; Protein: 9.4g

Ingredients

3 large eggs
2 cups milk
1 cup Greek yogurt
1/3 cup vegetable oil
1 cup sugar

1 ½ cups semolina
1/2 cup coconut, shredded
1/2 teaspoon baking powder
1 teaspoon pure vanilla extract
1/2 cup walnuts, ground

Directions

Thoroughly combine the eggs, milk, yogurt, oil, and sugar. Add in the semolina, coconut, baking powder, vanilla, and walnuts.
Let it rest for about 1 hour.
Bake in the preheated oven at 350 degrees F for approximately 40 minutes or until a tester inserted in the center of the cake comes out dry and clean. Transfer to a wire rack to cool completely before slicing and serving. Bon appétit!

Italian-Style Lemon Cheesecake

(Ready in about 2 hours + chilling time | Servings 9)
Per serving: Calories: 487; Fat: 30.7g; Carbs: 35.6g; Protein: 19.1g

Ingredients

16 ounces soft cheese
1 (16-ounce) container ricotta cheese
1 cup powdered sugar
1/2 cup honey
1 teaspoon vanilla extract
2 eggs, well beaten
2 tablespoons lemon juice
3 tablespoons all-purpose flour
3 tablespoons cornstarch
1 stick butter
2 cups Greek yogurt

Directions

Begin by preheating your oven to 350 degrees F. Spritz the sides and bottom of a springform pan with a nonstick spray.
Thoroughly combine the cheese, powdered sugar, honey, vanilla, eggs, lemon juice, flour, cornstarch, and butter.
Lastly, fold in the Greek yogurt and stir again to combine well. Pour the mixture into the prepared springform pan.
Bake your cheesecake for about 1 hour; heat off; leave in the oven for 1 hour more.
Allow your cheesecake to cool completely before slicing and serving. Bon appétit!

Chocolate Fudge Ice Pops

(Ready in about 10 minutes + chilling time | Servings 9)
Per serving: Calories: 177; Fat: 10.7g; Carbs: 19.6g; Protein: 4.7g

Ingredients

1 1/3 cups plain milk
2 tablespoons carob powder
1/4 cup cocoa powder
2 tablespoons honey
1/2 teaspoon ground cinnamon
A pinch of flaky sea salt
4 ounces milk chocolate chips
5 ounces dark chocolate chips

1 ½ cups Greek yogurt

Directions

In a saucepan, heat the milk, carob powder, cocoa powder, honey, cinnamon, and salt over medium heat.

Whisk until well combined and dissolved or about 6 minutes. Now, pour the warm milk mixture over the chocolate chips.

Beat the mixture using a wire whisk; afterwards, fold in the yogurt and whisk again.

Spoon the mixture into popsicle molds and freeze until solid, about 6 hours. Bon appétit!

Old-Fashioned Brownies

(Ready in about 35 minutes + chilling time | Servings 12)

Per serving: Calories: 400; Fat: 24.7g; Carbs: 40.2g; Protein: 5.7g

Ingredients

3 eggs
2 ounces honey
6 ounces sugar
12 ounces bittersweet chocolate
1/2 cup extra-virgin olive oil
2 ounces almonds, coarsely chopped
4 1/2 ounces all-purpose flour, sifted

Directions

Begin by preheating your oven to 330 degrees F. Line a baking pan with a parchment paper.

Beat the eggs, honey and sugar using an electric mixer at high speed for 4 to 5 minutes.

Microwave your chocolate until completely melted. Add in the olive oil, the egg mixture, and almonds.

Gradually add in the flour whisking constantly to avoid lumps; do not overmix the batter. Next, scrape the batter into the prepared baking pan.

Bake in the preheated oven for about 30 minutes, until the center is just set to the touch.

Allow your brownie to cool to room temperature before slicing and serving. Bon appétit!

Pistachio Penuche Fudge

(Ready in about 10 minutes + chilling time | Servings 12)

Per serving: Calories: 207; Fat: 17g; Carbs: 11.6g; Protein: 3.7g

Ingredients

12 ounces evaporated milk
4 tablespoons coconut oil
1 ½ cups white chocolate, broken into chunks
1/2 teaspoon ground cinnamon
A pinch of grated nutmeg
A pinch of sea salt
1/2 teaspoon vanilla bean paste
3/4 cup hulled pistachios, chopped

Directions

In a saucepan, heat the milk, coconut oil, chocolate, cinnamon, nutmeg, and salt; add in the vanilla bean paste and stir until creamy and smooth.

Fold in the pistachios and stir again to combine well. Scrape the mixture into a parchment-lined baking pan.

Place in your refrigerator until set and cut into squares. Enjoy!

Dried Fruit Compote (Hosafi)

(Ready in about 20 minutes + chilling time | Servings 4)

Per serving: Calories: 361; Fat: 5.4g; Carbs: 79.6g; Protein: 7.4g

Directions

1 cup dried apricots
1 cup dried figs
1/2 cup prunes
1/3 cup pistachios, hulled
4 tablespoons honey
1/2 teaspoon star anise
1 cinnamon stick
3-4 cloves
A pinch of grated nutmeg
A pinch of sea salt
3 ounces Greek yogurt, well-chilled

Directions

In a saucepan, place the fruits, pistachios, honey, and spices. Cover with the water by 1 inch. Bring to a boil and immediately reduce the heat to a simmer.

Let it simmer for about 18 minutes. Allow it to cool completely.

Serve in individual bowls, garnished with a dollop of well-chilled Greek yogurt. Enjoy!

Almond and Raisin Baklava

(Ready in about 35 minutes + chilling time | Servings 8)

Per serving: Calories: 532; Fat: 26.7g; Carbs: 71g; Protein: 5.1g

Ingredients

16 ounces crescent dough sheets
2 cups almonds, chopped
1 cup golden raisins
1 cup butter
1 cup granulated sugar
1/2 teaspoon ground anise
1/4 teaspoon grated nutmeg
1 teaspoon ground cinnamon
1/2 teaspoon almond extract
1/2 teaspoon vanilla extract
1 cup water
2 tablespoons lime juice
1/3 cup honey

Directions

Start by preheating your oven to 350 degrees F.

Unroll the dough and place two sheets of dough in a lightly greased pie pan. Brush with the butter and repeat until you have 8 sheets layered.

In a mixing bowl, combine the almonds and raisins. Spread about 3 tablespoons of the almond mixture on top. Top with two sheets of dough, brush with the butter, and repeat layering until you run out of ingredients.

End with 6 sheets of dough.

In a saucepan, bring the sugar, spices, water, lime juice, and honey, to a boil. Heat off; spoon half of the sugar syrup over the pie.

Bake in the preheated oven for approximately 30 minutes or until golden brown on the top. Spoon the remaining sugar syrup evenly over the hot baklava. Allow it to cool completely, and then, refrigerate for at least 1 hour. Bon appétit!

Classic Orange Cheesecake

(Ready in about 25 minutes + chilling time | Servings 12)

Per serving: Calories: 552; Fat: 34g; Carbs: 57.4g; Protein: 7.4g

Ingredients

50 Oreo cookies, crumbled
3 tablespoons coconut oil, at room temperature
22 ounces cream cheese, room temperature
1 cup Greek yogurt
Zest of 1 orange, finely grated
2 tablespoons orange liqueur
1/2 cup honey
1/2 cup sugar
1 cup double cream
1/2 cup powdered sugar
1 teaspoon vanilla extract
2 ounces dark chocolate, shaved

Directions

Thoroughly combine 35 Oreo cookies and coconut oil to form a crust; press the crust into a pie pan.

Mix the cream cheese with Greek yogurt, orange zest, orange liqueur, honey, and sugar until well combined. Spread this layer over the crust.

Then, beat the cream, powdered sugar and vanilla until stiff peaks form.

Slowly add in the remaining 15 Oreos; stir again to combine. Spoon the mixture into the pie pan.

Place your cheesecake in the refrigerator until ready to serve. Top with the chocolate and serve well-chilled!

Chocolate and Hazelnut Chickpea Blondies

(Ready in about 25 minutes + chilling time | Servings 12)

Per serving: Calories: 217; Fat: 11.3g; Carbs: 26.3g; Protein: 4.6g

Ingredients

12 ounces canned chickpeas, drained and rinsed
2 ounces hazelnuts, ground
1/4 cup butter, at room temperature
1/4 cup peanut butter
1/2 cup brown sugar
1/4 cup honey
1/2 teaspoon baking powder
1 teaspoon vanilla extract
1/2 teaspoon ground cinnamon
1/2 teaspoon ground cardamom
A pinch of grated nutmeg
A pinch of salt
1/2 cup dark chocolate, broken into chunks

Directions

Start by preheating your oven to 350 degrees F. Spritz a pie pan with a nonstick cooking spray.

Mix all ingredients, except for the chocolate, in your food processor or blender.

Fold in the chocolate chunks and gently stir to combine. Scrape the batter into the prepared pie pan.

Bake in the preheated oven for about 22 minutes or until a toothpick inserted into the center comes out dry and clean.

Transfer your cake to a wire rack to cool before slicing and serving. Bon appétit!

Grandma's Brownie Cupcakes

(Ready in about 35 minutes + chilling time | Servings 12)

Per serving: Calories: 354; Fat: 17.7g; Carbs: 48.4g; Protein: 4.4g

Ingredients

4 eggs
2 cups caster sugar
1 cup butter, melted
2 teaspoons pure vanilla extract
1/4 teaspoon grated nutmeg
1/2 teaspoon ground cinnamon
1/4 teaspoon ground cardamom
1 cup all-purpose flour
1 cup Dutch-processed cocoa powder
1/2 teaspoon salt

Directions

Begin by preheating your oven to 340 degrees F. Line a 12-cup muffin pan with cupcake liners.

Beat the eggs and sugar using a wire whisk for 4 to 5 minutes. Add in the butter and spices and beat again to combine well.

Sift in the flour, cocoa powder, and salt, whisking constantly to avoid lumps; do not overmix the batter.

Next, scrape the batter into the muffin pan.

Bake in the preheated oven for about 30 minutes, until a toothpick comes out mostly clean.

Allow your cupcakes to cool to room temperature before unmolding and serving. Bon appétit!

Authentic Samali with Orange Syrup

(Ready in about 1 hour 40 minutes + chilling time | Servings 10)

Per serving: Calories: 358; Fat: 17.4g; Carbs: 40.6g; Protein: 8.6g

Ingredients

4 large eggs
2 cups Greek yogurt
1/2 cup vegetable oil
3/4 cup sugar
1 ½ cups semolina
1 teaspoon baking powder
1/2 teaspoon sea salt
1/2 teaspoon ground cinnamon
1/4 teaspoon ground cloves
1/2 teaspoon vanilla extract
1/2 cup hulled pistachio nuts, ground

1 cup caster sugar
1 cup water
1 teaspoon crystallized ginger
Fresh juice from 1 orange

Directions

Thoroughly combine the eggs, Greek yogurt, oil, and sugar. Add in the semolina, baking powder, salt, cinnamon, cloves, vanilla, and ground pistachio nuts. Let it rest for about 1 hour.

Bake in the preheated oven at 350 degrees F for approximately 40 minutes or until a tester inserted in the center of the cake comes out dry and clean. Transfer to a wire rack to cool completely before slicing.

While your cake is baking, bring the water and caster sugar to a full boil; add in the ginger and orange juice; immediately turn the heat to a simmer.

Let the mixture simmer for about 8 minutes or until the syrup has thickened slightly.

Cut the cake into diamonds and pour the syrup over the top; allow it to soak for about 2 hours. Bon appétit!

Turkish Baked Pudding (Sütlaç)

(Ready in about 40 minutes + chilling time | Servings 4)
Per serving: Calories: 358; Fat: 17.4g; Carbs: 40.6g; Protein: 8.6g

Ingredients

3/4 cup Arborio rice, rinsed
6 cups whole milk
1 ½ cups sugar
2 tablespoons honey
1 teaspoon vanilla extract
A pinch of sea salt
1/4 teaspoon ground cardamom
3 teaspoons cornstarch
2 egg yolks whisked with 4 tablespoons of milk
1/2 teaspoon ground cinnamon

Directions

Begin by preheating your oven to 350 degrees F. Place the rice in a large saucepan and cover with enough water by about 1/2 inch. Bring it to a boil. Immediately reduce the heat to simmer; let it simmer for about 6 minutes. Add in the 5 cups of milk, sugar, honey, vanilla extract, sea salt, and cardamom. Let it cook for 9 to 10 minutes.

Now, whisk together the remaining 1 cup of milk and the cornstarch. Now, pour the mixture into the rice and stir until it has thickened. Heat off.

Spoon into lightly buttered ramekins and spoon the egg yolk mixture into the center of each ramekin.

Now, swirl the egg yolks from the center to the edges using the back of the spoon.

Bake the pudding for about 18 minutes until the tops are charred in spots. Let it cool on your countertop, then, place in your refrigerator until ready to serve.

To serve, dust with a sprinkle of ground cinnamon. Bon appétit!

OTHER FAVORITES

Favorite Homemade Granola

(Ready in about 40 minutes + chilling time | Servings 10)

Per serving: Calories: 337; Fat: 15.7g; Carbs: 43.2g; Protein: 9.6g

Ingredients
2 ½ cups rolled oats
1/2 cup walnuts, chopped
1 cup almond, slivered
1/4 cup extra-virgin olive oil
1 tablespoon ground cinnamon
1 tablespoon ground cardamom
1 tablespoon vanilla bean paste
1/2 cup sunflower seeds
1/2 cup pumpkin seeds
1 cup sultanas
1 cup golden raisins
4 tablespoons honey
1/2 cup chia seeds

Directions
Start by preheating your oven to 350 degrees F. Line a baking sheet with a piece of parchment paper.
Thoroughly combine all ingredients and spread the mixture on the prepared baking sheet.
Bake your granola for about 30 minutes, stirring it once or twice during the cooking time.
Allow your granola to cool down; then, store it in airtight containers. Bon appétit!

Tomato and Anchovy Sauce

(Ready in about 30 minutes | Servings 10)

Per serving: Calories: 155; Fat: 13.3g; Carbs: 6.3g; Protein: 4.6g

Ingredients
1/2 cup olive oil
6 cloves garlic, minced
4 scallion stalks, chopped
20 anchovy filets, mashed
1 cup Kalamata olives, pitted and chopped
1 teaspoon dried oregano
1 teaspoon dried rosemary
20 ounces crushed tomatoes
Sea salt and ground black pepper, to taste
1/2 cup Italian flat-leaf parsley, chopped

Directions
Heat the olive oil over medium heat. Once hot, sauté the garlic, scallions, anchovy filets, olives dried oregano, and rosemary for about 5 minutes.
Add in the tomatoes, sea salt and black pepper, bringing to a boil. Now, turn the heat to a simmer. Let it cook for 13 minutes more until the sauce has thickened.
Afterwards, stir in the parsley and continue to cook for 12 minutes more. Bon appétit!

Classic Aïoli Sauce

(Ready in about 10 minutes | Servings 10)

Per serving: Calories: 250; Fat: 27.9g; Carbs: 0.7g; Protein: 0.6g

Ingredients
2 egg yolks
3 garlic cloves
1 teaspoon Dijon mustard
1/2 teaspoon salt
3 tablespoons fresh lemon juice
1 ¼ cups extra-virgin olive oil

Directions
Mix the egg yolks, garlic, mustard, salt, and lemon juice in your blender at high speed for 2 to 3 minutes. While the machine is running, gradually pour in the olive oil until the mixture comes together.
Cover and place in your refrigerator until ready to serve. Bon appétit!

Authentic Yogurt Tahini Sauce

(Ready in about 10 minutes | Servings 4)

Per serving: Calories: 85; Fat: 6.1g; Carbs: 4.8g; Protein: 4.3g

Ingredients
1 teaspoon garlic, pressed
3 tablespoons tahini paste
8 tablespoons Greek-style yogurt
3 teaspoons fresh lime juice
1/4 teaspoon ground cumin
Sea salt and ground black pepper, to taste

Directions
In a mixing bowl, whisk all ingredients until well combined.
Serve the sauce well-chilled with veggie sticks for dipping.
Bon appétit!

Authentic Grandma's Tarama salad

(Ready in about 10 minutes | Servings 8)

Per serving: Calories: 380; Fat: 29.4g; Carbs: 23.1g; Protein: 7.5g

Ingredients
12 ounces stale bread, crust removed and soaked in water
4 ½ ounces tarama (fish roe)
1 red onion, finely chopped
4 tablespoons fresh lemon juice
1 cup extra-virgin olive oil

Directions
Squeeze the soaked bread well to remove the excess liquid. Transfer it to your food processor.
Add in the tarama and onion and process until the ingredients are well combined and mashed. Add in the lemon juice and blend again.
While the machine is running, slowly add in the olive oil, a little bit at a time, until the mixture is smooth and creamy.
Serve with pita or chips. Bon appétit!

Sicilian Chicken Marsala

(Ready in about 25 minutes | Servings 4)
Per serving: Calories: 334; Fat: 17.8g; Carbs: 12g;
Protein: 29.5g
Ingredients
1 pound chicken tenderloins
2 tablespoons besan
Sea salt and freshly ground black pepper
2 tablespoons olive oil
10 ounces Cremini mushrooms, sliced
1 red onion, chopped
2 cloves garlic, minced
1 cup chicken broth
1/2 cup dry Marsala wine
1 cup double cream
1/2 teaspoon red pepper flakes
1 teaspoon dried marjoram
1 teaspoon dried oregano
1/2 teaspoon dried savory
Directions
Toss the chicken with the besan, salt, and black
pepper.
Heat the olive oil in a frying pan over medium-high
heat. Once hot, sear the chicken until no longer pink
or about 5 minutes.
Add in the mushrooms and continue to cook for 2 to
3 minutes more until the mushrooms release the
liquid. Add a splash of wine to deglaze the pan.
Add in the remaining ingredients, partially cover, and
reduce the heat to a simmer. Let it simmer for 13
minutes more until thoroughly cooked. Bon appétit!

Authentic Tomato and Parmesan Panzanella

(Ready in about 25 minutes | Servings 4)
Per serving: Calories: 333; Fat: 19g; Carbs: 32.2g;
Protein: 11.5g
Ingredients
4 tablespoons extra-virgin olive oil, divided
8 slices baguette
1 pound green beans, trimmed and cut in half
1 ½ pounds heirloom tomatoes, halved
2 ounces parmesan cheese, grated
Sea salt and red pepper flakes, to taste
1 small red onion, thinly sliced
2 tablespoons fresh lime juice
1 teaspoon Dijon mustard
2 tablespoons fresh parsley, roughly chopped
Directions
Preheat the olive oil in a nonstick skillet over
medium-high heat. Now, toast the baguette slices for
about 10 minutes.
Meanwhile, in a saucepan, cook the water and green
beans over medium heat. Let it cook for about 10
minutes until the beans are al dente.
Drain and transfer the beans to a salad bowl; add in
the tomatoes, cheese, salt, pepper, onion, lime juice,
and mustard; toss to combine well.
Top with the toasted bread and fresh parsley. Bon
appétit!

Homemade Walnut Parsley Pesto

(Ready in about 25 minutes | Servings 4)
Per serving: Calories: 194; Fat: 19g; Carbs: 3.2g;
Protein: 3.8g
Ingredients
1/2 cup extra-virgin olive oil
1/3 cup walnuts, toasted
1 teaspoon fresh garlic
1/2 cup parsley leaves, firmly packed
1/4 cup fresh oregano leaves, firmly packed
8 Kalamata olives
1 tablespoon lime juice
Sea salt and ground black pepper
3 ounces parmesan cheese, grated
Directions
In your food processor, place all ingredients, except
for the cheese.
Process until uniform and creamy. Fold in the grated
parmesan cheese and stir to combine.
Bon appétit!

Sweet Tahini and Yogurt Sauce

(Ready in about 10 minutes | Servings 6)
Per serving: Calories: 106; Fat: 6.1g; Carbs: 12.3g;
Protein: 2.4g
Ingredients
1/4 cup tahini
1/2 cup Greek yogurt
2 tablespoons fresh lime juice
3 tablespoons honey
1/4 teaspoon ground cinnamon
1/4 teaspoon ground cardamom
Directions
Thoroughly combine all ingredients until everything
is well incorporated.
Serve with sliced fruit for dipping.
Bon appétit!

Wild Garlic Sauce

(Ready in about 10 minutes | Servings 10)
Per serving: Calories: 250; Fat: 26.1g; Carbs: 2.3g;
Protein: 2.7g
Ingredients
1 cup wild garlic, roughly chopped
1 cup extra-virgin olive oil
1/2 cup almonds
Sea salt and ground black pepper, to taste
1/2 cup feta cheese, crumbled
Directions
In your food processor, place the wild garlic, olive oil,
almonds, salt, and black pepper.
Process until uniform and creamy. Fold in the
crumbled feta cheese and stir until it is well
incorporated.
Bon appétit!

Roasted Pepper and Basil Pesto

(Ready in about 10 minutes | Servings 8)
Per serving: Calories: 105; Fat: 9.1g; Carbs: 3.6g;
Protein: 2.3g

Ingredients
4 red bell peppers
1/4 cup extra-virgin olive oil
1 teaspoon garlic
1/4 cup almonds
1/2 cup fresh basil
Sea salt and red pepper flakes, to taste
3 ounces Halloumi cheese, crumbled
Directions
Place the peppers on a parchment-lined baking pan.
Roast the peppers at 420 degrees F for about 25 minutes.
Allow the peppers to sit for 30 minutes, then, peel them and remove the seeds and membranes.
Transfer the peppers to a bowl of your food processor.
Add the olive oil, garlic, almonds, basil, salt, and red pepper to the bowl of your food processor. Mix until everything is well incorporated.
Add in the cheese and pulse for a few seconds more or until well combined. Bon appétit!

Gnocchi with Aromatic Herb Sauce

(Ready in about 15 minutes | Servings 4)
Per serving: Calories: 305; Fat: 23.8g; Carbs: 10.6g; Protein: 11.3g
Ingredients
1 pound gnocchi
3 tablespoons olive oil
1 teaspoon garlic, minced
2 tablespoons fresh parsley, chopped
2 tablespoons fresh basil, chopped
2 tablespoons fresh chives, chopped
1/2 cup vegetable broth
1/2 lemon, juiced and zested
Directions
Cook the gnocchi according to the package instructions; drain.
Heat the olive oil in a saucepan over medium-high heat. Now, sauté the garlic and herbs for about 3 minutes until fragrant.
Add in the vegetable broth and simmer for about 7 minutes more.
Toss the prepared gnocchi with the sauce and serve hot. Bon appétit!

Easy Silan Syrup

(Ready in about 2 hours 30 minutes | Servings 12)
Per serving: Calories: 160; Fat: 0.2g; Carbs: 42.5g; Protein: 1.3g
Ingredients
1 ½ pounds dates, pitted
7 cups hot water
Directions
In a medium saucepan bring the dates and water to a boil. Immediately turn the heat to a simmer.
Let it simmer for about 2 hours or until the mixture has thickened. Allow the mixture to cool to room temperature.

Now, pour the liquid through a strainer lined with cheesecloth into a bowl.
Bring the strained date liquid back to a boil; then, turn the heat to a simmer and let it simmer for another 30 minutes or until syrupy.
Your sauce will continue to thicken as it cools. Enjoy!

Tuna and Feta Cheese Lettuce Wraps

(Ready in about 10 minutes | Servings 8)
Per serving: Calories: 300; Fat: 8.6g; Carbs: 27.5g; Protein: 33.8g
Ingredients
8 ounces canned tuna in water, drained
2 Carmen peppers, deseeded and diced
2 San Marzano tomatoes, chopped
1 red onion, chopped
2 tablespoons sun-dried tomatoes, chopped
1 ½ tablespoons deli mustard
2 ounces feta cheese, crumbled
2 tablespoons fresh basil, chopped
2 tablespoons fresh parsley, chopped
2 tablespoons fresh scallions, chopped
Sea salt and ground black pepper, to taste
1 butterhead lettuce, torn into leaves
Directions
Place the lettuce leaves on a working surface.
Divide the remaining ingredients between the lettuce leaves. Wrap each of them and serve immediately. Bon appétit!

Basic Tomato Relish

(Ready in about 10 minutes + chilling time | Servings 12)
Per serving: Calories: 182; Fat: 18.4g; Carbs: 3.9g; Protein: 1.3g
Ingredients
2 pounds vine-ripened tomatoes
1 large red onion
1 cup extra-virgin olive oil
1 teaspoon sea salt
1 teaspoon mustard seed
1 teaspoon fennel seeds
1 teaspoon garlic, chopped
2 tablespoons fresh basil, chopped
2 tablespoons fresh parsley, chopped
1/2 cup white vinegar
Directions
Toss the tomatoes and onion with the olive oil and salt. Place under the preheated boiler for about 9 minutes.
Place the roasted vegetables in a bowl of your food processor; add in the remaining ingredients.
Blitz until finely chopped but not puréed. Keep in your refrigerator for up to 3 days. Bon appétit!

Arugula and Feta Pesto Sauce

(Ready in about 10 minutes | Servings 10)
Per serving: Calories: 75; Fat: 7.1g; Carbs: 0.8g; Protein: 1.3g
Ingredients

1 cup fresh arugula leaves, packed
1/4 cup fresh chives
1/4 cup fresh parsley
1/4 cup almonds
2 cloves garlic, peeled
1/2 cup feta cheese, crumbled
Sea salt and freshly ground black pepper, to taste
1 tablespoon lime juice, freshly squeezed
1/4 cup olive oil
Directions
In your food processor, place all ingredients, except
for the cheese.
Process until uniform and creamy. Fold in the
crumbled feta cheese and stir to combine.
Bon appétit!

Traditional Semolina Dumplings

(Ready in about 10 minutes | Servings 5)
Per serving: Calories: 92; Fat: 3.8g; Carbs: 10.4g;
Protein: 3.6g
Ingredients
6 tablespoons semolina flour
1/2 teaspoon garlic powder
1/4 teaspoon dried basil
1/4 teaspoon dried oregano
Sea salt and ground black pepper, to taste
1 egg, beaten
2 teaspoons olive oil
Directions
Bring a large saucepan of lightly salted water to a boil.
In a mixing bowl, thoroughly combine the garlic
powder, basil, oregano, salt, and black pepper.
Then, whisk in the egg and olive oil; stir to combine
well.
Drop the mixture by the teaspoonful into the boiling
water. Let it boil for 4 to 5 minutes until the
dumplings float to the surface.
Remove the cooked dumplings with a slotted spoon
and serve hot. Enjoy!

Authentic Matbucha Sauce

(Ready in about 35 minutes | Servings 10)
Per serving: Calories: 92; Fat: 6.8g; Carbs: 7.2g;
Protein: 1.6g
Ingredients
3 Carmen peppers, quartered
4 vine-ripened San Marzano tomatoes, halved
5 cloves garlic, peeled
1 large red onion, quartered
5 tablespoons olive oil
Salt and freshly ground pepper
1 teaspoon schug (hot sauce)
1 tablespoon balsamic vinegar
Directions
Start by preheating your oven 370 degrees F. Line a
baking pan with a piece of parchment paper.
Toss the peppers, tomatoes, garlic, and onion with
the olive oil, salt, black pepper, and hot sauce.

Arrange the vegetables onto the prepared baking pan
and roast for about 30 minutes or until tender and
slightly charred.
Process the roasted vegetables in your blender, along
with the hot sauce and balsamic vinegar.
Pulse to your desired consistency and transfer to a
serving bowl. Bon appétit!

Swiss Chard Wraps with Hummus and Feta

(Ready in about 10 minutes | Servings 4)
Per serving: Calories: 182; Fat: 14.5g; Carbs: 9.9g;
Protein: 5.6g
Ingredients
7 medium Swiss chard leaves, blanched
1/2 cup feta cheese, crumbled
2 ounces Kalamata olives, pitted and sliced
1 ripe tomato, chopped
4 tablespoons pine nuts, chopped
2 tablespoons fresh basil leaves, chopped
2 tablespoons fresh parsley leaves, chopped
Sea salt and ground black pepper, to taste
2 tablespoons olive oil
1 tablespoon fresh lemon juice
2 ounces hummus, preferably homemade
Directions
Blanch the Swiss chard in two cups of water for
about 30 seconds. Remove them with a slotted spoon.
Pat the leaves dry using a paper towel.
Divide the remaining ingredients between the Swiss
chard leaves; roll them up and serve immediately.
Bon appétit!

Skinny Cucumber Canapés

(Ready in about 10 minutes | Servings 4)
Per serving: Calories: 212; Fat: 5.5g; Carbs: 18.7g;
Protein: 24.6g
Ingredients
1 medium cucumber, cut into 12 thick rounds
12 prosciutto slices
12 Bocconcini balls
12 Campari tomatoes
1 teaspoon Italian seasoning mix
Directions
Top each cucumber piece with a slice of prosciutto,
Bocconcini ball, and Campari tomato.
Sprinkle the seasoning on them and arrange on a
serving platter.
Bon appétit!

Crackers with Grapes and Feta Cheese

(Ready in about 30 minutes | Servings 10)
Per serving: Calories: 159; Fat: 12.8g; Carbs: 8g;
Protein: 3.3g
Ingredients
1/2 cup all-purpose flour, plus extra to dust
1/2 teaspoon baking powder
1 teaspoon sea salt
1 tablespoon granulated sugar
1 stick butter

20 seedless grapes
20 basil leaves
20 feta cheese cubes

Directions

Start by preheating your oven to 370 degrees F. Line a cookie sheet with a parchment paper.

In a mixing bowl, thoroughly combine the flour, baking powder, salt and sugar. Cut in the butter and mix again until everything is well incorporated.

Bake your crackers in the preheated oven for about 13 minutes until firm and golden-brown around the edges. Rotate the cookie sheet once during the cooking time.

Allow your crackers to cool on a wire rack for about 15 minutes.

Divide the grapes, basil leaves, and feta cheese cubes between your crackers, secure with the cocktail sticks or toothpicks and serve immediately. Bon appétit!

The Best Mint Lemonade Ever

(Ready in about 30 minutes | Servings 10)

Per serving: Calories: 110; Fat: 0.1g; Carbs: 30g; Protein: 0.2g

Ingredients

5 cups water
3 medium lemons, peeled
1/2 cup honey
1 (1 ½ -inch) piece ginger root, peeled
1 ½ cups ice, crushed
2 tablespoons fresh mint leaves

Directions

Mix the water, lemon, honey, and ginger in your blender until well combined.

Pour the lemonade through a mesh strainer into a bowl.

To serve, place the crushed ice in five glasses. Pour in the lemonade and garnish with fresh mint leaves. Serve well-chilled and enjoy!

Herb Pita Crackers

(Ready in about 1 hour 25 minutes | Servings 9)

Per serving: Calories: 119; Fat: 1.8g; Carbs: 21.5g; Protein: 3g

Ingredients

2 cups all-purpose flour
1 teaspoon baking powder
Sea salt, to taste
1 teaspoon sugar
1 teaspoon dried basil
1/2 teaspoon dried oregano
1/2 teaspoon dried sage
2 tablespoons extra-virgin olive oil
2/3 cup water

Directions

Start by preheating your oven to 420 degrees.

In a mixing bowl, thoroughly combine the flour, baking powder, salt, sugar, basil, oregano, sage, and olive oil.

Gradually add in the water and beat with an electric mixer until the dough starts to stick together. Let your dough rest for about 15 minutes.

Using a rolling pin, roll out your dough as thin as possible. Transfer the dough to a parchment-lined baking sheet.

Bake for about 5 minutes; turn it over and continue to bake for about 5 minutes. Heat off; let it sit in the oven for about 1 hour to dry out.

Break the pita into pieces and serve with your favorite dipping sauce. Bon appétit!

Berry and Spinach Shake

(Ready in about 5 minutes | Servings 3)

Per serving: Calories: 139; Fat: 3.2g; Carbs: 24.4g; Protein: 4.3g

Ingredients

1 cup almond milk
3 cups baby spinach
1 large banana, peeled
1 cup mixed berries, fresh or frozen
1/2 cup pomegranate juice

Directions

Simply process all ingredients in your blender until well combined.

Pour into tall glasses and garnish with ice cubes, if desired.

Bon appétit!

Easy Greek Relish

(Ready in about 10 minutes | Servings 5)

Per serving: Calories: 122; Fat: 9.5g; Carbs: 6.9g; Protein: 3.1g

Ingredients

2 cups Greek cucumber, diced
2 medium tomatoes, diced
1 small red onion, diced
2 ounces Kalamata olives, pitted and sliced
1 tablespoon fresh lime juice
1 tablespoon red wine vinegar
2 tablespoons olive oil
1 teaspoon dried basil
1/2 teaspoon dried oregano
Sea salt and ground black pepper, to taste
2 ounces Halloumi cheese, crumbled

Directions

Toss all ingredients, except for the cheese, in a serving bowl. Taste and adjust the seasonings. Scatter the crumbled cheese over the top of your relish. Serve with toasted pita wedges and enjoy!

Kale and Hemp Pesto Sauce

(Ready in about 10 minutes | Servings 9)

Per serving: Calories: 135; Fat: 14.1g; Carbs: 1.9g; Protein: 1.1g

Ingredients

3 cups kale torn into small pieces
1/4 cup fresh basil
1 tablespoon fresh rosemary
1 tablespoon fresh oregano

1/4 cup hemp seeds, hulled
1/2 cup extra-virgin olive oil
Sea salt and ground black, to taste
1/2 teaspoon red pepper flakes, crushed
2 cloves garlic
Fresh juice of 1 lime
Directions
Process all ingredients in your blender until everything is well incorporated.
Serve with pasta, pita or crackers.
Bon appétit!

Cremini Mushroom Gnocchi
(Ready in about 10 minutes | Servings 4)
Per serving: Calories: 385; Fat: 25.1g; Carbs: 28.4g; Protein: 11.8g
Ingredients
1 pound gnocchi
4 tablespoons olive oil
1 pound Cremini mushrooms
1 teaspoon garlic, sliced
1/2 teaspoon red pepper flakes
1/2 teaspoon dried oregano
1/2 teaspoon dried basil
1/2 teaspoon mustard seeds
1/2 teaspoon dried marjoram
Salt, to taste
1 vine-ripened San Marzano tomato, crushed
2 ounces Pecorino-Romano cheese, grated
Directions
Cook the gnocchi according to the package instructions; drain.
Heat the olive oil in a saucepan over medium-high heat. Now, sauté the mushrooms and garlic for about 3 minutes until the mushrooms release the liquid.
Add in the seasonings and tomato. Let it simmer, covered, for about 7 minutes, until the sauce has thickened slightly.
Toss the prepared gnocchi with the sauce. Top with cheese and serve hot. Bon appétit!

Sardine and Avocado Lettuce Wraps
(Ready in about 10 minutes | Servings 8)
Per serving: Calories: 155; Fat: 9.9g; Carbs: 7.6g; Protein: 9g
Ingredients
1 small head romaine lettuce
2 tablespoons mayonnaise
1 tablespoon Dijon mustard
8 ounces canned sardines, bones removed and flaked
1 medium-sized avocado, pitted and diced
1 tablespoon capers, drained
1 sweet pepper, seeded and chopped
1 red chile pepper, seeded and chopped
1 small red onion, chopped
1 vine-ripened tomato, chopped
Directions
Place the lettuce leaves on a working surface.
Divide the remaining ingredients between the lettuce leaves. Wrap each of them and serve immediately.

Bon appétit!

Kale Roll-Ups with Avocado and Cheese
(Ready in about 10 minutes | Servings 2)
Per serving: Calories: 275; Fat: 21.3g; Carbs: 17.4g; Protein: 8.8g
Ingredients
4 large Lacinato kale leaves
4 tablespoons tomato relish
2 ounces feta, crumbled
1 medium-sized avocado, pitted and sliced
1 red onion, sliced
Directions
Blanch the kale leaves in 1 cup of water for about 30 seconds. Remove them with a slotted spoon. Pat the leaves dry using a paper towel.
Divide the remaining ingredients between the kale leaves; roll them up and serve immediately.
Bon appétit!

Italian-Style Salsa
(Ready in about 10 minutes | Servings 4)
Per serving: Calories: 138; Fat: 6.3g; Carbs: 17.4g; Protein: 4.8g
Ingredients
6 ounces canned garbanzo beans, drained
4 tablespoons scallions, chopped
1/2 teaspoon fresh garlic, minced
1 small cucumber, diced
1 large ripe tomato, diced
1 Carmen pepper, deseeded and diced
2 ounces green olives, pitted and sliced
1 red onion, diced
2 tablespoons fresh basil, roughly chopped
2 tablespoons fresh parsley, roughly chopped
1 tablespoon fresh mint, roughly chopped
1 tablespoon red wine vinegar
1 tablespoon lemon juice
1 tablespoon extra-virgin olive oil
Sea salt and ground black pepper, to season
Directions
Toss all ingredients in a serving bowl. Taste and adjust the seasonings.
Serve as an appetizer with the pita chips or as a side dish with chicken.
Bon appétit!

Whole-Wheat Digestive Biscuits with Seeds
(Ready in about 15 minutes | Servings 8)
Per serving: Calories: 168; Fat: 9g; Carbs: 18.4g; Protein: 4.2g
Ingredients
1 ½ cups whole-wheat flour
12 teaspoon baking powder
Flaky sea salt, to taste
1 teaspoon brown sugar
1 tablespoon Italian seasoning mix
2 tablespoons cumin seeds
2 tablespoons flax seeds

2 tablespoons sesame seeds
1/4 cup butter
1/3 cup water
Directions
Start by preheating your oven to 420 degrees F. Now, line a cookie sheet with a piece of parchment paper.
In a mixing bowl, thoroughly combine the flour, baking powder, salt, brown sugar, seasoning mix, and seeds. Cut in the cold butter and stir to combine well.
Gradually stir in the water until the dough starts to stick together. Roll the dough out and transfer it to the cookie sheet.
Next, use a sharp knife to create squares.
Bake your biscuits for about 12 minutes or until they are pale gold. Bon appétit!

Red Fruit Salad

(Ready in about 10 minutes | Servings 4)
Per serving: Calories: 188; Fat: 0.3g; Carbs: 48.4g; Protein: 1.6g
Ingredients
1 cup strawberries, hulled and sliced
1 cup sour cherries, pitted
1 cup raspberries
1 cup red seedless grapes
1/4 cup honey
2 tablespoons pomegranate juice
Directions
Toss all ingredients in a mixing bowl; toss to combine well.
Divide the fruit salad between individual bowls and serve well-chilled.
Bon appétit!

Authentic Romesco Sauce

(Ready in about 20 minutes | Servings 8)
Per serving: Calories: 213; Fat: 19.7g; Carbs: 8.4g; Protein: 2.7g
Ingredients
1/2 cup extra-virgin olive oil
2 slices crusty bread, torn into pieces
1/2 cup pine nuts, chopped
6 garlic cloves, chopped
Sea salt and ground black pepper, to taste
1 pound Roma tomatoes, chopped
2 roasted red peppers
1 tablespoon cayenne pepper
2 tablespoons fresh lime juice
2 tablespoons red wine vinegar
Directions
Start by preheating your oven to 350 degrees F. In a nonstick pan, toast the bread and pine nuts until they just begin to brown.
Add the contents of the nonstick pan to a food processor, along with the remaining ingredients. Process until uniform and smooth.
Spread the blended mixture out on a rimmed baking pan. Bake in the preheated oven for approximately 15 minutes.

Allow the sauce to cool and put it into an airtight container; keep in your refrigerator for up to a week.
Bon appétit!

Old-Fashioned Pickled Grapes

(Ready in about 10 minutes + chilling time | Servings 9)
Per serving: Calories: 63; Fat: 0g; Carbs: 15.4g; Protein: 0.3g
Ingredients
1/4 cup water
3/4 cup champagne vinegar
3/4 cup granulated white sugar
1 cinnamon stick
1/2 vanilla bean
1/4 teaspoon whole cloves
1/4 teaspoon black peppercorns
3/4 pound red grapes
Directions
In a saucepan, bring the water, vinegar, and sugar to a boil.
Add the remaining ingredients to a sterilized jar. Add the grapes to the jar.
Pour the hot vinegar mixture into the jar. Allow it to cool. Cover with the lid and refrigerate for at least 24 hours before serving.
Bon appétit!

Easy Pickled Radishes

(Ready in about 15 minutes + chilling time | Servings 4)
Per serving: Calories: 48; Fat: 0.1g; Carbs: 10.7g; Protein: 0.5g
Ingredients
1 cup radishes, slice off tops
2 teaspoons sea salt
1 teaspoon black peppercorns
1/2 teaspoon mustard seeds
1/2 teaspoon coriander seeds
1/2 cup apple cider vinegar
1/2 cup water
2 tablespoons honey
Directions
Cut the radishes into thin slices and transfer them to a canning jar. Add in the salt, black peppercorns, mustard seeds, and coriander seeds.
In a saucepan, bring the vinegar, water, and honey to a rapid boil; let it boil for a few minutes, stirring periodically.
Pour the brine over the radishes.
Allow it to cool to room temperature. Store in your refrigerator for up to 5 days. Bon appétit!

Spinach, Pecorino and Pistachio Pesto

(Ready in about 10 minutes | Servings 10)
Per serving: Calories: 183; Fat: 19.1g; Carbs: 2.3g; Protein: 1.9g
Ingredients
1 cup spinach, cleaned
1 teaspoon garlic
1/4 cup fresh basil leaves
1/4 cup fresh parsley leaves

1/2 teaspoon dried oregano
1/2 teaspoon dried savory
1/3 cup pistachio, hulled
3/4 cup extra-virgin olive oil
1/3 cup Pecorino-Romano cheese, grated
Sea salt and red pepper flakes, to taste

Directions

Add the spinach, garlic, basil, parsley, oregano, savory, and pistachio to a bowl of your food processor.

Process until well combined.

While the machine is running, gradually pour in the olive oil until the mixture comes together.

Fold in the cheese, stir to combine and season with salt and pepper to taste.

Bon appétit!

Gnocchi and Vegetable Skewers

(Ready in about 15 minutes | Servings 5)

Per serving: Calories: 283; Fat: 21.5g; Carbs: 19.2g; Protein: 7.1g

Ingredients

1 pound gnocchi
20 Kalamata olives, pitted
20 grape Campari tomatoes
20 feta cubes
20 basil leaves
3 tablespoons extra-virgin olive oil
1 teaspoon Italian herb mix

Directions

Cook the gnocchi according to the package directions.

Toss the prepared gnocchi, olives, tomatoes, feta, and basil leaves with the olive oil and Italian herb mix.

Thread the ingredients onto skewers.

Arrange the skewers on a serving platter and enjoy!

Classic Mediterranean Chutney

(Ready in about 5 minutes | Servings 5)

Per serving: Calories: 283; Fat: 21.5g; Carbs: 19.2g; Protein: 7.1g

Ingredients

2 Roma tomatoes, diced
1 tablespoon fresh lemon juice
1 tablespoon balsamic vinegar
1 tablespoon extra-virgin olive oil
1 tablespoon fresh mint leaves, roughly chopped
1 tablespoon fresh basil leaves, roughly chopped
1 tablespoon fresh parsley leaves, roughly chopped
1 tablespoon fresh cilantro leaves, roughly chopped

Directions

Toss all ingredients in a serving bowl. Taste and adjust the seasonings.

Serve as an appetizer with crostini.

Bon appétit!

Canapés with Pesto and Cheese

(Ready in about 30 minutes | Servings 9)

Per serving: Calories: 195; Fat: 11.5g; Carbs: 17.9g; Protein: 4.7g

Ingredients

1 ½ cups all-purpose flour
1/2 teaspoon baking powder
1/2 teaspoon flaky sea salt
1 teaspoon honey
1/3 cup butter, cold
1 ½ ounces almond milk
 1 cup feta cheese
4 tablespoons red pesto
2 ounces Kalamata olives, pitted and chopped

Directions

Start by preheating your oven to 420 degrees F. Now, line a cookie sheet with a piece of parchment paper.

In a mixing bowl, thoroughly combine the flour, baking powder, salt, and honey. Cut in the cold butter and stir to combine well.

Gradually stir in the milk until the dough starts to stick together. Roll the dough out and transfer it to the cookie sheet.

Next, use a sharp knife to create squares. Bake your biscuits for about 12 minutes or until they are pale gold. Allow your biscuits to cool for about 10 minutes. In a mixing bowl, thoroughly combine the cheese, red pesto, and olives. Divide the pesto/cheese mixture between your biscuits and serve immediately.

Bon appétit!

Breakfast Tahini Toast

(Ready in about 10 minutes | Servings 2)

Per serving: Calories: 186; Fat: 9.2g; Carbs: 22.1g; Protein: 7.2g

Ingredients

2 slice bread
2 tablespoons tahini
1 bell pepper, seeded and sliced
1 small-sized tomato, chopped
1 scallion stalk, chopped
Sea salt and red pepper flakes, to taste

Directions

Toast the bread slices and place them on serving plates.

Spread on the tahini. Top with the peppers, tomato, and scallions.

Sprinkle each toast with salt and red pepper and serve immediately. Bon appétit!

Healthy Grape Jam

(Ready in about 5 minutes | Servings 6)

Per serving: Calories: 86; Fat: 1.2g; Carbs: 17.7g; Protein: 1.2g

Ingredients

3 tablespoons chia seeds
1 ½ cups purple grapes
1/4 teaspoon ground cloves
1/3 teaspoon ground cinnamon
3 tablespoons honey

Directions

Grind the chia seeds in your blender or food processor.

Add in the remaining ingredients and blend until your desired consistency is reached.

Store in your refrigerator in a sealed container for up to 5 days. Bon appétit!

Salmon, Cheese and Almond Pâté

(Ready in about 10 minutes | Servings 9)
Per serving: Calories: 116; Fat: 8.4g; Carbs: 4.2g; Protein: 6.8g
Ingredients
1/2 cup pumpkin seeds
1/2 cup almonds
1 cup smoked salmon
2 tablespoons sun-dried tomatoes, chopped
4 tablespoons goat cheese
1 tablespoon fresh lemon juice
1 tablespoon Italian seasoning mix
2 cloves garlic
2 tablespoons olive oil
2 scallion stalks, sliced
1 tablespoon fresh basil, julienned
Directions
Grind the pumpkin seeds and almonds in your blender or food processor.
Add in the salmon, sun-dried tomatoes, cheese, lemon juice, Italian seasoning, garlic, and olive oil.
Puree the ingredients to your desired consistency.
Serve garnished with scallions and basil. Bon appétit!

Shortbreads with Feta and Olives

(Ready in about 45 minutes | Servings 10)
Per serving: Calories: 316; Fat: 24.6g; Carbs: 20.6g; Protein: 4.3g
Ingredients
2 cups all-purpose flour
1 cup butter
1 teaspoon powdered sugar
1/2 cup pecans, finely chopped
1 teaspoon flaky sea salt
1/4 teaspoon cracked black pepper
1/2 cup feta cheese, crumbled
2 ounces Kalamata olives, pitted and chopped
Directions
Mix the flour and butter until the mixture resembles fine breadcrumbs.
Add in the powdered sugar followed by pecans, salt, and black pepper.
Now, knead the dough until it is elastic and smooth; wrap the dough in clingfilm; place the dough in your refrigerator for about 30 minutes.
Using a floured rolling pin, roll out the dough to about 1/4-inch thickness. Then, cut small rounds using a cookie cutter; transfer the shortbreads to a parchment-lined baking sheet.
Bake in the preheated oven at 350 degrees F for about 12 minutes until lightly golden.
Mix the cheese and olives until well combined.
Now, sandwich shortbreads together with the feta/olive mixture and serve immediately. Bon appétit!

Mediterranean Mule Cocktail

(Ready in about 5 minutes | Servings 2)
Per serving: Calories: 376; Fat: 1.1g; Carbs: 81g; Protein: 3.7g
Ingredients
6 ounces fig vodka
1 ounce amaretto
1 ounce limoncello
1 cup ginger beer
1 tablespoon freshly squeezed lime juice
2 fresh figs, halved
Directions
Fill a tall glass with the crushed ice.
Pour in the vodka, amaretto, limoncello, ginger beer, and lime juice.
Stir to combine and garnish with figs. Enjoy immediately!

Herb Crisp Pita Bread

(Ready in about 20 minutes | Servings 6)
Per serving: Calories: 196; Fat: 9.3g; Carbs: 24.1g; Protein: 3.6g
Ingredients
1 ½ cups all-purpose flour
1 teaspoon baking powder
1/2 teaspoon flaky sea salt
1 teaspoon fresh rosemary, chopped
1 teaspoon fresh sage, chopped
1 teaspoon fresh thyme, chopped
1 teaspoon fresh basil, chopped
1/4 cup water
2 tablespoons Greek-style yogurt
1/4 cup olive oil
Directions
Start by preheating your oven to 420 degrees F. Now, line a baking sheet with a parchment paper.
Thoroughly combine the flour, baking powder, salt, and herbs. Make a well in the middle of this mixture and gradually pour in the water, yogurt, and oil. Mix until the dough comes together.
Knead the dough until it is smooth and elastic.
Divide the dough into 2 balls and roll them out, forming 2 round pitas about 1/4-inch thick.
Bake the round bread in the preheated oven for about 9 minutes. Repeat with another bread.
Break your pita into pieces and serve with hummus or tomato sauce, if desired. Bon appétit!

Truffle Oil and Sun-Dried Tomato Pesto

(Ready in about 10 minutes | Servings 10)
Per serving: Calories: 163; Fat: 17.1g; Carbs: 3.2g; Protein: 1.9g
Ingredients
1/2 cup almonds
4 cloves minced garlic
1/4 cup sun-dried tomatoes, chopped
1/2 cup fresh basil leaves
1 teaspoon dried oregano
1 teaspoon dried rosemary
1 tablespoon red wine vinegar
Sea salt and ground black pepper, to taste

1/2 cup extra-virgin olive oil
2 tablespoons truffle oil
Directions
Add the almonds, garlic, sun-dried tomatoes, basil, oregano, rosemary, and vinegar to a bowl of your food processor.
Process until well combined.
While the machine is running, gradually pour in the olive oil until the mixture comes together.
Afterwards, season with salt and pepper to taste. Bon appétit!

Grandma's Pickled Turnips

(Ready in about 10 minutes | Servings 5)
Per serving: Calories: 43; Fat: 0.3g; Carbs: 8.5g; Protein: 1.4g
Ingredients
2 cups water
1/4 cup sea salt
1/2 cup apple cider vinegar
1 pound turnips, peeled and cut into sticks
1 small red onion
1 teaspoon black peppercorns
1 teaspoon mustard seeds
1 teaspoon fennel seeds
2 bay leaves
2 cloves garlic, roughly chopped
Directions
Bring the water and salt to a boil over a moderate heat for about 4 minutes until the salt is completely dissolved.
Allow it to cool completely, and then, add in the vinegar.
Place the turnips and red onion in a jar and add in the remaining ingredients. Pour in the brine and seal the jar.
Place the turnips in your refrigerator until ready to serve. Bon appétit!

Corsican Canistrelli Biscuits

(Ready in about 35 minutes | Servings 8)
Per serving: Calories: 296; Fat: 15.5g; Carbs: 34.2g; Protein: 4.9g
Ingredients
1 ½ cups plain flour
1 cup chestnut flour
1 teaspoon sea salt
1 teaspoon brown sugar
1/2 teaspoon baking soda
1 teaspoon baking powder
1 teaspoon dried oregano
1/2 teaspoon dried rosemary
1/2 teaspoon dried basil
1/2 teaspoon ground bay leaf
1/2 cup colza oil
1/2 cup dry white wine
Directions
Start by preheating your oven to 350 degrees F. Now, line a cookie sheet with a silicone baking mat.
Thoroughly combine the flour, baking soda, baking powder, salt, sugar and dried herbs. Then, create a well in the middle of this mixture and gradually pour in the oil and wine.
Stir the mixture until the dough comes together. Then, knead the dough until it is elastic and smooth, but do not overwork it.
Roll the dough out to 1/2-inch thickness. Using a cookie cutter, cut the dough into diamonds.
Bake the canistrelli for about 25 minutes until golden brown around the edges. Rotate the pan halfway through the cooking time. Bon appétit!

Fig and Cranberry Chutney

(Ready in about 55 minutes | Servings 9)
Per serving: Calories: 56; Fat: 0.1g; Carbs: 14.2g; Protein: 0.2g
Ingredients
1/3 cup sugar
2 tablespoons honey
1/4 cup wine vinegar
1 tablespoon lime juice, freshly squeezed
2 ½ cups figs, fresh or frozen, quartered
1 shallot, chopped
1/3 cup dried cranberries
Sea salt, to taste
1/4 teaspoon ground allspice
1/3 teaspoon ground nutmeg
Directions
Heat the sugar and vinegar in a saucepan over medium-high flame. Add in the remaining ingredients and stir to combine well. Bring to a boil Immediately turn the heat to a simmer and let it cook for about 50 minutes, stirring periodically to prevent your chutney from sticking to the pan.
Store in a sealed container in a dry place. Bon appétit!

APPENDIX : RECIPES INDEX

Chocolate and Hazelnut Chickpea Blondies 141
Chocolate Fudge Ice Pops 139
Chunky Beef and Cannellini Bean Casserole 74
Chunky Hamburger Soup with Green Beans 77
Classic Aïoli Sauce 143
Classic Avocado and Campari Tomato Salad 41
Classic Baked Spaghetti 124
Classic Black-Eyed Peas with Herbs 94
Classic Chicken Parmigiana 62
Classic Chicken Salad 59
Classic Chicken Stroganoff 67
Classic Egg Salad with Herbs 110
Classic Fig Clafoutis 132
Classic Freekeh Salad 103
Classic Greek-Style Meatballs 77
Classic Italian Bruschetta 92
Classic Italian Stir-Fry 72
Classic Mediterranean Burritos 71
Classic Mediterranean Chutney 150
Classic Mixed Berry Cake 136
Classic Orange Cheesecake 141
Classic Pizza Dip 86
Classic Seafood Gumbo 29
Classic Shoulder Roast with Herbs 81
Classic Tabbouleh Salad 44
Classic Tomato and Orzo Soup 25
Classic Tomato-Braised Beans 98
Coffee and Nougat Semifrío 138
Colorful Cannellini Bean and Pea Soup 94
Corn, Vegetable and Herb Chowder 33
Cornbread with Feta and Sun-Dried Tomatoes 95
Corsican Canistrelli Biscuits 152
Country-Style Chicken Traybake 65
Couscous with Dried Fruits 100
Couscous with Tuna and Basil 47
Crackers with Grapes and Feta Cheese 146
Cream of Cauliflower Soup with Yogurt 114
Creamed Broccoli Soup with Pecorino-Romano 116
Creamed Fruit Salad 134
Creamed Lima Bean Salad 114
Creamed New Potato Soup 34
Creamed Shrimp Salad 32
Creamed Shrimp with Linguine 53
Creamy Apricot and Almond Dessert 137
Creamy Hummus with Greek Yogurt 84
Cremini Mushroom Gnocchi 148
Cremini Mushroom Risotto 95
Crock Pot Beef Sandwiches 75
Crunch Cereal with Cranberries 20
Crunchy Chickpea Stuffed Zucchini 40

D

Dad's Cloud Eggs 14

Date, Walnut and Tahini Balls 136
Decadent Green Bean Salad 26
Delicious Cucumber Rounds 115
Dijon Potato Salad 25
Double Cheese Chicken Casserole 61
Double Cheese Stuffed Mushrooms 87
Double-Cheese Broccoli Casserole 114
Dried Fruit Compote (Hosafi) 140

E

Easy Caprese Toast 20
Easy Cauliflower Parmigiana 38
Easy Chocolate Cream Pie 138
Easy Creamed Broccoli 41
Easy Garlicky Broccoli Rabe 40
Easy Greek Pizza 126
Easy Greek Relish 147
Easy Kamut with Sautéed Vegetables 103
Easy Oven-Roasted Broccoli 109
Easy Pan-Fried Halibut 54
Easy Pickled Radishes 149
Easy Pizza with Goat Cheese and Veggies 130
Easy Shrimp Kabobs 92
Easy Silan Syrup 145
Easy Stovetop Pepperoni Pizza 121
Easy Three Layer Dip 85
Easy Zucchini Croquettes 88
Easy Zuppa Toscana 76
Egg Cups with Tuna and Tomato 13
Egg Salad Niçoise 114
Eliopsomo (Olive and Herb Bread) 16

F

Family Roast Beef 78
Famous Clam Chowder 33
Famous Moroccan Yogurt Dip 92
Farro Bowl with Herbs and Cheese 96
Farro with Portabellas and Cheese 100
Farro with Roasted Veggies and Feta Cheese 98
Father's Day Pizza with Fefferoni 129
Fattoush (Traditional Lebanese Salad) 23
Favorite French Vichyssoise 33
Favorite Greek Keftedes 82
Favorite Homemade Granola 143
Fennel Quinoa Salad 94
Fig and Cranberry Chutney 152
Flaky Mini Pizza Rolls with Sardines 126
Flank Steak with Vegetables and Pasta 82
Fluffy Golden Cornbread 106
Fluffy Mini Frittatas 20
Freekeh Bowl with Roasted Peppers 104
French Toast with Cranberries 21
Fried Zucchini and Parmesan Cakes 37
Fruit Kabobs with Yogurt Deep 135
Fudge with Almonds 138

G

Garlic Carrots with Yogurt Dip 87
Garlic Marinated Cherry Tomatoes 85
Garlicky and Lemony Greek Potatoes 108
Garlicky Pita Triangles 89
Garlicky Roasted Brussels Sprouts 87
Giant Bean in Tomato Sauce 109
Gnocchi and Vegetable Skewers 150
Gnocchi with Aromatic Herb Sauce 145
Grandma's Brownie Cupcakes 141
Grandma's Pickled Turnips 152
Grandma's Sweet Cornbread 105
Great Northern Bean Salad 32
Greek Avgolemono Soup with Pastina 25
Greek Frozen Yogurt Dessert 133
Greek Kolokithokeftedes with Yogurt Sauce 93
Greek Lemon-Cheese Dip 92
Greek Makaronia me Kima 126
Greek Orzo Salad 30
Greek Parfait with Mixed Berries 135
Greek Pasta Spetsofai 125
Greek Pilaf with Chicken 64
Greek Pita Tostadas 14
Greek Steak Pitas 80
Greek Yogurt Fettuccine Alfredo 125
Greek-Style Baked Chicken 61
Greek-Style Chicken and Pasta Salad 66
Greek-Style Chicken Drumsticks 65
Greek-Style Chicken Lemon Soup 29
Greek-Style Chocolate Semifreddo 135
Greek-Style Corn on the Cob 88
Greek-Style Fish Pitas 57
Greek-Style Fruit Salad 137
Greek-Style Mushroom Lasagna 126
Greek-Style Pancakes with Blueberries 13
Greek-Style Potato Bites 87
Greek-Style Seafood Frittata 56
Greek-Style Steak Chowder 79
Greek-Style Summer Salad 23
Greek-Style Tangy Rice Bowl 94
Greek-Style Top Sirloin Steak 71
Green Apple Smoothie 13
Green Avocado and Hummus Dip 92
Green Bean and Egg Salad 28
Green Bean Pasta Salad 127
Green Beans with Feta Cheese 106
Green Beans with Halloumi Cheese 109
Grilled Cheese and Beef Sandwiches 79
Grilled Chicken Pitas 63
Grilled Chicken Salad 61
Grilled Chicken with Peanut Sauce 66
Grilled Green Bean Salad 116
Grilled Hash Brown Burgers 37
Grilled Mahi-Mahi Fish 52

Grilled Radicchio with Feta Cheese 39
Grilled Salmon Melt Sandwiches 14
Grilled Steak Salad with Cheese 75
Grilled Street Corn 84
Grilled Tofu Vegetable Kabobs 117
Grilled Tofu with Swiss Chard 108
Grilled Vegetable Kabobs 37
Grilled Veggie Pita Pockets 42
Ground Beef Soup with Sweet Corn 79
Ground Beef, Vegetable and Cheese Bake 77
Ground Turkey and Pasta Casserole 122
Guinness Beef Stew with Greek Yogurt 76

H

Halibut Fillets Pomodoro 57
Halibut Stew with Arborio Rice and Herbs 53
Hash Brown and Sardine Casserole 21
Healthy Grape Jam 150
Hearty Chicken and Bulgur Soup 60
Herb and Garlic Shrimp Skewers 88
Herb and Sun-Dried Tomato Bread 19
Herb and Wine Beef Stew 72
Herb Chicken with Orzo Pasta 68
Herb Crisp Pita Bread 151
Herb Millet Pilaf with Campari Tomatoes 40
Herb Mozzarella Chicken with Olives 70
Herb Pita Crackers 147
Herb Potato Wedges 85
Holiday Pot Roast 82
Homemade Potato Chips 84
Homemade Walnut Parsley Pesto 144
Hummus Stuffed Yams 43
Hummus, Feta and Vegetable Dip 113

I

Individual Egg Pizzas with Onion 122
Italian Berry Composta 139
Italian Chicken and Tortellini Soup 67
Italian Corn Muffins 100
Italian Meatballs in Marinara Sauce 80
Italian Rice with Mushrooms and Ricotta Salata 105
Italian Shrimp Pasta 47
Italian Tortini di Melanzane 90
Italian Zucchini and Prosciutto Pie 19
Italian-Style Cheesy Roasted Peppers 36
Italian-Style Lemon Cheesecake 139
Italian-Style Polenta Pie 104
Italian-Style Rice with Olives 97
Italian-Style Roasted Baby Bella Mushrooms 38
Italian-Style Salsa 148
Italian-Style Stuffed Peppers with Couscous 43
Italian-Style Zucchini Boats 39
Italian-Style Zucchini Lasagna with Mushrooms 115

Traditional Chicken and Olive Soup 68
Traditional Chicken Cacciatore 68
Traditional Greek Fasolada 97
Traditional Greek Paximadia 101
Traditional Greek Prune Compote 137
Traditional Greek Spanakokeftethes 18
Traditional Italian Cake with Almonds 136
Traditional Italian Caponata 44
Traditional Kagianas with Cherry Tomatoes 16
Traditional Kalo Prama 134
Traditional Lebanese Chicken Fattoush 60
Traditional Mediterranean Lokum 133
Traditional Minestrone Soup 28
Traditional Olive Oil Cake with Figs 133
Traditional Pita Bread 95
Traditional Semolina Dumplings 146
Traditional Shakshuka with a Twist 13
Traditional Socca with Spinach 15
Traditional Spaghetti Bolognese 119
Traditional Zuppa di Pesce 49
Truffle Oil and Sun-Dried Tomato Pesto 151
Tuna and Asparagus Frittata 50
Tuna and Cauliflower Gnocchi Gratin 56
Tuna and Chickpea Bruschetta 57
Tuna and Corn Fritters 15
Tuna and Feta Cheese Lettuce Wraps 145
Tuna Pasta Salad 118
Tuna Salad with Homemade Salsa 27
Tuna Salad with Tapenade Vinaigrette 31
Tuna, Kale and Yogurt Pie 17
Turkey and Mushroom Casserole 62
Turkey Wings with Horseradish Sauce 63

Turkish Baked Pudding (Sütlaç) 142
Turkish Irmik Helvasi 139
Turkish-Style Chocolate Halva 134
Turkish-Style Pilau 66
Tuscan Chicken Ribollita 65
Tuscan Fish and Bean Soup 51
Tuscan-Style Turkey Stew 59
Twisted Sautéed Beets 46
Tzatziki Chickpea Bowl 41

U

Ultimate Avocado Crostini 45

V

Vegetarian Pizza Sandwich 125
Vegetarian Skillet Pizza 119
Veggie Kabobs with Garlic-Yogurt Sauce 91

W

Whipped Feta Dip with Mint 88
White Bean Soup with Kale and Cheese 109
White Beans with Spinach 106
Whole-Wheat Digestive Biscuits with Seeds 148
Wild Garlic Sauce 144
Wild Mushroom Cappuccino 41
Wine-Braised Chicken with Leeks 70
Winter Hearty Chicken Pasta Casserole 69
Winter Salmon Salad with Aioli 32

Z

Za'atar Chickpea Salad 35
Zucchini Cakes with Feta and Dill 90
Zucchini Chips with Pine Nuts 86
Zucchini Polpette with Greek Sauce 112